THE HOLY SPIRIT IN WORSHIP MUSIC, PREACHING,
AND THE ALTAR
RENEWING PENTECOSTAL CORPORATE WORSHIP

THE HOLY SPIRIT IN WORSHIP MUSIC, PREACHING, AND THE ALTAR

RENEWING PENTECOSTAL CORPORATE WORSHIP

JOSH P.S. SAMUEL

CPT

CPT PRESS
CLEVELAND, TENNESSEE

The Holy Spirit in Worship Music, Preaching, and the Altar
Renewing Pentecostal Corporate Worship

Published by CPT Press
900 Walker ST NE
Cleveland, TN 37311
USA
email: cptpress@pentecostaltheology.org
website: www.cptpress.com

Library of Congress Control Number: 2017955530

ISBN-13: 978-1-935931-66-9

CONTENTS

ACKNOWLEDGMENTS AND DEDICATION

There are numerous people who have supported me throughout the process of putting this book together. In particular, I am deeply grateful:

To Dr Steven M. Studebaker, my supervisor for PhD studies at McMaster Divinity College, who provided incredible support for this work. I have especially appreciated his humble yet academically rigorous approach to research, writing, and mentorship. I have benefitted tremendously from his approach to supervision, and I cannot imagine trying to accomplish this work without his down-to-earth, challenging, encouraging, and sometimes humorous approach to academic work.

To Dr Gordon L. Heath, who provided great feedback on this work. I have appreciated his wise advice pertaining to historical issues related to this book, and regular encouragement whenever I met with him.

To Dr Wolfgang Vondey, who also provided valuable feedback on this work. He put a lot of work into his response, and I am appreciative of his willingness to engage with my work.

To the McMaster Divinity College community for being an incredible support throughout the years that I worked on this book. As Academic Dean, Dr Phil Zylla provided great support, including a meaningful response to this work. Dr Michael P. Knowles has been an excellent resource and support, not only related to his expertise in homiletics, but also through his encouraging words and prayers. Many others have been very supportive, including: Dr Stanley E. Porter, Dr Wendy Porter, Dr Mark J. Boda, Dr James C. Peterson, and Nina Thomas.

To the many friends, mentors, and scholars who have supported me, thank you. My apologies to those I may forget here, but I must try my best to acknowledge those who supported me in so many ways: Dr Jonathan Hong, Dr Dennis Ngien, Dr Lyman C.D. Kulathungam, Dr Jason Robinson, Dr Alex and Elaine Philip, Dr David Courey, Adrian and Tammy Isaacs, Dorian Persaud, Dr Randall Holm, Dr Glen Taylor, Dr Marion Taylor, Rev Jacob Thomas, Rev

Craig Burton, Rev Gordon Upton, Dr Brian Stiller, Dr Fred Penney, Linda Gibson, Allen and Sharon Alexander, Rev Rick Mootoo, Dr Puiwing Wong, Rev Daniel Yang, Dr Peter Neumann, Dr John D. Witvliet, and Dr Andrew Gabriel. I must also thank Dr Amos Yong (once co-editor of *Pneuma*) and all those involved at *Pneuma*, as well as the Society of Pentecostal Studies, who provided opportunity for me to explore some of these themes in a scholarly context.

To all the libraries and librarians who have supported me. Special thanks to Kimberly Pickett, the Senior Library Assistant at Mills Library at McMaster University, who has gone to great lengths to find numerous books for me through Interlibrary Loan. Thanks to Armen Svadjian and Norma Stuckless at the J. William Horsey Library at Tyndale University College and Seminary, who have been very accommodating to me for the many books I have needed throughout the years. Their friendship and support helped foster a very hospitable environment at Tyndale's library. Thanks to Nancy Warwick and Ruth Sadlier, of Master's College and Seminary library, for granting me privileges to obtain resources when needed. Thanks to the Peter Turkstra Library at Redeemer University College for also granting privileges to obtain resources.

To the churches and pastors who have supported and challenged my views on the church. They not only supported me, but gave me opportunity to serve and grow in so many ways. Thanks to Zion Gospel Assembly, Malvern Christian Assembly, North York Mandarin Alliance Church, Christian Life Centre, Cedarview Community Church, and Southside Worship Centre.

To the other various schools I attended in the past, where I grew in a variety of ways. Thanks to the University of Waterloo; Wycliffe College, the University of Toronto; and Tyndale Seminary. And special thanks to Master's College and Seminary, where I attended as a student when it was called Eastern Pentecostal Bible College. And now as Professor of Bible and Theology and Director of Worship and Creative Arts Ministry at Master's College and Seminary, I'm grateful for the faculty and staff who are incredibly supportive, students who have been very encouraging, and an excellent community experience at the school where God is glorified. Master's College and Seminary has been very good to me, and I'm grateful to God for the school.

To CPT Press. Thank you to Dr Lee Roy Martin and Dr John Christopher Thomas for support for this project and willingness to publish it alongside many other important works related to Pentecostalism in CPT Press.

To my extended family. Everyone on the Samuel family side and Varughese family side has been a blessing throughout the years, thank you.

To my in-laws. Dad, Rev Easaw Philip, and Mom, Aleykutty Philip, have been supporting me for a long time particularly through their prayers, especially since I grew up in the church where Dad was the Senior Pastor. Special thanks to the entire family, which includes: Anu, Lisbeth, Steven, Sarah, Timothy, Wesley, Gladis, Daniel, Abigail, Josh, Ruby, Hannah, and Levi. Each of them have been a blessing in different ways.

To the Samuel family. My mom, Kunjunjamma (Molly) Samuel, has been the most consistent source of encouragement and strength since I was born. She has always put her children ahead of her own needs, and has sought to do whatever she can to support us. She has shown me the importance of a relationship with God, prayer, and putting God first before anything else. Her example, prayers, and encouragement have been crucial for me. My dad, P. Stephen Samuel, has consistently sought to serve others, including me, in any way he can. His prayers have undoubtedly been important for me. I am especially proud of his miraculous change of heart, serving Christ faithfully. My sisters, brothers-in-law, nieces, and nephew have also been very important. Jenny, Jasmine, David, Krystal, Stéphane, Julia, and Daniel have always blessed me in so many ways, listening, supporting, praying, and sending emails of encouragement over these many years.

To my beautiful wife, Joyce, my two sons, Josiah and Jeremiah, and my daughter Joanna. Joyce has been an incredible blessing to me in so many ways. Her love, prayers, encouragement, and sacrifice have blessed me. She read and proofread elements of this work, and responded to various ideas I came up with, offering great advice throughout. She encouraged me during her own training and work as a medical doctor. I really cannot thank her enough. God truly brought the best and most beautiful woman of God for me into my life, and for that, I am grateful. Josiah, Jeremiah, and Joanna always bring joy whenever I return from my work. I always enjoy our times together, whether it is playing with toy cars ('Radiator Springs' style), clowning around, or singing and reading devotionals together. I am grateful to God for bringing wonderful children into our lives. Coming home to Joyce, Josiah, Jeremiah, and Joanna after research and writing is always something to which I look forward.

To God, for giving me the call, the opportunity, and the strength to complete this book. God has been tremendously faithful. I am grateful for his amazing grace. Thank you Father, Son, and Holy Spirit. To God be the glory.

Finally, I dedicate this work to six people. I have received love on a daily basis in so many ways throughout this journey from these people: my wife, two sons, daughter, mom, and dad. My wife, Joyce Samuel, my mom, Kunjunjamma (Molly) Samuel, and dad, P. Stephen Samuel, loved, prayed, and sacrificed on a regular basis throughout the years to help make this happen. My children, Josiah, Jeremiah, and Joanna Samuel, are three gifts of God we received while writing this work. My prayer is that my children grow to love God with all their hearts, souls, minds, and strength, and love their neighbours as themselves.

INTRODUCTION

The Spirit's Manifest Presence in Pentecostal Corporate Worship

But if all prophesy, an unbeliever or outsider who enters is reproved by all and called to account by all. After the secrets of the unbeliever's heart are disclosed, that person will bow down before God and worship him, declaring, 'God is really among you' (1 Cor. 14.24-25 NRSV).

Pentecostals often quote Acts 1.8 in order to distinguish themselves from other Christians, claiming Christ's promise of Spirit baptism as a defining experience for Pentecostals. But passages like 1 Cor. 14.24-25 should be mentioned alongside Acts 1.8. Pentecostal identity has been shaped by the anticipation of direct and present experiences of the Spirit – the Spirit's immediacy – in corporate worship, whereby participants in Pentecostal corporate worship might also claim that 'God is really among us'.[1] Experiencing the Spirit's immediacy is one of the primary objectives of Pentecostals when coming together for their church services, and is a theological foundation of Pentecostal corporate worship.[2] Thus, one of the best ways to understand Pentecostalism is not merely through doctrinal statements, but through the 'central Pentecostal expectation of a radical experience of the Spirit' – what is done here in this book.[3] This book examines contemporary

---

[1] A few important terms are defined in an upcoming section in this introduction.

[2] For a lengthy treatment on 'God's empowering presence', in Paul's letters in the New Testament, see Gordon D. Fee, *God's Empowering Presence: The Holy Spirit in the Letters of Paul* (Peabody: Hendrickson, 1994).

[3] Keith Warrington, *Pentecostal Theology: A Theology of Encounter* (London: T & T Clark, 2008), p. 20.

North American classical Pentecostal corporate worship, specifically the expressions of worship music, preaching, and the altar – places where Pentecostals expect to experience the Spirit's manifest presence. The goal of this book is to offer recommendations for the renewal of Pentecostal corporate worship. The aim of renewal is an attempt to strengthen the theology and practice of corporate worship – worship music, preaching, and the altar – as it relates to the emphasis on the Spirit's immediacy among Pentecostals today. I bring the worship practices of the Azusa Street Revival into this discussion because of Azusa's formative influence on the Pentecostal movement. I also examine Azusa's practices in order to show how they can and cannot be a source of renewal for contemporary Pentecostal corporate worship. Furthermore, I bring the views of other notable theologians and leaders into this discussion that can help point the way forward for renewal. Through this examination of the primacy of the Spirit's immediacy in Pentecostal corporate worship, both an appraisal of this theological foundation of Pentecostal corporate worship is offered and a robust Pentecostal theology of corporate worship is put forward.

Why Another Book on Corporate Worship?

There are several reasons why this study is important. First, while scholars have highlighted the important role of the Spirit's manifest presence in Pentecostalism, there is not sufficient analysis of this emphasis on the Spirit's work in Pentecostal corporate worship.[4] Examining Pentecostal corporate worship is crucial since this is the context where the present experience of the Spirit is chiefly expected to manifest.

Second, related to the previous point, an examination and analysis of Pentecostal *corporate worship* is important because Pentecostal corporate worship both 'reveals' who Pentecostals are and 'forms' who

---

[4] Examples of scholars who have noted the emphasis on the Spirit's immediacy, include Harvey Cox, *Fire From Heaven: The Rise of Pentecostal Spirituality and the Reshaping of Religion in the Twenty-First Century* (Cambridge: Da Capo, 1995), p. 15; Allan Anderson, *An Introduction to Pentecostalism* (Cambridge: Cambridge University, 2004), p. 14; and Peter D. Neumann, 'Encountering the Spirit: Pentecostal Mediated Experience of God in Theological Context' (PhD dissertation, University of St. Michael's College, 2010), p. 7.

they are becoming.[5] And though there is a growing corpus of scholarly work on Pentecostalism, works on issues related to Pentecostal corporate worship is one of the largest gaps in research.[6]

Finally, this study seeks to help leaders because it provides an examination and analysis of Pentecostal corporate worship, which is formative for discipleship. There are numerous challenges for Pentecostals connected to the Pentecostal emphasis on the Spirit's presence in corporate worship. Pentecostal churches in North America have had various challenges related to its corporate worship, such as those who chase after and subsequently imitate other revivals, indiscriminately follow fads related to worship, fall into emotionalism and manipulation, produce a worship context that is more about entertainment.

There are also some Pentecostal churches that choose to worship in ways that have little to do with the roots of Pentecostal corporate worship – found in places like Azusa – and the contemporary non-Western Pentecostal church, which favour a focus on the Spirit's immediacy in corporate worship. Some Pentecostal churches attempt to associate more with other evangelical approaches to corporate worship, and others who have experienced a decline in the expression of the gifts of the Spirit in worship.[7] A decline in the openness for the Spirit's presence in Pentecostal corporate worship may be best understood as arising due to various factors such as: institutionalism, uncertainty regarding what Pentecostal corporate worship is, a reac-

---

[5] Marva J. Dawn, *Reaching Out Without Dumbing Down: A Theology of Worship for the Turn-of-the-Century Culture* (Grand Rapids: Eerdmans, 1995), p. 4. Cf. Simon Chan, *Liturgical Theology: The Church as Worshiping Community* (Downers Grove: InterVarsity, 2006), p. 42 and Wolfgang Vondey, *Beyond Pentecostalism: The Crisis of Global Christianity and the Renewal of the Theological Agenda* (Grand Rapids: Eerdmans, 2010), p. 110.

[6] Martin Lindhardt, 'Introduction', in Martin Lindhardt (ed.), *Practicing the Faith: The Ritual Life of Pentecostal-Charismatic Christians* (New York: Berghahn, 2011), p. 1.

[7] Margaret M. Poloma, in 'North American Pentecostalism', argues that within North American Pentecostalism, there is an '"evangelicalization of Pentecostalism," where Pentecostal experiences become less common as Pentecostal churches adapt to the language and practices of a less experiential "seeker-sensitive" Protestantism'. Margaret M. Poloma, 'North American Pentecostalism', in Adam Stewart (ed.), *Handbook of Pentecostal Christianity* (DeKalb: North Illinois University Press, 2012), pp. 157.

tion against some of the abuses found in Pentecostal contexts, inse-
curity on the part of Pentecostals regarding practices that are not
always welcome in North American society, the influence of a secular
and scientific worldview, and generally a desire to be more accepted
by those who are not Christian.[8] Providing theological reflection on
the subject of the Spirit's work in Pentecostal corporate worship gives
Pentecostals an opportunity to address key issues involved in this di-
visive subject.

Methodology

This work is interdisciplinary because it delves into issues related to
the Spirit's presence, corporate worship, and Pentecostal history;
thus, it employs historical and systematic theology. First, it explores
some of the primary issues related to corporate Pentecostal worship
in North America today following the contours of three key worship
expressions in Pentecostal churches, namely, worship music, preaching, and the altar.[9] These three expressions – worship music, preaching, and the altar – are necessary and dominant elements of a Pentecostal corporate worship service. Elements of Pentecostal corporate
worship, like the reading of Scripture, testimonies, the Lord's Supper,
the announcements, financial giving, foot-washing, dance, and a ben-
ediction are found within Pentecostal corporate worship services, but

---

[8] See Margaret M. Poloma, 'The Symbolic Dilemma and the Future of Pentecostalism: Mysticism, Ritual, and Revival', in Eric Patterson and Edmund
Rybarczyk (eds.), *The Future of Pentecostalism in the United States* (Lanham: Lexington,
2007), pp. 108, 114; Vinson Synan, 'The Charismatic Renewal after Fifty Years', in
Vinson Synan (ed.), *Spirit-Empowered Christianity in the 21st Century* (Lake Mary: Charisma, 2011), p. 18; Robert Crosby, 'The Pentecostal Paradox: As the Global Chorus Grows, American Tongues Fall Silent'. No pages. Online: http://www.pa-
theos.com/Resources/Additional-Resources/Pentecostal-Paradox-Robert-
Crosby-01-27-2012, para. 14; Abby Stocker, 'Assemblies of God Surge, But Speaking in Tongues Slumps', *Christianity Today* (August 2013). No pages. Online:
http://www.christianitytoday.com/gleanings/2013/august/assemblies-of-god-
speaking-in-tongues-spirit-baptisms.html, paras. 8-9; Cary McMullen, 'Holding
their Tongues', *Christianity Today* (October 2009). No pages. Online:
http://www.christianitytoday.com/ct/2009/october/5.15.html, paras. 14, 18, 27-
31.

[9] Daniel E. Albrecht, *Rites in the Spirit: A Ritual Approach to Pentecostal/Charismatic
Spirituality* (JPTSup, 17; Sheffield: Sheffield University Press, 1999), p. 152.

are less dominant.[10] Finally, it explores and provides an analysis of the theological underpinnings related to the presence of the Spirit found in the various elements of corporate worship.

Corporate Worship among North American Pentecostals

To understand some of the key themes in this book, let me begin by explaining what I attempt to do here with regard to the theme of corporate worship among North American Pentecostals. In this work, the phrase 'corporate worship' is distinguished from 'worship' in the broad sense. 'Corporate worship' describes what occurs when believers gather together to worship God in a specific time and place.

Though the term 'ritual' could be used for 'corporate worship', the phrase 'corporate worship' is used because it reflects the language Pentecostals make use of for understanding their corporate worship services.[11] Furthermore, the term corporate worship is preferred because of the negative connotations the word ritual has among Pentecostals – 'ritual' is often associated with worship that lacks life, meaning, and the work of the Spirit.[12] I also refer to expressions or features of corporate worship throughout this work, which refer to practices like the sermon, the reading of Scripture, singing, the Lord's Supper, and other unique activities expressed during corporate worship. Though these expressions or features may also be referred to as

---

[10] Cecil B. Knight, 'The Wonder of Worship', in Cecil B. Knight (ed.), *Pentecostal Worship* (Cleveland, TN: Pathway Press, 1974), pp. 9, 13-14; Delton L. Alford, 'Music in Worship', in Cecil B. Knight (ed.), *Pentecostal Worship* (Cleveland, TN: Pathway Press, 1974), p. 66. Though this work does not engage in less dominant elements of Pentecostal corporate worship today, a few other works can benefit those exploring other elements of Pentecostal corporate worship. For instance, John Christopher Thomas and Kenneth Archer, both Church of God (Cleveland) theologians, argue that Pentecostals can relate five key Pentecostal theological affirmations with five sacraments. The five sacraments they focus on include water baptism, foot-washing, speaking in tongues, praying for healing and anointing those who are sick with oil, and the Lord's Supper (15-16). See John Christopher Thomas, '1998 Presidential Address: Pentecostal Theology in the Twenty-First Century', *Pneuma* 20.1 (Spring 1998), pp. 18-19; Kenneth J. Archer, *The Gospel Revisited: Towards a Pentecostal Theology of Worship and Witness* (Eugene: Pickwick, 2011), pp. 15-16. For a discussion on the Lord's Supper from scholars who have a Pentecostal-Charismatic perspective, see Wolfgang Vondey, *People of the Bread: Rediscovering Ecclesiology* (New York: Paulist, 2008); and Chris E.W. Green, *Toward a Pentecostal Theology of the Lord's Supper: Foretasting the Kingdom* (Cleveland: CPT, 2012).

[11] Albrecht, *Rites in the Spirit*, p. 22

[12] Albrecht, *Rites in the Spirit*, p. 21; Lindhardt, 'Introduction', p. 2.

'rites', I use terms like expressions or features because they are perceived with less suspicion among Pentecostals.[13] Like the word 'ritual', 'rites' can be perceived negatively by Pentecostals. And in order to reflect the Pentecostal movement accurately and to provide an analysis of Pentecostalism that may be received by Pentecostals themselves, it is best to use the language that is native to the tradition – namely, corporate worship.

Three expressions of corporate worship are highlighted in this book: worship music, preaching, and the altar. This is not because these are the only expressions found in Pentecostal corporate worship. Pentecostals may read Scripture, pray, partake of the Lord's Supper, include time for water baptisms, and include various other elements for a corporate worship service they deem necessary. However, worship music, preaching, and the altar, are primary expressions that are foundational for Pentecostal corporate worship services.[14]

Corporate worship is also distinguished from 'worship'. Harold M. Best provides a helpful definition of worship in the broad sense in light of passages like Rom. 12.1, when he states, '*Worship is the continuous outpouring of all that I am, all that I do and all that I can ever become*

---

[13] Albrecht, *Rites in the Spirit*, p. 22 Also see Monique M. Ingalls, 'Introduction: Interconnection, Interface, and Identification in Pentecostal-Charismatic Music and Worship', in Monique M. Ingalls and Amos Yong (eds.), *The Spirit of Praise: Music and Worship in Global Pentecostal-Charismatic Christianity* (University Park: The Pennsylvania State University Press, 2015), p. 4.

[14] This approach finds precedent in Daniel Albrecht's approach, as he acknowledges that while there are other elements – what he refers to as rites – included in Pentecostal corporate worship services, the three primary are worship music, preaching, and the altar. *Rites in the Spirit*, pp. 152-53. While some might consider worship music and preaching the two dominant rites for Pentecostal corporate worship, the altar cannot be neglected because of its interconnectedness to the rest of the corporate worship service. Aldwin Ragoonath claims that there would not even be 'Pentecostal preaching' apart from the altar call. *Preach the Word: A Pentecostal Approach* (Winnipeg: Agape Teaching Ministry, 2004), p. 37. Wolfgang Vondey contends that 'at the heart of the Pentecostal liturgy stands a theology of the altar – an archetype of Pentecost – that is the summit and source of sacramentality among Pentecostals' (95). See 'Pentecostal Sacramentality and the Theology of the Altar', in Mark J. Cartledge and A.J. Swoboda (eds.), *Scripting Pentecost: A Study of Pentecostals, Worship, and Liturgy* (London: Routledge, 2016), pp. 94-107; and Daniel Tomberlin, *Pentecostal Sacraments: Encountering God at the Altar* (Cleveland: Center for Pentecostal Leadership and Care, 2010), p. 31.

in light of a chosen or choosing god.[15] Best's description shows how worship is expressed by all people at all times, regardless of their backgrounds or religious affiliations. Though some of this book explores issues related to worship in the broad sense, the primary focus is corporate worship.

Second, this work focuses on a sustained treatment of contemporary *North American* Pentecostal corporate worship, though it has implications for non-Western Pentecostal approaches to worship.[16] While Pentecostals of various ethnic groups in North America have influenced Pentecostalism, it is impossible to provide a substantial treatment here of them for brevity's sake.[17] Furthermore, this discussion focuses on churches in North America that are English-speaking. The leaders discussed here, involved in Contemporary Worship Music (CWM) and contemporary preaching and the altar are all white, English-speaking leaders. All do, however, come from various backgrounds, such as Canada (Brian Doerksen and Charles T. Crabtree who has roots in Canada), Australia (Darlene Zschech), England (Matt Redman), and the United States (Ray H. Hughes, Charles T. Crabtree, and Haddon W. Robinson). One book cannot treat the global scene of Pentecostal worship without diminishing the various

---

[15] Harold M. Best, *Unceasing Worship: Biblical Perspectives on Worship and the Arts* (Downers Grove: InterVarsity, 2003), p. 18 (emphasis original).

[16] While this book does not explore non-Western Pentecostal-Charismatic approaches to corporate worship, there are sources that are helpful to explore other contexts of corporate worship. E.g., for a Charismatic African approach to corporate worship, see M.L. Daneel, *All Things Hold Together: Holistic Theologies at the African Grassroots* (Pretoria: Unisa, 2007); and Dana L. Robert and M.L. Daneel, 'Worship among Apostles and Zionists in Southern Africa, Zimbabwe', in Charles E. Farhadian (ed.), *Christian Worship Worldwide: Expanding Horizons, Deepening Practices* (Grand Rapids: Eerdmans, 2007), pp. 43-70.

[17] This book uses the terms 'African Americans' and 'Blacks' synonymously, which reflects a diversity of opinion regarding which term is best to use. In general, the phrases 'African American' and 'Black' refer to Africans who were originally brought to the United States through slavery, as well as their descendants. Since the only engagement with African Americans/Blacks in this work refers to those who have a connection with the United States' history of slavery – and not those who came to the United States through other avenues, like those who immigrated from the Caribbean – both terms are used. Furthermore, the use of both terms is reflected among those who came to the United States from Africa through slavery. E.g., see Frank Newport, 'Black or African American?', *Gallup* (September 28, 2007). Online: http://www.gallup.com/poll/28816/black-african-american.aspx, paras. 2-3, 8.

cultural nuances and differences among Pentecostal churches around the world. For this reason, this study is limited to Western approaches that affect contemporary Pentecostal corporate worship.

This study also focuses on the classical Pentecostal approach within the Pentecostal movement. The denominations in North America associated with classical Pentecostals include the Assemblies of God, the Church of God (Cleveland), the Church of God in Christ, the Pentecostal Assemblies of Canada, and the International Pentecostal Holiness Church.[18] Classical Pentecostals often identify the Azusa Street Revival as a significant part of their historical roots, and also maintain that the evidence of Spirit baptism is tongues.[19]

An analysis of CWM for probing the worship music of Pentecostals today is based both on the popular use of CWM among classical Pentecostal churches in North America, and because much of the music within CWM arises from and is influenced by those belonging to the Pentecostal-Charismatic tradition.[20] Three influential CWM leaders are examined here: Brian Doerksen, Darlene Zschech, and Matt Redman.[21] Understanding CWM from the perspective of leaders associated with the Pentecostal-Charismatic tradition ensures that the leaders are not only influential CWM leaders, but leaders that best

---

[18] The discussion here does not attempt to address the issues related to the Church of God in Christ because it is a predominantly African American denomination. The various cultural nuances of being a predominantly African American denomination means that this book cannot give it the extensive treatment it deserves. For an example of a Church of God in Christ leader addressing preaching, see Leonard Lovett, *Crock Pot Preaching: Toward a Preaching Methodology* (Cleveland: Derek, 2009).

[19] Vinson Synan, 'Classical Pentecostalism', in Stanley M. Burgess (ed.), *The New International Dictionary of Pentecostal and Charismatic Movements* (Grand Rapids: Zondervan, 2003), p. 553.

[20] Robb Redman, *The Great Worship Awakening: Singing a New Song in the Postmodern Church* (San Francisco: Jossey-Bass, 2002), pp. 22, 41, 48; Michael D. Macchia, 'Pentecostal', in Paul F. Bradshaw (ed.), *The New SCM Dictionary of Liturgy and Worship* (London: SCM Press, 2005), p. 84; and Mark Evans, *Open Up the Doors: Music in the Modern Church* (London: Equinox, 2006), pp. 15, 39, 60, 87.

[21] The use of the three particular CWM leaders discussed here finds precedent in Victoria Cooke, *Understanding Songs in Renewal* (Grove Renewal Series 4; Cambridge: Grove Books, 2001), p. 3. Unlike Cooke, however, Zschech is examined in this study – who is associated with Hillsong – rather than attempting to follow Hillsong broadly. Furthermore, Doerksen's views are examined, rather than Vineyard broadly, since Doerksen is associated with the Vineyard approach to worship music.

represent the popular approach to worship music among Pentecostals and Charismatics. Focusing on influential CWM leaders who are from the Pentecostal-Charismatic tradition also ensures that the dialogue is relevant for how worship music is conducted within the Pentecostal tradition.

The analysis of contemporary Pentecostal preaching is done by studying the approach of three leaders: Ray H. Hughes, Charles T. Crabtree, and Haddon W. Robinson.[22] Hughes and Crabtree both represent the approach of classical Pentecostal leaders. Hughes belonged (he passed away in 2011) to the Church of God (Cleveland) and Crabtree belongs to the Assemblies of God. Robinson is an Evangelical who has influenced Pentecostals primarily through his book, *Biblical Preaching*.

Finally, I must acknowledge my own background as a classical Pentecostal born and raised in Canada with an East-Indian background – all elements that influenced this study.[23] Rather than attempt to appear to be completely objective in this process of research – an impossibility for any author – it is important to share how my background has influenced why I think this subject is important and my understanding of the subject.[24] First, my personal involvement in

---

[22] The use of the three contemporary preachers to examine Pentecostal preaching, finds precedent in both Randall Holm, 'Cadences of the Heart: A Walkabout in Search of Pentecostal Preaching', *Didaskalia*. 15.1 (Fall 2003), pp. 13-27; and in an article I wrote, 'The Spirit in Pentecostal Preaching: A Constructive Dialogue with Haddon Robinson's and Charles Crabtree's Theology of Preaching', *Pneuma* 35.2 (2013), pp. 199-219. Holm examines the writings of three Pentecostal leaders to explore Pentecostal preaching, namely, Chester L. Allen, Ray H. Hughes, and Charles T. Crabtree. My article, however, only examines Crabtree and Robinson's views on preaching. Allen's work is not addressed in this study since the three leaders examined here are more contemporary leaders. Furthermore, focusing on only three leaders provides opportunity to offer a more substantial treatment of all the leaders' views. Holm, 'Cadences of the Heart', pp. 16-20; Samuel, 'The Spirit in Pentecostal Preaching', pp. 199-219. See chapter five for a more lengthy rationale for the use of these three leaders for this discussion.

[23] John Swinton and Harriet Mowat explain how reflexivity is an important dimension of research. They explain: 'Reflexivity is a mode of knowing which accepts the impossibility of the researcher standing outside of the research field and seeks to incorporate that knowledge creatively and effectively'. See *Practical Theology and Qualitative Research* (London: SCM Press, 2013), p. 59.

[24] Swinton and Mowat, *Practical Theology and Qualitative Research*, pp. 60-61.

Pentecostal churches has shown me the importance of the experience of the Spirit in corporate worship for Pentecostals. My experience, however, has also made me realise how the Pentecostal understanding and approach to the Spirit's manifest presence in corporate worship can be deficient theologically. Thus, my desire to discuss this subject does not come from any romanticised notions of the Pentecostal understanding and approach to the Spirit's felt presence in corporate worship. I critique the Pentecostal approach when necessary, while also acknowledging when the Pentecostal approach is theologically accurate.

Second, my personal involvement in the North American classical Pentecostal tradition and non-Western, non-Pentecostal traditions has broadened my view on corporate worship and has prepared me to address the issues of corporate worship within the North American classical Pentecostal movement. I was born and raised in Toronto, Ontario, Canada, and it is from within this context I have witnessed, participated in, led, and researched classical Pentecostal worship. I am a third-generation Pentecostal, involved in Pentecostal ministry, including ordained ministry with the Pentecostal Assemblies of Canada (PAOC). I have had opportunity to pastor for five years within a PAOC church and ministered in various classical Pentecostal churches, conventions, and conferences in Canada and the United States. I was also trained at Master's College and Seminary (a PAOC Bible College in Peterborough, Ontario, Canada), and am now the Director of Worship and Creative Arts Ministry and a Professor of Bible and Theology at this same college. But my associations and experience are not limited to just a North American brand of Pentecostalism.

I am Canadian but also of Indian background. My grandfather, P. M. Samuel, was the first president of the Indian Pentecostal Church of God (IPC), so I have a heritage in non-Western classical Pentecostalism. I also attended and later provided leadership at a local classical Pentecostal church in Toronto, Ontario, Canada, Zion Gospel Assembly, for the first eighteen years of my life, which consists primarily of Christians whose background is from Kerala, India. My experience in non-Western forms of Pentecostalism includes: ministry in Indian Pentecostal churches and conferences in North America and India; ministry in the Dominican Republic, teaching at Zion Bible College (IPC Bible College in Vijayawada, India) and teaching at

Universidad Teológica Pentecostal Cuba (AG Bible College in Havana, Cuba). My background in Pentecostalism, both Western and non-Western, is important because I can subsequently provide an analysis of Pentecostal corporate worship that is informed by both the scholarly discussion and personal experience. My involvement within the classical Pentecostal tradition, however, may be deemed as a negative point in order to provide an objective discussion on Pentecostal corporate worship. But I have been exposed to the worship practices in a variety of Christian traditions beyond Pentecostalism. I studied and participated in corporate worship at an Anglican seminary (Wycliffe College, University of Toronto) and interdenominational evangelical seminaries (Tyndale Seminary and McMaster Divinity College). I also taught and preached in various denominational and ethnic church contexts in North America (e.g., Alliance, Baptist, Presbyterian, Indian, Chinese, First Nations, Korean, and Sri Lankan). Being involved in various other Christian traditions has ensured that my understanding of corporate worship is broader than the Pentecostal tradition that I belong to.

The Historical Dimension of Pentecostal Corporate Worship: The Azusa Street Revival
Acknowledging the Azusa Street Revival as a critical influence upon North American Pentecostalism and looking to Azusa as a source of renewal for today's Pentecostal movement finds its precedent in the scholarship of D. William Faupel, Walter Hollenweger, Steven Land, Allan Anderson, and Cecil M. Robeck.[25] The early years of the Pentecostal movement form 'the heart and not simply the infancy of the

---

[25] The language of Azusa being a source of renewal is found in: D. William Faupel, *The Everlasting Gospel: The Significance of Eschatology in The Development of Pentecostal Thought* (JPTSup, 10; Blandford Forum: Deo, 2009), p. 309; Walter J. Hollenweger, 'Pentecostals and the Charismatic Movement', in Cheslyn Jones, Geoffrey Wainwright, and Edward Yarnold, SJ (eds.), *The Study of Spirituality* (Oxford: Oxford University Press, 1986), pp. 551-52; Steven Jack Land, *Pentecostal Spirituality: A Passion for the Kingdom* (Cleveland: CPT, 2010), pp. 1, 14-15; Allan Anderson, *An Introduction to Pentecostalism* (Cambridge: Cambridge University, 2004), p. 45. Cecil M. Robeck, Jr. claims that Azusa 'can still provide a new impetus toward an encounter with God and spiritual growth'. *The Azusa Street Mission and Revival: The Birth of the Global Pentecostal Movement* (Nashville: Thomas Nelson, 2006), pp. 10-11.

movement' and its 'spirituality'.[26] I discuss the corporate worship at
the Azusa Street Revival because it has been one of the most formative influences on the Pentecostal identity in North America. The
views and practices of those at Azusa provide examples for renewal
today, as well as approaches that cannot be repeated today. Whether
or not Azusa is the birthplace of Pentecostalism is not relevant for
this study.[27] Scholars have shown that there were various other contexts – such as India, Wales, Britain, the United States, Canada, and
Korea – where 'Pentecostal'-like phenomena erupted, such as
tongues, prior to and independent of the Azusa Street Revival.[28] But
though there were other contexts where experiences similar to the
Azusa Street Revival occurred independent of this revival, the practices (particularly the worship practices) at this revival were formative
for the entire movement worldwide – especially North American

---

[26] Faupel, *The Everlasting Gospel*, p. 309; Hollenweger, 'Pentecostals and the
Charismatic Movement', p. 551; Land, *Pentecostal Spirituality*, pp. 1, 14-15; Anderson,
Introduction to Pentecostalism, p. 45.

[27] For those who prefer to trace the origins of Pentecostalism to William J.
Seymour's leadership at Azusa, see Robeck, *The Azusa Street Mission and Revival*, 8,
239; Cox, *Fire from Heaven*, 149; and Walter J. Hollenweger, *Pentecostalism: Origins and
Developments Worldwide* (Peabody: Hendrickson, 1997), p. 18. For those who trace
the origins of Pentecostalism to Charles F. Parham's leadership at Topeka, Kansas,
see James R. Goff, Jr., *Fields White Unto Harvest: Charles F. Parham and the Missionary
Origins of Pentecostalism* (Fayetteville: University of Arkansas, 1988), pp. 11, 15 and
John Thomas Nichol, *Pentecostalism* (New York: Harper, 1966), p. 81.

[28] Anderson, *An Introduction to Pentecostalism*, pp. 35-38, 43; D.D. Bundy, 'Irving,
Edward', in Stanley M. Burgess (ed.), *The New International Dictionary of Pentecostal
and Charismatic Movements* (Grand Rapids: Zondervan, 2003), pp. 803-804; Vinson
Synan, *The Holiness-Pentecostal Tradition: Charismatic Movements in the Twentieth Century*
(Grand Rapids: Eerdmans, 1997), pp. 86-88; Paulson Pulikottil, 'One God, One
Spirit, Two Memories: A Postcolonial Reading of the Encounter Between Western
Pentecostalism and Native Pentecostalism in Kerala', in Veli-Matti Kärkkäinen
(ed.), *The Spirit in the World: Emerging Pentecostal Theologies in Global Contexts* (Grand
Rapids: Eerdmans, 2009), p. 83; Goff, *Fields White Unto Harvest*; Koo Dong Yun,
'Pentecostalism from Below: *Minjung* Liberation and Asian Pentecostal Theology',
in Veli-Matti Kärkkäinen (ed.), *The Spirit in the World: Emerging Pentecostal Theologies in
Global Contexts* (Grand Rapids: Eerdmans, 2009), p. 104. To explore the gifts of the
Spirit, including tongues, in the early church, see Ronald A.N. Kydd, *Charismatic
Gifts in the Early Church: An Exploration Into the Gifts of the Spirit During the First Three
Centuries of the Christian Church* (Peabody: Hendrickson, 1984).

classical Pentecostalism.[29] Numerous North American Pentecostal institutions and influential ministers admit to the Azusa Street Revival's influence upon their ministry.[30] Thus, understanding one of the most influential contexts for the development of Pentecostal corporate worship, the Azusa Street Revival, is critical. The Azusa Street Revival is not romanticised, however, for both its strengths and weaknesses are acknowledged here. Exploring Azusa's corporate worship allows Pentecostals to reckon with their roots and consider its relevance for their current practices.

Systematic Theology: The Immediacy of the Holy Spirit

The second major component of this study includes systematic theology, which focuses on the assumption of the immediacy of the Holy Spirit in Pentecostal corporate worship. In order to understand Pentecostal theology, you cannot just study statements of faith. Studying Pentecostal theology requires an analysis of Pentecostal spirituality.[31] And in the midst of studying Pentecostal theology, debates continue with regard to what is essential to Pentecostalism, such as Spirit baptism, the claim that there is no theological consistency, or

---

[29] Michael Bergunder, *The South Indian Pentecostal Movement in the Twentieth Century* (Grand Rapids: Eerdmans, 2008), pp. 6-8; Anderson, *An Introduction to Pentecostalism*, p. 43.

[30] They include: the Church of God in Christ, the Assemblies of God, the Church of God, the Pentecostal Assemblies of the World, the United Pentecostal Churches, the Vineyard Christian Fellowship, Victory Outreach, La Asamblea Apostólica de la Fe en Cristo Jesús, Inc. and its Mexican counterpart, La Iglesia Apostólica de la fe in Cristo Jesús, and the Trinity Broadcasting Network; and ministers such as Pat Robertson, Oral Roberts, T.D. Jakes, Kenneth and Gloria Copeland, and Canadian David Mainse. Robeck, *The Azusa Street Mission and Revival*, p. 11.

[31] Donald W. Dayton was one of the first to describe Pentecostalism through a theological lens, unlike others who might only focus on Spirit baptism, or even claim that there are no central theological impulses within Pentecostalism. Donald Dayton, *Theological Roots of Pentecostalism* (Grand Rapids: Francis Asbury, 1987), pp. 15-23; Steven Studebaker, 'Charismatic Theology'. Course at McMaster Divinity College, Hamilton, ON, Fall 2008. Others have likewise argued for the importance of understanding Pentecostal spirituality rather than just statements of faith. See Hollenweger, *Pentecostalism*, pp. 18-19; Cox, *Fire from Heaven*, p. 15; Veli-Matti Kärkkäinen, 'Pneumatologies in Systematic Theology', in Michael Bergunder, Allan Anderson, and A.F. Droogers (eds.), *Studying Global Pentecostalism: Theories and Methods* (Berkeley: University of California Press, 2010), p. 224.

theological diversity.[32] However, even in the debates about what is essential for Pentecostals, there is a prevalence of the assumption of the immediacy of the Holy Spirit among Pentecostal groups around the world.[33] An experience of the Spirit within one of the most important contexts for this experience – corporate worship – has not been sufficiently probed, and is one more reason why this study is important.[34]

Four elements of this work related to theology are necessary to explain, namely, the language of the Spirit's immediacy, the means of exploring this subject, this subject's relevance for other Christian traditions, and the implications of this study. First, though a number of authors use the language of the immediacy of God to describe the Pentecostal approach to God, they do not always explicitly take time to define this phrase.[35] Likewise, throughout this book, the views of several leaders and writers are examined who do not make use of the language of 'immediacy'. Rather, their views and practices presuppose a theology of the immediacy of God.[36] In this study, *the immediacy of God refers to a sensory experience of the presence of God through the*

---

[32] Hollenweger, *Pentecostalism*, pp. 18-19.

[33] For instance, Hollenweger rightly points out that Spirit baptism with the evidence of tongues is not emphasized globally among Pentecostals. And he also argues that a spirituality among Pentecostals is more notable than 'theology'. He points out tangible expressions of spirituality – emotionally and physically – which include things like dance, dreams, visions, and a general 'orality of liturgy'. The spirituality he points out, however, has the assumption of the immediacy of God as foundational. Anderson argues for theological diversity within Pentecostalism, but at one point in his writings, explains that the Pentecostal movement is 'concerned primarily with the *experience* of the working of the Holy Spirit and the *practice* of the gifts'. *Introduction to Pentecostalism*, pp. 10, 14 (emphasis original).

[34] Lindhardt, 'Introduction', p. 1.

[35] E.g., Anderson, 'Pentecostalism', p. 646; Mark A. Noll, *Turning Points: Decisive Moments in the History of the Christian Church* (Grand Rapids: Baker, 2nd edn, 2000), p. 302; Timothy C. Tennent, *Theology in the Context of World Christianity: How the Global Church is Influencing the Way We Think about and Discuss Theology* (Grand Rapids: Zondervan, 2007), p. 188.

[36] Anderson, 'Pentecostalism', p. 646. Daniel E. Albrecht, *Rites in the Spirit*, p. 24, explains that

> Pentecostal spirituality fosters a deep, even mystical, piety that emphasizes the immanent sense of the divine. The belief system accentuates an understanding that 'gifts of the Spirit', including the subjective religious experience of 'Spirit baptism' appear and operate as normative in the life of the Church. This conviction informs all of Pentecostal religious experiences and expressions.

Spirit. At times I may refer to the manifest presence of God, the present work of the Spirit, the felt presence of God, the experience of God, or the immediacy of God – these are all trying to capture the same idea. The immediacy of God is not mere religious experience in a broad sense – it is a theological issue within Christianity.[37] For Pentecostals, an experience of God is an experience of the Spirit, which is a 'personal encounter with the personal God of the Bible'.[38] The views in this book on the experience of God reflect the 'theological, cultural, and linguistic context' of classical Pentecostals in North America.[39] The assumption of the immediacy of God implies

---

Lindhardt also explains that '[i]n Pentecostal-charismatic worship, divine power is perceived as a physical force that mobilizes the senses and acts directly on and through the human body'. 'Introduction', p. 12.

[37] Steven M. Studebaker rightly notes that an exploration of the experience of the Spirit is not merely an issue of 'religious experience', but pertains to theology. He states that 'Pentecostals should give theological significance to what they take as the manifestation and experience of the Holy Spirit within their incipient tradition'. Steven M. Studebaker, *From Pentecost to the Triune God: A Pentecostal Trinitarian Theology* (Grand Rapids: Eerdmans, 2012), p. 12.

[38] Peter D. Neumann, 'Whither Pentecostal Experience? Mediated Experience of God in Pentecostal Theology', *Canadian Journal of Pentecostal-Charismatic Christianity* 3 (2012), p. 8.

[39] Neumann, 'Whither Pentecostal Experience?', pp. 11, 27. Neumann shows how Pentecostal scholars – particularly Simon Chan, Frank Macchia, and Amos Yong – have engaged with George A. Lindbeck's 'cultural-linguistic' model. For Lindbeck states that 'religion can be viewed as a kind of cultural and/or linguistic framework or medium that shapes the entirety of life and thought'. *The Nature of Doctrine: Religion and Theology in a Postliberal Age* (Philadelphia: Westminster, 1984), p. 32. Neumann shows how Chan, Macchia, and Yong try to help Pentecostals understand the experience of God in light of the influence of their own 'theological, cultural, and linguistic' contexts. Neumann shows how Chan stresses 'that experience of the Spirit occurs within and is shaped by the worshipping community. Spiritual experience is mediated through the Pentecostal subcultural-linguistic context, but also that of the broader Christian historical tradition.' Neumann, 'Whither Pentecostal Experience?', p. 21. E.g., see Simon Chan, *Pentecostal Theology and the Christian Spiritual Tradition* (JPTSup, 21; Sheffield: Sheffield Academic, 2000); and Chan, *Liturgical Theology*. Neumann shows how Macchia challenges Lindbeck's views on doctrine, showing that the experience of God through tongues transcends 'cultural-linguistic boundaries' (p. 29). Macchia acknowledges both the strengths and weaknesses of the Pentecostal approach, making use of the language of Spirit baptism, while also showing why a revision is required that draws upon 'the broader Christian tradition' (p. 30). E.g., see Frank D. Macchia, *Baptized in the Spirit: A Global Pentecostal Theology* (Grand Rapids: Zondervan, 2006). Finally, Neumann explains how Yong seeks to understand the experience of God as the Spirit mediating 'all

that God is present and active in this world through the Spirit. And this study shows how the experience of God may be sensed in various ways within Pentecostal corporate worship.

Second, examining the key expressions of Pentecostal corporate worship will demonstrate the theological core of Pentecostalism related to the Spirit's immediacy. Furthermore, for each chapter focused on specific expressions of worship, various categories such as the definition/nature of the activity, the preparation involved, and the actual presentation in corporate worship are explored theologically. In order to probe Pentecostal corporate worship, three broad expressions of worship are examined – worship music, preaching, and the altar.

Third, though this book focuses on the experience of the Spirit in Pentecostal corporate worship, other Christian groups may also highlight this type of corporate worship. Pentecostals, however, traditionally not only assume that it was and is important on occasion, but should be normative and is the indispensable theological presupposition of Pentecostal corporate worship and religious experience. Further, though this study focuses on North American classical Pentecostal worship, it has implications for other Christian traditions, most notably other Pentecostal and Charismatic contexts.

Finally, the implications of these concrete expressions of theology are numerous. By exploring various expressions of Pentecostal corporate worship, noting the assumption of the sensory experience of the Holy Spirit, one cannot help but recognise how this issue can

---

experience', so that the limitations of a theological framework can be overcome (p. 35). Thus, Yong is willing to dialogue with other religions and the sciences because of the Spirit who is 'universally present and active' (p. 34). E.g., see Amos Yong, *Discerning the Spirit(s): A Pentecostal – Charismatic Contribution to Christian Theology of Religions* (JPTSup, 20; Sheffield: Sheffield Academic, 2000); Amos Yong, *Spirit–Word–Community: Theological Hermeneutics in Trinitarian Perspective* (Eugene: Wipf and Stock, 2002); and Amos Yong, *Beyond the Impasse: Toward a Pneumatological Theology of Religions* (Grand Rapids: Baker, 2003); and Amos Yong, *The Spirit Poured Out on All Flesh: Pentecostalism and the Possibility of Global Theology* (Grand Rapids: Baker, 2005). For a fuller treatment of this subject, see Neumann, 'Whither Pentecostal Experience?' and Neumann, 'Encountering the Spirit'. The approach given here in this book follows the approach of Macchia more so than Chan and Yong, because the approach here is one that makes use of the theological framework found among classical Pentecostals in North America, while also being willing to make revisions where necessary.

be both helpful and damaging all at the same time. Should and can one always assume the Spirit's immediacy in expressions of corporate worship? What are the theological implications for those who do not tangibly experience the Spirit's in worship? How does one discern whether they are experiencing the Spirit? And if churches can make a difference to ensure the experience of the Spirit in corporate worship, to what extent should the church be making this a priority? When does the emphasis in corporate worship on an experience of the Spirit lead to manipulation and sensationalism? How leaders answer the above questions will determine the quality of corporate worship expressed by the church.

PART 1
THE AZUSA STREET REVIVAL'S APPROACH TO CORPORATE WORSHIP

1

'THE COMFORTER HAS COME' – THE AZUSA STREET REVIVAL

I received the baptism with the Holy Ghost and fire and now I feel the presence of the Holy Ghost, not only in my heart but in my lungs, my hands, my arms and all through my body and at times I am shaken like a locomotive steamed up and prepared for a long journey. O it is blessed to let the Lord have His way with you. I also speak in six foreign tongues given me at God's command. God has called me to Africa as a missionary, and told me to go to Monrovia, Liberia. He showed me the town which is on the west coast. I described the town and country to Bro. Mead, a missionary that had been there and he said it was a perfect description. Saints, pray much. Fast and pray.

– G.W. Batman[1]

Introduction

The Azusa Street Revival is one of the most famous revivals within Pentecostalism. This revival popularised Pentecostal spirituality worldwide, and has become iconic within the Pentecostal movement.[2] Many who experienced their own 'Pentecost' through this revival felt called to missions work and subsequently brought the Pentecostal message around the world. The Azusa Street Revival became international in scope. This chapter details the corporate worship of

---

[1] G.W. Batman. 'En Route to Africa', *AF* 1.4 (December 1906), p. 4.
[2] Robeck, *The Azusa Street Mission and Revival*, p. 10.

the Azusa Street Revival, focusing on worship music, preaching, and the altar.

Overview of the Azusa Street Revival

The Azusa Street Revival began in Los Angeles, California in 1906 under the leadership of William Seymour at the Azusa Street Mission. Though the mission experienced its most intense revivals during its first three years from 1906 to 1909, its ministry continued until 1936.[3] Azusa participants explain what happened among them in the revival's first official publication in 1906: 'The power of God now has this city agitated as never before. Pentecost has surely come and with it the Bible evidences are following, many being converted and sanctified and filled with the Holy Spirit, speaking in tongues as they did on the day of Pentecost.'[4] As news of the revival spread, people from all across the world came to the Azusa Street Mission to participate in this revival. Those who could not travel to Azusa sought their own 'Pentecost' in their local context in light of Azusa's influential message.

Corporate worship at the Azusa Street Revival was typically informal, spontaneous, expressive, emotional, and ecstatic, which was related to their value of the Spirit's immediacy in corporate worship.[5] While those at the Azusa Street Revival sought to draw closer to God in corporate worship through expressions like songs, preaching, and prayer, they 'frequently manifested some physical or mental change'.[6] Some of these 'manifestations' included being 'slain in the Spirit', shaking, jerking, involuntarily moving hands and feet, visions – and of course, tongues. 'As they focused upon Christ, several were overwhelmed by a sense of well-being or wholeness, in which they felt

---

[3] Cecil M. Robeck, Jr, 'Azusa Street Revival', in Stanley M. Burgess (ed.), *The New International Dictionary of Pentecostal and Charismatic Movements* (Grand Rapids: Zondervan, 2003), p. 315; Robeck, *The Azusa Street Mission and Revival*, p. 4.

[4] *AF* 1.1 (September 1906), p. 1.

[5] Joseph R. Guthrie explains that the corporate worship of early Pentecostals in general featured 'informality, spontaneity, congregational participation, and emotional outbursts'. 'Pentecostal Hymnody: Historical, Theological, and Musical Influences' (DMA dissertation, Southwestern Baptist Theological Seminary, 1992), p. 77.

[6] Robeck, *The Azusa Street Mission and Revival*, p. 186.

God's power, God's love, God's peace, God's joy, and God's presence'.[7] These early Pentecostals 'felt' God's nearness in worship, and they were emotionally, psychologically, physically, and spiritually affected. People witnessing this revival from the outside viewed it as epitomising 'the uninhibited expression of raw religious emotion'.[8] While past Christian revivals in the United States also included such emotion, Grant Wacker argues that others would view the 'uninhibited emotion' as 'central' to the worship of early Pentecostals.[9] But rather than seeking 'uninhibited emotion' merely for good feelings, these early Pentecostals connected their experience to a sign of the immediacy of the Holy Spirit in their worship, which ultimately pointed to Christ.

Sensing the tangible presence of God in corporate worship did not begin within the Christian community at the Azusa Street Mission – antecedents to this experience in corporate worship occurred throughout history. Scripture also includes various moments when people sensed God, from those who prophesied in the Old Testament to those who spoke in tongues in the New Testament. Concrete experiences of the Spirit are found in a number of instances in Scripture.[10] A number of historical antecedents to the worship at the Azusa Street Revival – apart from those described in Scripture – also occurred, which include African American spirituality, Revivalism, Methodism, the Holiness movement, and Proto-Pentecostal groups.[11] The Azusa Street Mission began as part of a broader resto-

---

[7] Robeck, *The Azusa Street Mission and Revival*, p. 186.

[8] Grant Wacker, *Heaven Below: Early Pentecostals and American Culture* (Cambridge: Harvard University, 2001), p. 99.

[9] Wacker, *Heaven Below*, p. 100.

[10] E.g. Saul prophesying in the company of prophets in 1 Sam. 10.9-11; and believers speaking in tongues in the Upper Room in Acts 2. For further exploration of this subject traced throughout Paul's letters in Scripture, see Fee, *God's Empowering Presence*.

[11] For more analysis of antecedents, see Synan, *The Holiness-Pentecostal Tradition*; Dayton, *The Theological Roots of Pentecostalism*; Edith L. Blumhofer, *Restoring the Faith: The Assemblies of God, Pentecostalism, and American Culture* (Urbana: University of Illinois Press, 1993); and Hollenweger, *Pentecostalism*.

ration movement at that time, known as the Apostolic Faith Movement.[12] Azusa leaders explain that their movement '[s]tands for the
restoration of the faith once delivered unto the saints – the old time
religion, camp meetings, revivals, missions, street and prison work
and Christian Unity everywhere'.[13] They later referred to their movement as the Pacific Apostolic Faith Movement, because of their division from Charles Parham.[14] Azusa leaders believed they were part
of a Christian movement that was witnessing the restoration of
Christian practices that began in the book of Acts, and in succession
with other traditions within the history of Christianity that sought
the restoration of apostolic Christianity.

The participants of the Azusa Street Revival were quite clear
about being in succession with various other movements, which they
believed brought the restoration of important Christian beliefs and
practices. Azusa leaders believed that God raised various leaders to
restore truth, especially when the church was 'preaching a partial
Gospel'.[15] They argued that Luther restored the teaching on justification by faith, Wesley brought back holiness, and Cullis reminded the
church of the doctrine of healing. They believed they were in conti-
nuity with such leaders by highlighting what they taught, and by restoring the biblical teaching on Spirit baptism.[16]

Five teachings became prominent at the Azusa Street Revival,
namely, salvation, sanctification, healing, the imminent second coming of Jesus Christ, and Spirit baptism – the Fivefold Gospel. During
a later stage of the Azusa Street Revival some divided over whether
entire sanctification was legitimate, often referred to as the 'finished-
work controversy'.[17] The early Pentecostals, however, could also be
described as focusing on four key teachings – salvation, the imminent
return of Jesus, healing, and Spirit baptism – since many later Pentecostals eventually rejected the teaching on entire sanctification. But

---

[12] Also see S.L. Ware, 'Restorationism in Classical Pentecostalism', in Stanley
M. Burgess (ed.), *The New International Dictionary of Pentecostal and Charismatic Movements* (Grand Rapids: Zondervan, 2003), pp. 1019-21.
[13] *AF* 1.1 (September 1906), p. 2.
[14] *AF* 1.3 (November 1906), p. 2.
[15] *AF* 1.2 (October 1906), p. 1.
[16] *AF* 1.2 (October 1906), p. 1.
[17] See R.M. Riss, 'Finished Work Controversy', in Stanley M. Burgess (ed.), *The
New International Dictionary of Pentecostal and Charismatic Movements* (Grand Rapids:
Zondervan, 2003), pp. 638-39.

the early Pentecostals' focus on sanctification is important to understand as the emphasis on holiness and being set apart continued – whether explicitly or implicitly (e.g. even when in the extreme form of legalism).[18] Thus, the role of holiness and being set apart – including the other key teachings mentioned here – are still important for understanding the identity of Pentecostalism. The early Pentecostal movement often referred to these four or five key teachings as part of the 'full gospel', which reveals how these teachings were core, formative teachings for them.[19]

Among the key teachings, three represent stages in the Christian life among Pentecostals: beginning with salvation, then sanctification, and finally Spirit baptism. And all three are often described as occurring while the Spirit of God is felt during corporate worship. One excerpt from *AF* shows how the three stages occurred within their corporate worship context at the Azusa Street Mission. The article reveals:

> Many are praising God for the old barn-like building on Azusa Street, and the plain old plank beside which they kneeled in the sawdust when God saved, sanctified and baptized them with the Holy Ghost. Those who know God feel His presence as soon as they cross the threshold.[20]

'Saved, sanctified, and baptised in the Holy Ghost' was a recurring phrase representing key stages of Christian growth. And those 'who know God' could 'feel His presence' when they came into their worshipping context. God's felt presence in their worship provided the context for the three stages to occur.

The Azusa leaders described the three stages in the Christian life in the following way. According to the Azusa participants, the first stage in the Christian life is salvation. The 'First Work' is about being justified, which 'is that act of God's free grace by which we receive remission of sins'.[21] Salvation must be understood within the context of humanity's sinful condition. People must repent, have godly sor-

---

[18] Dayton, *Theological Roots of Pentecostalism*, pp. 21-22.

[19] See *AF* 1.1 (September 1906), p. 2; Allan Anderson, *Spreading Fires: The Missionary Nature of Early Pentecostalism* (Maryknoll: Orbis, 2007), p. 294.

[20] *AF* 1.1 (September 1906), p. 3.

[21] *AF* 1.1 (September 1906), p. 2.

row for sin, confess sin, forsake sinful ways, and seek restitution. Justification is a critical first step for anyone, as people put their faith in Jesus Christ and receive forgiveness of sins.[22] Justification is called the 'First Work' because it precedes and is distinguished from two other important stages of Christian growth.

Azusa participants explain that sanctification 'is the second work of grace and the last work of grace. Sanctification is that act of God's free grace by which he makes us holy.'[23] A few comments on their views on this are necessary. First, when they refer to sanctification, they are referring to entire sanctification – Seymour explains that through sanctification one experiences 'freedom from all sin'.[24] They believe that even after people are justified, believers still experience 'warfare' due to 'old inherited sin' from Adam.[25] But by believing God's Word about sanctification, 'inherited sin' is taken away and '[e]verything is heavenly in your soul' – one is made holy.[26] Furthermore, believers will recognise when this happens, as they believe that the 'Spirit of God witnesses in your heart that you are sanctified'.[27] They do not, however, describe any specific objective experience to look for to know when one is sanctified, other than the Spirit's witness to one's 'heart'. The assurance of sanctification, then, is another instance where they focus on an experience of the Spirit.[28]

Sanctification was an important experience, as it was required for those who wanted to experience Spirit baptism. Azusa leaders believed that sanctification was a necessary step towards Spirit baptism, because the disciples were likewise sanctified prior to their experience of Spirit baptism. The Azusa leaders pointed out that Jesus described his disciples as 'clean' because of the 'Word' that he spoke to them prior to their experience of Spirit baptism.[29] They argued that the

---

[22] *AF* 1.1 (September 1906), p. 2. They make reference to a variety of scriptures, such as Prov. 28.13; Isa. 55.7; Ezek. 33.15; Mt. 9.13; Mk 1.14-15; Lk. 15.21; 18.18; 19.18; Jn 3.8; Acts 10.42-43; 17.30-31; Rom. 3.25; and 2 Cor. 7, 9, 11.

[23] *AF* 1.1 (September 1906), p. 2. They make reference to various Scripture passages, such as Jn 17.15, 17; 1 Thess. 4.3; 5.23; Heb. 13.12; 2.11; and 12.14.

[24] *AF* 1.1 (September 1906), p. 2.

[25] *AF* 1.1 (September 1906), p. 3.

[26] *AF* 1.1 (September 1906), p. 3.

[27] *AF* 1.1 (September 1906), p. 3.

[28] *AF* 1.1 (September 1906), p. 3.

[29] *AF* 1.1 (September 1906), p. 2. Cf. Jn 13.10; 15.3

disciples, and believers today, cannot experience Spirit baptism without sanctification. Christians need to be holy before the Spirit can baptise a believer.

Finally, one of the unique teachings at the Azusa Street Revival was their belief in Spirit baptism, and its evidence being speaking in tongues. Various other groups had already taught on salvation, sanctification, healing, and the imminent return of Christ – all important teachings among Pentecostals. But Spirit baptism, as they taught it, was a novel idea for their time. Parham taught Seymour about this experience. Parham 'invented', or discovered, this teaching in 1901 – just five years prior to the Azusa Street Revival.[30] Prior to Parham's belief on Spirit baptism, Christians had often associated Spirit baptism with salvation, or like Holiness believers, associated Spirit baptism with sanctification.[31]

The early Pentecostals at Azusa explain that 'The Baptism with the Holy Ghost is a gift of power upon the sanctified life; so when we get it we have the same evidence as the Disciples received on the Day of Pentecost (Acts 2:3,4) in speaking in new tongues'.[32] A few comments are necessary to explain their view on Spirit baptism. First, they distinguish this experience from justification and sanctification, noting that these two earlier experiences are works of grace, while Spirit baptism is a 'gift of power'. Sanctification is the 'last work of grace' because one becomes – by God's grace – holy through sanctification. After sanctification, one is consecrated to receive Spirit baptism.[33]

Second, Spirit baptism is based on the Father's promise described by Christ in Lk. 24.49 and Acts 1.4-8, and the subsequent reception of the promise described in Acts 2.[34] The Azusa Street leaders argue that Christ gave his disciples the '[p]romise of the Father', Spirit baptism, so that the disciples would receive 'power from on high' when the Holy Spirit comes on them.[35] The Spirit's empowerment of the disciples would enable them to witness to Jesus Christ in 'Jerusalem,

---

[30] Hollenweger, *Pentecostalism*, pp. 20-21; Goff, *Fields White Unto Harvest*, p. 164.

[31] *AF* 1.1 (September 1906), p. 1.

[32] *AF* 1.1 (September 1906), p. 2. They make reference to various Scripture passages, such as Acts 10.45, 46; 19.6; 1 Cor. 14.21.

[33] *AF* 1.4 (December 1906), p. 2.

[34] *AF* 1.4 (December 1906), p. 2.

[35] *AF* 1.1 (September 1906), p. 2.

and Judea, and in Samaria, and unto the uttermost parts of the earth'.[36] The disciples could receive this promise if they were willing to 'wait' for it. In Acts 2, the disciples wait for the promise and 'were all filled with the Holy Ghost, and began to speak with other tongues, as the Spirit gave them utterance'.[37] The early Pentecostals' comment on Acts 2.4, stating: 'We see here that they ALL spoke in other tongues'.[38] Azusa leaders, thus, contended that tongues is 'the Bible evidence' of Spirit baptism.[39] Since their view of what type of 'tongues' they received changed over time, a few comments on this issue follow.

Initially, the Azusa Street participants believed they received human, foreign languages – *xenolalia* – when they were baptized in the Holy Spirit, which related to their belief in the imminent return of Christ. Like the experience of believers in the book of Acts, they believed that these tongues would enable them to preach the gospel to people of other countries. And the Pentecostals' experience of Spirit baptism led to their emphasis on the mission to preach the gospel to all nations.[40] They believed that the end times were imminent due to the sign of tongues. The reception of tongues convinced them that God was speeding up the process for world evangelization just prior to Christ's imminent return. This implication of Spirit baptism, the imminent return of Christ, points to one other early emphasis that contributed to what they called the 'full gospel'. Tongues provided them with new unlearned languages, which enhanced the missions effort to all nations. They assumed that they would not have to secure lengthy language training because of tongues received.[41] The message of Joel 2.23 provided rationale for their views on the Spirit: 'He gave the former rain moderately at Pentecost, and he is going to send upon us in these last days the former and latter rain. There are greater things to be done in these last days of the Holy

---

[36] *AF* 1.1 (September 1906), p. 2.

[37] *AF* 1.1 (September 1906), p. 2.

[38] *AF* 1.1 (September 1906), p. 2 (emphasis original).

[39] *AF* 1.1 (September 1906), p. 2.

[40] *AF* 1.1 (September 1906), p. 1. Anderson, *Spreading Fires*, pp. 27, 37, 65.

[41] And though there were some reports of believers speaking new languages in different countries, this teaching received less emphasis, in favour of tongues not necessarily being a new language on earth (e.g. it could be a language of angels). For further information, see Anderson, *Spreading Fires*, pp. 57-68.

Ghost.'[42] While this revival began in a humble setting on Azusa Street, it launched missionary workers, and a whole new movement spread across the globe. An experience of the Spirit through Spirit baptism led to one other key belief, namely, the imminent return of Christ.

Finally, healing was another early focus among those in the movement associated with the Azusa Street Revival, which also points to an experience of God. Azusa leaders stated that people must believe God that he is able to heal, referencing various texts from Scripture. The leaders quoted Exod. 15.26, for instance, where God explains, 'I am the LORD who heals you'.[43] Seymour focused on the role of the atonement for healing, stating: 'Sickness and disease are destroyed through the precious atonement of Jesus. O how we ought to honor the stripes of Jesus, for "with his stripes we are healed."'[44] The above concludes this broad treatment of Azusa. The primary teachings found at the Azusa Street Revival included salvation, sanctification, Spirit baptism, the imminent return of Jesus Christ, and healing. The above discussion reveals how each key teaching is related to an experience of God, most notably in corporate worship. What is important now, then, is an examination of Azusa's approach to the three key expressions of corporate worship among Pentecostals, worship music, preaching, and the altar.

The Azusa Street Revival and Worship Music

The Spirit's immediacy became a crucial factor for various expressions of music at the Azusa Street Revival. I provide an analysis of worship music at the Azusa Street Revival by focusing on four themes for worship music: the definition/nature of worship music, songwriting, preparing songs for the service, and the presentation of worship music (the same themes I use for my discussion of contemporary

---

[42] *AF* 1.1 (September 1906), p. 4. Using the version of Scripture used in *AF*, the passage explains, 'Be glad then, ye children of Zion, and rejoice in the Lord your God: For he hath given you the former rain moderately, and he will cause to come down for you the rain, the former rain and the latter rain the first month'. *AF* 1.1 (September 1906), p. 4.

[43] *AF* 1.1 (September 1906), p. 2. Also 2 Kgs 20.5; Jer. 32.27; Ps. 103.3; Jas 5.14; Mt. 8.16,17; Mk 16.16-18.

[44] *AF* 1.1 (September 1906), p. 2.

worship music in chapters two and three). Leaders at Azusa believed that they had a superior approach to corporate worship music because of the influence of the Spirit's work on their approach to singing and the songs sung. First, those at Azusa did not take time to define the nature of worship music because music was valued for the pragmatic purposes of experiencing the Spirit. Second, they delved into writing worship songs, relying on the Spirit's present work for this practice. Third, they did not value the preparation of worship songs for a specific service, because they expected a spontaneous visitation of the Spirit to govern the worship music. Fourth, the Spirit's immediacy was emphasised in various ways during the presentation of worship music, found in their views on the role of instruments, spontaneous singing from memory, the chosen songs to sing, and singing in tongues.

The Definition/Nature of Worship Music

The Azusa participants did not take time to define or describe the nature of worship music. They understood the use of music in corporate worship primarily related to its function of experiencing the Spirit. Defining worship music was not an important discussion for them. How it functioned for their purposes, however, was important. Thus, more discussion on how it can or should be used is developed and explained below.

Writing Worship Songs

Azusa participants emphasised the role of an experience of the Spirit for songwriting in three ways. First, song writers at Azusa viewed the Spirit as the source of inspiration for their new songs.[45] These lay music composers claimed a special experience of God that led to the development of songs. Throughout the *AF*, the editors include nineteen songs written by advocates of the revival.[46]

The second way that these new songs were linked to an experience of the Spirit relates to how these songs were used. Four of the nineteen original songs in the *AF* include only titles or short excerpts, but are included within the context of a testimony. From these testimo-

---

[45] *AF* 1.3 (November 1906) 3; *AF* 1.5 (January 1907) 3; Stephen Dove, 'Hymnody and Liturgy in the Azusa Street Revival, 1906–1908', *Pneuma* 31 (2009), p. 255.
[46] Dove, 'Hymnody and Liturgy in the Azusa Street Revival', p. 254.

nies, all four songs functioned as a means to prepare for Spirit baptism.[47] Though the content of all four songs do not explicitly focus on Spirit baptism, the songs function as a transitional expression of worship just as the individual is about to receive Spirit baptism.

Third, by linking these new songs to the Spirit's influence, Azusa song writers were able to teach various theological themes. As stated earlier, the four songs found within testimonies include various themes, such as pneumatology and Christology. Of the fifteen songs with the full text in the *AF*, there is greater variety of theological themes: eleven emphasise Christology, three pneumatology, and one the triune God.[48] The leaders at Azusa understandably highlighted pneumatology in light of their new experience of Spirit baptism, but they deemed Christology a central teaching of their movement. Of the three songs focused on pneumatology, two include the role of Jesus for salvation. But of the eleven songs emphasising Christology, none make reference to the Spirit. Prioritising Christ in songs shows that they viewed the goal of the Spirit's immediacy as primarily for the exaltation of Christ. These songs functioned as a corrective to anyone who considered the Spirit's immediacy, particularly the experience of Spirit baptism, as a primary focus among them.[49] A key function of the Spirit's present work was to exalt Christ.

Preparing for Congregational Singing

Azusa participants opposed planned song selections for services because of their view of spontaneity and the present work of the Spirit, and they valued Spirit baptism for singing in tongues. First, planning the songs to sing in advance reflected a human-led approach to worship music for services. But sensing what song to sing during a service reflected a greater reliance on the Spirit's present leadership *during* a service. Letting the Spirit choose what songs to sing during a service assumed that spontaneity reflected a more Spirit-led approach for worship music.[50] Thus, Azusa participants emphasised what happened at the moment during worship services because they valued the Spirit's spontaneous work among them.

---

[47] *AF* 1.3 (November 1906) 3; *AF* 1.5 (January 1907) 3; Dove, 'Hymnody and Liturgy in the Azusa Street Revival', pp. 254-55.

[48] See Dove, 'Hymnody and Liturgy in the Azusa Street Revival', p. 256.

[49] Dove, 'Hymnody and Liturgy in the Azusa Street Revival', p. 257.

[50] Frank Bartleman, *Azusa Street* (Vinson Synan (intro.); Alachua: Bridge-Logos, 2nd edn, 1980), p. 62.

Second, Azusa participants emphasised the need of Spirit baptism in order to sing in tongues. The spirituality of participants was more important than musical excellence, since Spirit baptism provided opportunity for participants to join in the most important expression of worship music in their view: singing in tongues. A more detailed explanation of singing in tongues is included under the following theme on presenting worship music, since it was music expressed in the present moment during services.

The Presentation of Worship Music
The direct and present work of the Spirit influenced Azusa's presentation and act of worship music in four ways. First, the role of instruments for corporate worship music at the Mission appears paradoxical – but understandable in light of the emphasis on the Spirit's immediacy.[51] On the one hand, Frank Bartleman frowned upon the use of instruments, and those involved in the publication of *AF* deemed them unnecessary. Instruments were deemed as unnecessary because Azusa participants experienced the Spirit's immediacy to sing songs spontaneously from memory and when they sang in tongues – all moments not requiring musical accompaniment.[52] Bartleman rebuked the 'jazzy' music of the day.[53] On the other hand, the *AF*, as early as the first edition, reported that people received the 'gift of playing on instruments'.[54] Jennie Evans Moore, Seymour's eventual wife, explained, 'the Spirit led me to the piano, where I played and sang under inspiration, although [*sic*] I had not learned to play'.[55] Playing an instrument that you could not previously play was a miracle and a sign of the Spirit's immediacy.

The use of instruments for worship music was eventually embraced because some appeared to sense the Spirit's immediacy when

---

[51] David Douglas Daniels, III, also acknowledges that the use of instruments became a topic for debate among early Pentecostals. '"Gotta Moan Sometime": A Sonic Exploration of Earwitnesses to Early Pentecostal Sound in North America', *Pneuma* 30 (2008), p. 17.

[52] Bartleman, *Azusa Street*, p. 62; *AF* 1.1 (September 1906), p. 1; *AF* 1.3 (November 1906) 1; Robeck, *The Azusa Street Mission and Revival*, pp. 144-45; Guthrie, 'Pentecostal Hymnody', pp. 83-84.

[53] Bartleman, *Azusa Street*, p. 62.

[54] *AF* 1.1 (September 1906), p. 1.

[55] *AF* 1.9 (May 1907), p. 3. Also see Jon Michael Spencer, *Protest and Praise: Sacred Music of Black Religion* (Minneapolis: Fortress, 1990), p. 173.

instruments were used.[56] How leaders decided to include the use of instruments, like a piano, is not explicitly explained by leaders in the primary sources. But leaders' focus on the Spirit's immediacy in corporate worship appears to be the determining factor for the inclusion of instruments. First, Moore gave regular leadership for Azusa's music ministry. And since she gained the gift of playing the piano through the Spirit, the use of a piano for worship music would be the next logical step since that experience of the Spirit affirmed the use of a piano for her worship. Second, Bartleman concedes that those at Azusa moved away from not using musical instruments and hymnbooks, to finally opening up to these musical practices. And though he rebukes the 'jazzy' religious music of his day, he acknowledges that this new approach to music moved 'the toes'.[57] The physical and emotional demonstrations through worship music gave early Pentecostals a sense of the Spirit's immediacy. Ecstatic experiences like singing in tongues and spontaneous singing led to physical and emotional demonstrations, which were deemed as manifestations of the Spirit. But 'jazzy' religious music could also lead to physical and emotional demonstrations – without requiring ecstatic musical expressions – so that participants could likewise feel that the Spirit moved. Thus, instruments were included in the corporate worship music of the early Pentecostals due to their focus and expectation for an experience of the Spirit.

Second, the Azusa participants sang spontaneous songs from their memory, as opposed to reading from a hymnbook. Bartleman argues that spontaneous songs from memory are superior, and explains that: '[a]ll the old well known hymns were sung from memory, quickened by the Spirit of God'.[58] Bartleman reflects an early Pentecostal approach to corporate worship, that values spontaneity, since it would appear that believers were yielded to the leading of the Spirit in that present moment for the choice of songs.[59] Songs that are prepared in advance for the worship service would appear to some early Pentecostals as following a more human-led approach to worship music.

---

[56] Bartleman, *Azusa Street*, p. 62; cf. Guthrie, 'Pentecostal Hymnody', p. 84.
[57] Bartleman, *Azusa Street*, p. 62.
[58] Bartleman, *Azusa Street*, p. 62.
[59] Cf. Guthrie, 'Pentecostal Hymnody', p. 79.

Third, the songs sung at Azusa also reveal the importance of the Spirit's immediacy. The song sung 'every day', which became somewhat of a theme song, is 'The Comforter Has Come'.[60] This song testifies to the Spirit's presence among them in their corporate worship gathering.[61] 'The Comforter Has Come' found fulfillment in their lives together through their experience of Spirit baptism. Azusa Street participants viewed the refrain of the song, which describes the Spirit as the promise of the Father, as referencing Christ's admonition to his disciples to wait for the promise of the Father: Spirit baptism.[62]

Related to Azusa's key theme of Spirit baptism, a few other themes emerge from the song, 'The Comforter Has Come'. 'The Comforter Has Come' also communicates the experience of 'healing' and 'deliverance', important values of the Azusa Street Revival. Participants reported healings of various kinds. Further, the song emphasises the importance of evangelism. The message and experience Azusa participants received through the Spirit, led them to tell others about the 'matchless grace divine' available to all who deserve hell.

A number of other songs regularly sung focused on Christ and his work on the cross – since the Spirit's present work was to lead to the goal of exalting Christ.[63] The songs featured Christ's redemptive work related to his blood – such as: 'Under the Blood', 'The Blood Is All My Plea', 'Are You Washed in the Blood?', 'Saved by the Blood of the Crucified One', and 'Hallelujah! 'Tis Done'.[64] 'Heavenly Sunlight' is another popular song sung at the revival, which is also about Christ, but focuses more on the immediacy of Christ in a believer's life.

Finally, singing in tongues featured prominently in the worship at Azusa as an experience of the Spirit's present work. Though other Christian gatherings included spontaneous hymn singing, and even songs like 'The Comforter Has Come', singing in tongues distinguished worship at the Azusa Street Revival from other Christian

---

[60] *AF* 1.3 (November 1906), p. 1; Robeck, *The Azusa Street Mission and Revival*, p. 145.

[61] See Robeck, *The Azusa Street Mission and Revival*, pp. 145-46.

[62] Acts 1.4-5.

[63] *AF* 1.5 (January 1907), p. 2.

[64] *AF* 1.3 (November 1906), p. 1; Robeck, *The Azusa Street Mission and Revival*, p. 146.

gatherings.[65] Jennie Evans Moore was the first Azusa participant to sing in tongues. She prayed for the gift of singing in tongues on April 9, 1906.[66] Because singing in tongues featured so prominently at Azusa, and especially because it demonstrates their emphasis on the Spirit's present work, six points on singing in tongues follow.

First, how Azusa participants sang in tongues is important to understand. Only those who were baptised in the Spirit could speak in tongues. Participants believed that when someone was singing in tongues, the Spirit was singing through that person.[67] Someone might stand up and sing in tongues using a familiar tune from a song like 'Jesus Savior, Pilot Me' and 'Nearer My God to Thee'.[68] Or participants might sing in tongues through an unfamiliar – and possibly original – musical tune.[69]

Second, when people sang in tongues as a group, it was so valued that those at Azusa referred to the group's song as a 'Heavenly Chorus'.[70] Singers would sing in their various tongues, and hearers apparently considered it harmonious.[71] Whether or not such harmonies were acoustically perfect is not as important as the idea that it was perfect to the ears of hearers – 'the ears of faith'.[72]

Third, singing in tongues required an interpretation. The gift of interpretation through song confirmed the Spirit's work through tongues. After singing in tongues, the Spirit gives the interpretation through a song in English.[73] Probably one of the most revealing insights into singing in the Spirit at the Azusa Street Revival comes from a reported interpretation of a song sung in tongues:

With one accord, all heaven rings
With praises to our God and King;
Let earth join in our song of praise,

---

[65] Robeck suggests that this phenomenon has roots in African American spirituality, most notably the 'Negro chant' found in 'praise houses' during and after the times of slavery. See *Azusa Street Mission and Revival*, p. 150.

[66] *AF* 1.9 (May 1907), p. 3; Spencer, *Protest and Praise*, p. 155.

[67] *AF* 1.5 (January 1907), p. 3.

[68] *AF* 1.3 (November 1906), p. 1; *AF* 1.4 (December 1906), p. 1.

[69] *AF* 1.3 (November 1906), p. 1; *AF* 1.4 (December 1906), p. 1.

[70] *AF* 1.6 (February-March 1907), p. 4; Daniels, 'Gotta Moan Sometime', p. 27.

[71] *AF* 1.1 (September 1906), p. 1.

[72] Spencer, *Protest and Praise*, p. 161.

[73] *AF* 1.4 (December 1906), p. 2.

And ring it out through all the days.[74]

In this interpretation, the lines were not only poetic (the lines rhymed), but the song gives expression to how Azusa participants viewed singing in tongues. It was not just a song sung among humans – like other hymns in English they might sing. Singing in tongues enabled humans to participate in the song of praise in the heavens. It provided opportunity for singing in 'one accord'. Such songs originate in heaven, not earth, so that these songs could be called 'heavenly' songs.

Fourth, singing in tongues authenticated the Spirit's immediacy in Azusa's worship for some who attended. When Frank Bartleman first heard singing in tongues, he said that he had a 'great hunger' to receive it.[75] He believed it 'would exactly express' his 'pent-up feelings'.[76] Bartleman explains: 'It brought a heavenly atmosphere, as though the angels themselves were present and joining with us. And possibly they were.'[77] H.L. Blake explains that it was not speaking in tongues that convinced him that God was present in the meetings.[78] Rather, he explains that the singing in tongues – as well as testimonies – convinced him of God's presence and his need for Spirit baptism with the evidence of tongues.[79] Singing in tongues was not merely for an ecstatic musical experience. Singing in tongues witnessed to something beyond its aesthetic beauty, for it brought conviction among its hearers through the songs, the harmonies among singers, and the interpretations. It convinced people of their need for the type of spirituality found among the participants of the revival. Furthermore, singing in tongues influenced those opposed to Azusa. Bartleman explains that this practice made it difficult for people to ridicule the movement, and it even quieted some others.[80]

Fifth, understanding the rationale Azusa participants gave for singing in tongues can also help contemporary Pentecostals discern whether or not this type of singing can be expected today. The earli-

---

[74] *AF* 1.1 (September 1906), p. 4.
[75] Bartleman, *Azusa Street*, pp. 61-62.
[76] Bartleman, *Azusa Street*, pp. 61-62.
[77] Bartleman, *Azusa Street*, pp. 61-62.
[78] *AF* 1.6 (February 1907), p. 5; Spencer, *Protest and Praise*, p. 158.
[79] *AF* 1.6 (February 1907), p. 5.
[80] Bartleman, *Azusa Street*, pp. 61-62.

est mention of singing in tongues is Moore's testimony of the experience. According to her report, she prayed and received the gift of singing in tongues.[81] She does not explain why she desired to sing in tongues. The editors of *AF* link singing in tongues to the message of 1 Cor. 14.14-16, focusing solely on the importance of interpreting tongues that are spoken or sung.[82] The editors of *AF* do not, however, explain how singing in tongues is an experience founded upon Scripture. Their one reference to Scripture, as explained above, only implicitly suggests a biblical precedent for singing in tongues, as they argue for the need for the interpretation of songs in tongues.

Finally, singing in tongues demonstrates the centrality of the Spirit's immediacy in the corporate worship at Azusa. Because this singing was ecstatic, not traditional, and not dependent on musical training, Azusa participants could suggest that it was the one expression of music that linked the songs of heaven with the songs of earth. Not learned at a school of music, or from a hymnbook – it came from God. Singing in tongues was the direct work of the Spirit. The participants' view of singing in tongues as 'music from heaven' was restricted to this type of singing. They described singing in tongues as God dropping 'down sweet anthems from the paradise of God, electrifying every heart'.[83] They simply stated that this expression of songs is 'heaven below'.[84] These songs are in the Spirit because the Spirit sings his own songs through humans.[85] Those at Azusa needed no instruments in these cases of singing in tongues, since they state that after the Spirit 'touches' them, 'the Holy Ghost plays the piano in all of our hearts'.[86] In their view, humans did not have control of the words sung, unlike known songs – the Spirit was in complete control of this musical expression. Singing in tongues derived entirely from the presence and work of the Spirit in the worship experience. After careful analysis of the way Azusa participants included music in their times for corporate worship, it is clear that the goal of the Spirit's manifestation influenced their approach to worship music in various ways.

---

[81] *AF* 1.9 (May 1907), p. 3.
[82] *AF* 2.9 (May 1908), p. 2.
[83] *AF* 1.4 (December 1906), p. 2.
[84] *AF* 1.4 (December 1906), p. 2.
[85] *AF* 1.5 (January 1907), p. 2.
[86] *AF* 1.4 (December 1906), p. 2.

The Azusa Street Revival – Preaching and the Altar

The Spirit's immediacy – particularly the experience of Spirit baptism – influenced the understanding of preaching and the altar among those involved with the Azusa Street Revival in various ways related to five themes on preaching and the altar: Spirit baptism, the definition/nature of preaching, how to prepare for preaching, the preaching event, and the response to the sermon at the altar. Before describing the various ways the Spirit's immediacy influenced Azusa's understanding of preaching and the altar, why Spirit baptism became foundational to their views must first be addressed.

Spirit Baptism

Those at Azusa found rationale for their view on Spirit baptism from Christ's promise in Lk. 24.49 and Acts 1.4-8, and the subsequent reception of his promise by his disciples in the Acts 2 narrative.[87] Christ commanded his disciples to wait for the promise of the Father – Spirit baptism – which is power to be Christ's witnesses throughout the world when the Spirit comes on them. In Acts 2, the disciples wait for this promise and 'were all filled with the Holy Ghost, and began to speak with other tongues, as the Spirit gave them utterance'.[88] Since they all spoke in tongues when receiving Spirit baptism, the Azusa leaders viewed tongues as 'the Bible evidence' of Spirit baptism.[89]

Initially, Azusa Street participants believed they received human, foreign languages – *xenolalia* – when they were baptized in the Holy Spirit. Azusa participants believed that these tongues would enable them to preach the gospel to people of other countries – much like those in the book of Acts were able to do on the Day of Pentecost.[90] They believed that the end times were imminent due to the sign of tongues – God was speeding up the process for world evangelization just prior to Christ's imminent return. The eschatological implication of Spirit baptism, the imminent return of Christ, is one of their early key emphases. These tongues provided them with new unlearned languages, which they believed enhanced evangelism to all nations. They

---

[87] *AF* 1.4 (December 1906), p. 2.
[88] *AF* 1.1 (September 1906), p. 2.
[89] *AF* 1.1 (September 1906), p. 2.
[90] Acts 2.1-12.

assumed that they would not have to secure lengthy language training to share the gospel in an unknown language.

Azusa participants eventually experienced both success and failure when it came to preaching in tongues in contexts where English – or their own native tongue – was not spoken. Some reported that they were able to preach in tongues with success – communicating in the native language of the context.[91] Others, however, were not able to preach in the native tongue of the context they were ministering in.[92] Though later Pentecostals refocused their attention from xenolalia tongues (a human language) to unknown tongues, the implications of being missions-focused persisted.[93] The implications of early Pentecostals' views on Spirit baptism for preaching are crucial, though, as it influenced the ethos of Pentecostal preaching.

The Definition/Nature of Preaching

The Azusa leaders did not take time to define preaching, but the little they said showed how the Spirit's immediacy was crucial for preaching, since they associated preaching with prophesying. They equated the consequence of Spirit baptism with prophesying, described in Acts 2.17-18. Because the Spirit is indiscriminately poured out on all through Spirit baptism, anyone who is baptised in the Spirit can prophesy. Seymour described prophesying as preaching 'in your own tongue, which will build up the saints and the church'.[94]

But prophesying could be expressed through both testifying or preaching in their view.[95] Testimonies were an important part of their corporate worship services, so that they allotted time for testimonies, which preceded the preaching.[96] Seymour explained that some people think that they are called to be a vocational minister and subsequently preach because they speak in tongues. He explained that those who think they should be a vocational minister and preach because they speak in tongues do not realise that they 'preach in testifying'.[97] Testifying and preaching may have been viewed similarly, since they

91 *AF* 1.9 (May 1907), p. 3.
92 Robeck, *The Azusa Street Mission and Revival*, p. 243.
93 *AF* 1.1 (September 1906), p. 1. Anderson, *Spreading Fires*, pp. 27, 57-68.
94 *AF* 1.5 (January 1907), p. 2.
95 *AF* 1.5 (January 1908), p. 2.
96 *AF* 1.3 (November 1906), p. 1.
97 *AF* 1.3 (November 1906), p. 3.

could both 'build up the saints and the church'.[98] What exactly is preaching was not explained in detail in the written record left by Azusa participants.

Finally, Azusa leaders understood that people who were not baptised in the Spirit could preach if they were anointed.[99] Thus, though prophesying is an explicit result of Spirit baptism, preaching was not restricted to those who experienced Spirit baptism. The anointing of the Spirit enabled Christians to preach without an experience of Spirit baptism. Those who were baptised in the Spirit, however, could experience greater results from their ministry.[100] Azusa participants likely did not go to great lengths to explain what preaching is, since they were more interested in explaining what Spirit baptism is.

Preparing to Preach

The Azusa participants' understanding of the preparation for preaching was influenced by a stress on the Spirit's immediacy in six ways. First, their views affected who can preach. Seymour stated that Christ chooses and ordains people for ministry.[101] And while 'the visible church' may give credentials for ministers, the 'main credential' for ministers is the experience of Spirit baptism.[102] Rather than theological education, the primary need for potential preachers is an experience of Spirit baptism.[103] Spirit baptism is important because this experience of the Spirit gives life, power, and authority to witness throughout the world.[104]

An experience of Spirit baptism led to the inclusion of various types of people who could preach, who otherwise might be rejected in churches at the time. The Azusa Street Revival occurred during a time of intense racism in the United States. That people of various ethnic backgrounds could preach within a racially integrated meeting because of an experience of Spirit baptism was radical. African-American Seymour was the lead pastor at Azusa, and others of various ethnic backgrounds were acknowledged as equal participants in

---

[98] *AF* 1.5 (January 1907), p. 2.
[99] *AF* 1.6 (February–March 1907), p. 4.
[100] *AF* 1.6 (February–March 1907), p. 4.
[101] *AF* 1.9 (June–September 1907), p. 3.
[102] *AF* 1.9 (June–September 1907), p. 3.
[103] *AF* 1.9 (June–September 1907), p. 3.
[104] *AF* 1.9 (June–September 1907), p. 3.

leadership and preaching. Azusa participants did not just accept people of various ethnic backgrounds, but accepted women and children
– also groups marginalized for ministry – as potential preachers because of their experience of Spirit baptism.[105]

A key Scripture that provided rationale for an inclusive approach
to preaching because of an experience of Spirit baptism is based on
Peter's preaching in Acts 2, when he refers to Joel 2.28-32. In Acts
2.16-18, Peter comments on the experience of Spirit baptism,
whereby people began speaking in tongues on the Day of Pentecost,
explaining:

> This is what was spoken through the prophet Joel: 'In the last days
> it will be, God declares, that I will pour out my Spirit upon all
> flesh, and your sons and your daughters shall prophesy, and your
> young men shall see visions, and your old men shall dream dreams.
> Even upon my slaves, both men and women, in those days I will
> pour out my Spirit; and they shall prophesy.'

In the above passage, Peter declares that the Spirit has been
poured out, so that 'sons', 'daughters', and 'slaves, both men and
women' would 'prophesy'. The Spirit given on the Day of Pentecost
has been given without respect to age, gender, or social status. In the
view of those leading at Azusa, to prophesy meant one might testify
or preach.[106] Thus, since Peter taught that Spirit baptism is the indis-
criminate experience of the Spirit to prophesy – that is, preach or
testify – all believers who experience Spirit baptism may also preach.

Second, though Spirit baptism became a critical one-time experience necessary for preachers, a fresh anointing of the Spirit was also
critical for preachers at Azusa. An anointing – also called 'the unction
of the Holy Spirit' – can be experienced multiple times and is available both before and after an experience of Spirit baptism.[107] In Jn
20.21-22, Jesus' disciples received an anointing of the Spirit prior to
Spirit baptism, when Jesus breathed on them and said: 'Receive the
Holy Spirit'.[108] The disciples received the Spirit on this occasion – an

---

[105] *AF* 1.10 (September 1907), p. 3; *AF* 1.5 (January 1908), p. 2; *AF* 1.2 (October 1906), p. 3.
[106] *AF* 1.12 (January 1908), p. 2. Since no one is credited with this idea, one can
assume that at least the leadership at Azusa affirmed this position.
[107] *AF* 1.4 (December 1906), p. 2.
[108] *AF* 1.4 (December 1906), p. 2.

anointing – prior to their experience of Spirit baptism. The disciples' experience shows that an anointing is available prior to Spirit baptism, and that Spirit baptism is distinct from an anointing.

A fresh anointing of the Spirit is crucial for preachers, for the Spirit is willing to anoint 'His ministers afresh for every service'.[109] Though preachers may have learned how to preach without a fresh anointing, it is best that preachers refuse to preach unless they have experienced a fresh anointing.[110] To maintain an ongoing fresh anointing of the Spirit, those at Azusa gave a number of recommendations. First, preachers must obey the Word of God, Scripture. They must live 'in the word of God with perfect obedience'.[111] Second, preachers must exhibit the fruit of the Spirit, most notably love.[112] Those who fail to express the fruit of the Spirit in their lives, exhibit anger, speak evil, or backbite.[113] Third, in order to discern whether they are anointed to preach for a specific occasion, they need to pray and seek God's will. To ensure they are anointed to preach, potential preachers must get on their knees, pray for God's will, and ask God to use them to preach with a fresh anointing or set them aside.[114] If God provides a fresh anointing, preachers will know as they will quickly 'feel the power going all over' them.[115] Preachers who feel that power, must 'yield to the will of God' to preach.[116]

Being anointed to preach was so crucial for those at Azusa that the congregation gave discernment regarding who was or was not anointed to preach. If someone preached from 'human understanding only', rather than through the Spirit's anointing, the congregation would weep.[117] For instance, if a presumptuous non-anointed preacher arose to preach, Mother Jones, an African-American woman, would quickly and quietly go to the minister and state: 'Brother … Can't you see that you are not anointed to preach?' Her question would cause the preacher to stop. Eventually, all Mother

[109] *AF* 1.9 (June–September 1907), p. 2.
[110] *AF* 1.9 (June–September 1907), p. 2.
[111] *AF* 1.11 (October–January 1908), p. 2.
[112] *AF* 1.11 (October–January 1908), p. 2.
[113] *AF* 1.11 (October–January 1908), p. 2.
[114] *AF* 1.9 (June–September 1907), p. 2.
[115] *AF* 1.9 (June–September 1907), p. 2.
[116] *AF* 1.9 (June–September 1907), p. 2.
[117] A.C. Valdez, Sr, with James F. Scheer, *Fire on Azusa Street* (Costa Mesa: Gift Publications, 1980), pp. 79-80.

Jones had to do was stand up when a non-anointed person attempted to preach, and the person would stop preaching.[118] The response of the congregation at Azusa reveals the importance of a fresh anointing of the Spirit for preaching.

Third, an experience of Spirit baptism was crucial for power in preaching at Azusa. Spirit baptism is crucial for preachers, for it gives power for bold preaching. Prior to an experience of Spirit baptism, the Apostle Peter denied Christ before people.[119] But after an experience of Spirit baptism, the Apostle Peter received power to preach boldly.[120] And like Peter, believers who experience Spirit baptism will receive power to preach boldly.

Fourth, the Spirit's work is involved in giving authority to the preacher, for both Christ and the Spirit give authority for preaching in the views of leaders at Azusa. Christ gives authority for those who may be leaders in the church, since Christ chooses and ordains people to be leaders in the church.[121] The Spirit is also involved in giving authority for preaching, so that Spirit-baptised preachers can witness throughout the world and perform the same miraculous works as Jesus.[122]

Fifth, an experience of the Spirit with the evidence of tongues led to a strong missionary focus. The early Azusa participants believed that their reception of tongues was the reception of a known human language. Azusa leaders relate the Great Commission with tongues explaining:

> The gift of languages is *given with the commission*, 'Go ye into all the world and preach the Gospel to every creature'. The Lord has given languages to the unlearned Greek, Latin, Hebrew, French, German, Italian, Chinese, Japanese, Zulu and languages of Africa, Hindu and Bengali and dialects of India, Chippewa and other languages of the Indians, Eskimaux, the deaf mute language and, in fact the Holy Spirit speaks all the languages of the world through his children.[123]

---

118 Valdez, *Fire on Azusa Street*, p. 80.
119 *AF* 1.10 (September 1907), p. 3; cf. Lk. 22.54-62.
120 *AF* 1.10 (September 1907), p. 3; cf. Acts 4.
121 *AF* 1.9 (June–September 1907), p. 3; (October–January 1908), p. 3.
122 *AF* 1.9 (June–September 1907), p. 3; (October–January 1908), p. 4.
123 *AF* 1.1 (September 1906), pp. 7-8 (emphasis original).

Tongues are directly connected with the commission to preach to those of other language groups. God gives tongues, a real language, in order to preach the gospel in a language that is understandable to each unique group in the world. They also believed that Jesus was coming back soon, so there was a need to send out missionaries shortly in anticipation of this event.[124] Rather than spend years learning theology and languages, an experience of Spirit baptism for God's power and a foreign language was an effective way to reach the world quickly with the preaching of the gospel.[125] As noted earlier, though the emphasis on human languages received through Spirit baptism declined (in favour of viewing tongues as unknown languages), the missionary impulse continued among the early Pentecostals.

Finally, an experience of Spirit baptism does not negate the need to study Scripture, for Scripture plays an important role for preachers. First, preachers – including those who have experienced Spirit baptism – must study Scripture on a regular basis. A thorough knowledge of Scripture helps provide discernment for believers, and ensures that people are not led into false experiences of the immediacy of God. Those who fail to study Scripture regularly may 'become fanatical', 'led by deceptive spirits', 'have revelations and dreams contrary to the word', and give false prophecies, beginning to think they are better than other Christians.[126] Seymour encourages preachers to read, meditate, and hear portions of Scripture every day with prayer, ensuring that they practice what is learned in Scripture.[127] Though Seymour highlights the important role of Scripture in a preacher's life, he does not give guidance on how to study it systematically for a particular sermon. He only delves into the need for regular time in Scripture for one's lifestyle as a preacher. It is likely that sermons

---

[124]   In *AF* 1.1 (September 1906), p. 1, they state their anticipation through prophecies that foretold this belief:

> Many are the prophesies spoken in unknown tongues and many the visions that God is giving concerning His soon coming. The heathen must first receive the Gospel. One prophecy given in an unknown tongue was interpreted, "The time is short, and I am going to send out a large number in the Spirit of God to preach the Full Gospel in the power of the Spirit."

[125] Anderson, *Spreading Fires*, p. 27.

[126] *AF* 1.11 (October–January 1908), p. 2.

[127] William J. Seymour, *The Doctrines and Discipline of the Azusa Street Apostolic Faith Mission of Los Angeles, California* (ed. Larry Martin; The Complete Azusa Street Library, Vol. 7; repr., Joplin: Christian Life, 2000), p. 107.

arose out of one's own regular study of Scripture – rather than a purposeful study of Scripture for a sermon. It is for this reason that unlike the inclusion of a separate upcoming section on contemporary preaching that delves into the preparation of sermons, this discussion on Azusa is limited to one section on preparing to preaching.

The Preaching Event

The Azusa participants' understanding of the preaching event was influenced by a focus on the present work of the Spirit in three ways. First, the Spirit's work in preaching relates to the centrality of preaching Christ and his redemptive work at Azusa. There is no time to preach anything else but Christ, because the Spirit does not have 'time to magnify anything else but the Blood of our Lord Jesus Christ'.[128] Preaching Christ and his redemptive work on the cross works in co-ordination with the Spirit's primary role of magnifying Christ and his redemptive work. When people fail to make Christ central in their preaching, a living relationship with Christ diminishes in people. When people preach about other topics, such as what people should eat, how people should dress, human-constructed doctrines, and opposing other churches, it shows that the 'love of God' is absent in the life of a preacher.[129] But when Christ is exalted, Christ draws everyone unto himself.[130] When people focus on solely preaching 'Christ and him crucified', people would not have to convince others of the authenticity of the ministry at Azusa – God would convince people that the ministry is a genuine work of God.[131] William H. Durham also explains that a focus on preaching Christ and him crucified alone led to an immediacy of God among the people, whereby the Spirit fell on those who 'heard the Word'.[132] Maintaining the centrality of preaching Christ and his redemptive work includes five benefits: the goal aligns with the Spirit's primary role of magnifying Christ and his redemptive work, a living relationship with Christ is maintained, Christ draws people unto himself, God convinces people that the ministry is a genuine work of God, and is a crucial means by which

---

[128] *AF* 1.5 (January 1907), p. 2.
[129] *AF* 1.5 (January 1907), p. 2.
[130] *AF* 1.5 (January 1907), p. 2.
[131] *AF* 1.4 (December 1906), p. 4.
[132] *AF* 1.12 (January 1908), p. 1.

hearers of preaching may experience the Spirit's work as they respond to the preaching.

Second, Azusa leaders valued openness to spontaneous leadings of the Spirit for preaching. Sermon manuscripts were unnecessary, since preachers should rely on the spontaneous leading of the Spirit.[133] Even who would preach was not predetermined, since only those led by the Spirit and anointed to preach for the moment were encouraged to preach.[134]

Third, Azusa participants stressed the uncompromised preaching of biblical truth, which generates supernatural results, though is also accompanied by opposition.[135] Thus, preachers must be willing to experience some persecution as a result of preaching the uncompromised truth.[136] Signs and wonders accompany those who follow Christ and preach the gospel, but so does opposition and persecution.[137] Azusa participants witnessed Christ's 'promise fulfilled in some of the persecutions that attend the preaching of the full gospel'.[138] Azusa's discussion on uncompromised biblical preaching also has implications for the altar and response because they acknowledge the role of opposition following faithful preaching.

The Response to the Sermon – the Altar

Those at Azusa stressed the direct work of the Spirit in response to the sermon in six ways, which includes opposition following faithful biblical preaching described above.[139] First, those at Azusa highlighted the importance of signs – revealing the immediacy of God – as accompanying the preaching of the Word. In the first issue of the *AF*, Seymour explained: 'God is now confirming His Word by granting signs and wonders to follow the preaching of the Full Gospel in

---

[133] Bartleman, *Azusa Street*, pp. 62-63; Roberts Liardon, *The Azusa Street Revival: When the Fire Fell* (Shippensburg: Destiny Image, 2006), p. 109.

[134] *AF* 1.9 (June–September 1907), p. 2.

[135] *AF* 2.13 (May 1908), p. 2; *AF* 1.11 (October–January 1908), p. 4.

[136] *AF* 1.11 (October–January 1908), p. 4.

[137] *AF* 1.3 (November 1906), p. 1.

[138] *AF* 1.5 (January 1907), p. 3. Though the Azusa participants do not reference any particular passage, a few that may pertain include: Mt. 10.16-22; Jn 15.18-21, 16.1-4, and 17.14-18.

[139] To avoid duplication, see the immediate earlier discussion on this subject of supernatural results and opposition following faithful biblical preaching.

Los Angeles'.[140] Seymour explains how this idea is based on the Mk 6.17-20, quoting and commenting on the passage:

And these signs shall follow them that believe; in My name shall they cast out devils; they shall speak with new tongues; they shall take up serpents; and if they drink any deadly thing, it shall not hurt them; they shall lay hands on the sick and they shall recover ... And they went forth and preached everywhere, the Lord working with them, and confirming the Word with signs following. Praise His dear name, for He is just the same today.[141]

Signs not only accompany preaching, but confirm the preaching. And since Jesus 'is just the same today', preachers can expect signs to accompany their preaching.

Second, those at Azusa believed that the Spirit's work may lead hearers to respond to a sermon while it is being preached, which may cause them to come to the altar during the sermon. Preaching of the 'Word in the Spirit' is so powerful that 'people are shaken on the benches'.[142] The 'power falls on people' through the Spirit during testimonies or sermons, leading to the immediacy of God among the people; they may experience salvation, sanctification, Spirit baptism, or a healing.[143]

Third, they emphasised an altar experience where both preachers and hearers experienced the immediacy of God for the altar time. They explain: 'As soon as it is announced that the altar is open for seekers for pardon, sanctification, the baptism with the Holy Ghost and healing of the body, the people rise and flock to the altar ... Coming to the altar, many fall prostrate under the power of God'.[144] The call to the altar is not emphasised, for it is through the 'simple declaring of the Word of God ... in the Spirit' that causes people to come to the altar.[145] While someone is speaking, the Spirit suddenly falls 'upon the congregation', followed by God himself giving the

---

140 *AF* 1.1 (September 1906), p. 2.
141 *AF* 1.9 (June–September 1907), p. 3.
142 *AF* 1.3 (November 1906), p. 1.
143 *AF* 1.3 (November 1906), p. 1.
144 *AF* 1.3 (November 1906), p. 1.
145 *AF* 1.3 (November 1906), p. 1.

altar call.[146] The preacher's role is just to know 'when to quit' preaching, since God calls people to the altar as hearers experience the Spirit's work through the Spirit's power and conviction.[147] The preacher's call to an altar is so infused with the Spirit's work, that hearers view the call as coming from God alone. Leaders may also pray with seekers at the altar. Ardell K. Mead explains, for instance, how Seymour, Florence Crawford, and 'another sister laid their hands' on her so she might receive Spirit baptism.[148]

Fourth, Spirit baptism also gives power for greater results at the altar than the type of results that may arise from a preacher who just has an anointing of the Spirit. W.H. Durham's experience with preaching illustrates the difference the anointing and Spirit baptism make for preaching. Durham explains that prior to his experience of Spirit baptism he was involved in the ministry of preaching, and experienced the Spirit's power for preaching so that people responded to preaching at the altar, experiencing salvation, sanctification, and healing.[149] Following his own experience of Spirit baptism, Durham explains: 'I had such power on me and in me as I never had before'.[150] Hearers of Durham's preaching responded at the altar and experienced an immediacy of God prior to his experience of Spirit baptism, but the response to Durham's preaching following his experience of Spirit baptism increased greatly. While he could count the number of people at the altar who responded to his preaching prior to his experience of Spirit baptism, his experience of Spirit baptism enabled him to witness altars so full that it was difficult for him to personally meet with each person at the altar.[151] Thus, Spirit baptism provides power for greater results at the altar.

Finally, Azusa participants' view of the altar was shaped by their emphasis on maintaining a contemporary 'Upper Room' experience, whereby participants experienced the immediacy of God. The Azusa Street Mission is described as having an 'Upper Room' experience in two ways: their entire meeting was considered an 'Upper Room' experience and they called an upper level room at the Mission an Upper

---

[146] Bartleman, *Azusa Street*, p. 65.
[147] Bartleman, *Azusa Street*, p. 65.
[148] *AF* 1.3 (November 1906), p. 3.
[149] *AF* 1.6 (February–March 1907), p. 4.
[150] *AF* 1.6 (February–March 1907), p. 4.
[151] *AF* 1.6 (February–March 1907), p. 4.

Room. Azusa leaders explain, '[i]t is a continual upper room tarrying at Azusa Street'.[152] But those at Azusa also describe their 'Upper Room' as a large room on a level above their usual meetings for corporate worship. Azusa participants explain that people may study the Bible in this room, but more often than not it is highlighted as a place for people seeking God for provision for finances, healing, and Spirit baptism – an experience of the immediacy of God.[153] While the message in the lower room at the Azusa Mission focused on the need for a direct experience of the Spirit, the Upper Room also provided a regular context to experience the Spirit. Thus, Azusa's understanding of preaching and the altar was linked to the Spirit's immediacy in various ways.

Conclusion

This chapter shows that the Azusa Street Revival included an emphasis on the Spirit's immediacy in corporate worship in several ways. The Azusa Street Revival made Spirit baptism the climax of their corporate worship expression, so that a tangible sense of the Spirit's immediacy – particularly tongues – was expected. More importantly, this expectation for the Spirit's immediacy as the pinnacle of worship became normative for corporate worship in general at Azusa. The next two parts of this book continues to tackle three critical elements of contemporary Pentecostal corporate worship, namely, worship music, preaching, and the altar. The upcoming discussion is not just descriptive in nature, but provides a constructive theological appraisal. Understanding Azusa will also help with the upcoming analyses.

---

[152] *AF* 1.5 (January 1907), p. 1.
[153] *AF* 1.1 (September 1906), p. 4; 1.2 (October 1906), p. 3; 1.3 (November 1906), p. 1; 1.6 (February–March 1907), p. 6.

PART 2
SINGING WITH THE HEAVENLY CHOIR: THE PENTECOSTAL APPROACH TO WORSHIP MUSIC

2

AN INTRODUCTION TO PENTECOSTAL CONTEMPORARY WORSHIP MUSIC

The previous section examined how Azusa included the role of the present work of the Spirit in corporate worship. In order to understand the emphasis on the Spirit's present work in the worship music found in North American Pentecostal churches today, it is crucial to provide an account of how worship music developed among Pentecostals from the Azusa Street Revival onwards, culminating in Contemporary Worship Music (CWM). CWM is prevalent in North American churches. CWM influences both Pentecostal and non-Pentecostal traditions, and both Pentecostals and non-Pentecostals contribute to the production of CWM. In the past thirty years, CWM in North America has become such an influential form of worship within corporate worship settings that some have equated their understanding of worship with worship music alone.[1] But worship is more than CWM. The theology of CWM must be addressed because of its influence and use among Pentecostal churches.

Methodology

To understand the methodology for part two of this work, the terminology and outline used here must be explained. First, the phrases congregational singing and worship music are distinguished from the

---

[1] See Calvin M. Johansson, 'Music in the Pentecostal Movement', in Eric Patterson and Edmund Rybarczyk (eds.), *The Future of Pentecostalism in the United States* (Lanham: Lexington, 2007), pp. 61-62.

more broad term – worship – though some may use these phrases interchangeably.[2] Second, this work does not provide an elaborate system of distinguishing the different types of songs used in corporate worship. The Apostle Paul referred to 'psalms, hymns, and songs from the Spirit' in Eph. 5.19 and Col. 3.16. But since Paul never explained how these types of songs differed from each other, there are no conclusive distinctions.[3] Thus, I do not attempt to distinguish psalms, hymns, and spiritual songs because the distinctions are not clear. Pentecostals, though, have made other distinctions between three categories of music, namely, hymns, gospel songs, and choruses. A hymn is generally 'ancient or modern', and 'is a metrical poem with multiple stanzas, often without a refrain (chorus). A gospel song usually has multiple stanzas plus a memorable refrain. A chorus is a mini-poem consisting of a refrain, but usually without stanzas or with only one stanza.'[4]

Finally, CWM is a contemporary movement within Protestantism. CWM is 'worship music in the genres of popular music' produced since the 1970s by 'North American Protestant recording and publishing companies, churches, and individuals'.[5] CWM styles may include 'rock, folk, pop, gospel, R & B, reggae, country, and hip hop'.[6]

Second, part two of this book includes three major sections, which is covered over chapters two, three, and four. The three major sections are: 1) a brief historical account of worship music in Pentecostal churches, which led to the use of CWM; 2) a description of CWM by probing the views of three influential CWM leaders: Brian Doerksen, Darlene Zschech, and Matt Redman; and 3) a constructive theological appraisal of CWM. The third section provides an appraisal of CWM by discerning how Azusa and other biblical-theological resources can be a source of renewal in order to provide the way forward for worship music in corporate Pentecostal worship services.

---

[2] Best, in *Unceasing Worship*, also uses the language of 'congregational singing' over the term worship (155).

[3] Guthrie, 'Pentecostal Hymnody', pp. 36-40. Even in Joseph Guthrie's dissertation, entitled 'Pentecostal Hymnody', he never offers a clear definition of a hymn.

[4] Barry Liesch, *The New Worship: Straight Talk on Music and the Church* (Grand Rapids: Baker, exp. edn, 2001), pp. 23-24.

[5] Redman, *The Great Worship Awakening*, p. 47.

[6] Redman, *The Great Worship Awakening*, p. 47.

Brief History of Worship Music in the Pentecostal Church

To begin this discussion of worship music in Pentecostal churches, it is important to explore some of the turning points that have shaped the use of worship music among Pentecostals. Though a number of factors relate to worship music in Pentecostal churches, the focus here is on elements that showcase an experience of the Spirit in Pentecostal worship music. The various uses of music throughout the history of Pentecostalism are briefly described, with a broad description of the early years, followed by a key juncture in the 1960s that ushered in the use of CWM today.[7] A detailed description of the Azusa Street Revival's use of worship music is not provided here, since it was already covered in chapter one.

Early Pentecostal Worship Music Up to the 1950s

An experience of the Spirit was an important feature of the worship music of the early period of Pentecostalism (roughly up until the 1950s by their emphasis on participation and pragmatism. First, the Spirit could be expected to move anyone to sing – all could participate.[8] Anyone in the meeting could initiate a song, and everyone would follow with 'wholehearted, even boisterous, music making'.[9] Women, blacks, and even children participated, primarily because it was assumed that it was the Spirit that led them.[10] Second, Pentecostals chose the form of music that best served their interest of experiencing the Spirit – they were pragmatic in their approach to worship music.[11] 'Music was employed which gave a desired result; no other criterion need be considered.'[12] 'Rhythm and innovation' were 'hallmarks of the early Pentecostal musical ethos', and they were generally open to various types of instruments to use, such as horns, guitars, banjos, accordions, fiddles, and drums that facilitated an experience

---

[7] This discussion relies on important features highlighted by Calvin M. Johansson, Grant Wacker, and Larry Eskridge.

[8] Johansson, 'Music in the Pentecostal Movement', p. 51; Wacker, *Heaven Below*, pp. 103-105.

[9] Johansson, 'Music in the Pentecostal Movement', p. 51.

[10] Wacker, *Heaven Below*, pp. 103-105.

[11] Johansson, 'Music in the Pentecostal Movement', pp. 51-53.

[12] Johansson, 'Music in the Pentecostal Movement', pp. 51-52.

of the Spirit.[13] The art form was not as important as the role of supernatural signs and wonders.[14] The only art forms rejected were
those forms primarily associated with mainline Protestant denominations.[15] The reason the art forms of mainline Protestant denominations were rejected is because these denominations were viewed as
'spiritually dead' – as opposed to open to an experience of the
Spirit.[16] So, for instance, if mainline Protestant denominations used
formal liturgy, Pentecostals preferred spontaneity.[17] Music served a
function, namely, to be open to an experience of the Spirit, particularly through signs and wonders.

Pentecostal Worship Music beyond the 1950s
The attitude of Pentecostals beyond the 1950s towards different art
forms changed by their developing relationship with non-Pentecostals, so that art forms previously deemed unusable for an experience
of the Spirit were welcomed. Three trends related to the relationship
between Pentecostals, other Christian traditions, and American culture provided significant implications for the use of music in Pentecostal churches. The three trends are the rise of the charismatic
movement among mainline Protestant traditions and Roman Catholicism, the popular appeal of Pentecostalism found on TV, and the
eventual rise of CWM.[18]

The first trend relates to the rise of the charismatic movement,
whereby previously rejected art forms were now accepted since charismatics using them experienced the Spirit. During the 1950s and
1960s, some adherents belonging to Roman Catholicism, Anglican-
ism, and other denominations began to accept the classical Pentecostal notion of Spirit baptism with the evidence of tongues.[19] The charismatic movement, however, has been more open to other gifts of

---

[13] Larry Eskridge, 'Slain by the Music', *Christian Century* 123.5 (March 7, 2006),
p. 18. Eskridge's article draws on his thesis: 'God's Forever Family: The Jesus People Movement in America, 1966-1977' (PhD thesis; Stirling University, Scotland,
2005).

[14] Johansson, 'Music in the Pentecostal Movement', pp. 51-52.

[15] Johansson, 'Music in the Pentecostal Movement', p. 51.

[16] Johansson, 'Music in the Pentecostal Movement', p. 51.

[17] Johansson, 'Music in the Pentecostal Movement', p. 51.

[18] Eskridge, 'Slain by the Music', p. 19.

[19] Johansson, 'Music in the Pentecostal Movement', p. 55; P.D. Hocken, 'Charismatic Movement', in Stanley Burgess (ed.), *The New International Dictionary of Pentecostal and Charismatic Movements* (Grand Rapids: Zondervan, 2003), pp. 477-85.

the Spirit beyond tongues as evidence of Spirit baptism.[20] The rise of the charismatic movement influenced the music of the Pentecostal movement, as Pentecostals became more open to art forms the early Pentecostals rejected, such as hymns, choirs with formal vestments, organs, musical methods developed by non-Pentecostals, and the hiring of music ministers to serve on staff at churches.[21] The charismatic movement 'looked to the developing body of folk masses and new hymnody' rather than traditional hymns or Gospel music found in Pentecostal churches.[22] This new movement's approach to music found its way into Pentecostal circles, so that the music of 'mainstream American Christianity' gained ground among Pentecostals. Since other Christian fellowships experienced the Spirit while using other art forms, these same forms could be welcomed by Pentecostals as well.

The second trend relates to Pentecostals embracing an entertaining style to worship music, due to the 'power, prosperity and respectability' of ministers who became influential on TV.[23] With the advent of influence through TV, noted by prominent ministers like Oral Roberts, Pentecostals 'adapted their musical presentations to the expectations of American TV audiences'.[24] Pentecostals incorporated the musical approach that the majority of Americans appreciated – that which was more 'Hollywood' and entertaining.[25] Experiencing the Spirit through entertaining worship music became acceptable.

The third trend demands more attention here as it delves into the rise of CWM, and the link between popular music and an experience of the Spirit. This trend is a critical one, and three key elements that led to the rise of CWM are discussed: the role of the Jesus People movement, the establishment of Christian music media companies, and the Vineyard movement. First, the Jesus People movement refers to a group of young people in the 1960s in California, who converted to Christianity from a lifestyle of drug use and sexual promiscuity.[26]

---

[20] Hocken, 'Charismatic Movement', 517.
[21] Johansson, 'Music in the Pentecostal Movement', p. 55.
[22] Eskridge, 'Slain by the Music', p. 19.
[23] Eskridge, 'Slain by the Music', p. 19.
[24] Eskridge, 'Slain by the Music', p. 19.
[25] Eskridge, 'Slain by the Music', p. 19.
[26] Terry W. York, *America's Worship Wars* (Peabody: Hendrickson, 2003), pp. 13-16.

A number of them belonged to a church called Calvary Chapel, led by Chuck Smith Sr. The worship services at Calvary Chapel included the use of rock music, informal clothing, and the expression of charismatic gifts such as tongues.[27] The use of popular music – rock music – in a church's worship service was a distinct feature of this church's music. This new expression of worship music birthed a new approach to music and corporate worship within churches, and its influence began to spread.

CWM eventually arose into a major influence on worship music throughout churches in North America through Christian music media companies. One of the most recognised producers of worship music within the Christian market today, Maranatha! Music, finds its roots in the Jesus Movement. Chuck Smith Sr. of Calvary Chapel spearheaded Maranatha! Music.[28] Maranatha! Music's purpose today is to introduce 'new songs' and promote 'its classics to the church through song publishing, music in stores and church leadership training'.[29] It wants to 'continue to shepherd the 'Jesus Music' of today by serving the church with the song of faith'.[30]

The birth of CWM, initiated by the Jesus People Movement, and popularised at Calvary Chapel, led to the rise of various other popular artists and songs for corporate Christian worship.[31] Another major producer of CWM, Integrity, developed in the 1980s.[32] The mission of Integrity is revealing: 'Helping people worldwide experience the manifest presence of God'.[33] The experience of God is crucial for Integrity's approach to CWM. Integrity promotes an 'experience' of the 'manifest presence of God'. The prevailing approach of CWM

---

[27] York, *America's Worship Wars*, p. 15; Maranatha Music. 'About Maranatha! Music'. Online: http://maranathamusic.com/about.

[28] Maranatha Music, 'About Maranatha! Music'.

[29] Maranatha Music, 'About Maranatha! Music'.

[30] Maranatha Music, 'About Maranatha! Music'.

[31] Redman, *The Great Worship Awakening*, pp. 47-50.

[32] Redman, *The Great Worship Awakening*, p. 55. This company has recently been bought by another company, David C. Cook, but continues its work. David C. Cook. 'David C. Cook Acquires Integrity Music from Integrity Media Inc'. Online: http://davidccook.ca/news.php?area=&aid=928.

[33] Integrity Music. 'About: Our Mission'. Online: http://integritymusic.com/about/.

corresponds with Pentecostal spirituality.[34] CWM even extends its influence beyond just companies who self-describe themselves as 'Christian', as some of the largest distributors in the world produce CWM.[35]

The third factor contributing to the rise of CWM is the Vineyard movement, most notably through its leaders, John and Carol Wimber.[36] Vineyard also emphasised an experience of the Spirit for worship music. Though there are others who influenced CWM, a discussion on the Wimbers is important because of their influence on Vineyeard. Furthermore, examining the Wimbers' views is helpful since two of the three CWM leaders discussed in this study – Brian Doerksen and Matt Redman – explicitly acknowledge John Wimber's influence on their approach to worship music.[37] John and Carol Wimber were part of the Calvary Chapel movement, but eventually left it to help establish the Vineyard Church. Vineyard's influence upon CWM was especially significant during the 1980s.[38] Experiencing the Spirit became an important part of their approach to worship music, as they linked this experience to three key things: songs addressed to Christ, miracles, and the structure of a song service that has intimacy with God as the goal.

First, Carol Wimber explains that times in her home gatherings where they 'experienced God deeply', were those times when they sang songs 'personally and intimately to Jesus'.[39] She

---

[34] Redman, *The Great Worship Awakening*, p. 55.

[35] Redman, *The Great Worship Awakening*, p. 67.

[36] Pete Ward, *Selling Worship: How What We Sing Has Changed the Church* (Milton Keynes: Paternoster, 2005), pp. 69, 98-101, 106-107, 135, 145, 180; William A. Dyrness, *A Primer on Christian Worship: Where We've Been, Where We Are, Where We Can Go* (Grand Rapids: Eerdmans, 2009), p. 66.

[37] For an extended discussion on the various figures and developments of CWM, see Ward, *Selling Worship* and Redman, *The Great Worship Awakening*. Brian Doerksen explains that in November 1989, John Wimber led a training session on songwriting that brought together thirty-five songwriters – including him – from the Vineyard. 'Song Writing', in John Wimber (ed.), *Thoughts on Worship* (Anaheim: Vineyard Music Group, 1996), p. 101. Redman's influence: Ward, *Selling Worship*, pp. 103-109; Redman, *The Unquenchable Worshipper*, p. 88.

[38] Barry Liesch, 'How We Arrived at Worship Choruses'. Online: http://208.86.154.138/~worship/how-we-arrived-at-worship-choruses.

[39] John Wimber, 'Worship: Intimacy with God', in John Wimber (ed.), *Thoughts on Worship* (Anaheim: Vineyard Music Group, 1996), pp. 1-2.

differentiated 'songs about Jesus' from 'songs to Jesus'.[40] Personal, intimate songs to Jesus 'both stirred and fed the hunger for God' within her.[41] The manifestation of God was notably apparent through songs that directly addressed Christ, and became a significant approach within CWM.

Second, both John and Carol Wimber acknowledged how miracles can be associated with worship music through the manifestation of the Spirit. Carol Wimber describes a critical juncture in 1981 for the Wimber's ministry – and subsequently for Vineyard – as it relates to songs of worship. During a meeting in York, England, she states that the Spirit moved so that '[b]lind eyes saw, the deaf heard, and the lame walked'.[42] During the entire meeting the Spirit moved among the people, a young boy aged thirteen or fourteen sang when the Spirit fell on him. Her remark on this experience is telling, when she states, 'John and I understood that night, that for us, the Vineyard, that song and singing would always be attached to the presence and manifestation of the Holy Spirit'.[43] Singing, then, would become an important activity if one were to expect a manifestation of the Spirit in their influential approach.

Third, John Wimber's approach to how the structure of a song service is designed anticipates an experience of the Spirit. Wimber suggests five phases for worship music, which has been influential on how sets of songs are chosen for a worship service within CWM.[44] The first phase is the 'call to worship, which is a message directed toward the people or toward God'.[45] The second is 'engagement,

---

[40] Wimber, 'Worship', p. 2.

[41] Wimber, 'Worship', p. 2.

[42] Carol Wimber, 'The Flame of God's Presence', in Christy Wimber (ed.), *The Way In is the Way On: John Wimber's Teachings and Writings on Life in Christ* (Boise: Ampelon, 2006), p. 107.

[43] Wimber, 'The Flame of God's Presence', p. 107.

[44] Liesch, *The New Worship*, pp. 53-66. Liesch explains that around the same time that Wimber developed this five-phase model, Judson Cornwall – a Pentecostal – independently developed a similar five-phase approach. Cornwall's model follows a journey into the Holy of Holies, using images of the Old Testament pattern for worship. The five phases are: 'Songs of Personal Testimony in the Camp', 'Through the Gates with Thanksgiving', 'Into His Courts with Praise', 'Solemn Worship inside the Holy Place', and 'In the Holy of Holies'. The focus is on Wimber here, however, since Wimber's approach made a greater influence upon CWM. Liesch, *The New Worship*, pp. 71-73; Liesch, 'How We Arrived at Worship Choruses'.

[45] Wimber, 'Worship', p. 4.

which is the electrifying dynamic of connection to God and to each other … In the engagement phase we praise God for who he is through music as well as prayer'.[46] At this phase, 'the manifest presence of God is magnified and multiplied'.[47] The third phase is one of 'expression', in light of being 'awakened' to God's presence.[48] This phase can include physical and emotional expression. The fourth phase develops from the third phase of expression, whereby worship moves to 'a zenith, a climactic point, not unlike physical lovemaking'.[49] After expressing to God what is in one's heart, mind, and body, it is time for God to respond by visiting with his people.[50] 'His visitation is a byproduct [*sic*] of worship'.[51] The last phase is 'the giving of substance'.[52] Wimber refers to the giving of one's whole life, and can include anything from money, love, hospitality, or information.[53] Though all these phases are important, all are focused on the goal of intimacy with God. He defines intimacy 'as belonging to or revealing one's deepest nature to another (in this case to God), and it is marked by close association, presence, and contact'.[54] Wimber describes the experience of intimacy with God as 'the highest and most fulfilling calling men and women may know'.[55] Intimacy with God – experiencing God – is not only the goal of worship, but is the supreme calling of all people. This whole process requires the Spirit to lead the worship music as well, which may include prophecies, tongues, and interpretation.[56] While Pentecostal churches have been influenced by various other groups that may relate to art forms, it is clear that the Vineyard influence – via CWM – not only affects the Pentecostal use of art forms but the approach to the Spirit's manifestation for worship music. With a broad understanding of the development

---

[46] Wimber, 'Worship', pp. 4-5.
[47] Wimber, 'Worship', p. 5.
[48] Wimber, 'Worship', p. 5.
[49] Wimber, 'Worship', p. 5.
[50] Wimber, 'Worship', p. 6.
[51] Wimber, 'Worship', p. 6.
[52] Wimber, 'Worship', p. 6.
[53] Wimber, 'Worship', p. 6.
[54] Wimber, 'Worship', p. 4.
[55] Wimber, 'Worship', p. 7.
[56] Wimber, 'Worship', p. 4.

of worship music within Pentecostalism, a movement that has integrated CWM into their approach, a closer look at the views of the three CWM leaders follows.

An Introduction to Contemporary Worship Music Leaders

Part two of this work highlights the approach of three influential CWM leaders: Brian Doerksen, Darlene Zschech, and Matt Redman. First, each leader's background is described, which reveals their importance and influence within CWM. Next, the three leaders' views related to four key themes are discussed: the definition/nature of worship music in this chapter, followed by songwriting, preparing for songs of worship, and presenting worship music in chapter three. The descriptive discussion in chapters two and three are followed by a theological analysis of this subject in chapter four.

In order to examine worship music in Pentecostal churches, an examination of the artists who are writing, composing, and performing their music for the Christian masses is critical. CWM music leaders influence the words congregations sing, the type of music churches use, and how worship music is understood. Both the words and musical styles communicate and influences individuals and groups.[57] Theologians have sometimes viewed theological activity as predominantly cerebral, but have come to recognise that it is very much an embodied activity, whereby music is incredibly influential.[58] The approach of the three artists is crucial to understand because they also have a significant influence on the general approach to worship music through various other avenues. The three artists – and

[57] Jeremie S. Begbie, *Resounding Truth: Christian Wisdom in the World of Music* (Grand Rapids: Baker Academic, 2007), p. 45; Peter Althouse and Michael Wilkinson, 'Musical Bodies in the Charismatic Renewal: The Case of Catch the Fire and Soaking Prayer', in Monique M. Ingalls and Amos Yong (eds.), *The Spirit of Praise: Music and Worship in Global Pentecostal-Charismatic Christianity* (University Park: The Pennsylvania State University Press, 2015), pp. 29-44.

[58] Amos Yong, 'Conclusion: Improvisation, Indigenization, and Inspiration: Theological Reflections on the Sound and Spirit of Global Renewal', in Monique M. Ingalls and Amos Yong (eds.), *The Spirit of Praise: Music and Worship in Global Pentecostal-Charismatic Christianity* (University Park: The Pennsylvania State University Press, 2015), pp. 281-82.

other CWM leaders like them – tour internationally, present at conferences on the subject of worship, and educate through writing and videos.[59] In the examination of each leader, their understanding of worship music and the role of the Spirit's manifestation is highlighted throughout.

Background of Key CWM Leaders

Let's begin with a Canadian leader, Brian Doerksen. He is considered '[o]ne of the founding fathers of modern worship music'.[60] He was born and raised in Abbotsford, British Columbia, Canada. He is a popular musician associated with the Vineyard movement, serving in various ministry contexts, including the UK and Canada.[61] He served as a worship pastor at South West London Vineyard and a trainer for songwriters and song leaders in the Vineyard movement in England, Scotland, and Ireland. He now serves at a church called 'The Bridge' in Abbotsford, British Columbia, Canada, which he helped plant in 2006.[62] Some popular songs he has written or co-written, include 'Refiner's Fire', 'Light the Fire Again', 'Eternity', 'Faithful Father', 'Come, Now is the Time to Worship', 'Faithful One', 'Hallelujah (Your love is amazing)', 'Holy God', and 'The River'.[63] He received a Juno award – a Canadian music award – for his album 'Holy God', awarded as the Contemporary Christian/Gospel album of the year in 2008.[64] Doerksen's influence as one of the 'founding fathers' of and contemporary influences on CWM reveal why his approach to worship music is crucial for understanding CWM.

Darlene Zschech is one of the most popular song leaders associated with the music developed at Hillsong Church in Australia. Hillsong Church is the largest church in Australia, with approximately 20,000 attending its weekend services, with church plants in London,

---

[59] Also see Michelle K. Baker-Wright, 'Intimacy and Orthodoxy: Evaluating Existing Paradigms of Contemporary Worship Music', *Missiology: An International Review* 35.2 (April 2007), p. 176.

[60] Andree Farias, 'Think About God: Pioneer Doerksen on What's Wrong with Worship Music', *Christianity Today* 51.7 (July 2007), p. 59.

[61] Brian Doerksen, 'BrianDoerksen.com'. Online: http://briandoerksen.com.

[62] Doerksen, 'BrianDoerksen.com'.

[63] Julie Bogart (ed.), *All About Worship* (Anaheim: Vineyard Music Group, 1998), p. 58; Doerksen, 'BrianDoerksen.com'.

[64] Doerksen, 'BrianDoerksen.com'.

Paris, Kiev, Ukraine, and New York.[65] The church belongs to the Australian Christian Churches (Assemblies of God in Australia), and is led by co-pastors Brian and Bobbie Houston.[66] The music of Hillsong is so influential that 'Hillsong Music Australia (HMA) claims annual worldwide sales in excess of two million albums'.[67] HMA intentionally wants to influence the church's music internationally, explaining that '*Hillsong Music is a vital component in the ministry that God has entrusted to Hillsong Church, its primary function being to resource the church worldwide*'.[68] Zschech acknowledges the international influence of Hillsong through worship music, and their intentional desire to influence while exalting Christ 'with powerful songs of faith and hope'.[69] And beyond just resourcing the church worldwide with 'fresh songs of worship', Hillsong explains that they have 'a deep passion to see people connect with the Living God in a real and personal way'.[70] Zschech joined Hillsong Church during the mid 1980s, and was involved in various capacities, such as a backup vocalist, Vocal Director, Worship Pastor, and leader for international tours until 2010.[71] Though Zschech is now a co-senior pastor with her husband Mark Zschech at Hope Unlimited Church (also affiliated with Australian Christian Churches, the Assemblies of God in Australia) on the Central Coast of New South Wales, Australia, she still associates with Hillsong for projects related to worship music.[72]

---

[65] Cassandra Zinchini, 'Taking Revival to the World: Australia's Largest and Most Influential Church Extends Its Reach to London, Paris and Kiev', *Christianity Today* 51.10 (October 2007), p. 34.

[66] Zinchini, 'Taking Revival to the World', pp. 34-36; Australian Christian Churches, 'Our History'. Online: http://www.acc.org.au/AboutUs/OurHistory.aspx.

[67] Evans, *Open Up the Doors*, p. 97.

[68] Quoted in Evans, *Open Up the Doors*, p. 9 (emphasis original).

[69] Darlene Zschech, 'The Role of the Holy Spirit in Worship: An Introduction to the Hillsong Church, Sydney, Australia', in Teresa Berger and Bryan D. Spinks (eds.), *Spirit in Worship – Worship in the Spirit* (Collegeville: Liturgical, 2009), p. 285.

[70] Hillsong Live, 'About Hillsong LIVE', Online: http://live.hillsong.com/about.

[71] Evans, *Open Up the Doors*, p. 108; Jimmy Stewart, 'Darlene Zschech Leaving Hillsong to Co-Pastor Church', *Charisma Magazine* (November 3, 2010). No pages. Online: http://www.charismamag.com/site-archives/570-news/featured-news/1096-darlene-zschech-leaving-hillsong-to-co-pastor-church, paras. 1 and 6.

[72] Darlene Zschech, 'Biography'. Online: http://www.darlenezschech.com/biography; Hope Unlimited Church, 'About Us'. Online: http://www.hopeuc.com/

Zschech's most popular song, 'Shout to the Lord', was sung by an estimated twenty-five million Christians around the world each week around the year 2009.[73] Bill Hybels rightly argues: 'When church historians reflect on the worship revolution that happened around the turn of the 21st century, Darlene Zschech will be credited for playing a major role'.[74] And though she now provides leadership at another church in Australia, and there are other influential artists that have arisen out of Hillsong (e.g., Geoff Bullock, Reuben Morgan, Joel Houston, Russell Fragar, and Marty Sampson), Zschech's international influence and continued association with Hillsong gives reason for a focus on her approach to worship music.[75]

Redman is an influential leader who has written numerous popular songs, such as: 'The Heart of Worship', 'Better is One Day', 'Once Again', 'Blessed Be Your Name', 'You Never Let Go', and '10,000 Reasons'.[76] He has participated in and led songs for notable ministries such as New Wine, Soul Survivor, and the Passion movement, which have had a tremendous influence upon millions of young people around the world.[77] These ministries have conducted numerous conferences, and have become important venues that Redman's songs have been launched around the world. One of the features of conferences like Passion is vibrant worship music led by some of the most well-known names in CWM.[78] He is currently supporting a

---

#/home/about-us; Australian Christian Churches, 'About ACC'. Online: http:// www.acc.org.au/AboutUs.aspx; Felicia Howard, 'Hillsong's Darlene Zschech Leaves After 25 Years of Service', *The Christian Post* (October 28, 2010). Online: http://www.christianpost.com/news/hillsongs-darlene-zschech-leaves-after-25-years-of-service-47404.

[73] Zinchini, 'Taking Revival to the World', p. 35; Teresa Berger and Bryan D. Spinks (eds.), *The Spirit in Worship – Worship in the Spirit* (Collegeville: Liturgical Press, 2009), p. 296.

[74] Bill Hybels, 'Endorsements', in Darlene Zschech, *Extravagant Worship: Holy, Holy, Holy is the Lord God Almighty Who Was and Is, and Is to Come* (Bloomington: Bethany, 2002), p. 13.

[75] See Evans, *Open Up the Doors*, pp. 107-108.

[76] Matt Redman, 'Bio'. Online: http://www.mattredman.com/bio.

[77] Redman, 'Bio'; Passion. 'About'. Online: http://www.268generation.com/3.0/#!about/story; Cooke, *Understanding Songs in Renewal*, p. 5.

[78] E.g., Chris Tomlin has led songs at the Passion conferences, and currently leads music at the Passion City Church in Atlanta, Georgia, which is led by Louie Giglio. See Mark Moring, 'Interview: Redman's Reasons'. Online: http://www.christianitytoday.com/ct/2011/julyweb-only/redmansreasons-july12.html.

church plant in London.[79] his popularity and influence as a CWM leader is an important reason his approach is also examined here.

CWM and the Definition/Nature of Worship Music

To begin this examination of CWM leaders' approach to worship music, it is critical to begin with their foundational views on what worship in general is in relation to worship music. How they distinguish worship and worship music is important, in order to discern how they deem worship music fits within the overall expression of worship of God. The distinctions between worship and worship music are also important to consider since the two concepts are sometimes wrongly viewed as synonymous within the church. The role of the Spirit's immediacy in worship and worship music is highlighted in their views.

Brian Doerksen

Doerksen focuses on worship that generates intimacy with God the Father, whereby the Spirit's manifestation for worship is assumed.[80] Doerksen explains that when believers gather to worship, it is 'quite rare' that they worship God as Father.[81] This is problematic because the central reason Jesus came is to 'restore us to right relationship with the Father'.[82] A lack of relationship with the Father has created a 'deep longing' for God the Father in the hearts of people.[83]

The emphasis on intimacy with God the Father appears to have arisen out of an acknowledgement that human fatherly affection has been lacking in many people's lives, including Doerksen's relationship with his father. Doerksen longed for his parents' 'affirmation and affection' growing up, but he did not receive what he hoped for.[84] When Doerksen eventually became a father, his daughter once said: 'Daddy … I want you to hold me'.[85] He wept as he realised that these are the

---

[79] Redman, 'Bio'.

[80] E.g., Wimber, 'Worship', p. 3.

[81] Brian Doerksen, 'The Call to Worship the Father', in Julie Bogart (ed.), *All About Worship* (Anaheim: Vineyard Music Group, 1998), p. 55.

[82] Doerksen, 'The Call to Worship the Father', p. 55.

[83] Doerksen, 'The Call to Worship the Father', p. 55.

[84] Doerksen, *Make Love, Make War: Now is the Time to Worship* (Colorado Springs: David C. Cook, 2009), p. 73.

[85] Doerksen, *Make Love, Make War*, p. 73.

words he always wanted to say to his human father – and 'ultimately' to God the Father.[86] Doerksen relays that when he first sang the song he wrote, 'Father, I Want You to Hold Me', John Wimber thanked him after he heard it.[87] Wimber explained: 'When I was a young boy, my alcoholic father left, and you just put into song what I have wanted to say to my Father in heaven my whole life'.[88] There is a strong correlation in both Doerksen and Wimber between the lack of human fatherly affection and subsequent desire to experience a close relationship with a father. Focusing on intimacy with God the Father, then, appears to be the ultimate experience of fatherly affection.

Doerksen shows why and how worship of God the Father can be restored through the story of Jesus' encounter with the Samaritan woman at the well in Jn 4.1-30.[89] The primary teaching revolves around Jesus' statement in verse 23: 'true worshipers will worship the Father in spirit and truth, for the Father seeks such as these to worship him'. Both the object of one's worship and how one worships is significant.[90] Since people 'can only worship if God has breathed life into' their 'spirits', 'worship is always a gift'.[91] Worshiping 'in spirit' consists of 'our spirit surrendering to and communing with God's Spirit'.[92] And '[t]o worship in truth is to know who God truly is – in this context, as father [*sic*]. This knowledge is not just based on what people think or feel, but on the Word of God and the incarnation of Jesus'.[93] Furthermore, 'we must come to God honestly as we are'.[94] The good news of Jesus is that people can become children of God so that they can know the Father intimately and honestly.[95]

The overall approach to worship that has intimacy with God the Father as the goal of worship, includes an assumption of the Spirit's manifestation. Since worship must include surrendering to and communing with the Spirit, an approach that has intimate worship of the

---

[86] Doerksen, *Make Love, Make War*, p. 73.
[87] Doerksen, *Make Love, Make War*, p. 75.
[88] Doerksen, *Make Love, Make War*, p. 75.
[89] Doerksen, 'The Call to Worship the Father', p. 55.
[90] Doerksen, 'The Call to Worship the Father', p. 55.
[91] Doerksen, 'The Call to Worship the Father', p. 58.
[92] Doerksen, 'The Call to Worship the Father', p. 58.
[93] Doerksen, 'The Call to Worship the Father', p. 58.
[94] Doerksen, 'The Call to Worship the Father', p. 58.
[95] Doerksen, 'The Call to Worship the Father', p. 58.

Father as the goal is based on an experience of the Spirit in worship. This reveals how Doerksen's approach to worship can be easily adapted among Pentecostal congregations who already anticipate an experience of the Spirit in corporate worship.[96]

Doerksen's songs reveal his theology of worship; that worship should promote communion with the Father – a privilege in light of the Father's character. One popular song, 'Faithful Father', communicates the Father's love and grace, and willingness to welcome people even when they break his heart. 'Faithful Father' is a song of praise for who God is and what he does from the time Doerksen's life began – God has been faithful. Doerksen closes this song, writing: 'Father, I love the way you hold me close and say my name. I know when my life is through my heart will find its home in you'.[97] Doerksen emphasises intimacy with the Father in light of his faithful character. This example, though, is not to say that Doerksen writes songs only about the Father and intimacy – he has addressed a wide range of subjects in his songs. 'Faithful Father', though, reflects a central impulse in his overall approach to worship music.

Doerksen's exaltation of the worship music component of the corporate worship setting relates to his views on the immediacy of God experienced through worship music. His views on leading songs of worship reveal his inclination to exalt the role of worship music. He considers '[l]eading worship … the most sacred, delightful responsibility in the church'.[98] 'Positions' like 'instruction' and 'correction' are 'important'.[99] But leading songs of worship deals with 'the longing of the human heart'.[100] This longing responds to the question: 'when can I go meet with God?'[101] Song worship leaders have the opportunity to respond to this longing by figuratively saying through the songs, 'what about now?'[102] This is 'an incredible and

---

[96] For instance, Cecil B. Knight argues that it is the work of the Spirit that distinguishes Pentecostal corporate worship. The manifestation of the Spirit's gifts in corporate worship is more crucial than forms for Pentecostals. 'The Wonder of Worship', p. 12.

[97] Brian Doerksen, 'Faithful Father'. Mercy/Vineyard Publishing, 1996.

[98] Brian Doerksen, 'Faithful One'. *Equip: Vineyard Worship Resources*. 2004.

[99] Doerksen, 'Faithful One'.

[100] Doerksen, 'Faithful One'.

[101] Doerksen, 'Faithful One'.

[102] Doerksen, 'Faithful One'.

awesome responsibility' for those who lead songs of worship.[103] Meeting with God relates to Doerksen's emphasis on intimacy with God the Father in worship, which again is about the immediacy of God.

This brief look at Doerksen's views reveals his focus on the immediacy of God, with a focused attention on intimacy with God the Father in worship. Because he focuses on intimacy with God in worship, and implicitly anticipating the Spirit's immanent work in worship, he is able to connect his worship music with the overall approach within Pentecostal contexts. Furthermore, his approach to worship and worship music both anticipate an experience of the Spirit for genuine worship.

Darlene Zschech

The role of the Spirit's immediacy figures prominently in Zschech's views of both worship and worship music. Her views on worship in general arise out of her understanding of the role of the Triune God for worship, and what worshipping in spirit and truth means. Zschech follows a Trinitarian approach to worship, stating:

Worship, at every level, begins and ends with God as the priority – God showing us the Father's heart of love for us, God counseling, comforting, and guiding us through the voice of the precious Holy Spirit, and God in the person of Jesus Christ who is our Mediator and Way-Maker into the throne room of heaven.[104]

She argues that worship begins with God, since it is God who '*first loved us*'.[105] The human response involved in worship 'is an active expression of our love toward God'.[106] Human response, though, is enabled by the Spirit's work – for the Spirit counsels, comforts, and guides. Love for God is reflected in one's deeds and words, and generally 'involves the giving of ourselves totally to the Lord'.[107] In the midst of so many approaches to worshipping, she explains that

---

[103] Doerksen, 'Faithful One'.

[104] Darlene Zschech, *The Art of Mentoring: Embracing the Great Generational Transition* (Bloomington: Bethany, 2011), pp. 182-83.

[105] Zschech, *The Art of Mentoring*, p. 178; Darlene Zschech, *Extravagant Worship: Holy, Holy, Holy is the Lord God Almighty Who was and Is, and Is to Come* (Bloomington: Bethany, 2001), p. 30.

[106] Zschech, *The Art of Mentoring*, p. 178; Zschech, *Extravagant Worship*, p. 30.

[107] Zschech, *Extravagant Worship*, p. 30.

'[w]orship should be a way of life, with many facets of expression'.[108] The numerous ways of worshipping God include expressions like music, feasting, sacrifices, offerings, walking, and jumping.[109] What is essential, apart from the various methods available for worship, is that '[t]he Lord enjoys the diversity of sincere worship when expressed through His Spirit and in truth'.[110]

She picks up on this idea of worshipping in 'Spirit/spirit' and 'truth' developed by Jesus, describing the appropriate approach for worship. '[T]he act of worship must be in spirit (from our rational consciousness) and truth (consistent with the rest of our lives) (John 4:24)'.[111] Worship involves both the role of the human spirit – one's 'rational consciousness' – and the Holy Spirit. In order for there to be true worship of God, one must genuinely worship God with one's rational consciousness – the human spirit – through God's Spirit. An experience of the Spirit is a crucial link to the human spirit for worship of God. Furthermore, one must also worship in a way that it is truthful – what one is saying or doing is consistent with one's lifestyle – there is integrity. The worship of God through music is not restricted to 'great singers or musicians', 'radical demonstrations of praise', or 'quiet and personal times' – these are issues that are not important.[112] What is important is that people 'need to be in a personal relationship with our great God and live with the truth of His greatness reflecting through all we are becoming and all we do'.[113] Thus, worship is enabled by the Spirit and is all-encompassing, so that worship music is just one expression of worship.

Zschech views an experience of the Spirit as essential for worship music for a number of reasons. Though a long quote, her thoughts on music here are revealing, when she states,

> music was created to carry, capture, and communicate the presence of God, but over generations it has been taken out of the hands of all people and given *exclusively* into the hands of the extremely gifted, skilled, pretty, young, and brilliant – not to mention

---

[108] Zschech, *Extravagant Worship*, p. 31.
[109] Zschech, *Extravagant Worship*, pp. 31-32.
[110] Zschech, *Extravagant Worship*, p. 31.
[111] Zschech, *Extravagant Worship*, p. 32.
[112] Zschech, *Extravagant Worship*, p. 32.
[113] Zschech, *Extravagant Worship*, p. 32.

the extremely lucky. Only a few are now allowed to sing and personally enjoy contributing to the expression of music found on the planet.[114]

Zschech believes that music, in its purest form designed by God, had two very important purposes. First, music is linked to the presence of God. She does not explicitly elevate music over other expressions of worship, but her views on music show that she assumes the manifestation of God for songs of worship. Second, music was to be available to all people. Regrettably, music has been solely assigned to very gifted musicians. These two values find its way into Zschech's various discussions on worship music.

In Zschech's thoughts on worship music, she makes clear that the manifestation of God should be assumed for all types of songs for worship, both old and new. There are a variety of new songs that may be sung that are sent by God that may be about praise, something prophetic, unity, intimacy, war, 'peace and righteousness', 'grace and forgiveness', 'mercy and compassion', 'strength and justice', and 'power and might'.[115] While there are new songs to be written, the 'great anthems' sung over the centuries by people like Charles Wesley must also be included for congregational singing.[116]

Zschech identifies five characteristics of 'praise and worship' music that are all connected to experiencing the presence of God. Her descriptions of each follow and reveal the common assumption of the manifestation of God. The first is celebration and exaltation. Celebration of God may lead to being 'lost in worship', raising your voice and hands, throwing your head back, dancing, and rejoicing,

---

[114] Darlene Zschech, *The Kiss of Heaven: God's Favor to Empower Your Life Dream* (Bloomington: Bethany, 2003), p. 142.

[115] Zschech, *Extravagant Worship*, p. 191. Two types of prophetic messages are included in the New Testament, prediction and proclamation – or otherwise referred to as foretelling and forthtelling. See J.P. Baker, 'Prophecy, Prophets', in I.H. Marshall *et al.*(eds.), *New Bible Dictionary* (Leicester: Inter–Varsity, 3rd edn, 1996), p. 974. Apart from Zschech's discussion on Russell Fragrar receiving a prophetic message that is predictive (*Extravagant Worship*, 193), most of the prophetic songs discussed here refer to a message of proclamation – forthtelling. Since the distinction between these two types of prophecies does not affect the overall discussion on prophetic songs of praise for this book, the two types are not distinguished throughout this work.

[116] Zschech, *Extravagant Worship*, p. 191.

'purely because you are in God's presence'.[117] The second relates to evangelism and sharing the gospel. As you genuinely worship through song – like Paul and Silas – people will 'see the presence of God in your life', and 'they will run toward salvation'.[118] The third is warfare, whereby the 'enemy has no chance in the middle of people who are consumed by the presence of God'.[119] The fourth is healing, so that prophetic songs may bring 'words of life, comfort, and healing'.[120] The song itself does not minister, but 'it is the anointing on that song that breathes life where maybe there was none'.[121] The last is characterised as one of seeking God, whereby people '[m]inister to God in His presence', '[s]ee God move mightily in His church', and '[w]atch God change you from the inside out!'[122] Whether Zschech explicitly states the relation to these five characteristics of worship music to God's manifest presence or the anointing (being 'set apart for God and his work' through the Spirit's enablement), it is clear that an experience of God is linked to the various characteristics of worship music in Zschech's thought.[123] In sum, Zschech views the Spirit's manifestation as crucial for the enablement of worship, and an essential experience in all types of worship music.

Matt Redman
Redman does not distinguish worship and worship music, preferring to focus on worship in general. His view of worship includes the importance of the Spirit's manifestation for worship of the Father through the Son. To uncover Redman's understanding of worship, it is fitting to focus on one of his most popular songs related to this subject, 'Heart of Worship'. The song arose out of a decision made by the pastor of his local church. The pastor at the church, Mike Pilavachi, decided to remove the sound system and band for a season of ministry, so they could offer an alternative offering to God rather than something musical.[124] The meetings were initially awkward, with

---

[117] Zschech, *Worship*, p. 22.
[118] Zschech, *Worship*, p. 24-25.
[119] Zschech, *Worship*, p. 26.
[120] Zschech, *Worship*, p. 27.
[121] Zschech, *Worship*, p. 27.
[122] Zschech, *Worship*, p. 28.
[123] Evans, *Open Up the Doors*, p. 100.
[124] Matt Redman, *The Unquenchable Worshipper: Coming Back to the Heart of Worship* (Ventura: Regal, 2001), p. 103.

prolonged periods of silence and little singing. But Redman states, 'we soon began to learn how to bring heart offerings to God without any of the external trappings we'd grown used to'.[125] This led to the development of his song, 'Heart of Worship', which reflects an approach to worship that is not dependent on music. Worship, Redman proclaims in this song, is 'all about ... Jesus'. And he even includes a note of apology in the song for what people have made it about – most often music. But God is searching 'much deeper within ... looking into' people's hearts, whereby worship is about Jesus.[126]

Redman's song, 'Gifted Response', reveals a Trinitarian approach to worship. The lyrics open up, explaining:

This is a gifted response
Father we cannot come to You by our own merit
We will come in the name of Your Son
As He glorifies You
And in the power of Your Spirit

Though a short excerpt, it reflects a Trinitarian theology of worship. Worship is a gifted response, since worship is possible through Christ, in the power of the Spirit. Worship begins with God, not with what humans do. The human act is merely a response to the gift of worship. The Triune God is involved in the human response, for while people worship Jesus, the Father and Spirit are included in their worship of a Triune God. People 'join with Jesus as He glorifies His Father'.[127] And the Spirit reveals Christ's lordship and 'takes us into the Son's relationship with the Father'.[128] The experience of the Spirit for worship is acknowledged, in that worship is offered 'in the power of the Spirit'. People can worship the Father through the Son because of the Spirit's present work. All three CWM leaders acknowledge the role of an experience of the Spirit for worship in general, while both Doerksen and Zschech give greater attention to the role of the Spirit's manifestation for worship music.

---

[125] Redman, *The Unquenchable Worshipper*, p. 103.
[126] Redman, *The Unquenchable Worshipper*, p. 104.
[127] Matt Redman, *Facedown* (Eastbourne: Kingsway, 2004), p. 61.
[128] Redman, *Facedown*, p. 61.

Conclusion

CWM is the choice of Pentecostals for their use of songs in local church services today. CWM leaders, Doerksen, Zschech, and Redman demand the attention of those wanting to understand and discern the way forward for Pentecostal corporate worship music. Thus, the next two chapters continue the exploration of CWM through the lens of the three leaders described above, providing both a description and analysis of their views.

3

FROM SONGWRITERS TO CONGREGATIONAL SINGING IN CONTEMPORARY WORSHIP MUSIC

In order to delve deeper into the theological ramifications of CWM leaders' approach to worship music, this chapter describes three important themes in CWM: songwriters writing worship songs, local churches preparing to sing CWM songs, and the presentation and act of congregational singing. Each leader's approach to the three themes is described, followed by an analysis in the next chapter. The role of the immediacy of God for worship music is highlighted throughout.

CWM and Writing Worship Songs

Before the musicians play their instruments, vocalists sing on the platform, and congregations join in singing, there are a number of elements that leaders argue contribute to the actual presentation of worship music. This section examines the development of worship music, particularly songwriting.

Brian Doerksen
Doerksen assumes the Spirit's manifestation for successful songwriting in his views on five key concepts: the anointing, being made in God's image, Scripture, the church, and being called and gifted to write songs. He also provides three recommendations for the craft of songwriting, and though not explicitly associated with the immediacy of God, they are helpful to acknowledge since his goal for wor-

ship music is an experience of God. First, Doerksen assumes an experience of God for the anointing in order to write new and successful songs. 'Anointed' songs are 'timeless, used everywhere, cross denominational lines, cross musical styles lines, and get recorded on multiple albums'.[1] Anointed songs are 'God ordained', and 'the undefinable [*sic*] element that moves us deeply in our spirit and makes us say, "That's God!"'[2] People acknowledge God's presence when songs are anointed.

Doerksen describes two instances when he experienced the Spirit so that anointed songs developed. First, 'Come, Now is the Time to Worship' is one of Doerksen's most popular songs, and he explains that it arose during a period of doubting God and his goodness.[3] While he was walking, praying, singing, and speaking 'out Scriptures', he 'heard' an 'idea', which 'felt like the "frequency of worship"'.[4] He was in a 'realm where God is completely real', and he 'immediately sensed the presence of God'.[5] He 'intuitively knew' he was 'tuning into God's invitation' to worship, which goes out continually as described in Psalm 19.[6]

Second, while writing the song, 'Father, I Want You to Hold Me', he experienced an ongoing sense of God's presence. He explains, 'as I wrote a few phrases and started singing them back to God, I kept experiencing waves of God's presence washing over me'.[7] A theological idea eventually led to the development of music to accompany the lyrics that were also developing from this one idea.[8] Doerksen's explanation reveals his understanding of the divine element, but also reveals the human responsibility to respond by crafting a suitable musical piece. Writing songs out of an encounter with the Spirit can only arise from a genuine expression of one's relationship with God. He encourages songs for corporate worship that are initially developed

---

[1] Doerksen, 'Song Writing', p. 102.
[2] Doerksen, 'Song Writing', p. 102.
[3] Doerksen, *Make Love, Make War*, p. 18.
[4] Doerksen, *Make Love, Make War*, p. 19.
[5] Doerksen, *Make Love, Make War*, p. 19.
[6] Doerksen, *Make Love, Make War*, p. 19.
[7] Doerksen, *Make Love, Make War*, p. 74. Another example of the immediacy of God provoking the development of songs includes his popular song, 'Refiner's Fire'. Doerksen, *Make Love, Make War*, p. 88.
[8] Doerksen, *Make Love, Make War*, pp. 19-20, 73-74.

in the writers' own private devotion to God. For he admits, songwriters 'basically write the songs that we need to sing'.[9] Writers should not try to write songs that become internationally popular, but songs they can 'sing in their private time with God'.[10]

Next, Doerksen affirms the role of an experience of God for songwriting based on humans being made in God's image.[11] He explains that '**all creativity comes from God**', for God created humans in his image.[12] While humans cannot create out of nothing like God, they can 'transform chaos into order and art'.[13] People can participate with God's creativity, which can lead to 'art that is *filled with both passion and God's presence*'.[14] Songwriting includes a divine element, because creativity finds its source in the God humans reflect – being made in his image. Several sources of inspiration for songs, all associated with God, include: Scripture, one's relationship with God, the church, the church's teaching, sung prayers, revelation and understanding, and prophetic words.[15]

Third, Scripture should play a primary role in the development of the songs. Scripture can be included by directly singing the text of Scripture, 'fresh' songs that are paraphrases of Scripture, or songs that find their inspiration from Scripture.[16] He argues for a more holistic theology in songs of worship, and notably does this by focusing on the lack of songs of lament in churches today. Though Doerksen does not explicitly link his views on songs of lament to the Spirit's manifestation, his view fosters honest and intimate relationship with God. The connection between songs of lament and the Spirit's presence is explained in the following chapter. For now, his argument for the inclusion of songs of lament is important and follows.

Songs of worship produced today, Doerksen argues, can often be relegated to 'the big, shiny, happy anthems'.[17] But this culture of

---

[9] Doerksen, *Make Love, Make War*, p. 22.

[10] Doerksen, *Make Love, Make War*, p. 22.

[11] Doerksen, 'Song Writing', p. 87.

[12] Doerksen, 'Song Writing', p. 87 (emphasis original).

[13] Doerksen, 'Song Writing', p. 87.

[14] Doerksen, 'Song Writing', pp. 87-88 (emphasis added).

[15] Doerksen, 'Song Writing', pp. 96-100.

[16] Doerksen, 'Song Writing', pp. 96-97; *Make Love, Make War*, pp. 191, 105, 125, 222.

[17] Doerksen, *Make Love, Make War*, p. 147.

'happy appearances and upbeat performances is keeping some brokenhearted people away from churches'.[18] Writers must 'bring the whole experience of life into worship like the Psalms do. ... from our grief to our joy'.[19] Regrettably, some leaders are unwilling to allow believers to bring their 'sorrow, pain, and suffering into God's presence'.[20] Solely including songs of celebration and joy, to the neglect of honest songs of grief and lament, is a form of flattery. Flattery occurs when people sing songs they think 'God wants to hear' – what they think will bring them God's favour.[21] This type of flattery, though, is a form of 'false worship' that Scripture warns against.[22] Churches must include songs of grief and lament in their songs of worship. People must be able honestly to express to God what is in their hearts in worship.[23]

Doerksen's song, 'How Long O Lord', is a song of lament based on Psalm 13. In the song, he follows the approach of the Psalmist, beginning with questions before God as forms of lament:

How long O Lord will you forget me
How long O Lord
Will you look the other way
How long O Lord
Must I wrestle with my thoughts
And every day
Have such sorrow in my heart

But he moves on to a request before God in this song:

Look on me and answer,
O God my Father
Bring light to my darkness
Before they see me fall

One departure from Psalm 13 is his use of 'O God my Father' for the psalmists' address, who uses the phrase, 'O LORD my God'.[24]

---

[18] Doerksen, *Make Love, Make War*, p. 147.

[19] Brian Doerksen, 'Songs of Lament: An Interview with Brian Doerksen (Part 2)'. Interview by Jim Coggins. May 15, 2008. Online: http://canadianchristianity.com/songs-lament-interview-brian-doerksen-part-2-3424/.

[20] Doerksen, *Make Love, Make War*, p. 156.

[21] Doerksen, *Make Love, Make War*, p. 158.

[22] Doerksen points out Ps 78.36-37. Doerksen, *Make Love, Make War*, pp. 158-59.

[23] Doerksen, *Make Love, Make War*, p. 159.

[24] Psalm 13.3.

The change of address reflects Doerksen's emphasis – and the Vineyard emphasis – on relating to God as Father. He ends, however, with a declaration of trust and worship, much like the psalmist includes hope in the midst of lament:

But I trust
In Your unfailing love
Yes my heart will rejoice
Still I sing of your unfailing love
You have been good
You will be good to me[25]

This song does not merely wallow in sorrow. It includes the various components that suffering often involves: doubts, questions, and supplication. But it ultimately ends on an exclamation of trust and rejoicing for God who is loving and good. The song is not only based on a Psalm, but offers something unique for those wrestling with suffering – it offers hope because of who God is.

Fourth, Doerksen delves into the importance of songs that arise out of what is happening in a church, which implicitly involves the Spirit's present work in a church. These songs may arise out of one's experience in the life of the church, the type of teaching going on in the church, or a prophetic word received.[26] His song, 'Song for the Bride', arose out of prophetic words he received.[27] Rather than trying to follow popular trends in worship music, songwriters should be prophetic. Being prophetic is about knowing what is going to happen in advance, so that the songs are available when they are needed.[28] This prophetic call for songwriters should 'inform and shape' their writing.[29]

Doerksen also views the church as the community that provides the sounding board for songs of worship – whereby other believers acknowledge whether a song is anointed or not. Some may declare that 'God gave me this song'.[30] But rather than declaring what God

---

[25] Doerksen, *Maker Love, Make War*, p. 142.

[26] Doerksen, 'Song Writing', pp. 97-99.

[27] Doerksen, 'Song Writing', p. 99.

[28] Brian Doerksen, 'Focusing Your Worship Ministry on God'. *Christian Musician Summit: CMS Overlake 2007 Mini-Sessions.* November 9–10, 2007. Online: http://www.youtube.com/watch?v=PtDhS4X816c.

[29] Doerksen, 'Focusing Your Worship Ministry on God'.

[30] Doerksen, 'Song Writing', p. 88.

has apparently done, it is more constructive to let others declare that a song is 'inspired' by God.[31] The local church can provide a helpful 'initial screening' for songs, to filter out songs that should or should not be sung by the church both at the local and international level.[32]

His views on the call to write songs also assume the Spirit's immediacy, for he argues that only those who are called and gifted by God should write songs.[33] Even those who may be 'gifted worship leaders' may not be songwriters.[34] The church must be honest with those who are and are not gifted for songwriting.[35]

Finally, Doerksen shares three other important elements for the craft of songwriting, though not explicitly tied to the Spirit's manifestation, still lead to the goal of intimacy with God. The three recommendations he makes include: having one '[u]niversal song vision' that reflects the heart of the songwriter and church, using a variety of forms, and making use of a memorable melody.[36] These recommendations are deemed as helpful means to facilitate the Spirit's manifestation for worship music. In sum, Doerksen's focus on an experience of God for songwriting finds an explicit role in his thoughts on the anointed song, intimacy with God the Father, being made in God's image, the role of Scripture, the church's role, and being called and gifted by God to write songs. His three recommendations for the craft of songwriting can also help facilitate God's present work for worship music.

Darlene Zschech

Zschech values the experience of God for songwriting, explicitly related to the need for three elements: the anointing, the role of prophetic songs, and the use of Scripture for worship music. Two other factors involved in songwriting in Zschech's view that are not explicitly tied to the Spirit's immediacy for worship music – but nonetheless help facilitate the Spirit's immediacy for worship music – are also explained here. First, Zschech explains that Hillsong has 'an anointing

---

[31] Doerksen, 'Song Writing', p. 88.
[32] Doerksen, 'Song Writing', p. 88.
[33] Doerksen, 'Song Writing', p. 88.
[34] Doerksen, 'Song Writing', p. 88.
[35] Doerksen, 'Song Writing', p. 88.
[36] Doerksen, 'Song Writing', pp. 89-90, 102.

for a new song'.[37] The anointing is about being 'set apart for God and his work' through the Spirit's work.[38] Thus, the underlying foundation for writing songs of worship is an experience of the Spirit in the writer's life – the anointing. From the outflow of the anointing in one's life, the rest of her recommendations for writing songs of worship can occur.

Zschech encourages songwriters to write prophetic songs, which reveals her reliance on an experience of God to receive songs from God.[39] God sends 'new songs for us to sing', so that it is important to search for 'songs that bring a prophetically fresh sound, something straight from the Father's heart'.[40] Songs are 'birthed' through writers who go 'to the throne room of God'.[41] Songs are 'sent' to the writers through the Spirit's present work.

Receiving songs is not restricted to God immediately sending these songs through the Spirit, but through other mediators from God. She provides a revealing story about a 'prophetic word spoken over Russell Fragar', who was Hillsong's music pastor from 1989–2001.[42] She heard this message regarding Fragar: 'And the angel of the Lord will stand at the foot of your bed at night and sing songs over you, O great scribe'.[43] Who this 'angel of the Lord' is, is not clear. But she speaks positively of this message, describing it as having 'songs sung to you straight from heaven that bring revelation, not just beautiful music'.[44] She does not elaborate on this idea, and does not claim to have personally experienced anyone other than God directly giving her a song. Her desire for songs from heaven is not restricted to receiving songs directly from God, but from those from God's heavenly realm. The experience of God is still valued, though,

---

[37] Evans, *Open Up the Doors*, p. 100. Evans quotes Zschech from a Hillsong conference panel discussion that occurred on July 15, 1999.

[38] Evans, *Open Up the Doors*, pp. 100-101.

[39] Delton L. Alford, a Church of God leader, also affirms the importance of prophecy and music. He states that 'Music is an appropriate medium for expressing the power of the prophetic word today', founded upon the idea in Joel 2.28 that the Spirit will be poured out on all people now. *Ministering Through Music* (ed. Donald S. Aultman; Cleveland, TN: Pathway Press, 2002), p. 163.

[40] Zschech, *Extravagant Worship*, pp. 191, 193.

[41] Zschech, *Extravagant Worship*, p. 191.

[42] Russell Fragar, 'About Russell'. Online: http://www.russellfragar.com.

[43] Zschech, *Extravagant Worship*, p. 193.

[44] Zschech, *Extravagant Worship*, p. 193.

since the songs are received from an angel of God. Such an experience, while not stated by Zschech, assumes the Spirit's enabling work for relationship with God and his angels.

Third, Zschech argues that '[t]he strongest praise and worship songs are Scripture put to music', based on her expectation for the manifestation of God through Scripture. Including Scripture for worship music is important because 'the Bible is the living, breathing, infallible Word of God'.[45] She follows up these comments with her view that Scriptural songs reflect 'our expression and feelings toward God', which 'are very intimate'.[46] Whenever she begins writing worship songs, she opens the Bible and sings songs of worship from a Psalm because '[t]here is nothing more inspiring'.[47] Her song, 'Shout to the Lord', for instance, came about both through a difficult period in her family life, and subsequently reading Psalms 96–100.[48] Scripture put to music facilitates an experience of God, as Scripture is the 'living, breathing' Word of God, and enables singers to experience intimacy with God through heart-felt biblical songs.

Zschech also acknowledges the role of worship music as a tool to teach the Word of God, for songs can 'make the Word memorable and settle the message into our hearts'.[49] What is important, though, is that these songs that teach are coordinated with the local church's current teaching. The songs found in her albums were often influenced by the teaching of Brian Houston, the senior pastor at Hillsong. This idea reveals the need for worship music to complement what is going on during the rest of the worship service theme-wise, rather than being unrelated.

Finally, Zschech makes two other recommendations for songwriting, though not explicitly connected to the experience of God, implicitly lead to the goal of an experience of God. First, she encourages songwriters to '[a]lways work on the skill of writing'.[50] Writers

---

[45] Zschech, *Extravagant Worship*, p. 199.

[46] Zschech, *Extravagant Worship*, p. 199.

[47] Zschech, *Extravagant Worship*, p. 198.

[48] Darlene Zschech, '100 Huntley Interview with Darlene Zschech Part 1'. Online: http://www.youtube.com/watch?v=yXHHE4Qvwoo&feature=related.

[49] Zschech, *Extravagant Worship*, p. 196.

[50] Zschech, *Extravagant Worship*, p. 198.

must listen beyond their musical preferences, as the 'greatest musicians and singers are the greatest listeners'.[51] Writers should compose inclusive songs, so that all can join in singing – not just good singers.[52] Furthermore, writers should work at making songs memorable.[53] Working hard at songwriting, learning from other musicians, writing songs available for anyone to sing, and making songs memorable are just some of the recommendations she makes for songwriters to help develop their skills.

Second, Zschech also encourages songwriters to be critical of their songs. There are a number of ways songwriters can be critical of their music. Writers need to be open to revising songs in order to 'dig deeper' for new thoughts and new expressions lyrically to gain 'clarity and meaning'.[54] They must do this with a 'prayerful, contemplative' approach.[55] Writers must also be open to constructive criticism from those they trust.[56] Congregational feedback as a whole is also crucial, as they are 'the greatest road test for congregational songs. If after a few weeks the song doesn't fly – let it go!'[57] The congregation's acceptance and affirmation of a worship song is the most important filter for the inclusion of worship songs. In sum, Zschech expects the experience of God for songwriters, reflected in her views that writers should be anointed, prophetic songs should be encouraged, and Scriptural music is needed. Factors contributing to good worship music, implicitly tied to the goal of the experience of God, include the need to work at the craft of songwriting and being critical of one's songs.

Matt Redman

Redman's views on prophetic worship songs and including Scripture in songs explicitly reveals his value for the Spirit's manifestation for writing songs. He also shares three recommendations for songwriting not explicitly linked to the Spirit's immediacy, but nonetheless helps facilitate the Spirit's present activity for worship music. Beginning

---

[51] Zschech, *Extravagant Worship*, p. 198.
[52] Zschech, *Extravagant Worship*, pp. 196-97.
[53] Zschech, *Extravagant Worship*, p. 197.
[54] Zschech, *Extravagant Worship*, p. 197.
[55] Zschech, *Extravagant Worship*, p. 197.
[56] Zschech, *Extravagant Worship*, p. 197.
[57] Zschech, *Extravagant Worship*, p. 197.

with prophetic songs, Redman believes that songwriting can contribute to a form of 'prophetic worship'.[58] Songs that are written with the prophetic in mind, describe God's particular message for 'the many different seasons of church life'.[59] Redman considers his song, 'The Heart of Worship', as a song that was a form of 'prophetic worship'.[60] Since those in his congregation lost their 'focus in gathered worship', changes needed to be made, which eventually brought about true worship.[61] His song 'described and gave voice to what God was doing' among them.[62]

In order to write prophetic songs, leaders must make changes. Leaders need to change their priorities, which affect their use of time. Since many people's lives are full of activities, there is little room to hear God's 'still small voice'.[63] 'Creativity and the prophetic are so often birthed in the place of stillness.'[64] Thus, by cultivating a 'quiet heart', listening for God's 'inspiring whispers', it is possible to receive and write a 'fresh' song for the congregation.[65]

Second, Redman also believes that the use of Scripture in song is a means of experiencing God. When songs are saturated with Scripture, both unbelievers and believers may experience 'the awakening power of truth' as songs are sung.[66] He explains how this works in his life, whereby Scripture initiates 'the wake–up call' in his 'soul' and subsequently strengthens his 'walk with God'.[67] Thus, songwriters must read and study Scripture to ensure their songs are saturated with Scripture. For as Jesus states, '[o]ut of the overflow of the heart, the mouth speaks (Mt. 12.34)'.[68]

---

[58] Matt Redman, 'Worship-Leading Essentials: (Part 5) The Powerful Insights of the Prophetic', in Matt Redman, *Inside Out Worship* (vol. 2; Eastbourne: Kingsway, 2005), p. 98.

[59] Redman, 'Worship-Leading Essentials (Part 5)', pp. 98-99.

[60] Redman, 'Worship-Leading Essentials (Part 5)', pp. 99-100.

[61] Redman, 'Worship-Leading Essentials (Part 5)', p. 99.

[62] Redman, 'Worship-Leading Essentials (Part 5)', p. 99.

[63] Matt Redman, 'Cultivating a Quiet Heart', in Matt Redman (comp.), *The Heart of Worship Files* (Ventura: Regal, 2003), pp. 179-80.

[64] Redman, 'Cultivating a Quiet Heart', p. 179.

[65] Redman, 'Cultivating a Quiet Heart', pp. 179-80.

[66] Matt Redman, 'Worship-Leading Essentials: (Part 2) The Awakening Power of Truth', in Matt Redman, *Inside Out Worship* (vol. 2; Eastbourne: Kingsway, 2005), pp. 31-32.

[67] Redman, 'Worship-Leading Essentials: (Part 2)', p. 28.

[68] Redman, 'Worship-Leading Essentials: (Part 2)', pp. 30-31.

Following the 'awakening' through the inclusion of Scriptural truth in songs, Redman states that the song must provide the opportunity for singers to respond. 'The best worship songs poetically, relevantly and biblically capture the truths of God, and the same time also give the worshipper a way of responding to these truths.'[69] Tim Hughes' song, 'Here I Am to Worship', is an example of including biblical truth and an opportunity for response. The verses describe the incarnation of Jesus, while the chorus provides this response: 'Hear I am to worship. Here I am to bow down, Here I am to say that You're my God'.[70] The song provides important biblical truth to generate an awakening – which initiates an experience of the immediacy of God – while giving opportunity for people to respond to God.

Redman also offers three recommendations for those interested in writing melodies, while not explicitly related to experiencing the immediacy of God, can help facilitate the experience of God for worship music. First, '[t]he best congregational melodies work *in* worship because they began *as* worship'.[71] This recommendation implicitly, though, suggests that the new worship song previously led an individual to worship that included an experience of the immediacy of God. Second, write songs that are memorable.[72] Third, extra thought on 'chord progressions' is important for a good match between 'tune and cord'.[73] Thus, Redman stresses the importance of the experience of God in his approach to writing prophetic songs and including Scriptural truth in songs. Redman, however, also acknowledges the human dynamics of what constitutes good music, including it being: birthed in personal worship, memorable, and musically appropriate – all elements that facilitate an experience of God through worship music.

CWM and Preparing for Congregational Singing

After the songs of worship have been written and available for use by congregations, churches are responsible for integrating the songs

---

[69] Redman, 'Worship-Leading Essentials: (Part 2)', p. 32.

[70] Redman, 'Worship-Leading Essentials: (Part 2)', p. 32.

[71] Redman, 'Thoughts on Songwriting', 32.

[72] Matt Redman, 'Thoughts on Songwriting (Part 1): Making Melody', in Matt Redman (comp.), *The Heart of Worship Files* (Ventura: Regal, 2003), p. 32.

[73] Redman, 'Thoughts on Songwriting', pp. 32-33.

into their worship services. A number of dynamics are involved for integrating songs as they prepare for the actual presentation of the worship songs for corporate worship. Various elements involved in this integration of songs include God, pastors, song leaders, a band, and the congregation. How these three leaders describe this type of preparation follows.

Brian Doerksen

The Spirit's manifestation is explicitly assumed for the preparation of congregational singing in two ways in Doerksen's thought. Song leaders must facilitate intimacy with God for all and prepare for spontaneous prophetic songs. Doerksen also shares two other recommendations for song leaders that he does not explicitly relate to the Spirit's manifestation, but help facilitate an experience of the Spirit. These are the fraction principle and understanding who is available.

First, the goal of facilitating intimacy with God for all people through songs is crucial for song leaders preparing for corporate worship. Doerksen's view on the responsibilities of a song leader are consistent with the established 'three main values' for worship within the Vineyard: intimacy, integrity, and accessibility.[74] Intimacy with God, however, stands out among the three and contributes to his approach that highlights the experience of God for worship music. A 'relational encounter' in songs is important, so that songs are not just 'about God', but address him personally.[75] Even the Vineyard movement, a movement Doerksen associates with, has influenced CWM by encouraging a structure for choosing worship songs – described by John Wimber as the 'phases' of worship – whereby intimacy with God is the goal.[76]

Related to the previous value of intimacy, the second value of accessibility ensures all may experience God through worship music. His goal as a song leader is to 'make intimate worship accessible through my song, our song'.[77] This should ensure that both the leader

---

[74] Jeremy Cook, 'Vineyard Worship Values'. Inside Worship: A Vineyard Resource for Worship. Online: http://www.insideworship.com/2011/about/vineyard-worship-values.

[75] Doerksen, 'Faithful One'. See Carol Wimber's precedent-setting view on this idea in chapter 2.

[76] Wimber, 'Worship', pp. 4-6.

[77] Doerksen, 'Faithful One'.

and the congregation can sing the songs as their 'own'.[78] This is about singing songs that allow everyone 'to express their hearts to God'.[79] The leader may need to include both old and new songs. A leader must avoid being overly creative to the detriment of accessibility. Thinking and praying through the choice of songs can ensure that everyone can 'own' the song.[80] Choosing the appropriate song may require the leader to '[a]llow God's presence to breath on it', sensing God's direction for the decision.[81] The song leader anticipates the immediate presence of the Spirit who guides the choice of songs, so that they are accessible to all to experience intimacy with God through the music.

In order for the immediacy of God to be experienced by all, the third value of integrity must be exhibited by leaders. The goal is creating 'a safe place where' people 'can express their worship to God'.[82] When people lack integrity – when their 'walk doesn't match their talk' – leaders lose their authority.[83] And this lack of authority leads to a loss of that 'sense of safety' for people to worship through music.[84] Integrity can be lost through a lack of character. Integrity can also be lost when leaders try to manipulate people to 'perform'.[85] While emotion may occur in worship, genuine worship comes 'out of real relationship'.[86] Emotions are not manufactured.[87] Likening a song leader to a best man at a wedding, a leader must value being as 'invisible or unnoticed as possible'.[88]

Integrity is also connected to mercy. Scripture reveals that love for God is linked to loving others who are in need.[89] If people fail to love those in need, their songs are 'false'.[90] In Amos 5.22-23, God states, 'Take away from me the noise of your songs; I will not listen to the

---

[78] Doerksen, 'Faithful One'.
[79] Doerksen, 'Faithful One'.
[80] Doerksen, 'Faithful One'.
[81] Doerksen, 'Faithful One'.
[82] Doerksen, 'Faithful One'.
[83] Doerksen, 'Faithful One'.
[84] Doerksen, 'Faithful One'.
[85] Doerksen, 'Faithful One'.
[86] Doerksen, 'Faithful One'.
[87] Doerksen, 'Faithful One'.
[88] Doerksen, 'Faithful One'.
[89] Doerksen, 'Faithful One'.
[90] Doerksen, 'Faithful One'.

melody of your harps. But let justice roll down like waters, and right-eousness like an ever-flowing stream.' When someone does not re-spond to others with mercy, their heart is hardened as they make 'worship just about the musical moment'; but they eventually witness 'emptiness' in worship.[91] When someone shows mercy, however, their 'heart' and 'authority in worship' can 'flourish and grow'.[92] This re-quires worshippers getting involved in serving others in need.[93]

The values of integrity – and accessibility – in worship music also requires a variety of types of songs, which is critical in order to ex-perience God. Variety ensures that the unique expression that each person needs to sing reflects the broad spectrum of people in the congregation. 'Upbeat, joyful songs' are more popular forms of CWM.[94] But to limit songs to only one type of expression neglects other needs within the congregation. There may be people who are broken and need to sing a song of brokenness.[95] Some may require songs of lament.[96] This ensures that songs are accessible and sung with integrity.

Second, Doerksen acknowledges the role of spontaneous pro-phetic songs – an approach that assumes and values the Spirit's man-ifestation for worship music. These are songs whereby God releases songs to sing over his people.[97] Doerksen explains that you may even just receive a 'phrase' from God that 'comes into your mind as you are leading worship or a phrase from a Scripture'.[98] But he writes, '[m]ake sure you 'practice this in private and small groups before you do it with a large group!'[99] He encourages a form of planned sponta-neity. And while these songs may be 'powerful', they should not be 'overdone'.[100] Practising this approach can help leaders feel confident about being spontaneous in their song leading.[101]

---

91 Doerksen, 'Faithful One'.
[91] Doerksen, 'Faithful One'.
[92] Doerksen, 'Faithful One'.
[93] Doerksen, 'Faithful One'.
[94] Doerksen, *Make Love, Make War*, p. 147.
[95] Doerksen, *Make Love, Make War*, p. 147.
[96] Doerksen, *Make Love, Make War*, p. 147.
[97] Doerksen, *Make Love, Make War*, p. 252.
[98] Doerksen, *Make Love, Make War*, p. 252.
[99] Doerksen, *Make Love, Make War*, p. 252.
[100] Doerksen, *Make Love, Make War*, p. 252.
[101] Bob Sorge also makes a case for balancing the need for preparation with openness for spontaneity, because when song leaders follow the Spirit, people have

Finally, Doerksen offers two key principles for arranging bands preparing for worship: the fraction principle and understanding who is available to be involved.[102] Though he does not explicitly link these two principles to an experience of God, they facilitate the goal of intimacy with God. The fraction principle is the idea that 'the goal of every equation in worship is one'.[103] So if there are five musicians, each provides one-fifth of the equation in order to equal one. The problem of musicians is to offer 'one' whole, as opposed to one-fifth, so that there are five different things going on during the songs.[104] This also ensures that the band comes together unified as a team, with 'one heart, one sound', playing 'one sound'.[105]

The second principle for bands is to reckon with who is available for the band.[106] This deals with matching the skill level of musicians with the type of music to use. Rather than attempting to copy professionally produced albums, the goal is for the band to sing simply so that the congregation 'can join in and sing'.[107] While complex arrangements may be possible, depending on the skill level of musicians, simplicity often accomplishes more for the purpose of corporate worship music.[108] Thus, while Doerksen explicitly assumes the immediacy of God for the preparation of worship music through a focus on intimacy with God and prophetic songs, he also encourages the facilitation of an experience of God through the fraction principle and being aware of who is available for the worship band.

Darlene Zschech

Zschech includes the importance of the Spirit's immediacy in preparation for the presentation of worship music by her stress on character and preparation that includes singing in the Spirit. First, her comments found in a letter she sent to Hillsong's song leaders and music directors reveal her link between character and the experience of God. She stated: '*The more preparation you commit to the rehearsal, the more*

---

the opportunity to encounter God. See *Following the River: A Vision for Corporate Worship* (Greenwood: Oasis House, 2004), pp. 27-33.

[102] Doerksen, 'Faithful One'.

[103] Doerksen, 'Faithful One'.

[104] Doerksen, 'Faithful One'.

[105] Doerksen, 'Faithful One'.

[106] Doerksen, 'Faithful One'.

[107] Doerksen, 'Faithful One'.

[108] Doerksen, 'Faithful One'.

room you'll have to step out in the prophetic, to play the unexpected, to release the 'MOMENTS' in church life that make a service special.[109] The prophetic, the unexpected, and those moments she speaks about refers to instances during congregational singing that people experience the manifestation of God. Preparation includes good leadership, being supportive, loving, punctual, and prepared musically – essentially being a person of good character.[110]

Zschech expounds on the type of character required for those leading worship songs, advocating for eight important values – which includes a personal experience of God. First, leaders must know Christ, and make him their first priority in life.[111] Second, leaders must be able to testify of a personal encounter with God. A testimony of the experience of God brings both 'passion' to your gifts of worship and 'a powerful conviction on others because they can see what God has done in you'.[112] Third, people must 'serve God with excellence' because He is 'an excellent God'.[113] As Ps. 33.3 states, 'Sing to him a new song; *play skillfully*, and shout for joy'.[114] Fourth, leaders need to serve God through their musical talents, which bring joy to the one who serves.[115] Fifth, unity is 'essential' because it is a testimony of the church to the world revealing God's love found through Jesus.[116] God blesses unity.[117] Believers must commit to unity, forgiveness, praying for unity, and spiritual growth.[118] Sixth, leaders must commit to being friends with band members.[119] Seventh, people must be generous with others. Eighth, since 'creative people tend to live in the "feelings" department', they must be determined in their faithfulness to God.[120] Creative people must discipline their minds to 'agree with God's Word'.[121] Thus, while Zschech values the Spirit's manifestation

---

[109] Zschech, *Extravagant Worship*, p. 184 (emphasis original).
[110] Zschech, *Extravagant Worship*, p. 184 (emphasis original).
[111] Zschech, *Extravagant Worship*, p. 126.
[112] Zschech, *Extravagant Worship*, pp. 126-27.
[113] Zschech, *Extravagant Worship*, p. 127.
[114] Zschech, *Extravagant Worship*, p. 127 (emphasis original).
[115] Zschech, *Extravagant Worship*, p. 129.
[116] Zschech, *Extravagant Worship*, pp. 130-32.
[117] Zschech, *Extravagant Worship*, pp. 130-32.
[118] Zschech, *Extravagant Worship*, pp. 130-32.
[119] Zschech, *Extravagant Worship*, p. 133.
[120] Zschech, *Extravagant Worship*, pp. 135-38.
[121] Zschech, *Extravagant Worship*, pp. 135-38.

for those special moments in corporate worship, she recognises the importance of godly character among song leaders, which includes a personal experience of God.

Second, Zschech values an experience of the Spirit's immediacy in rehearsals by singing in the Spirit.[122] She explains, '[s]ometimes in our rehearsals, we play and sing in the spirit [*sic*]. This helps to encourage and equip our team to operate and move under the anointing of the Holy Spirit. When we lead the congregation with confidence, they will follow.'[123] Singing in the Spirit is about singing songs in tongues or in English – what she deems as 'free worship'.[124] Singing in the Spirit in English is about singing a prophetic song, whereby the Spirit reveals the heart of God in a message through song.[125] Singing in the Spirit – whether in tongues or a prophetic song – reflects the Pentecostal heritage of Hillsong, which values a charismatic, spontaneous, Spirit-led approach to singing. Her approach to singing in the Spirit shows that the band's experience of the Spirit prior to the actual presentation not only provides them the opportunity to experience an anointing of the Spirit during preparation, but confidence for the anointing of the Spirit for the musical presentation. In sum, Zschech highlights the experience of God in the preparation for worship music in her belief that those involved in leading the worship music must be people of character – which includes a personal experience of God. Leaders must also be open to singing in the Spirit during rehearsals – both in tongues and prophetically – in order to experience the Spirit during the actual presentation of worship music.

Matt Redman

Redman values the Spirit's immediacy for preparation in three ways: he encourages preparing for spontaneity in worship music, he views

---

[122] Zschech, *Extravagant Worship*, p. 184.

[123] Darlene Zschech, *Worship: Hillsongs Australia Leadership Series* (Castle Hill: Hillsongs Australia, 1996), p. 96. In order to distinguish worshipping in the 'spirit', which Zschech recommends for worship based on John 4 (explained earlier), these practices are referred to as singing in the 'Spirit' throughout this discussion. Zschech, *Extravagant Worship*, pp. 31-32. Furthermore, using the language of singing in the Spirit is consistent with Stephen Dove's work, who describes how this type of singing was reflected at Azusa (referenced later in this work). See Dove, 'Hymnody and Liturgy in the Azusa Street Revival'.

[124] Zschech, *Worship*, p. 95.

[125] Zschech, *Worship*, pp. 95-96.

worship as more spiritual than musical, and he values Scriptural songs. First, spontaneity is something Redman values in the presentation of worship music, and is subsequently something he admits requires preparation. The little Redman writes about rehearsals and musical excellence, revolves more around spontaneity and what he deems as the importance of the spiritual over the musical.

Redman's views on spontaneity are due to his view of both the Spirit's and Father's work. First, spontaneous changes may occur during worship music due to the Spirit's leading.[126] Second, leaders may be led 'to do the unexpected', for '[i]f we do what the Father is doing, when He is doing it, God will break into our services in powerful and surprising ways'.[127] Preparing for unplanned moments ensures leaders are ready when God 'breaks' into the corporate worship service, which is ultimately about helping to ensure the entire congregation can experience the Spirit. Leading an entire band with various skills and expectations can be demanding, which is why spontaneity must be 'rehearsed'.[128] Rehearsing for spontaneity may sound contradictory, but leaders need to train musicians and computer operators to 'flow with the spontaneous'.[129] This can be done during rehearsals by trying to run 'songs one into the other seamlessly', trying 'different endings', and 'playing songs in various keys, so you can adapt them to link with different songs'.[130] While it is important for bands to respect 'the discipline of a well-rehearsed song', they should also be 'able to flow with any changes of direction and approach that seem appropriate'.[131]

Second, though Redman values good musicianship, music is always secondary to the Spirit's immediate work in worship music be-

---

[126] Redman, 'Worship-Leading Essentials: (Part 5)', p. 96.

[127] Redman, *The Unquenchable Worshipper*, p. 54.

[128] Matt Redman, 'Cell, Congregation, Celebration: Worship Leading in Three Contexts', in Matt Redman (comp.), *The Heart of Worship Files* (Ventura: Regal, 2003), pp. 115-16.

[129] Redman, 'Cell, Congregation, Celebration', p. 116. Delton L. Alford also explains that the strength of Pentecostal churches is the freedom to follow the Spirit for corporate music, though he admits that a coordinated effort at organization and structure is important. *Music in the Pentecostal Church* (Cleveland, TN: Pathway Press, 1967), pp. 60-61.

[130] Redman, 'Cell, Congregation, Celebration', p. 116.

[131] Redman, 'Cell, Congregation, Celebration', p. 116.

cause worship music is spiritual. This focus on the Holy Spirit in worship music is because worship is 'a spiritual event long before it is ever a musical event'.[132] While linking songs in a set of songs, playing well, and excellence in music is 'vital', 'the key is in remembering there can never be a substitute for the Holy Spirit of God. If He's not involved, we'll know it, and no amount of good musicianship or skillful arrangements will ever be able to fill that gap.'[133]

Third, including biblical truth in songs is critical because it facilitates the Spirit's immediacy. Reading Scripture awakens hearts for a deeper relationship with God.[134] And song leaders who are students of Scripture will ensure that they choose songs for worship that 'bleed the Word of God'.[135] And by choosing songs that reflect biblical truth, people can ensure that they are 'rallying around the essential focus points' of their faith, while also defending their 'services from misleading theology'.[136] Redman does not point out what are all the 'essential focus points' of the faith, but does single out the cross as central for Christianity.[137] In sum, Redman values the Spirit's immediacy in preparation, through his focus on rehearsing for spontaneous leadings of the Spirit, prioritizing the Spirit's work over musical excellence, and the importance of Scripture being foundational as one prepares for congregational singing. After an examination of all three leaders, it is clear that all three leaders value the importance of the immediacy of God in the preparation for worship music through their various recommendations.

CWM and the Presentation of Worship Music

While CWM leaders encourage preparation for congregational singing, the act of congregational singing also includes various elements, such as the role of God, song leaders, the band, and congregation. How they understand worship music should be expressed during a corporate worship service is significant. The views of Doerksen, Zschech, and Redman follow.

---

132 Redman, *The Unquenchable Worshipper*, p. 59.

133 Redman, *The Unquenchable Worshipper*, p. 59.

134 Redman, 'Worship-Leading Essentials: (Part 2)', p. 28.

135 Redman, 'Worship-Leading Essentials: (Part 2)', p. 29.

136 Redman, 'Worship-Leading Essentials: (Part 2)', p. 29.

137 Redman, 'Worship-Leading Essentials: (Part 2)', p. 30.

Brian Doerksen

Doerksen highlights the immediacy of God during congregational singing, acknowledging how an experience of God can be more certain with some prewritten songs over others, and through spontaneous prophetic songs. First, when some prewritten songs are sung at the right time, one can sense 'God's presence come and it connecting with people'.[138] The message of that song may even relate to the message being preached by the pastor – possibly unknown to the song leader.[139] But what is key, is that the message of the song is what 'God is saying for that particular meeting'.[140] The Spirit's immediacy is crucial, then, for Doerksen expects God to be present and to speak.

Doerksen shares some insights on the Spirit's work through the experience of leading his song, 'Father, I Want You to Hold Me'. As he sang the song, people began to weep. This occurred as 'the Spirit of God opened up the "father-wound" in their hearts and the song gave voice to the heart's cry'.[141] Two things stand out in his comment. First, it is the Spirit that works through the songs of worship to bring about change. The Spirit can reveal a message needed for that time through a song. Second, good songs for worship include lyrics that give voice to what the congregation wants and needs to express. The Spirit enabled people to know that a song about the Father is what their hearts needed to express.

Second, Doerksen is open to spontaneous prophetic songs that arise while leading worship music. To sing this type of song, leaders must '[a]sk God to release' them 'to sing His heart over His people'.[142] This may be a 'phrase' that comes to one's mind while leading the songs, which may be directly from Scripture. And as stated earlier, a form of planned spontaneity helps facilitate this, whereby leaders 'practice' this approach in small groups before doing it in a large group.[143] Thus, both prewritten and prophetic songs can serve the purpose of experiencing the immediacy of God, whereby God is present in the service to speak through the songs.

---

138 Doerksen, 'Faithful One'.
139 Doerksen, 'Faithful One'.
140 Doerksen, 'Faithful One'.
141 Doerksen, *Make Love, Make War*, p. 75.
142 Doerksen, *Make Love, Make War*, p. 252.
143 Doerksen, *Make Love, Make War*, p. 252.

Darlene Zschech

The Spirit's immediacy is pronounced in Zschech's thoughts on the presentation of worship music through five ways. The five include: expecting the Spirit's manifestation to a greater degree through worship music, focusing on the goal of an experience of the Spirit, showing the need for discerning the Spirit's work, encouraging singing in the Spirit – both in tongues and prophetically, and her views on the roles of song leaders that explicitly and implicitly value the Spirit's immediacy. First, Zschech's view on what happens when the presentation of worship music in church begins, reveals why the Spirit's manifestation is especially linked with worship music. She contends that

> [e]very time the praise and worship teams with our musicians, singers, production teams, dancers, and actors begin to praise God, His presence comes in like a flood. Even though we live in His presence, His love is *lavished* on us in a miraculous way when we praise Him![144]

Her statement reveals two vital points. First, the immediacy of God is always expected during congregational singing. Second, while she recognises the immediacy of God in day-to-day activities when she states that 'we live in His presence', she expects the immediacy of God to a greater degree through worship music. For she states that it is during congregational singing that God's love is '*lavished*' on believers.

Second, experiencing God's presence – through the Spirit – is an essential goal of congregational singing in Zschech's view. She is 'captivated by the presence of God'.[145] An awareness of the Spirit being near, she explains, 'messed with' her 'own initial "safer" understanding of worshiping in spirit'.[146] Since Scripture shows that no one can 'say "Jesus is Lord" except by the Holy Spirit', it is important to highlight the Spirit who alone can ensure 'worship being in truth'.[147] To ensure this, her 'goal has been to develop a Spirit-infused culture – revealed in our day-to-day lives, bringing with it an unfolding revelation of the Father, Son, and Holy Spirit in our

---

[144] Zschech, *Extravagant Worship*, p. 56 (emphasis original).
[145] Zschech, 'The Role of the Holy Spirit in Worship', p. 286.
[146] Zschech, 'The Role of the Holy Spirit in Worship', p. 286.
[147] Zschech, 'The Role of the Holy Spirit in Worship', p. 286.

midst'.[148] 'Spirit-inspired worship' is crucial for a revelation of God.[149] Whether Zschech deems 'Spirit-inspired worship' songs as comparable with Scripture – inspired by the Spirit – is not clear since she does not clarify those statements.

'Holy Spirit Rain Down', though written by Russell Fragar, is sung by Zschech on multiple Hillsong albums.[150] The song reflects an expectation for the Spirit's immediacy in congregational singing:

Holy Spirit, rain down, rain down
Oh Comforter and Friend
How we need Your touch again
Holy Spirit, rain down, rain down
Let Your power fall
Let Your voice be heard
Come and change our hearts
As we stand on Your word
Holy Spirit, rain down

The song reflects the goal of the immediacy of God, namely, the Spirit's 'touch', 'power', 'voice', and transformation.

Third, Zschech is aware of the potential problems of highlighting the Spirit's immediacy in music ministry, and encourages discernment. One cannot 'manufacture the Holy Spirit'.[151] The Spirit's work is not about hype and 'excitement', which are 'very transient' things that eventually fade away.[152] One cannot 'replace or fake His presence'.[153] 'When the Holy Spirit moves on a meeting, He builds, refines, comforts, and is very pure … Once the Holy Spirit gets hold of you, He will fire you up and you will be different from the inside out.'[154] Song leaders must ensure, then, that they do not try to force people to worship or try to 'manufacture' an experience of

---

[148] Zschech, 'The Role of the Holy Spirit in Worship', p. 287.

[149] Zschech, 'The Role of the Holy Spirit in Worship', pp. 289, 290.

[150] See Hillsong, *Touching Heaven, Changing Earth (Live)*. Hillsong Music Australia, 2010; Hillsong, *Simply Worship 3 (Live)*. Hillsong Music Australia, 2010; and Hillsong, Hillsong. *Shout to the Lord: The Platinum Collection featuring Darlene Zschech* (Hillsong Music Australia, 2000).

[151] Zschech, *Worship*, p. 86.

[152] Zschech, *Worship*, p. 86.

[153] Zschech, *Worship*, p. 86.

[154] Zschech, *Worship*, p. 86.

the Spirit.[155] Leaders must not manipulate worship music in order to generate an experience of the Spirit that is not genuine.[156]

Fourth, Zschech's views on singing in the Spirit, and the spontaneity it requires, reflects her desire for the Spirit's immediacy during congregational singing. When churches 'sing in the spirit [*sic*], in almost free worship', they 'simply express themselves in other tongues or in English'.[157] Singing in the Spirit in English is about singing prophetic songs. Song leaders and musicians should expect the Spirit's immediacy for a successful time of congregational singing. Zschech, however, does not mention this idea of 'singing in the Spirit' in any of her later books on worship. Only in her first book published in 1996, shortly after her rise to fame through the song, 'Shout to the Lord', is this idea found. References to 'singing in the Spirit' may not be emphasized in latter products for the mass market to appeal to a broader audience.

Songs in the Spirit are spontaneous and reflects her desire not to be tied to a preplanned song service limited by songs that are written down. New 'songs in the spirit' are important during congregational singing.[158] Prophetic songs occur when musicians 'bring forth … *revelation* … from the very heart of God'.[159] When singing a song in the spirit, musicians may use various types of melodies, phrases, chords, or even 'no music at all'.[160] 'When the Holy Spirit turns up, He brings a sound all of His own.'[161] As you allow the Spirit to lead, 'He will guide and help you'.[162]

Finally, Zschech discusses the roles of song leaders, which both explicitly and implicitly reflect her desire for the Spirit's immediacy in worship music. She states that song leaders have three roles. First, '**[w]e are to lead the whole congregation into God's presence so that each one of them will be ministered to while spending time**

---

[155] Zschech, *Worship*, pp. 84-87.
[156] Zschech, *Worship*, pp. 84-87.
[157] Zschech, *Worship*, p. 95.
[158] Zschech, *Worship*, p. 95.
[159] Zschech, *Worship*, p. 95 (emphasis original).
[160] Zschech, *Worship*, p. 95.
[161] Zschech, *Worship*, p. 95.
[162] Zschech, *Worship*, p. 95.

with the Father'.[163] The goal is God's presence, whereby people experience intimacy with the Father. There is a need for all to be sensitive to the Spirit as they lead people into God's presence.[164] Second,
they are to '**cover and lead the singers and musicians**'.[165] They
must be fully acquainted with the band and musical direction of the
songs. Third, they are to '**prepare the congregation for the preaching of the word**'.[166] There is an important link between congregational singing and the ministry of the Word. The time of singing is
not an end in and of itself, though it includes important elements like
an experience of God. Congregational singing must support the ministry of the Word. In sum, Zschech prioritizes the Spirit's immediacy
for the presentation of worship music ministry, notably in her views
on a greater expectation of the Spirit's immediacy in worship music,
the goal of an experience of the Spirit, discerning the Spirit's work,
singing in the Spirit, and the three roles of song leaders.

Matt Redman

The Spirit's immediacy is highlighted in Redman's conviction that the
Spirit is the essential worship leader.[167] Seven implications of his view
that the Spirit is the essential worship leader include: song leaders
must experience the Spirit's immediacy through godly character,
Christ is exalted, authority to lead is received, the role of spontaneity,
the pastoral and prophetic must be exhibited, the Spirit may lead individuals within the congregation, and songs should ultimately lead
to a greater experience of the Spirit. 'The Holy Spirit of God is the
ultimate worship leader', since people 'worship by the Spirit of God
(Philippians 3:3)'.[168] The Spirit, then, 'is the agent and orchestrator of
our worship'.[169] Without the Spirit's involvement in worship,

---

[163] Zschech, *Worship*, p. 82 (emphasis original).

[164] Zschech, *Worship*, pp. 47-77.

[165] Zschech, *Worship*, p. 82 (emphasis original).

[166] Zschech, *Worship*, p. 83 (emphasis original). Also see Bob Sorge, *Exploring Worship: A Practical Guide to Praise and Worship* (Canandaigua: Oasis House, 1987), p. 118.

[167] Bob Sorge also acknowledges that a human may be a 'worship leader', but the Spirit must be the 'divine Worship Leader'. Sorge, *Exploring Worship*, pp. 77, 153-96.

[168] Matt Redman, 'The Real Worship Leader', in Matt Redman (comp.), *The Heart of Worship Files* (Ventura: Regal, 2003), p. 80.

[169] Redman, 'The Real Worship Leader', p. 80.

'[n]othing meaningful, spiritual or true happens'.[170] The implications for song leaders, then, who are often referred to as worship leaders is that they should be referred to as 'lead worshippers'.[171] The seven implications of the Spirit leading worship follow.

First, song leaders must experience the Spirit through godly character. Redman refers to song leaders as 'lead worshippers'. Since song leaders are not worship leaders, but lead worshippers, their role is to be an example for others, as they listen for the Spirit's promptings.[172] And in order to experience this type of Spirit-led worship, 'we need to make sure we're in step' with the Spirit 'in our everyday lives'.[173] This is about ensuring people's lives are appropriate dwelling places for the Spirit, since a 'worshipper needs to be full of the Holy Spirit'.[174] Referring back to John Wimber's thoughts, Redman explains that the 'real test' for leaders is not about producing 'great worship music', but the exhibition of godly character.[175]

Second, Christ is exalted when the Spirit leads worship. The 'major role' of the Spirit is to bring glory to Jesus Christ.[176] Thus, rather than being a worship leader – which is actually the role of the Spirit – a human leader is just a 'lead worshipper' who follows the Spirit who glorifies Jesus.[177] The human leader, then, is a *lead* worshipper because they are an example for others to follow. This takes the pressure off of humans, since humans cannot 'make worship happen' – people must 'always worship by the Spirit of God'.[178] Worshipping by the Spirit ensures that 'lead worshippers' remain dependent on God rather than rely on mere musical excellence.[179] Those who rely

---

[170] Redman, 'The Real Worship Leader', p. 80.

[171] Redman, 'The Real Worship Leader', p. 80.

[172] Redman, *The Unquenchable Worshipper*, p. 24.

[173] Redman, *The Unquenchable Worshipper*, p. 24; cf. Guthrie, 'Pentecostal Hymnody', p. 153.

[174] Redman, *The Unquenchable Worshipper*, p. 24.

[175] Redman, *The Unquenchable Worshipper*, p. 88. Redman does not reference where this idea from Wimber comes from.

[176] Redman, *The Unquenchable Worshipper*, p. 58.

[177] Redman, *The Unquenchable Worshipper*, p. 58.

[178] Redman, *The Unquenchable Worshipper*, p. 58.

[179] Redman, *The Unquenchable Worshipper*, pp. 58-59; Matt Redman, 'Worship-Leading Essentials: (Part 1) The Gentle Persuasion of Authority', in Matt Redman (comp.), *Inside Out Worship* (vol. 2; Eastbourne: Kingsway, 2005), p. 18.

merely on musical excellence, rather than allowing the Spirit to lead, miss out on some important things Redman expands on that follow.

Third, Redman explains that those who rely on musical excellence over the Spirit who leads, lack 'the gentle persuasion of authority'.[180] This authority is 'a God-given anointing – a divine hand of favor upon a person that leads to spiritual successes in ministry'.[181] Authority comes through the 'Holy Spirit's authority resting upon them'.[182] This success does not come 'by might, nor by power, but by His Holy Spirit'.[183] By depending on God, 'the power of God upon us will always be the deciding factor' on the authority lead worshipers have.[184]

Fourth, Redman encourages song leaders to follow the present lead of the Spirit during the actual presentation of worship music by being open to spontaneity. While leaders may have a plan for songs to be sung, they should be open to spontaneity. Redman believes that '[t]here's nothing more exciting than a dynamic worship time where God breaks in with such freshness that no one really knows where we're going next'.[185] While trying to balance the need for form and spontaneity, the human leader relies on the Spirit's leading, who ultimately takes worship music to 'the throne room'.[186] This throne room represents the immediate presence of a majestic God. This may happen through a means the human leader may have never encountered before.[187] He describes one experience of this occurring, whereby through a time of worship through music a group experienced 'an otherly moment – a heightened sense of the glory and grace of God'.[188] This moment occurred through 'spontaneous singing and prayer … in the power of the Holy Spirit before the throne of God'.[189] These moments cannot be 'manufactured or formularized' since they are due to grace. People must wait for them. Individuals

---

[180] Redman, 'Worship-Leading Essentials: (Part 1)', pp. 16-18.

[181] Redman, 'Worship-Leading Essentials: (Part 1)', p. 16.

[182] Redman, 'Worship-Leading Essentials: (Part 1)', p. 16.

[183] Redman, 'Worship-Leading Essentials: (Part 1)', p. 16. Cf. Zech. 4.6.

[184] Redman, 'Worship-Leading Essentials: (Part 1)', p. 19.

[185] Redman, *The Unquenchable Worshipper*, p. 57.

[186] Redman, *The Unquenchable Worshipper*, p. 57.

[187] Redman, *The Unquenchable Worshipper*, p. 57.

[188] Matt Redman, 'Worship-Leading Essentials: (Part 9) The Constant Expectation of the Heavenly', in Matt Redman (comp.), *Inside Out Worship* (vol. 2; Eastbourne: Kingsway, 2005), p. 165.

[189] Redman, 'Worship-Leading Essentials: (Part 9)', p. 165.

can only 'prepare' their 'hearts and create an environment of dependence'.[190] Leaders must ask the Spirit to '[u]sher us today into the depths of God'.[191]

Fifth, there is a dual role of the prophetic and pastoral in a song leaders' approach to following the Spirit's lead for worship music.[192] Leaders must ask the Spirit for the 'insights' to lead prophetically, and 'wisdom' to lead pastorally.[193] Prophetic worship is not simply about being spontaneous – though it may include that. Rather it is about receiving 'insight' from the Spirit 'to show us where and how He is leading', so that people follow him.[194] Leaders need to remain focused on Jesus; even when they may be led to do something deemed 'a little unusual'.[195] While leaders may make mistakes while endeavouring to follow this approach, they can learn from their mistakes.[196] This approach requires 'a mixture' of being 'Holy Spirit led' and using their 'God-given' head.[197]

Song leaders must also view themselves as a pastor as they lead – to be willing to shepherd those they lead.[198] Since people are more important than music, wisdom ensures that a musician submit to the pastor in them.[199] And as a musician, this may mean not overburdening people with too many new, fresh songs. They must ensure that others are willing to join in the journey in congregational singing.[200]

---

[190] Redman, 'Worship-Leading Essentials: (Part 9)', p. 166.

[191] Redman, 'Worship-Leading Essentials: (Part 9)', p. 168.

[192] Redman, *The Unquenchable Worshipper*, pp. 57-58. Similarly, Alford argues that '[m]inisters and leaders need to understand both the priestly and prophetic roles they are expected to fulfill in a congregation. The priestly role is to serve the people of God in worship, training, nurture, and mission. Music ministers attempt to meet needs, both felt and expressed. The prophetic role is to share the good news of the Lord. The songs they lead tell of salvation, healing, and blessings, as well as foretell His glorious coming'. *Ministering Through Music*, p. 96.

[193] Redman, *The Unquenchable Worshipper*, pp. 57-58.

[194] Redman, 'Worship-Leading Essentials: (Part 5)', pp. 96-97.

[195] Redman, 'Worship-Leading Essentials: (Part 5)', p. 98.

[196] Redman, 'Worship-Leading Essentials: (Part 5)', p. 98.

[197] Redman, 'Worship-Leading Essentials: (Part 5)', p. 98.

[198] Matt Redman, 'Worship-Leading Essentials: (Part 3) The Shepherding Instincts of a Pastor', in Matt Redman (comp.), *Inside Out Worship* (vol. 2; Eastbourne: Kingsway, 2005), pp. 49-50.

[199] Redman, 'Worship-Leading Essentials: (Part 3)', p. 51.

[200] Redman, 'Worship-Leading Essentials: (Part 3)', p. 51.

Sixth, Redman does not neglect the active role of the congregation during congregational singing, particularly in light of his view that song leaders should be viewed as a 'lead worshipper'.[201] First, 'not all worship has to originate from the stage'.[202] But the 'lead worshipper' still has a 'responsibility to be aware' of how 'God may want to lead through others'.[203] In a corporate worship context 'anyone can feel free to start a song and move in a direction he or she feels the Holy Spirit is leading'.[204] There may be times when lead worshippers are uncertain of the direction the congregational singing should go, but good things can arise from someone 'within the congregation'.[205] This inclusive approach to who may lead during congregational singing is somewhat surprising in light of Redman's involvement in professional productions. His view of the Spirit's immediacy, however, shapes his approach. For it is as people sense the Spirit's immediate leading that brings greater authority for congregational singing than any preplanned, produced songs of worship.

Lastly, Redman shares that the 'journey' in a worship music set has the immediacy of God as the goal.[206] He likes the language of 'journey' when describing a worship gathering, as he views it as 'a progression'.[207] Each particular worship gathering is a 'little journey' that is part of a 'bigger pilgrimage' believers are on that lasts for years.[208] Each 'little journey' – those particular gatherings for worship music – begin with a 'call to worship' or '"announcement" song', which 'awakens us to worship and reminds us of the magnitude of what we do in our time together'.[209] In the progression, 'every song' is 'a step further into the depths of God – an expectation of encounter'.[210] In the segment of corporate worship dedicated to worship music, each set has the immediacy of God as the goal throughout the journey.

---

[201] Redman, *The Unquenchable Worshipper*, p. 59.
[202] Redman, *The Unquenchable Worshipper*, pp. 59-60.
[203] Redman, *The Unquenchable Worshipper*, pp. 59-60.
[204] Redman, *The Unquenchable Worshipper*, p. 60.
[205] Redman, *The Unquenchable Worshipper*, p. 60.
[206] Matt Redman, 'Insights: Congregational Worship as Journey', in Matt Redman (comp.), *Inside Out Worship* (vol. 2; Eastbourne: Kingsway, 2005), p. 162.
[207] Redman, 'Insights', p. 162.
[208] Redman, 'Insights', p. 163.
[209] Redman, 'Insights', p. 162.
[210] Redman, 'Insights', p. 162.

Redman's song, 'Lord Let Your Glory Fall', reflects his desire for the immediacy of God as the goal for a worship music set along one's journey with God. The lyrics include the people's request that God's glory would fall 'as on that ancient day'. That 'day' refers to when God's presence came like a cloud, and the priests were overwhelmed by his glory in 2 Chronicles 5–7.[211] Redman's musical reflections on this story show that his desire – and for all who sing the song – is that God is not only present among them, but might even manifest his presence in a visible, tangible way.[212] When God's glory falls, the people are 'overwhelmed'. This song reflects Redman's longing for God's manifest presence, activity, and favor among his people through song. In sum, Redman highlights the Spirit's immediacy for the presentation of worship music by stressing that the Spirit is the essential worship leader. And because of his stress on the Spirit as the worship leader, the Spirit's immediacy becomes crucial for seven elements of worship music. The seven include: the need for song leaders to have godly character, full of the Spirit; the Spirit who exalts Jesus; authority that is received through the Spirit's work; the value of spontaneity; leaders who are both prophetic and pastoral; the Spirit's manifestation among the congregation; and the immediacy of God as the goal of the journey with God through worship music.

Conclusion

An examination of the three CWM leaders reveals that they all acknowledge the importance of the Spirit's immediacy for worship music. Whether their approaches relate to their views on worship in general, songwriting, preparing, or presenting songs for congregational singing, the Spirit's immediacy is a crucial component for worship music. They do not, however, always explicitly describe the importance of the Spirit's immediacy for worship music, but recognise that things like godly character and musical excellence helps facilitate

---

[211] Debra Akins, 'Song Story: Matt Redman's'. *Crosswalk.com*, April 28, 2003. Online: http://www.crosswalk.com/church/worship/song-story-matt-redmans-1197457.html, para. 7.

[212] Bob Sorge concurs, arguing that the story in 2 Chronicles 5–7 provides an important example and goal for worshippers today. That experience of God 'was a very special manifestation of the presence of God, and it is the same type or nature of manifestation that we seek today!' *Exploring Worship*, p. 29.

the Spirit's immediacy. The CWM approach to worship music affects how corporate worship is conducted within Pentecostal churches in general. Understanding the implications of the CWM approach is important in order to provide an analysis for worship music in Pentecostal churches. The next chapter provides an analysis of CWM with respect to worship music for Pentecostal churches.

4

ANALYSIS OF CONTEMPORARY WORSHIP MUSIC

The previous two chapters provided an important discussion on worship music according to three CWM leaders, which showcased how the present work of the Spirit in corporate worship is crucial in their thought. This chapter, thus, analyzes CWM and how it relates to the Pentecostal emphasis on the immediacy of God, showing what may or may not be appropriate elements for worship music in Pentecostal churches today. I provide an appraisal of CWM, which shows what should or should not be maintained by Pentecostals for worship music. The appraisal of CWM includes two key components: 1) discerning whether or not the Azusa Street Revival's use of music is a source of renewal for Pentecostals and 2) going beyond Azusa, engaging with various biblical-theological resources in order to articulate a more robust theology of worship music for Pentecostals.

A Constructive Appraisal of CWM Using Azusa and Other Theological Resources

This constructive theological appraisal of worship music in Pentecostal churches discusses the three CWM leaders treated in chapter two. Key theological themes in each leader's approach with an emphasis on the immediacy of God in worship music are addressed, which provide both promise and problems for Pentecostal corporate worship music. Since the key theological themes that arise among the three leaders have implications for various aspects of worship music, this appraisal is not divided by the four themes used in the previous discussions. Rather, the three leaders' approaches are discussed somewhat chronologically, appraising Doerksen, Zschech, and then Redman. The last two theological themes addressed in the appraisal apply to all three CWM leaders.

God the Father

The Vineyard movement has brought significant attention to intimacy with the Father in worship. There is a strong correlation in both Doerksen and Wimber between the lack of human fatherly affection and subsequent desire to experience a close relationship with a father. Embracing God the Father offers both of them the ultimate substitute father. Expressing and receiving affection with God the Father through songs of worship is powerful because it is done through a very emotional medium – music. And since worship music offers the ultimate experience of intimacy with God – in light of Doerksen's views – it follows that it offers the ultimate experience of intimacy with God the Father.

Azusa does not offer much regarding intimacy with the Father through worship music, or worship in general. At Azusa, Spirit baptism became a crucial new teaching for the formation of the early Pentecostal movement. Because of the early Pentecostals' emphasis on Spirit baptism, the role of the Father they emphasised was the Father's promise of Spirit baptism. Thus, the emphasis on the Father related primarily to being viewed as the giver of Spirit baptism, rather than one with whom believers could experience intimacy. Since Azusa does not offer substantial thought on intimacy with the Father, an examination of Rom. 8.15b-16 follows that substantiates Doerksen's emphasis.

Doerksen's emphasis on God the Father provides a number of strengths for worship music for Pentecostals, primarily because it links the Spirit's immediacy to intimacy with the Father. First, it brings Paul's thoughts in Romans 8 to bear upon corporate worship. Christians can call out to and experience intimacy with God the Father. In Rom. 8.15b-16, Paul explains, 'When we cry, "Abba! Father!" it is that very Spirit bearing witness with our spirit that we are children of God' (NRSV). The Spirit's present work points to a believer's identity as a child of God the Father.

Second, though Pentecostals emphasise the Spirit's immediacy, early Pentecostals surprisingly did not emphasise worshipping God the Father like those in the Vineyard movement. Paul explains that the Spirit witnesses with the believer's spirit – a direct reference in Scripture to the Spirit's immediacy for the believer – so that they can cry out to God the Father in worship. Pentecostal churches have done well by emphasising Jesus Christ and the Spirit – this has occurred from the time of the Azusa Street Revival. The Father, however, is often only mentioned as the one who gifts believers with Spirit baptism. But the Spirit's role is not just relegated to power for witness (Spirit baptism) and exalting Christ (Jn 15.26). A more thorough view of the Spirit's work must include the Spirit who also bears witness to the believer's identity, which is intimately tied to God the Father. The Spirit's present work enables the believer to worship God with the intimate language of 'Abba! Father!'

Doerksen's emphasis on intimacy with God the Father is not only relevant for Christians, but also for those who are not Christian. Contemporary North American society is noted for a deficiency in fathers who are present in the lives of their children.[1] An emphasis on God the Father can benefit contemporary society in numerous ways. First, it can enable those who do not have an earthly father involved in their life to relate to God as Father, who is faithful, loving, and good.[2] This benefits believers, but also provides a point of contact for evangelism. Unbelievers may be drawn to God the Father, who through the Son and Spirit, may be worshipped and known intimately. Second, an emphasis on God the Father can provide an example of the type of character needed for fathers – one, for example, who is faithful, loving, and good.[3]

Songs of Lament

Doerksen's desire for a more holistic approach in songs for worship, particularly the role of songs of lament, contributes to a Pentecostal focus on the immediacy of God because these songs can be sung 'in the Spirit'. Contemporary Pentecostals are stereotyped as 'happy,

---

[1] See 'The Fatherless Child: It is a Unique Cultural Moment for the Church to Act like a Family', *Christianity Today* 51.10 (October 1, 2007), p. 25.

[2] E.g., Exod. 34.6-7; Ps. 103.13; Lk. 18.19; 1 Jn 4.7-12.

[3] Some may view the emphasis on God the Father as patriarchal, it should not be viewed in a limiting human way, since God is not human (Num. 23.19; 1 Sam. 15.29); God uses language of being motherly to describe His care for His people (Isa. 66.15; Mt. 23.37), and both males and females are equally made in God's image (Gen. 1.27).

clappy' Christians because of their desire to focus on upbeat, joyful songs. But while Doerksen may be considered one of the pioneers of the CWM, his inclusion of a variety of songs – that includes lament – is not being heeded.[4] Doerksen admits that most leaders want songs that are upbeat and joyful.[5] His admonitions have been ignored by leaders. Some leaders even rebuked his desire to sing a song of lament during a time of loss. But songs of lament encourage intimacy. These types of songs ensure that worshippers are being honest before God, especially for those who are suffering. But can songs of lament be used in a Pentecostal context where the Spirit's immediacy is prioritized?

Those at Azusa do not appear to have sung songs of lament. Though they lamented the worldliness of society and the need for repentance through spoken word and writing, songs of lament do not appear to have been sung. Azusa does not provide impetus for contemporary Pentecostals to adopt songs of lament. But Scripture and the Pentecostal emphasis on the Spirit's immediacy leads to the need for adopting songs of lament.

Songs of lament can be led by the Spirit according to Scripture – the Spirit's immediacy is not restricted to 'happy, clappy' songs. Scripture presents the Spirit's role in lament. First, Rom. 8.18-27 reveals that believers 'inwardly groan' during this earthly life of weaknesses.[6] This occurs as believers wait to be free from the 'bondage to decay' to experience 'the redemption of our bodies'. But the Spirit 'helps' people with their 'weaknesses' and inability to know how to pray. The Spirit 'intercedes with sighs too deep for words'.[7] In the midst of human frailty, the Spirit intercedes through us, which may include prayers of lament.

Second, Scripture includes songs that are prayers of lament. Some notable laments include portions in the Psalms and Lamentations.

---

[4] Also see Andrew M. McCoy, 'Salvation (Not Yet?) Materialized: Healing as Possibility and Possible Complication for Expressing Suffering in Pentecostal Music and Worship', in Monique M. Ingalls and Amos Yong (eds.), *The Spirit of Praise: Music and Worship in Global Pentecostal-Charismatic Christianity* (University Park: The Pennsylvania State University Press, 2015), pp. 45-59.

[5] Doerksen, *Make Love, Make War*, pp. 147, 154-56.

[6] See Rom. 8.23-26.

[7] See Luke A. Powery, 'Lament: Homiletical Groans in the Spirit'. Paper presented at the annual meeting of the Academy of Homiletics, Boston, MA, November 21, 2008, pp. 23-26.

And since these laments are part of Scripture, they are inspired by the Spirit and beneficial for believers' edification.[8] God validates laments. The Spirit intercedes on behalf of human weaknesses – 'sighing' for individuals. But he also provides songs of lament that people can sing with in Scripture, and use as a model for new songs of lament.

Pentecostals often lack a thorough theology of suffering, and the use of songs of lament can help correct this problem.[9] The introduction of songs of lament can benefit the church, and the exclusion of these types of songs impoverishes Pentecostal worship in two ways. First, Pentecostals will lack genuine intimacy with God in worship without songs of lament.[10] While upbeat praise songs are appropriate and biblical, an overreliance on this approach in worship music can stifle the believer's ability to worship genuinely, 'in spirit and in truth'.

Second, an unwillingness to sing songs of lament suppresses concerns related to suffering.[11] Pentecostals are forced to deny their pain and the injustices of the world, particularly when they are forced to solely sing upbeat, joyful songs. The exclusion of lament among Pentecostals may be one factor contributing to the growth of the Word Faith movement among Pentecostals. Those involved in this approach to the gospel are known for failing to admit to the role of suffering in a faithful believer's life.[12] But Jesus is the believer's example – who led by a path of suffering.[13] Jesus did not deny his suffering. And during Christ's time on the cross, it was Psalm 22 – a Psalm of lament – that he uttered to his Father.[14] Believers suffer for failing to

---

[8] 2 Timothy 3.16-17. Also see Powery, 'Lament', pp. 23-26.

[9] See David J. Courey's analysis of a lack of a theology of suffering among Pentecostals in 'What Has Wittenberg to do with Azusa?: Luther's Theology of the Cross and Pentecostal Triumphalism' (PhD diss., McMaster Divinity College, 2011); but see Martin William Mittelstadt, *The Spirit and Suffering in Luke-Acts: Implications for a Pentecostal Pneumatology* (JPTSup, 26; New York: T&T Clark, 2004); Samuel Solivan, *The Spirit, Pathos and Liberation: Toward an Hispanic Pentecostal Theology* (JPTSup, 14; Sheffield: Sheffield Academic, 1998); and John Christopher Thomas, *The Devil, Disease, and Deliverance: Origins of Illness in New Testament Thought* (Cleveland, TN: CPT Press, 2010).

[10] See Walter Brueggemann, *The Psalms and the Life of Faith* (Patrick D. Miller (ed.), Minneapolis: Fortress, 1995), p. 102.

[11] See Brueggemann, *The Psalms and the Life of Faith*, p. 104.

[12] See Robert M. Bowman, Jr, *The Word-Faith Controversy: Understanding the Health and Wealth Gospel* (Grand Rapids: Baker, 2001).

[13] E.g., see 1 Pet. 2.19-25.

[14] Brueggemann, *The Psalms and the Life of Faith*, pp. 70-71.

include songs of lament in their worship – an important expression that can be led by the Spirit. Doerksen's commendation to include songs of lament is an important counterbalance to the reliance on upbeat, joyful songs among Pentecostals. And the inclusion of these songs of lament is consistent with the Pentecostal emphasis on the Spirit's immediacy because songs of lament can be led by the Spirit.

Singing in Tongues

Zschech's teaching on singing in tongues is an important practice for Pentecostals to address and adopt. This type of singing is important for Pentecostals to understand because it welcomes the charismatic dimension of spirituality to worship music.[15] While all the gifts of the Spirit are charismatic, the phrase charismatic in its contemporary sense in the church more often focuses those deemed as more 'miraculous', such as tongues, prophecy, and healing – those most often associated with Pentecostals and Charismatics.[16] Out of the three CWM leaders examined here, only Zschech makes reference to the practice of singing in tongues.

Singing in tongues, however, is only addressed in Zschech's first written work on worship music; none of her subsequent works address the subject. Zschech's and Hillsong's global appeal among non-Pentecostals and non-Charismatics may have led to her minimizing this experience. Or it may have to do with her publisher's desires for a wider appeal. Her first book was published by Hillsong, while subsequent books have been published by larger Christian publishers that may prefer to reach audiences beyond Pentecostals and Charismatics. A diminishing emphasis on singing in tongues, though, reflects a diminishing experience of this practice among Pentecostals today. The lack of discussion and experience of singing in tongues requires examination, beginning with its role at Azusa.

As stated earlier, the Azusa Street Revival included singing in tongues, and became a prominent practice within the community. One person even deemed it more convincing of the Pentecostal mes-

---

[15] Zschech, *Worship*, p. 95.

[16] Millard J. Erickson, 'Charismatic gifts', *The Concise Dictionary of Christian Theology* (Wheaton: Crossway, rev. edn, 2001), p. 31; Millard J. Erickson, 'Charismatics', *The Concise Dictionary of Christian Theology* (Wheaton: Crossway, rev. edn, 2001), p. 31.

sage than speaking in tongues. Singing in tongues was so highly regarded, though, that when they sang together in unison, they described it as a 'heavenly choir' joining with the angels in harmony to sing a 'heavenly song'.[17] The early Pentecostals, however, did not provide a 'theological rationale' for linking tongues and song.[18] Early Pentecostals may have been so fixated on arguing for tongues as the initial evidence for Spirit baptism, that an apologetic for singing in tongues was neglected. But if it is a legitimate Christian practice, Pentecostals must reckon with its relevance for worship music today.

Pentecostals can look to 1 Cor. 14.15b for a biblical rationale for the practice of singing in tongues.[19] In a discussion on tongues in 1 Cor. 14.14-15, Paul states: 'For if I pray in a tongue, my spirit prays but my mind is unproductive. What should I do then? I will pray with the spirit, but I will pray with the mind also; I will sing praise with the spirit, but I will sing praise with the mind also'. Jon Michael Spencer explains,

> Most writers, even of biblical commentaries, refer to the 'a' section of this verse and skip over the 'b' section. Some commenting on the verse do not acknowledge the parallelism in its two parts and fail to realize that Paul was actually referring to singing in tongues.[20]

While the subject of singing in tongues in this passage is often ignored, New Testament scholars James D.G. Dunn, Gordon D. Fee, and Craig S. Keener argue that Paul is referring to singing in tongues when he writes about singing praise with his spirit.[21] Dunn, commenting on this passage, refers to singing in tongues as a type of

---

[17] *AF* 1.1 (September 1906), p. 1.

[18] Spencer, *Protest and Praise*, p. 154.

[19] Spencer, *Protest and Praise*, p. 154.

[20] Spencer, *Protest and Praise*, p. 154, n. 3. Cf. Joseph A. Fitzmyer, *First Corinthians* (The Anchor Yale Bible, 32; New Haven: Yale University Press, 2008), p. 516.

[21] E.g., James D.G. Dunn, *Jesus and the Spirit: A Study of the Religious and Charismatic Experience of Jesus and the First Christians as Reflected in the New Testament* (London: SCM, 1975), p. 238; Fee, *God's Empowering Presence*, pp. 230-31; Craig S. Keener, *1–2 Corinthians* (The New Cambridge Bible Commentary; Cambridge: Cambridge University Press, 2005), p. 114. Cf. Craig Blomberg, *1 Corinthians* (The NIV Application Commentary, Grand Rapids: Zondervan, 1994), p. 270.

'*charismatic hymnody*'.[22] An analysis of this biblical passage for singing in tongues is surprisingly not highlighted among early or modern day Pentecostals.[23]

The interpretation of songs in tongues is also crucial, and those at Azusa advocated for the interpretation of songs in tongues based on 1 Cor. 14.14-16. Interpretation is not merely for 'spoken' tongues – tongues given through the medium of music also requires an interpretation. Keener addresses the interpretation of tongues sung through 1 Cor. 14.15. He argues that '"praying" and "singing with the mind" (14.15) refers to interpreting the prayer or song in a tongue'.[24] The context of the passage reveals that Paul is addressing the need for interpretation of tongues (1 Cor. 14.13) for the edification of all who are in attendance (1 Cor. 14.16-17). So, while a believer may sing in tongues in private, singing in tongues without someone to interpret within the corporate context is inappropriate. But in a context where people are seeking God for the gift of singing in tongues, an interpretation may not be readily available if believers are just maturing in their expression of the gifts of the Spirit. Nevertheless, in contexts where people are seeking God for the gift of singing in tongues, an interpretation should be encouraged and commended to establish the principle of interpreting tongues. If believers who already practice

---

[22] Dunn, *Jesus and the Spirit*, p. 238 (emphasis original). Fee follows Dunn's approach, also referring to this type of singing as 'charismatic hymnody'. See Fee, *God's Empowering Presence*, p. 230. Also see Guthrie, 'Pentecostal Hymnody', pp. 42-45.

[23] E.g., Delton L. Alford, a prominent Church of God leader who led the Division of Music at Lee College (Cleveland, TN), comments on the relevance of 1 Cor. 14.14-16 for Pentecostals in *Music in the Pentecostal Church*. He explains that singing in the spirit is about singing 'in a spiritual or spirited manner', allowing the personality of the singer to come through, which the Spirit leads (p. 34). He contrasts singing with the spirit with singing with the mind by explaining that singing with the mind is about singing something that is 'understandable or intelligible' to the hearer (p. 34). He incorrectly contrasts these types of singing by assuming that singing with the spirit is more emotional while singing with the mind is intellectual (p. 34). However, more recent Pentecostal scholars have explored singing in tongues. See C.M. Johansson, 'Singing in the Spirit', *Paraclete* 24.2 (1990), pp. 20-23; Dove, 'Hymnody and Liturgy in the Azusa Street Revival', pp. 243-63; K.E. Alexander, 'Heavenly Choirs in Earthy Spaces: The Significance of Corporate Spiritual Singing in Early Pentecostal Experience', *Journal of Pentecostal Theology* 25.2 (2016), pp. 254-68; and M.L. Archer, *'I Was in the Spirit on the Lord's Day': A Pentecostal Engagement with Worship in the Apocalypse* (Cleveland, TN: CPT Press, 2014), pp. 73-109, 315-16.

[24] Keener, *1–2 Corinthians*, p. 114.

singing in tongues desire to sing in tongues in a corporate setting, though, they must ensure that someone can interpret.

This discussion on singing in tongues is important because of its historical precedent at Azusa, its biblical precedent, and subsequently its legitimacy as a charismatic expression of worship music for believers today. Singing in tongues may have been neglected because of the lack of theological rationale for it among Pentecostals. But as argued here, there is adequate theological rationale for it, and can be a source of renewal within the church.

Discerning a Genuine Work of the Spirit

Zschech acknowledges the temptations for those involved in worship music who desire the Spirit's manifestation, and shares helpful insights into discerning a genuine work of the Spirit in corporate worship. She shares important insights throughout her works on discerning between what is and is not the Spirit's work through worship music. It may be that because she ministers primarily within a classical Pentecostal context, she recognises the temptations among those who stress the Spirit's work. For those who emphasise the Spirit's work can be tempted to manipulate worship music to accomplish things that appear to be in the Spirit. She explains that when ministers seek to manipulate worship music so that hype and excitement are the goal in corporate worship, the affect is 'a temporary sense of feeling good'.[25] Feeling good has often been a gauge to detect whether the worship music has been successful in some Pentecostal churches. Zschech, however, rightly argues that the Spirit's work in worship music brings transformation that leads to Christ-likeness.[26] She encourages those involved in leading worship music not to be led by feelings, but to have faith the Spirit is leading even when he does not appear to be.[27] Zschech's encouragement is a helpful antidote to those who feel compelled to manipulate worship music to appear Spirit-led.

Looking back to Azusa, Seymour eventually described the ultimate evidence of Spirit baptism to be love. The presence of God generated holiness, not just emotional ecstasies. Character became more crucial than the ecstasy and excitement of a worship service in

---

[25] Zschech, *Worship*, p. 86.
[26] Zschech, *Worship*, p. 86.
[27] Zschech, *Extravagant Worship*, p. 184.

Seymour's view. And though he did not specifically address worship music, his thoughts can be linked to the outcomes of worship music. Becoming a person of Christ-like character, evidencing love, supplants mere feelings of ecstasy and excitement all in the perceived name of the Spirit's present work.

Another CWM leader, Israel Houghton, provides a means by which the immediacy of God can be maintained in worship music, while ensuring social justice is not abandoned for apparent feelings of God through worship music. The emphasis on the Spirit's immediacy related to music is often relegated to bodily sensations – weeping, joy, dancing, and insights for a song to write. Houghton acknowledges that CWM can lose sight of social justice in favor of mere feelings of the Spirit through worship music. Houghton's desire for God's constant presence in his life, reflected in his song 'Deeper', reveals a common thread among Pentecostals that desire the immediacy of God in worship, with the added dimension of social justice. For 'worship is a natural progression toward justice'.[28] Jesus' admonition to serve those in need – 'the least of these' – ultimately leads to social justice.[29] For as people 'find them', people 'find Him!'[30] God is present when we minister to those in need. The immediacy of God is not relegated to sensory feelings while singing songs of worship, but to ministry to those in need – 'the least of these'. This is a helpful connection that is beneficial for the future of Pentecostal worship music, making the connection between worship songs, the immediacy of God, and social justice.[31]

Linking the Spirit's immediacy in corporate worship music to social justice may not have been made explicit by those at Azusa, but

---

[28] Israel Houghton, *A Deeper Level* (New Kensington: Whitaker House, 2007), p. 131.

[29] Cf. Mt. 25.31-46.

[30] Cf. Mt. 25.45.

[31] Amos 5.23-24 also includes God's displeasure with those who sings songs of worship without addressing issues of social justice. Wen Reagan also contends that Israel Houghton is making a connection between being blessed to being a blessing, so that Houghton reflects what he refers to as 'soft prosperity', with a link to the prosperity gospel movement. See 'Blessed to be a Blessing: The Prosperity Gospel of Worship Music Superstar Israel Houghton', in Monique M. Ingalls and Amos Yong (eds.), *The Spirit of Praise: Music and Worship in Global Pentecostal-Charismatic Christianity* (University Park: The Pennsylvania State University Press, 2015), pp. 215-29.

they did link the Spirit's immediacy to the inclusion of the marginalized in society within their corporate worship context and movement. Azusa leaders believed that Spirit baptism was available to all people, regardless of colour, gender, social status, or age. And their inclusive view of Spirit baptism led to their view that all may equally minister, so that an experience of the Spirit initiated an eradication of social injustice regarding who can minister – an important point also discussed in part three of this book on preaching and the altar.[32] In sum, when discerning the Spirit's immediacy in worship, it is crucial to maintain that while sensory feelings of the Spirit may be apparent for those experiencing the immediacy of God, feelings are not the goal. Song leaders must not attempt to manufacture sensory feelings of God. Rather, Christ-likeness, love, and social justice are some of the fruit of the immediacy of God in worship music.

The Spirit as Worship Leader

Redman's view that the Spirit ultimately leads worship is an important teaching on the role of the Spirit for worship, and can be a helpful antidote to those who attempt to manufacture the Spirit's immediacy through worship music. In many Pentecostal churches, there is at least one assigned 'worship leader' – which typically refers to the person who leads the band and congregation in songs. 'Worship leaders' are found in non-Pentecostal churches as well. With the Pentecostal

---

[32] See chapter 5 that shows Azusa leaders' views on including the marginalized in ministry because of the Spirit's immediacy. Though Bobby C. Alexander's work on Pentecostal ritual, *Victor Turner Revisited*, focuses primarily on an African American Pentecostal congregation called The House of the Lord, he makes an important association of Spirit baptism with social justice. He explains that for those at The House of the Lord,

> the doctrine of 'baptism in the Spirit' does not so much induce egalitarianism as provide theological justification (through divine sanction) for opposing the dominant social structure. Separating participants from the statuses and roles they hold within the everyday social order relaxes some of the demands of everyday status distinctions. No longer obligated to mediate their encounters with one another through everyday social roles, participants appear to interact with one another more directly, more spontaneously, and have a sense of community. Bobby C. Alexander, *Victor Turner Revisited: Ritual as Social Change* (ed. Susan Thistlethwaite; American Academy of Religion Academic Series 74; Atlanta: Scholars, 1991), pp. 89-90.

In Alexander's analysis, Spirit baptism – the Spirit's immediacy – provides impetus for social justice because this inclusive experience provides divine approval for the disenfranchised to confront inequities within the social order.

emphasis on the Spirit's role in worship, it is surprising that contemporary Pentecostal churches have not picked up on Redman's views. As stated earlier, Redman argues that the Spirit is the 'ultimate worship leader', based on Phil. 3.3.[33] Since the Spirit is the worship leader, he refers to those traditionally labelled the worship leader as the lead worshiper. Lead worshipers merely provide an example for others to follow, as these leaders follow the Spirit's lead.

The Azusa Street Mission also referred to the Spirit as the leader of their corporate worship services. When believers arrived, its proponents claimed, they would immediately recognise that the Spirit led the meetings.[34] After Parham's criticism of the revival, those at Azusa stated that they were too hasty in recognising Parham as their leader.[35] Rather, they explained that Jesus was their leader, 'the great Shepherd', and Seymour their 'humble pastor' whom the Spirit made as overseer.[36] The language of 'leader' over the revival and movement includes a dual emphasis on the Spirit and Jesus. Jesus is the leader of the movement, while the Spirit leads the corporate worship services.[37] The Spirit even sings 'songs through them' as they sang in tongues.[38] They do not, however, make reference to Phil. 3.3 in their newsletter to substantiate the idea of the Spirit as the worship leader.

An examination of Phil. 3.3 is helpful because Paul explains that believers 'worship in the Spirit of God'. To understand this passage, it must be set in the context of Paul dealing with a faction in the church in Philippi. He contrasts two groups of people. One group of people put their confidence for righteousness in 'the flesh'. These people consider their Jewish pedigree – notably circumcision – as their means to righteousness. Paul states that he belongs to those who put their confidence for righteousness through faith in Jesus Christ – not physical circumcision. But of the second group, he states, 'we are the circumcision, who worship by the Spirit of God and glory in

---

[33] Redman, 'The Real Worship Leader', p. 80.

[34] *AF* 1.3 (November 1906), p. 1.

[35] *AF* 1.4 (December 1906), p. 1.

[36] They cite Acts 20.28 as precedence for this idea. *AF* 1.4 (December 1906), p. 1.

[37] *AF* 1.1 (September 1906), p. 1; *AF* 1.11 (October-January 1908), p. 4.

[38] *AF* 1.1 (September 1906), p. 1.

Christ Jesus and put no confidence in the flesh' (ESV). Since an extensive study of this biblical passage is not possible here, a few short remarks follow.

The word for worship that Paul uses here is what is often used by the Jewish people for the temple service.[39] External laws or rituals cannot lead to the worship of God though. Paul explains that the Spirit's initiative within the believer enables them to worship God.[40] This refers to worship as a lifestyle whereby believers trust Christ – glorying in Christ – rather than any other thing. Worshipping by the Spirit is not relegated to a corporate worship context. This reveals that Redman's point about the worship leader is not just significant for the segment of music during a service. The Spirit should lead all aspects of a corporate worship service, such as the preaching and the altar. And of course, the Spirit must lead worship in all aspects of one's life. But for purposes of this chapter on worship music, Redman's point is necessary for a number of reasons.

By classifying song leaders as worship leaders, churches are elevating song leaders to something that is impossible theologically. When humans are considered the worship leader, they are taking on a role that only the Spirit can take. The exalted role of a human will lead to false perceptions of worship in both the mind of the song leader and congregants. If the people respond with lively singing, the song leader may take responsibility for this success. But if the people do not respond with lively singing, the song leader assumes responsibility. This song leader may wonder where they went wrong – whether musically or spiritually. But if song leaders recognise that only the Spirit leads worship, it will not only release them from the pressure of trying to get people to worship, but also rely more on the Spirit to lead. Redman recognises these benefits through a change of focus on who leads worship.[41]

Another problematic issue related to the idea that a song leader is a worship leader – partially corrected by Redman – arises because congregational singing has often become synonymous with worship

---

[39] Richard R. Melick, *Philippians, Colossians, Philemon* (New American Commentary 32; Nashville: Broadman and Holman, 1991), p. 129; Gerald F. Hawthorne and Ralph P. Martin. *Philippians* (Word Biblical Commentary 43; Nashville: Thomas Nelson, rev. edn, 2004), pp. 175-76.

[40] Hawthorne and Martin, *Philippians*, p. 176.

[41] Redman, *The Unquenchable Worshipper*, p. 58.

in many churches. If the most important function of the church – worship – is being done through music, the song leader becomes the most crucial believer within the congregation. If the church is to survive, it must have the most skilled song leader. And if it is up to the song leader to get congregants to sing – 'worship' – there will be a temptation to get people to sing with exuberance through any means possible. Hype, emotionalism, and entertainment are just some of the means by which churches are tempted to use to ensure congregants sing – to 'worship'. Redman's view points to a more healthy approach to the issue of worship leading, for it is the Spirit who leads.

There is a human element in song leading, so that Redman applies the phrase 'lead worshipper' to song leaders. 'Lead worshippers' lead by example. While there are negative implications of being a 'lead worshipper', which is explained in an upcoming section on the elevation of worship music, one positive implication of his view is that not all the songs may be led by those on the stage. Someone among the congregation may be led by the Spirit as they worship through song.[42] This inclusive approach to participation coincides with the early period at the Azusa Street Revival.

Those at the Azusa Street Revival experienced tensions between the approach of relying on people within the congregation who spontaneously lead out in songs and being dependent on leaders who preplan and choose songs in advance of gatherings. Initially songs were sung spontaneously from memory among the congregation.[43] Bartleman preferred this spontaneous approach, whereby no human leaders selected or led the songs. He considered this spontaneous approach to be Spirit-led.[44] He admits, however, that human song leaders eventually arose who chose the songs and Azusa participants began to make use of hymnbooks.[45] And though others like Bartleman were opposed to these changes, they were not able to reverse the changes.[46] He likened this change to 'murdering the Spirit'.[47]

At the Azusa Street Revival, there was difference of opinion regarding how the Spirit might lead the songs of worship. Since the

---

[42] Redman, *The Unquenchable Worshipper*, p. 60.
[43] Bartleman, *Azusa Street*, p. 62.
[44] Bartleman, *Azusa Street*, p. 62.
[45] Bartleman, *Azusa Street*, p. 62.
[46] Bartleman, *Azusa Street*, p. 62.
[47] Bartleman, *Azusa Street*, p. 62.

early church's use of music for worship is unclear, and the teachings in Scripture on worship music allow for freedom, there is room for flexibility.[48] But it is this flexibility that can become a source of conflict, since people have varying opinions and preferences regarding how songs of worship are sung. Today, there can be human song leaders who are appointed from within the congregation, to lead them as they follow the Spirit. But others – not appointed as song leaders – should be able to lead a song as the Spirit leads. Pastoral leadership should give guidance for this practice in the church. For the Spirit has gifted some to oversee functions of the church. And a pastor can ensure that what is being sung is faithful to the nature of God and the church.

Regardless of who is leading the songs, though, whether they are an appointed or non-appointed song leader, churches must recognise the varying gifts and talents God has given his people. Not everyone is called to lead musically. Having a poor singer lead songs is a disservice to everyone involved. It deprives people from thriving in their own gifting – both those who are good singers and those who are not good singers. Good singers should be given the opportunity to share their gifts and talents with the church. And those who are not good singers, are also gifted in another area of ministry to strengthen the church. Having poor song leaders deprives both believers and unbelievers from receiving ministry through the various gifts of the church that are needed – even beyond music ministry. In sum, Redman's admonition that the Spirit is the essential worship leader is a crucial position that must be adopted by Pentecostals, because it acknowledges the limited ability of song leaders to lead worship, while also giving room for the Spirit to lead worship music from within the congregation.

The Elevation of Worship Music

All three CWM leaders elevate worship music over other expressions of worship because of the link between worship music and the immediacy of God. Beginning with Doerksen's views, he elevates worship music by prioritizing the role of the song leader over all other positions in the church. The primary problem in Doerksen's views that leads to the elevation of worship music over other elements of worship, is his belief that those involved in leading worship music are

---

[48] Best, *Unceasing Worship*, pp. 146-47.

the most important part of the corporate worship service. Since song leaders and band members are leading the form of worship that leads to the immediacy of God, whereby people can 'meet with God', a sense of elitism can be created among song leaders.[49] Those involved in leading songs may be deemed as the most important part of the corporate worship service, whereas all other elements are considered less important. Though Doerksen argues strongly for a lifestyle of worship, he admits that he considers leading worship music as 'the most sacred, delightful responsibility in the church'.[50] Doerksen recognises other forms of worship, but there is a hierarchy in his thoughts on corporate worship. There are three negative implications of this view, which follow.

First, viewing worship music as more important than other expressions of corporate worship can affect churches by extending the time for worship music, and limiting time for other expressions of worship. Singing in Pentecostal churches is often one of the longest forms of worship during corporate worship services. There may be times when churches devote their entire service for singing. Singing for extended periods of time is not the problem. Rather, the problem is when other forms of worship are minimized or neglected. First, Christians may neglect other forms of worship. Expressions like preaching may need to be shortened, Scripture is not read, and communion is often dismissed on a regular basis. Expressions of worship that do not appear to convey intimacy with God – the Spirit's immediacy – are either ignored or given less prominence. The greatest evidence of this shift in views of worship is the language used for the time allotted for songs of worship during corporate worship – this time is often just referred to as 'worship'. When church members explain that they enjoyed the 'worship' at a service, what they often mean is that they enjoyed their experience of singing songs of worship.

The early participants at Azusa did not elevate the role of worship music over other expressions of worship. Since other expressions of worship in their context of revival meetings might display the apparent immediacy of the Spirit, music was not the sole means for seemingly ecstatic experiences of God. For instance, those at Azusa report

---

[49] Doerksen, 'Faithful One'.
[50] Doerksen, 'Faithful One'.

that someone fell 'under the power of God' after being baptised in water.[51] Azusa participants were not as reliant on the emotional stirrings of music to feel like the Spirit was moving among them. But they eventually welcomed more 'jazzy' music that physically moved them, which indicates that they began to rely less on ecstatic experiences for the Spirit immediacy and more on upbeat worship music for a sense of the immediacy of God. To rely on ecstatic experiences for a sense of the immediacy of God may have been easier during the height of the revival, but to do so continually can understandably be a difficult goal during worship services under ordinary circumstances. Upbeat worship music is understandably a quick, easier way to experience something that feels like the immediacy of God, because of its powerful effects physically and emotionally. Bartleman argues that Azusa participants were beginning to rely on upbeat worship music, rather than charismatic expressions like singing in tongues for a sense of the immediacy of God. This may regrettably be the same route that some contemporary Pentecostals are on, for they often rely on worship music as a quick route to sense what seems to be the immediacy of God. The tensions involved among those who expect the immediacy of God through worship music are explicit at Azusa, and show that those at Azusa were not immune to how corporate worship is affected by the powerful medium of music. So rather than show the way forward, Azusa shows that the tension of relying on worship music for the immediacy of God is typical among those who expect and focus on the Spirit's immediacy in corporate worship.

The second negative implication of Doerksen's view on song leading is that he elevates the role of song leaders and worship bands. Those with the best sounding voices and musical skills are often considered great worshippers. Song leaders may often be called upon to explain 'worship' – since they apparently know more about it than those not musically inclined. This is often the case today among churches who value worship music – like Pentecostals – for while some scholars who may on occasion be called upon to describe worship, musicians are often called upon to explain what the worship of God is about. Doerksen, Zschech, and Redman are all called upon to

---

[51] *AF* 1.6 (February-March 1907), p. 4.

share at conferences on worship, and while they have excellent insights into worship, they have reached the level of 'expert' status within the church because of their experience and influence with worship music.

Finally, Doerksen's elevation of worship music during corporate worship services makes music and all those involved in leading music disproportionately influential on the life of the church. To put this into perspective, pastors who lead churches and corporate worship services are often the ones who preach the Word. The work of song writers and leaders, however, take up as much time – or more than – the lead pastor during a service because of the length of time for songs. Musicians influence the songs people sing, and the teaching people receive through worship music. People may forget a pastor's sermon, but songs often linger in people's minds because songs are often more memorable.[52] These memorable songs, however, include theology as well – as the sermon does. Pastors are often expected to complete years of training in theology, internships, and undergo the scrutiny of denominational leaders regarding their theology and character. Song leaders, however, are often expected only to be skilled musically and to receive some sort of approval from the pastor, often through church membership.

All song leaders should not be required to undergo the same rigour as pastors in order to serve – though this may be an excellent option for some. The church includes believers with various callings and gifts, so that all may serve. The Spirit is given for all believers to serve and edify others.[53] But if churches find it necessary to ensure that those involved in influential positions of leadership – pastors – who lead and teach in the church undergo rigorous training and scrutiny, does it not follow that there are similar expectations for song leaders? Doerksen recognises this problem of lack of training for musicians relative to pastors, and makes an effort to train musicians.[54] There should be some theological training provided for those writing and choosing the songs that teach. And since song leaders have found themselves in influential positions in the church, there must be an emphasis on issues related to discipleship and character in the lives

---

[52] Doerksen, *Make Love, Make War*, p. 224.

[53] 1 Corinthians 12.7.

[54] Doerksen, 'Song Writing', p. 87; Doerksen, *Make Love, Make War*, p. 223.

of these leaders. The elevation of worship music, because of the CWM approach that favours worship music for an experience of the immediacy of God, cannot continue. This elevation leads to unhealthy expressions of Christian worship because it neglects other expressions of worship, and creates a sense of elitism among those involved in worship music.

Doerksen recognises the problem of elevating worship music, even if his views lead in this direction. For instance, his local church and recent album offers some helpful suggestions to counter the approach to worship music that exalts the band. His church meets in a 'round', so that 'the congregation faces each other in four sections like a diamond'.[55] He explains that 'the band stands off to one end while the speaker is on the other end'.[56] Doerksen's recent album release, 'Level Ground', seeks to capture this idea. He had the musicians and singers placed among the people, rather than on stage.[57] The early Pentecostals at Azusa arranged themselves in a similar way, seated in a way that was more like a round.[58] The seats at Azusa were on the same level, and there was no elevated platform where people led.[59] Arranging the setting for corporate worship may be a lot of work today, but can benefit the church's corporate worship since setup and architecture communicates. While elevated platforms were previously used for activities like preaching, bands and musical instruments have come to dominate these contexts for corporate worship.[60] Recognising that worship music is just one among many other important expressions of worship is critical for the future of Pentecostal corporate worship today.

Though Zschech acknowledges the importance of a lifestyle of worship, her views on music and the importance of the immediacy of God in her approach to ministry implicitly leads to elevating worship music. First, she states that 'music was created to carry, capture,

---

[55] Doerksen, *Make Love, Make War*, p. 178.
[56] Doerksen, *Make Love, Make War*, p. 178.
[57] Doerksen, 'BrianDoerksen.com'.
[58] Hollenweger, *Pentecostalism*, pp. 23-24.
[59] Hollenweger, *Pentecostalism*, pp. 23-24.
[60] John D. Witvliet, 'Beyond Style: Rethinking the Role of Music in Worship', in Tim A. Dearborn and Scott Coil (eds.), *Worship at the Next Level: Insight from Contemporary Voices* (Grand Rapids: Baker, 2004), p. 168.

and communicate the presence of God'.[61] The expression of music in its primal form involves the immediacy of God. Second, she acknowledges that she is not only 'captivated by the presence of God', but aims at a 'Spirit-infused culture' in her day to day life.[62] What this means is that the music – with its original goal of communicating God's presence – offers a key context for the pursuit of a Spirit-infused culture. This approach is not necessarily explicit in Zschech's thought, but the value of worship music is undeniably crucial for an experience of God through the Spirit. Since issues related to the elevation of worship music is addressed in the critique of Doerksen, it is not repeated here to avoid duplicating that discussion that has similar implications.

While Redman's views on the Spirit's leadership of worship and subsequent view of song leaders as 'lead worshippers' has positive implications, the phrase, 'lead worshipper' still elevates the role of song leaders. The phrase 'lead worshipper' does not go far enough in providing a biblical term to acknowledge the role of a song leader. The phrase still exalts worship music over all other functions of a corporate worship service, and even the life of worship itself. The term 'lead worshiper' falsely implies that the best example for worship will likely only arise among musicians. If someone cannot sing well or even play an instrument, they will not be leading a band for congregational singing. This implicitly means that unskilled musicians cannot be considered a 'lead worshipper' within a local church body. Even if unskilled musicians are allowed to lead a song, which Redman encourages, it is best to label those who lead songs of worship as a song leader. Since the Spirit is the ultimate worship leader, as Redman acknowledges, associating the leadership of worship to a human inevitably leads to an unhealthy exaltation of those involved in leading worship music. Once again, since the elevation of song leaders is addressed in the critique of Doerksen's views in the previous section, those issues are not repeated in order to avoid duplicating that discussion.

Prophetic Songs of Praise

All three leaders acknowledge the role of prophetic songs led by the Spirit – a charismatic approach to worship music that emphasises the

---

[61] Zschech, *The Kiss of Heaven*, p. 142.
[62] Zschech, 'The Role of the Holy Spirit in Worship', pp. 286-87.

Spirit's immediacy.[63] Doerksen maintains that prophetic worship music may be either 'prewritten' or 'spontaneous songs sung from God's heart'.[64] This can come about as one asks God to 'release' one to 'sing His heart over His people'.[65] This may be a phrase that comes to one's mind, or a phrase from Scripture.[66] A prophetic message is a message from God for the particular needs of the church at that time. One should 'practice' this type of song in small groups before singing this way with larger groups.

Zschech calls prophetic songs a form of singing in the Spirit. She acknowledges that these songs occur spontaneously, explaining they take place 'in almost free worship'.[67] Like Doerksen, she recognises the place of this type of singing in a small group – a rehearsal – before practicing it before a larger group.[68]

Finally, Redman also refers to prophetic songs, and argues that they may be songs prepared beforehand or sung spontaneously.[69] And like both Doerksen and Zschech, he admits that spontaneity needs to be 'rehearsed' so that leaders, musicians, and technical operators are prepared when spontaneous singing occurs during the actual presentation.[70] Presenting a prophetic song requires the reception of 'insights' from God for the particular 'season' of a church.[71] As stated earlier, he considers his song 'The Heart of Worship' a prophetic song because it 'described and gave voice to what God was doing' among those in his church.[72]

Those at Azusa did not use the language of 'prophetic songs' for worship music as do the CWM leaders, but they could acknowledge both their prewritten songs of worship for particular seasons of

---

[63] An emphasis on the prophetic role in song is also found in Sorge's work, *Exploring Worship*. He states that 'God intends that those in leadership, especially musical leadership, function under a prophetic anointing'. Sorge, *Exploring Worship*, p. 126.

[64] Doerksen, *Make Love, Make War*, p. 235.

[65] Doerksen, *Make Love, Make War*, p. 252.

[66] Doerksen, *Make Love, Make War*, p. 252.

[67] Zschech, *Worship*, p. 95.

[68] Zschech, *Worship*, p. 96.

[69] Matt Redman, *Inside Out Worship* (vol. 2; Eastbourne: Kingsway, 2005), p. 97.

[70] Redman, 'Cell, Congregation, Celebration', pp. 115-16.

[71] Redman, 'Worship-Leading Essentials: (Part 5)', pp. 98-99.

[72] Redman, 'Worship-Leading Essentials: (Part 5)', p. 99.

church life and spontaneous songs as 'prophetic'. While Azusa participants professed to prophesy through spoken word, viewing some songs that they sang as prophetic was more implicit than explicit.[73] A prewritten song they might view as prophetic was 'The Comforter Has Come'. As stated earlier, this song became an anthem for the mission. Since they viewed their reception of the Spirit through Spirit baptism as a turning point in church history, it is only fitting that this song was sung regularly.

Participants at Azusa also remained open to spontaneous songs led by the Spirit. For instance, a man in *AF* referred to as 'Bro. Burke' shares a testimony on how he received Spirit baptism.[74] In the midst of praying for Spirit baptism, he explains that the Spirit 'rushed through' him bodily one day.[75] And the next day he began to sing a spontaneous song at home: 'The power, the power, the Pentecostal power, is just the same today'.[76] This example shows how a spontaneous song reflected what Azusa participants might deem as 'prophetic', because this song conveyed the message from God that his prayer for Spirit baptism and power was available for him that day.[77] He eventually began to sing 'The Comforter has Come'.[78] Burke's shift in songs implicitly conveys to readers that he received Spirit baptism at that point. This incident shows how both a spontaneous song and prewritten song functioned together prophetically for Burke. The spontaneous song prepared him for Spirit baptism, and the prewritten song acknowledged what the Spirit was doing in his life at the moment.

The Azusa participants' newly composed songs, both spontaneous and prewritten songs for worship, reflect a similar CWM expectation for prophetic songs of worship because those who received the songs viewed them as God's particular message for their particu-

---

[73] *AF* 1.1 (September 1906), p. 4.

[74] *AF* 1.3 (November 1906), p. 3.

[75] *AF* 1.3 (November 1906), p. 3.

[76] *AF* 1.3 (November 1906), p. 3.

[77] Burke's spontaneous song reflects an emphasis on Spirit baptism, but there is evidence of spontaneous songs of worship addressing the theme of Christology as well. Myrtle Shideler sang 'Jesus' blood covers me, I was blind but, hallelujah, now I see'. Shideler sang this song as a preparation for Spirit baptism. See *AF* 1.5 (January 1907), p. 3.

[78] *AF* 1.3 (November 1906), p. 3.

lar context. Azusa participants did not give a rationale for their 'prophetic' songs, but they appeared to experience the Spirit's immediacy as they composed new songs.[79] The songs served a prophetic role for their particular time and place. Azusa's songs focused on central teachings promoted at Azusa, such as pneumatology and Christology. As stated in the previous section, Spirit baptism played an important role in some of these new songs, whether it was a song to prepare for Spirit baptism or by lyrics that featured the experience of Spirit baptism. And though Spirit baptism was an important emphasis at Azusa, the new songs at Azusa were predominantly focused on Christology. Most of the songs composed by Azusa participants were about Christ, and the two out of three songs about pneumatology included teachings on Christ. Most of the songs about Jesus contain lyrics dealing with the atoning work of Jesus through his blood and Christ's second coming. And the songs prominently teaching about Jesus, do not teach at all on the Spirit. The Azusa participants primarily exalted Jesus through the new songs they composed, and can be deemed as prophetic. The April 1907 edition of *AF* – representing the half-way mark of the more popular time of the revival – contains fifty-seven articles.[80] And of these fifty-seven articles, forty-four reference Spirit baptism.[81] These new 'prophetic' songs at Azusa provided a corrective to the potential for fixation on the Spirit's immediacy alone.[82] The *AF* does not provide any indication that some songs were welcomed and others dismissed by leaders based on theology. But the *AF* includes a message that the Spirit's role is to magnify Christ, not anything else.[83] So while Azusa leaders may not have critiqued the songs at Azusa, they critiqued the actual and potential issue of people magnifying an experience of the Spirit over the exaltation of Christ. And this general critique of the Spirit's role may have also influenced the songs people composed. The role of these new songs, which can be deemed as prophetic at Azusa, cannot be

---

[79] Burke's and Shideler's experiences of composing new songs, explained earlier in this chapter, are examples of Azusa participants experiencing the Spirit's immediacy while composing a new song. *AF* 1.3 (November 1906), p. 3; *AF* 1.5 (January 1907), p. 3.

[80] Dove, 'Hymnody and Liturgy in the Azusa Street Revival', p. 256.

[81] Dove, 'Hymnody and Liturgy in the Azusa Street Revival', p. 256.

[82] Dove, 'Hymnody and Liturgy in the Azusa Street Revival', p. 257.

[83] *AF* 1.5 (January 1907), p. 2.

understated for contemporary Pentecostals. Two lessons can be learned for contemporary Pentecostals related to songs for worship.

The first lesson Pentecostals can learn from Azusa regarding their prophetic songs relates to the content of these songs – the Spirit's immediacy is not the goal of worship music or the Christian life in general. Those at Azusa recognized that the Spirit's immediacy leads to the exaltation of Jesus Christ. But they could have also explained other goals of the Spirit's present work, such as intimacy with the Father and social justice (concerns discussed earlier). An experience of the Spirit through songs solely for that experience is not biblical.[84] The Spirit does not exalt himself.

The second lesson Pentecostals can learn from Azusa regarding prophetic songs relates to the function of their songs – the Spirit's present work for the composition of a prophetic song can provide a powerful impetus for transformation in the church. Songs are a powerful medium of communication within corporate worship, especially when they are memorable and made for maximum participation. They can be learned quickly and remembered often longer than other mediums like sermons. Though Azusa never referred to their new songs as 'prophetic', the songs functioned similarly to the approach commended by the CWM leaders considered here. The Spirit enables people to write songs or sing spontaneously to communicate a message from God pertinent for a particular time and place.

The question, remains, though, is there any biblical precedent to prophesy through prewritten or spontaneous songs? First, Scripture includes prewritten songs that are prophetic. The Psalms exhibit some of the best examples of songs that are prophetic. For instance, Psalm 22 is considered prophetic because it communicates a Spirit-inspired message relevant for the original audience and future believers joining in this lament. Psalm 22 is a messianic psalm because it communicates Christ's suffering and vindication.[85] Christ uttered the words of Ps. 22.1 while on the cross.[86] Singing songs directly from or influenced by Scripture can be prophetic, particularly when the message conveys a particular message for the life of a particular church context.

---

[84] John 16.14.

[85] Geoffrey W. Grogan, *Psalms* (The Two Horizons Old Testament Commentary; Grand Rapids: Eerdmans, 2008), p. 72.

[86] See Mt. 27.46 and Mk 15.34.

Second, spontaneous prophetic songs also have precedent in Scripture. 1 Chronicles 25.1-3 and 1 Sam. 10.5 reveal that spontaneous songs of worship may be prophetic in nature.[87] Heeding the CWM leaders' recommendations to sing a spontaneous prophetic song is valid and can be meaningful. The leaders' recommendation to prepare for spontaneous songs is also important for all those involved in leading the songs – such as singers, musicians, and technical support. While leaders should not be manipulative, they should teach all those involved what could happen when spontaneous prophetic songs arise, and how to appropriately respond.

While all three leaders rightfully acknowledge the value of prophetic songs of worship, there is room for strengthening how this can be done within the church. Just like tongues require interpretation, songs of prophecy require evaluation. But in all three leaders' thoughts on prophetic songs, none delve into the need for prophetic evaluation.[88] The leaders do, however, encourage artists in general to be willing to receive constructive criticism of their songs, particularly songs that are prewritten. They encourage being open to criticism, ensure that songs are Scriptural, and recommend that local churches be the filter for songs – these are all helpful guides for the evaluation of prewritten songs. But they do not explicitly address how one might evaluate spontaneous prophetic songs. At Azusa, there is no indication that leaders critiqued spontaneous songs – though they critiqued the general theology and experience of Azusa participants. The evaluation of spontaneous prophetic songs, however, is necessary.

Scripture includes the rationale for prophetic evaluation. First, Paul makes clear that prophetic evaluation is necessary. Paul explains in 1 Cor. 14.29 that after someone shares a prophecy within a corporate setting, other believers must 'weigh what is said'. In 1 Thess. 5.20-21, Paul admonishes believers to welcome prophecies, but 'test everything'. Scripture is clear that prophecies must be evaluated.

Second, Paul makes clear how prophecies must be evaluated. He recognises that some believers have a gift of the Spirit that involves discernment.[89] Like the gift of tongues requires the complimentary

---

[87] Keener, *1-2 Corinthians*, p. 114; Sorge, *Exploring Worship*, p. 128.

[88] See Zschech, *Worship*, pp. 93-97.

[89] 1 Corinthians 12.29; James D.G. Dunn, *1 Corinthians* (New Testament Guides; Sheffield: Sheffield Academic, 1995), pp. 82-83.

gift of interpretation in a corporate worship context, prophetic messages requires the complimentary gift of discernment.[90] A few tests in Scripture for discerning between true and false prophecies include the character of the person sharing a message – most notably love – and the message must conform to the teachings of Scripture, glorify Christ, and build up the church.[91] Prophecies left unevaluated can leave a church coerced into something the Spirit is not saying. Because songs deemed prophetic can often be put forward spontaneously within a church setting, pastors must ensure that feedback is given on songs rather than allow the song to be sung without a response from the leadership of the church.

Conclusion

After an analysis of CWM through the three CWM leaders, it is clear that Pentecostals are both strengthened and weakened by a reliance on CWM for worship music. First, the strengths of CWM for Pentecostal worship music must be highlighted. Doerksen helps the church focus on an important part of the Godhead – the Father. Pentecostals have always focused on Jesus in worship, and the Spirit's role in worship has always been acknowledged. But the Father can be forgotten in Pentecostal contexts. Doerksen's emphasis is helpful because it reminds Pentecostals that Scripture shows that the Spirit's immediacy also leads to intimacy with the Father. Doerksen's admonition to sing songs of lament is another important contribution, because these songs can help complement the already accepted upbeat, joyful songs of worship used in Pentecostal churches. Songs of lament can be 'in the Spirit', and gives opportunity for genuine worship from the range of circumstances represented in a congregation.

Zschech gives many important recommendations for worship music. First, the role of singing in the Spirit – in tongues – must be addressed. While Zschech explains the importance of this practice in

---

[90] Cecil M. Robeck, Jr, 'Prophecy, Gift of', in Stanley M. Burgess (ed.), *The New International Dictionary of Pentecostal and Charismatic Movements* (Grand Rapids: Zondervan, 2003), pp. 1004-1005.

[91] Matthew 7.20; Jn 16.14; 1 Cor. 12.2-3; 13.2; 14.3, 37-38; 1 Jn 4.1-3, 6. Baker, 'Prophecy, Prophets', pp. 973-74; Frank Macchia, 'Signs of Grace: Towards a Charismatic Theology of Worship', in Lee Roy Martin (ed.), *Towards a Pentecostal Theology of Worship* (Cleveland: CPT Press, 2016), pp. 162-64.

her early work on worship music, there is no mention of it in anything later she writes. Neither Doerksen nor Redman make mention of it in their writings. And while it may be understandable that publishers want books by these popular leaders to be widely accessible beyond those who are Pentecostal or Charismatic, there is precedent for singing in tongues in both Scripture and at the Azusa Street Revival. Singing in tongues should be encouraged, as long as Paul's insights on interpretation are heeded within a corporate context. Second, she recognises the temptations many song leaders face who expect the Spirit's immediacy through worship music, and rightly provides discernment to ensure people do not try to 'manufacture' the Spirit. Further, the fruit of the immediacy of God in worship music cannot just be relegated to good sensory feelings, but must include Christ-likeness, love, and social justice.

Redman also reminds those involved in worship that it is the Spirit who is the 'ultimate worship leader'. His view is an important corrective to churches who view song leaders as worship leaders. Redman's position has precedent at Azusa. Song leaders should never be called worship leaders, because the Spirit alone leads worship.

Though CWM offers beneficial insights into worship music for Pentecostals, there are weaknesses found in CWM that Pentecostals must be aware of and correct. While all three leaders acknowledge that worshipping God is more than just singing songs of praise – worship is a lifestyle – they inadvertently elevate worship music over other expressions of worship. Doerksen favors the role of leading worship music over any other position in the church. Zschech connects the primal goals of music with the presence of God, while also emphasising an experience of God's presence in ministry. Her ministry approach inevitably leads to an exaltation of worship music. Even Redman attempts to sway the emphasis off of song leaders of worship music by changing the titles of these leaders from worship leader to lead worshiper. But even this change of title does not take away the elevation of those within a band – they are still the primary example for 'worship'. The exaltation of worship music has regrettably led some to associate worship solely with worship music. But worship music or congregational singing should never just be called worship. A narrow view of worship neglects to give adequate attention to worship that encompasses all of one's life, as well as other expressions of corporate worship (e.g., preaching) that are necessary for the life and health of the church.

Finally, all three leaders also acknowledge the role of prophetic songs of worship – this is to be commended. Though Azusa participants did not refer to their new songs as 'prophetic', the new songs functioned similarly to what CWM leaders espouse for prophetic songs. The Spirit's present work can lead to prophetic songs that benefit the church and provide impetus for transformation. Prophetic songs have precedent in Scripture. The current emphasis on professionalism in music can sometimes make worship music overly predictable. Including the prophetic in worship music can ensure that leaders are expecting fresh insights from Scripture and the Spirit for the season that the church is experiencing. However, none of the three leaders explicitly take on the importance of responding to spontaneous prophetic songs of worship with discernment. Their views on discernment are implicit, for they express caution in songwriting to ensure that the teachings are Scriptural. But a more explicit approach for ensuring leaders and pastors 'weigh in' on spontaneous songs can ensure the congregation is not being led in the wrong direction.

After the expression of worship music in Pentecostal corporate worship, preaching and the altar often follow in services. The next section reflects this progression in Pentecostal services, examining how the Spirit's immediacy is a crucial factor for a Pentecostal approach to preaching and the altar.

PART 3
POWER IN THE PULPIT AND PROSTRATE AT THE ALTAR: THE PENTECOSTAL APPROACH TO PREACHING AND THE ALTAR

5

AN INTRODUCTION TO PENTECOSTAL
PREACHING AND THE ALTAR

Part two of this book showed that an emphasis on the Spirit's present work in worship music is being maintained by a CWM approach, which is the popular approach to worship music among Pentecostals today. After an expression of worship music in Pentecostal services, though, preaching and the altar are key features that regularly follow. Thus, part three of this work offers an examination and analysis of some important issues related to the emphasis on the Spirit's immediacy in preaching and the altar among Pentecostals in North America – with implications for Evangelicals and Charismatics.[1] With that end in mind, chapters five and six include a comparison and contrast of three approaches to preaching and the altar. Classical Pentecostals Ray H. Hughes and Charles T. Crabtree will be examined primarily through their books, both entitled *Pentecostal Preaching*. Baptist preacher Haddon W. Robinson's perspective will be drawn from his *Biblical Preaching*, which has been an influential evangelical approach to preaching.[2] Chapter seven provides a theological appraisal of the three leaders' approaches to preaching and the altar, delving into two

---

[1] Portions of part three have been published. See Samuel, 'The Spirit in Pentecostal Preaching'.

[2] Haddon Robinson, *Biblical Preaching: The Development and Delivery of Expository Messages* (Grand Rapids: Baker, 2nd edn, 2001). Unless noted, all subsequent citations refer to the second edition of Robinson's book. Charles T. Crabtree, *Pentecostal Preaching: Empowering Your Pulpit with the Holy Spirit* (Springfield: Gospel Publishing House, 2003); Ray H. Hughes, *Pentecostal Preaching* (Cleveland, TN: Pathway Press, rev. edn, 2004).

things: 1) how the approach to preaching and the altar among those at the Azusa Street Revival may or may not be a source of renewal for contemporary Pentecostal preaching and the altar; and 2) how other pertinent biblical-theological resources can provide the way forward for preaching and the altar in Pentecostal corporate worship services.

Methodology

Two preliminary remarks are necessary to understand the methodology used in this section on preaching and the altar. First, why use Hughes, Crabtree, and Robinson as dialogue partners? Hughes and Crabtree have been preachers and denominational leaders in classical Pentecostal denominations in the United States and thus represent a traditional approach to preaching and the altar among classical Pentecostals.[3] Although not a Pentecostal, Robinson's views on preaching and the altar have influenced the approach to preaching among Pentecostals today.[4] This discussion is limited in that it focuses on Western approaches and challenges for preaching and the altar, and all three authors are white leaders from the United States; nevertheless, it has relevance for anyone who is concerned with Pentecostal preaching and the altar. Further, this discussion is limited to just three approaches to preaching and the altar because it allows for a sustained and systematic analysis.

Second, for the theological analysis of preaching and the altar, five categories are examined: 1) the authors' definition of preaching and the altar; 2) the preparation required for people involved in preaching; 3) preparing the message/sermon 4) the preaching event; and 5) the altar.[5] The category focusing on the preparation for preaching

---

[3] Charles T. Crabtree, 'Dr. Charles T. Crabtree Biography'. No pages. Online: http://crabtreeandramona.com/charlesBio.htm; Hughes, *Pentecostal Preaching*.

[4] 'The Heresy of Application: An Interview with Haddon Robinson', *Leadership Journal* 28.4 (Fall 1997), p. 20. Online: http://www.christianitytoday.com/le/1997/fall/714020.html; Bryan Chapell, *Christ-Centered Preaching: Redeeming the Expository Sermon* (Grand Rapids: Baker, 2nd edn, 2005), p. 13; and Kenton C. Anderson, *Choosing to Preach: A Comprehensive Introduction to Sermon Options and Structures* (Grand Rapids: Zondervan, 2006), pp. 11, 38.

[5] See Richard Lischer, 'Introduction: The Promise of Renewal', in Richard Lischer (ed.), *The Company of Preachers: Wisdom on Preaching, Augustine to the Present*

underscores the response to God's call to preach. Preparing the message/sermon involves the various aspects involved in constructing a sermon. The preaching event includes all that is involved when the sermon is delivered. The altar may also be called an altar service, since it involves that component of a corporate worship service that follows in response to the sermon. In chapter seven, a constructive analysis of the three approaches, engaging Azusa and other pertinent theological resources, are put forward to provide a more robust theology of preaching and the altar for Pentecostals.

Background of Key Leaders

Ray H. Hughes represents a classical Pentecostal leader and preacher. He ministered in various capacities for many years within the Church of God, Cleveland, Tennessee – a classical Pentecostal denomination. Though he recently passed away in 2011 – at the age of 87 – his extensive influence as a classical Pentecostal leader is grounds to include him in this discussion.[6] Hughes' 'educational accomplishments include Lee College, A.A., D.Litt.; Tennessee Wesleyan College, B.A.; University of Tennessee, M.S., Ed.D.'.[7] He served as 'an evangelist, pastor, state overseer, international director of youth and Christian education, president of Lee College, and three terms as the top executive of the Church of God, Cleveland, Tennessee'.[8] He, however, viewed himself primarily as an evangelist.[9] He ministered in various other Pentecostal contexts in the United States and around the world, serving as the president of the Pentecostal Fellowship of North America, president of the Pentecostal World Conference, and preaching at four Pentecostal World Conferences.[10] He also gained

---

(Grand Rapids: Eerdmans, 2002), pp. xiii-xvi; Thomas G. Long, *The Witness of Preaching* (Louisville: Westminster John Knox, 2nd edn, 2005), pp. 15-18.

[6] Ministry Today, 'Former Church of God Leader Ray H. Hughes Sr. Dies'. Online: http://ministrytodaymag.com/index.php/ministry-news/19099-former-church-of-god-leader-ray-h-hughes-sr-dies.

[7] Ray H. Hughes, *Classical Pentecostal Sermon Library* (vol. 1; Cleveland, TN: Pathway Press, 2011), p. 16.

[8] Hughes, *Pentecostal Preaching*.

[9] Hughes, *Pentecostal Preaching*, pp. 117-18.

[10] Ministry Today, 'Former Church of God Leader Ray H. Hughes Sr. Dies', para. 2.

broader appeal beyond Pentecostals, serving as the president of the National Association of Evangelicals.[11]

Charles Crabtree also represents a classical Pentecostal leader and preacher. He is an ordained minister within the Assemblies of God (AG) in the United States – a classical Pentecostal denomination. He served in various capacities within AG for many years. He was born in Halifax, Nova Scotia, Canada, but his base of ministry is in the United States. He graduated from Central Bible College in Springfield, Missouri, with a Bachelor of Arts in Bible, and later received an honorary Doctor of Divinity degree from Northwest University of the Assemblies of God in Kirkland, Washington.[12] He pastored two AG churches, First Assembly in Des Moines, Iowa and Bethel Church in San Jose, California, over a period of 25 years.[13] He eventually became the assistant general superintendent of the Assemblies of God in the USA for 14 years – resigning from his denominational post in 2007.[14] He presently serves as the president of Northpoint Bible College, which is a college associated with the Assemblies of God in Springfield, Missouri.[15] He ministers in a variety of contexts throughout the States and the world. Since this work focuses on North American Pentecostalism, it is important to note that he has been welcomed for ministry among classical Pentecostals in Canada. In 2009, for instance, he spoke as the keynote speaker for a week of ministry at Lakeshore Pentecostal Camp, which is a ministry of the Eastern Ontario District of the Pentecostal Assemblies of Canada (PAOC).[16] His work on Pentecostal preaching provides a good representative of what the AG – and other classical Pentecostals in

---

[11] Ministry Today, 'Former Church of God Leader Ray H. Hughes Sr. Dies', para. 1.

[12] Northpoint Bible College, 'Charles Crabtree'. Online: http://northpoint.edu /academics/faculty/charles-crabtree.

[13] Crabtree, 'Dr. Charles T. Crabtree Biography'.

[14] Ken Horn, 'Charles T. Crabtree: A focus on discipleship and unity', *Pentecostal Evangel* (September 2007). No pages. Online: http://pentecostalevangel.ag.org/ Articles2007/4873_Crabtree.cfm.

[15] Northpoint Bible College, 'Accreditation'. Online: http://northpoint.edu/ about/accreditation.

[16] See Eastern Ontario District – PAOC. Online: http://www.eod.paoc.org/ camps.html. Lakeshore Pentecostal Camp. Online: http://www.lakeshorepente-costalcamp.com.

North America – would consider a traditional classical Pentecostal approach to preaching and the altar.

Examining the preaching approach in two classical Pentecostal leaders, Crabtree and Hughes, is understandable. But why include Robinson, who is not a Pentecostal? Robinson is important because of his influence on Pentecostal preachers. He is currently the Harold John Ockenga Distinguished Professor of Preaching at Gordon-Conwell Theological Seminary, has been president and professor of homiletics at Denver Seminary, and has also been a professor of homiletics at Dallas Theological Seminary.[17] The first edition of his book, *Biblical Preaching*, came out in 1980, and by one estimate in 1997, his text is 'used in 120 seminaries and Bible colleges'.[18] He also 'teaches on the daily program "Radio Bible Class" and, in a 1996 poll conducted by Baylor University, was named one of the twelve most effective preachers in the English-speaking world'.[19]

Robinson's views on preaching are used here for an examination of contemporary Pentecostal preaching and the altar for a number of reasons. First, Robinson's ideas on expository preaching have been very influential on contemporary Pentecostal preaching. In Bible colleges and seminaries associated with classical Pentecostal denominations in the United States and Canada, *Biblical Preaching*, is often a required or recommended text for classes on homiletics.[20] Further-

---

[17] See Robinson, *Biblical Preaching*.

[18] 'The Heresy of Application'.

[19] 'The Heresy of Application'.

[20] For instance, the ministerial credentials program within the International Pentecostal Holiness Church (IPHC) offers a 'Homiletics I' course for potential ministers. The only book required for this first course on preaching for IPHC ministers is Robinson's *Biblical Preaching*. In the fall of 2005, Robinson's book was used at the Assemblies of God Theological Seminary for a course entitled, 'Communicating the Message', taught by Doug Oss. In the fall of 2013, Robinson's book was used at Christian Life College (associated with the United Pentecostal Church International), for a course entitled 'Homiletics II', taught by Richard Bishop. In the fall of 2006, Robinson's book was used at Urshan Graduate School of Theology (associated with the United Pentecostal Church International), for a course entitled 'Introduction to Preaching', taught by Jeffrey C. Garner. In 2009, Robinson's book was used at Lee University (associated with the Church of God in Cleveland, TN), for an independent studies course entitled 'Expository Preaching'. Robinson's *Biblical Preaching* was a regular textbook in homiletics classes throughout the 1980s and 1990s at Eastern Pentecostal Bible College, now known as Master's College and Seminary. Specifically, as early as 1982 (his book first came out in 1980), Robinson's

more, Robinson himself has personally trained ministers within classical Pentecostal denominations in North America.[21]

While other books are now also being used in courses on homiletics in Pentecostal classrooms, Robinson's work has been an important influence on the authors of some of the most widely-used
books on preaching. For instance, Bryan Chapell's work, *Christ-Centered Preaching: Redeeming the Expository Sermon* is another popular book
on expository preaching.[22] Chapell emphasizes the need for sermons
to be Christ-centered and redemptive. Yet Chapell acknowledges
Robinson's important role as 'expository preaching's senior states-
man'.[23]

Another more recent work that has found its way into Pentecostal
preaching courses is Kenton Anderson's book, *Choosing to Preach*.[24]

book was the required textbook for the introductory course on preaching, which
was taught by Tom Miller. I attended Master's College from 1996–2000, and Robinson's book was required for the course, 'Homiletics I', taught by David Kennedy.
Master's College and Seminary is associated with the PAOC, and has been the official denominational school for four districts within the PAOC, including Eastern
Ontario, Western Ontario, Quebec, and the Maritimes. During the 1990s, the Pentecostal Assemblies of Newfoundland and Labrador (PAONL) also used Eastern
Pentecostal Bible College as their official denominational school. See
www.mcs.edu. The PAONL uses Tyndale University College and Seminary as their
official theological training institution as of 2007. Pentecostal Assemblies of Newfoundland and Labrador, 'Tyndale University College and Seminary'. But even at
Tyndale, one of the required texts for a 2008 course 'Preaching', taught by Daniel
L. Wong, was Robinson's *Biblical Preaching*.

[21] E.g., In February 2002, Robinson was invited to co-teach with one of his
former students, Fred Penney, at Master's Seminary (associated with the PAOC).
Robinson and Penney taught an intensive course entitled, 'Expository Preaching'.
In October 2003, Robinson taught and preached at the IPHC National Pastors'
Conference in Nashville, Tennessee. Robinson was also invited to teach AG min-
isters for a seminar entitled, 'Biblical Preaching for the 21st Century', at the 2007
General Council of the AG.

[22] E.g., Chappel's book was a required course textbook in two courses taught
by Pentecostal professors who teach preaching. Fred Fulford taught Expository
Preaching at Summit Pacific College in the Spring of 2010 and Fred Penney taught
Homiletics II at Master's College and Seminary in the Winter of 2009 both requiring Chappel's book for their courses.

[23] Chapell, *Christ-Centered Preaching*, p. 13.

[24] One course, however, is taught by Anderson himself at Canadian Pentecostal
Seminary in Langley, British Columbia. Canadian Pentecostal Seminary, 'Canadian
Pentecostal Seminary'. While he is the dean of Northwest Baptist Seminary, he
teaches Pentecostals since these schools are all part of the Associated Canadian

Anderson also emphasizes expository preaching, and admits that Robinson's book 'has done more to shape the teaching of preaching among evangelicals over the last twenty-five years' than any other book.[25] So while Chapell and Anderson have written works now found in homiletics courses taken for Pentecostal ministry, they too acknowledge the influence of Robinson on the ethos of evangelical preaching, which has influenced the Pentecostal approach to preaching.

Another example of Robinson's influence relates to his influence on the PAOC – the largest classical Pentecostal denomination in Canada. Though a growing number of Pentecostals are obtaining doctorates within the PAOC, Fred Penney is one of the few PAOC professors of preaching whose doctorate has a focus on preaching. Penney earned his degree at Gordon-Conwell Theological Seminary, and his mentor and supervisor for his thesis was Robinson.[26] Penney has been called upon to teach courses on preaching for Master's College and Seminary in Peterborough, Ontario, which is a PAOC sponsored school. And during a course on preaching he taught in 2002 at Master's, he brought in Robinson to co-teach the course.

Thus, Crabtree's and Hughes' works are important representatives to discern what classical Pentecostal leaders consider a traditional approach to Pentecostal preaching and the altar. Robinson, however, shows what type of approach to preaching that Pentecostals training for preaching and the altar are being influenced by, particularly at Bible Colleges and Seminaries. And though Crabtree and Hughes have some different emphases from Robinson, the variety showcases the variety of approaches found in Pentecostal churches in North America today.

The Definition/Nature of Preaching

To begin an examination of these leaders' approach to preaching, their foundational views on what preaching is must be discussed.

Theological Schools. The other school Anderson's book is currently being used for a course on preaching is Master's College and Seminary, in Peterborough, Ontario, Canada. Potter, *Homiletics I*.

[25] Chapell, *Christ-Centered Preaching*, pp. 11, 38.

[26] See Fred Penney, 'Applying a Spiritual Warfare Cosmology to Preaching' (DMin thesis, Gordon-Conwell Theological Seminary, 1999).

How they distinguish preaching from other forms of verbal communication is important, showing what they believe makes a sermon
within the context of the church's corporate worship. Because the
subject of an altar is a shorter subject than preaching, a discussion
on the altar is only given in chapter six. Delaying the treatment of the
altar also helps avoid duplication of discussions.

Ray H. Hughes

Hughes' views on preaching include the importance of the Spirit's
immediacy throughout in three ways. The three include: the priority
of preaching for those called to vocational ministry, how sermons are
distinguished from messages from God, and three crucial ingredients
for powerful preaching.[27] First, Hughes gives greater prominence to
the ministry of preaching than any other responsibility for those
called to vocational ministry. People called to vocational ministry are
'first and foremost' preachers.[28] Vocational ministers, then, must
'have skill in the art of preaching'.[29] Preaching involves both primary
and secondary objectives. The primary goal in preaching is 'to communicate the Word of God'.[30] The '[s]econdary goals are to inform,
to teach, to challenge and to inspire'.[31] Thus, the primary objective
for ordained ministers is to communicate the Word of God through
preaching.

Second, Hughes distinguishes a 'sermon' from a 'message' dependent on an experience of the immediacy of God in the preacher's
preparation.[32] People can learn to prepare a sermon through a course
in homiletics, but preachers receive a message to preach from God.
Even the most thorough study to construct a sermon is useless unless
a preacher first sees 'the face of God' to receive a message.[33] And
though a preacher must study the Scripture thoroughly, they must call

---

[27] Joseph Kendall Byrd attempts to explain Hughes' definition of preaching;
but, for my purposes, his definition ends up being deficient because he focuses
solely on Hughes' goals in preaching. See 'Formulation of a Classical Pentecostal
Homiletic in Dialogue with Contemporary Protestant Homiletics' (PhD dissertation, The Southern Baptist Theological Seminary, 1990), pp. 65-66.

[28] Hughes, *Pentecostal Preaching*, p. 78.
[29] Hughes, *Pentecostal Preaching*, p. 78.
[30] Hughes, *Pentecostal Preaching*, p. 78.
[31] Hughes, *Pentecostal Preaching*, p. 78.
[32] Hughes, *Pentecostal Preaching*, p. 93.
[33] Hughes, *Pentecostal Preaching*, p. 93.

upon and depend upon 'the aid of God's Holy Spirit' while preparing and studying to construct a message.[34]

Though Hughes distinguishes a 'sermon' from a 'message', he does not consistently distinguish these terms throughout his work. He often refers to sermons the same way he views 'messages'. The terms 'sermon' and 'message' are often synonymous – whereby a 'sermon' is also considered a message received from God.[35] Nevertheless, Hughes prioritizes the Spirit's immediacy for faithful Christian preaching.

Third, Hughes describes three essential ingredients to powerful preaching that highlights the Spirit's immediacy, which also necessitates an altar. The three elements of powerful preaching include: 'the Word, the Holy Spirit, and interaction between pulpit and pew'.[36] First, the 'inherent, foundational power of preaching' is in the Word of God, and is associated with the immediacy of God because '[t]he Bible is the Word of God just as much as if God spoke every single word of it with His own lips, [*sic*] (2 Peter 1:21)'.[37] Thus, 'the Bible is a miracle' primarily because it has 'one Author', the Spirit, who inspired the various human authors.[38] Scripture is the Word of God, whereby people experience the immediacy of God by receiving the very words of God. Scripture, then, is the authority for the church and is the 'source of all preaching'.[39]

The second element is the Spirit, 'the operational power of preaching', who brings 'the power and anointing of God' on someone's preaching, whereby the preacher experiences the Spirit's immediacy.[40] The preacher not only experiences the Spirit's presence in preaching, but affects listeners, attesting that the preacher is called, awakening people to regeneration, and convincing people of the message being preached.[41] Power in preaching is derived through the

---

[34] Hughes, *Pentecostal Preaching*, pp. 93-100.

[35] E.g., Hughes refers to Peter's message in Acts 2 as a sermon and a 'masterpiece'. This 'sermon', of course follows Peter's experience of Spirit baptism, a crucial experience of the Spirit's immediacy for preaching in his thought, which shows that Hughes is not consistent in distinguishing a sermon and message.

[36] Hughes, *Pentecostal Preaching*, p. 12.

[37] Hughes, *Pentecostal Preaching*, pp. 17-18.

[38] Hughes, *Pentecostal Preaching*, pp. 17-18.

[39] Hughes, *Pentecostal Preaching*, p. 15.

[40] Hughes, *Pentecostal Preaching*, p. 19.

[41] Hughes, *Pentecostal Preaching*, pp. 19-20.

Spirit, not mere intellect, persuasiveness, eloquence, and style.[42] The Spirit's 'anointing' provides 'forcefulness' to the message that is not available to an 'ordinary speech' lacking the anointing.[43]

A few comments are required to explain what Hughes believes the anointing is and is not. The anointing is not equated with being loud, excitement, demonstrations, pulpit mannerisms, or being inspired like an artist, politician, or writer – though one who is anointed may display these attributes.[44] Rather, the anointing is somewhat 'mysterious and miraculous', whereby preachers 'often speak and act beyond themselves'.[45] Preachers may be led by the Spirit to share 'a word of knowledge, a word of wisdom, or a revelation' that comes 'right out of heaven'.[46] During an experience of an 'exceptional anointing', God may open 'up a fresh avenue of thought', which may include new sermons.[47] Though preachers must prepare for preaching through research and study, the Spirit makes 'their words live'.[48] The Spirit may also lead to a prophetic unction that takes the message beyond the preacher's prepared outline or manuscript.[49] Thus, preachers must prepare themselves by depending on the Spirit, particularly through prayer, communion with God, reading Scripture, assimilating the truths of Scripture, and meditating on the promises in Scripture.[50]

The third essential element of powerful preaching is 'the connection between pulpit and pew'. Through this connection, the congregation can respond to a sermon, primarily at an altar, and experience the supernatural so that God's present work is manifest.[51] Preaching is connected to the altar. Preachers must give hearers the opportunity to respond to a sermon, so that people can experience the supernatural, which includes 'signs, wonders, healings, and miracles'.[52] Be-

---

[42] Hughes, *Pentecostal Preaching*, p. 19.
[43] Hughes, *Pentecostal Preaching*, pp. 19.
[44] Hughes, *Pentecostal Preaching*, pp. 20, 23-24.
[45] Hughes, *Pentecostal Preaching*, p. 24.
[46] Hughes, *Pentecostal Preaching*, p. 24.
[47] Hughes, *Pentecostal Preaching*, pp. 24-25; Holm, 'Cadences of the Heart', p. 19.
[48] Hughes, *Pentecostal Preaching*, p. 24.
[49] Hughes, *Pentecostal Preaching*, p. 25.
[50] Hughes, *Pentecostal Preaching*, p. 21.
[51] Hughes, *Pentecostal Preaching*, pp. 27, 155.
[52] Hughes, *Pentecostal Preaching*, p. 155.

cause the congregation's response is a critical component of preaching, preachers must be adequately acquainted with their hearers' lives.[53] But even an emphasis on knowing the congregation well does not neglect the role of the Spirit's present work, for the Spirit 'applies the Word to the hearts and lives of listeners'.[54] And since the Spirit applies the Word to hearers, a preacher must submit to the Spirit's will, even when hearers do not respond as the preacher expects.[55] Thus, Hughes' views on preaching privileges the role of the immediacy of God, in that a message must be received from God, Scripture provides the Word from God for preaching, and the Spirit ultimately leads the preaching to a supernatural response at the altar.

Charles T. Crabtree

Crabtree does not define preaching in general, but the way he distinguishes Pentecostal preaching from other forms of Christian preaching reveal some key elements of Christian preaching. His views also reveal that the Spirit's immediacy underlies his theological assumptions about preaching. Key elements of all Christian preaching include the Word as foundational, Jesus Christ as central to the message, and the Spirit being the one who draws people to salvation.

First, the Word is foundational to preaching because of its link to the immediacy of God. Crabtree states that 'Scripture proceeds from God, and is therefore invested with divinity that makes it as authoritative and efficient as a word orally spoken by God directly to us'.[56] Scripture is 'God-breathed', so that books on preaching must acknowledge Scripture as 'the basis for all preaching'.[57] Though Scripture includes 'variant readings', the variants are minute, so that no major doctrine in the church is compromised.[58] Since Scripture is God-breathed and subsequently authoritative, preachers must be cautious toward scholarship that questions the authority of Scripture.[59]

Finally, the last two elements – the centrality of Jesus and the Spirit's drawing power – are intimately connected, so that the Spirit's

---

[53] Hughes, *Pentecostal Preaching*, p. 27.
[54] Hughes, *Pentecostal Preaching*, p. 29.
[55] Hughes, *Pentecostal Preaching*, p. 29.
[56] Crabtree, *Pentecostal Preaching*, pp. 46-47.
[57] Crabtree, *Pentecostal Preaching*, p. 43.
[58] Crabtree, *Pentecostal Preaching*, p. 50.
[59] Crabtree, *Pentecostal Preaching*, pp. 46-49.

immediacy is necessary. Jesus Christ is the central message in preaching, but the Spirit can only reveal Christ for who he is so that people may receive salvation and make Christ their Lord.[60] Though Scripture is God-breathed, people must experience the Spirit's immediacy through illumination to understand Scripture.[61] The Spirit 'brings life to dead words'.[62] For as Paul writes, 'The letter kills, but the Spirit gives life'.[63] Preachers must have a 'Spirit-filled mind' in order to go beyond the mere 'letter itself' to 'the meaning behind the letter'.[64] Paul explains that '[t]he man without the Spirit does not accept the things that come from the Spirit of God'.[65] Thus, Scripture is authoritative for preaching since Scripture is God-breathed. But the preacher must rely on the Spirit's present work through illumination to understand the truth of Scripture – which ultimately centers on Jesus. Thus, preaching in general requires the immediacy of God, found in three interrelated elements of Scripture, Jesus, and the Spirit.

Crabtree differentiates Pentecostal preaching from other forms of Christian preaching, explaining that Pentecostal preachers experience a qualitatively greater experience of the Spirit's present work, which subsequently leads to a greater experience of God's presence for preaching and the altar. All Christians receive 'an enduement' of the Spirit at salvation, so that the Spirit enables preachers who are not Pentecostal.[66] But when preachers receive Spirit baptism with the evidence of tongues – a classical Pentecostal understanding of Spirit baptism – preachers receive a 'special enduement of power' from the Spirit for preaching.[67] Spirit baptism better enables preachers to 'emphasise Jesus Christ and Him crucified' and base the sermon on Scripture. Pentecostal preaching 'will also be accompanied by the living works of Christ in supernatural demonstration'.[68] While non-Pentecostal preachers – like Billy Graham – may experience tremendous

---

[60] Crabtree, *Pentecostal Preaching*, pp. 33-34.

[61] Crabtree, *Pentecostal Preaching*, pp. 115-16.

[62] Crabtree, *Pentecostal Preaching*, p. 115; 2 Cor. 3.6.

[63] Crabtree, *Pentecostal Preaching*, p. 115; 2 Cor. 3.6.

[64] Crabtree, *Pentecostal Preaching*, p. 115.

[65] Crabtree, *Pentecostal Preaching*, p. 115; 1 Cor. 2.14.

[66] Crabtree, *Pentecostal Preaching*, p. 30.

[67] Crabtree, *Pentecostal Preaching*, p. 31.

[68] Crabtree, *Pentecostal Preaching*, p. 35.

results in preaching as it relates to salvation, Pentecostal preachers are empowered to experience other supernatural results. Some supernatural results include: overcoming demonic activity; being sensitive to the Spirit's leading, even when spontaneous; an expression of the gifts of the Spirit; and miracles.[69] Thus, Pentecostal preaching is distinguished from non-Pentecostal Christian preaching, solely because Spirit baptism enables preachers to experience the Spirit's present work to a greater degree. The experience of Spirit baptism leads to a response that generates a greater experience of the immediacy of God through the supernatural – most notably at an altar.

Finally, Crabtree elevates the role of preaching over all other expressions of corporate worship, stating that preaching is central for Pentecostal churches – likely because preaching leads to an immediacy of God through salvation and the supernatural. Preaching is central so that all other expressions of corporate worship 'must support and lead to a more effective pulpit'.[70] Thus, Crabtree's general views on preaching and the altar delve frequently into the importance of the immediacy of God. The key ways the immediacy of God is showcased in his views on preaching and the altar include the ideas that: preaching is based on Scripture, which provides the Word of God; the Spirit enables people to understand the central message of Jesus Christ; and an altar is a key component for Pentecostal preaching because it provides opportunity for an experience of the supernatural.

Haddon W. Robinson

Robinson's understanding of preaching is shaped by his view that the immediacy of God is experienced through the reading and hearing of Scripture – God's primary means of communication. Further, the Spirit applies Scripture to preachers and subsequently for those who hear a sermon. First, Scripture is crucial for humanity to receive and hear because 'God speaks through the Bible', and 'is the major tool of communication by which He addresses individuals today'.[71] Scripture is an authoritative Word from God. Since Scripture is the Word of God, preachers must 'preach the Word' – the Scriptures[72] For '[t]hrough the preaching of the Scriptures, God encounters men and

---

[69] Crabtree, *Pentecostal Preaching*, p. 35.
[70] Crabtree, *Pentecostal Preaching*, p. 10.
[71] Robinson, *Biblical Preaching*, p. 20.
[72] Robinson, *Biblical Preaching*, p. 20.

women to bring them to salvation (2 Tim. 3:15) and to richness and ripeness of Christian character (vv. 16-17)'.[73] 2 Timothy 3.15-17 reveals that the Scriptures are invested with the same authority as a Word from God.[74] When Scripture is not foundational for a message prepared for preaching, the preaching lacks divine authority and fails to be Christian preaching.[75] Only when Scripture is foundational to the sermon, is the sermon an authoritative word from God.

Expository preaching is the best approach to preaching that ensures that preaching is based on Scripture. Expository preaching carries 'the force of divine authority' so that the immediacy of God is experienced through God's communication with people.[76] Preaching includes the 'interaction' of three elements: 'God, the preacher, and the congregation', so an understanding of expository preaching must include these three elements.[77] Taking these three elements into consideration, expository preaching can be defined as

> *the communication of a biblical concept, derived from and transmitted through a historical, grammatical, and literary study of a passage in its context, which the Holy Spirit first applies to the personality and experience of the preacher, then through the preacher, applies to the hearers.*[78]

The content of the message is founded upon and driven by the results of one's study of Scripture. Since Scripture is a Word from God, ensuring faithful witness to Scripture in preaching requires rigorous study.

The second element in Robinson's understanding of expository preaching that includes the immediacy of God, is the idea that the Spirit applies the biblical concept studied to the preacher, and subsequently applies the biblical concept to the hearers of preaching. First, the Spirit's immediacy provides the application of the biblical concept for the preacher through their study. This reveals that 'God's dealing with the preacher' is 'at the center of the process'.[79] This is

---

[73] Robinson, *Biblical Preaching*, p. 20.

[74] Robinson, *Biblical Preaching*, p. 20.

[75] Robinson, *Biblical Preaching*, p. 20.

[76] Robinson, *Biblical Preaching*, p. 20.

[77] Robinson, *Biblical Preaching*, p. 21.

[78] Robinson, *Biblical Preaching*, p. 21 (emphasis original).

[79] Robinson, *Biblical Preaching*, p. 25.

because 'God is more interested in developing messengers than messages'.[80] Who the preacher becomes after the Spirit's application of Scripture is crucial. And since the primary way that the Spirit confronts people is through Scripture, preachers 'must learn to listen to God before speaking for God'.[81]

Second, the Spirit's immediacy is available through the preaching, whereby the Spirit applies the biblical concept to the hearers of a sermon. To ensure the Spirit applies the biblical concept, preachers must work at developing applications that arise out of the study of Scripture, and adequately address the social context of the hearers.[82] Thus, Robinson's understanding of preaching includes the immediacy of God, so that preachers must preach the Scriptures. Scripture is the Word of God, and one should expect the Spirit to apply the Scripture to both the preacher and congregation.

Conclusion

The approach to preaching among Pentecostals has been significantly shaped by an emphasis on an experience of the Spirit, the authority of Scripture, and an altar experience for miracles to occur, evidenced in Hughes' and Crabtree's approach. But the inclusion of Robinson's approach to preaching shows the affinities between Pentecostals and Evangelicals in North America today, particularly related to the authority of Scripture for preaching. The ethos of Pentecostal preaching, however, is not entirely consistent because of the variety of impulses represented in Hughes, Crabtree, and Robinson. Thus, the next two chapters continue the exploration of preaching and the altar within Pentecostalism through the lens of the three leaders described above, providing both a description and analysis of their views.

---

[80] Robinson, *Biblical Preaching*, p. 27.
[81] Robinson, *Biblical Preaching*, p. 27.
[82] Robinson, *Biblical Preaching*, pp. 28-29.

6

FROM PREACHING TO THE ALTAR

The previous chapter revealed how the Spirit's present work among Pentecostals is being maintained among some Pentecostal leaders, though there are divergent approaches in light of the Evangelical influence upon Pentecostals (evidenced in Haddon Robinson's approach to preaching). This chapter follows up on the previous one, describing four themes involved in preaching: the preparation necessary to be a preacher, the preparation required for sermons, the event of preaching, and the altar. Each leader's approach to the four themes is described, followed by an analysis in the next chapter. How an emphasis on the direct and present work of the Spirit in Pentecostalism relates to these three leaders' approach is highlighted throughout.

Preparing to Preach

Before someone can develop and preach a sermon, certain qualities are necessary to be an effective Christian preacher. The types of requirements found among these leaders include the need to be called of God to preach, an experience of Spirit baptism, being continually filled with the Spirit, character, and being gifted by God to preach. The unique requirements highlighted by Hughes, Crabtree, and Robinson follows.

Ray H. Hughes
The immediacy of God is a key qualification for Pentecostal preaching in Hughes' views on the need for a call of God, Spirit baptism, a fresh anointing, and one's self-concept for preaching. But he also

delves into the need for character, which is not explicitly linked to the immediacy of God. First, regardless of whether or not someone experiences the call of God through miraculous or ordinary means, potential preachers must 'first look into the face of Jesus and hear His straightforward, unequivocal command, "Take up … (your) cross daily, and follow me" (Luke 9:23)'.[1] This call gives 'inner conviction' and 'certain knowledge' that God is giving 'direction', and that he is 'the Employer' and 'Judge'.[2] Only God calls ministers to preach, so the church's role is just to sanction a minister's call.[3] Those God calls, God also 'qualifies' for the task they are called to.[4] And though the call and qualification are inseparable, 'the gift of ministry must be rekindled and cultivated'.[5] Furthermore, the primary evidence of the call of God on the preacher's life is that he or she is living out the call to 'holy living'.[6]

Second, Hughes argues for the need of an experience of the Spirit's immediacy for prophetic preaching, available through Spirit baptism. 'Preaching at its best is prophetic'.[7] Prophetic preachers speak 'for God'.[8] Preachers 'receive authority to speak through the Spirit', and their 'message comes through the Holy Spirit'.[9] For instance, Peter received the empowerment of the Spirit on the Day of Pentecost (found in Acts 2) to preach prophetically.[10] Prophecy is 'a distinctive gift of Pentecost'.[11] For Peter explained that their experience of the Spirit – Spirit baptism – on the Day of Pentecost fulfills Joel's prophecy that the Spirit would enable people to prophesy.[12] Spirit baptism 'is an experience subsequent to a clean heart and is an enduement of power for service with the initial evidence of speaking

---

[1] Hughes, *Pentecostal Preaching*, pp. 49-50.

[2] Hughes, *Pentecostal Preaching*, p. 52.

[3] Hughes, *Pentecostal Preaching*, p. 69.

[4] Hughes, *Pentecostal Preaching*, p. 53.

[5] Hughes, *Pentecostal Preaching*, p. 53.

[6] Hughes, *Pentecostal Preaching*, p. 51.

[7] Hughes, *Pentecostal Preaching*, p. 153.

[8] Hughes, *Pentecostal Preaching*, p. 138.

[9] Hughes, *Pentecostal Preaching*, p. 138.

[10] Hughes, *Pentecostal Preaching*, pp. 142-43.

[11] Hughes, *Pentecostal Preaching*, p. 137.

[12] Hughes, *Pentecostal Preaching*, p. 137.

with other tongues as the Spirit gives utterance'.[13] Spirit baptism provides power for preaching in order to: witness 'convincingly', overcome 'obstacles' and withstand 'opposition', evangelise, and ultimately help to fulfill the Great Commission.[14] Thus, to preach prophetically, preachers must experience the Spirit's immediacy through Spirit baptism.

Hughes believes certain conditions must be met to receive Spirit baptism. First, only Christians can be baptised in the Spirit. Jesus explains that the 'world', or unbelievers, cannot receive Spirit baptism.[15] Second, though one may be a Christian, being converted and 'born of the Spirit', Spirit baptism is a distinct experience from salvation.[16] Even Paul recognised that some Christians may believe in Christ, but not have experienced Spirit baptism yet.[17] Thus, Spirit baptism is available only to Christians and is a distinct and subsequent experience to salvation.

Hughes shares three steps for Christians to experience Spirit baptism. And though he acknowledges that Spirit baptism is available to all believers, not just ordained vocational ministers, how this experience shapes preachers is highlighted here.[18] The first is to '[c]onfess your spiritual emptiness, then claim your rightful heritage as a believer'.[19] Spirit baptism is available to all preachers who claim the promise of this experience, which gives divine power to preach.[20] Second, '[t]his fullness of God is obtained only when you come to the position that you can say, "Cost what it may, I am willing to make

[13] Ray H. Hughes, 'The Baptism with the Holy Ghost', in Ray H. Hughes (ed.), *Who is the Holy Ghost? A Study of the Person and Work of the Holy Spirit* (Cleveland, TN: Pathway Press, rev. edn, 2004), p. 149.

[14] Ray H. Hughes, 'The Holy Ghost and Power', in Ray H. Hughes (ed.), *Who is the Holy Ghost? A Study of the Person and Work of the Holy Spirit* (Cleveland, TN: Pathway Press, rev. edn, 2004), p. 87; Ray H. Hughes, 'Speaking in Tongues', in Ray H. Hughes (ed.), *Who is the Holy Ghost? A Study of the Person and Work of the Holy Spirit* (Cleveland, TN: Pathway Press, rev. edn, 2004), p. 118.

[15] Ray H. Hughes, 'How to Receive Power', in Ray H. Hughes (ed.), *Who is the Holy Ghost? A Study of the Person and Work of the Holy Spirit* (Cleveland, TN: Pathway Press, rev. edn, 2004), p. 126.

[16] Hughes, 'How to Receive Power', p. 125; 'The Baptism With the Holy Ghost', pp. 143-53.

[17] Hughes, 'How to Receive Power', pp. 125-26; Acts 19.1-2.

[18] Hughes, 'How to Receive Power', pp. 127-28.

[19] Hughes, 'How to Receive Power', p. 127.

[20] Hughes, 'How to Receive Power', pp. 127-28.

my full surrender to God and appropriate the blessing for myself'".[21] Preachers must purge themselves of being 'full of self, preconceived ideas and prejudices', which keeps them from an experience of Spirit baptism.[22] Thirdly, after one's 'heart is truly prepared, the Bible says, He gives "the Holy Spirit to them that ask him" (Luke 11:13)'.[23] And after asking for Spirit baptism, preachers must '[a]ccept this blessing'.[24] They must yield their 'faculties to the Spirit', for they do 'not initiate the utterance'.[25] While a person 'is not passive', they do 'not form the words to be spoken of' on their 'own accord'.[26] The Spirit gives a person 'the words', and people merely speak 'as the Spirit gives utterance'.[27]

Third, Hughes believes that 'maintaining' a 'fresh anointing' of the Spirit – a continual experience of the Spirit's immediacy – is crucial in the life of the preacher in order to preach best.[28] Preachers can remain 'sensitive to the Spirit' to maintain a 'fresh anointing' primarily 'through prayer and fasting'.[29] An experience of the Spirit's anointing further enables preachers to preach prophetically. Preachers can remain yielded to the Spirit through eight ways. The eight include: cultivating a 'personal relationship with Christ'; practicing 'intercessory prayer'; seeking 'God for a message, not just a sermon'; speaking from one's 'heart and soul'; asking God to direct one's 'performance in the pulpit'; remaining 'sensitive to the Spirit'; being 'bold in … obedience'; and expecting results when one preaches.[30]

Fourth, Hughes argues that a preacher's 'self-concept' determines 'the joy and success' of his or her ministry, delving into both explicit

[21] Hughes, 'How to Receive Power', p. 128.
[22] Hughes, 'How to Receive Power', p. 128.
[23] Hughes, 'How to Receive Power', p. 128.
[24] Hughes, 'How to Receive Power', p. 128.
[25] Ray H. Hughes, 'Speaking With Tongues at Will'. Online: http://rayhhughes.com/uploads/SPEAKING_WITH_TONGUES_AT_WILL.doc.
[26] Hughes, 'Speaking With Tongues at Will'
[27] Hughes, 'Speaking With Tongues at Will'
[28] Hughes, *Pentecostal Preaching*, p. 139.
[29] Hughes, *Pentecostal Preaching*, p. 139. Though Hughes uses masculine language for all preachers in general, he is open to both male and female preachers. Hughes, *Pentecostal Preaching*, p. 167.
[30] Hughes, *Pentecostal Preaching*, p. 152.

and non-explicit associations with the immediacy of God.[31] Five concepts, found in Scripture, are concepts that God applies to the identity of a preacher. First, preachers experience an immediacy of God because they are *'ordained of God'*.[32] God initiates the call to preach, choosing and ordaining preachers.[33] Second, *'Preachers are ministers of Christ'*, because the ministry of preaching is done in Christ's name.[34] Third, *'Preachers are stewards of God'* since they must manage 'God's affairs on earth'.[35] Fourth, *'Preachers are ambassadors of God'*, speaking 'in Christ's name and with His authority'.[36] Fifth, *'Preachers are ministers of reconciliation'*, which includes reconciliation with God and people.[37] The five concepts regarding the identity of the preacher are important because it helps preachers understand who they are as God views them.[38]

Finally, Hughes shares six attributes necessary for the preacher that are not explicitly related to the Spirit's immediacy, but show his concern for the preacher's character.[39] These characteristics show evidence of a preacher's calling.[40] The first is a love and care for people. More than any other characteristic, a genuine love for people contributes to the success of preachers who may not be very skilled as public speakers.[41] Second, the conversation of a preacher is crucial, since he or she is viewed as a spokesperson for God.[42] Preachers, for instance, must ensure that they are faithful to the verbal commitments they make and be careful of the type of humour they use.[43] Third, preachers must conduct their personal life with self-discipline.[44] Fourth, preachers must show respect for their family, peers, and others in

---

[31] Hughes, *Pentecostal Preaching*, p. 52.
[32] Hughes, *Pentecostal Preaching*, pp. 68-69 (emphasis original).
[33] Hughes, *Pentecostal Preaching*, pp. 68-69.
[34] Hughes, *Pentecostal Preaching*, p. 69 (emphasis original).
[35] Hughes, *Pentecostal Preaching*, p. 70 (emphasis original).
[36] Hughes, *Pentecostal Preaching*, p. 71 (emphasis original).
[37] Hughes, *Pentecostal Preaching*, p. 72 (emphasis original).
[38] Hughes, *Pentecostal Preaching*, p. 72.
[39] Byrd also acknowledges these issues in Hughes' approach. See 'Formulation of a Classical Pentecostal Homiletic', pp. 92-94.
[40] Hughes, *Pentecostal Preaching*, p. 51.
[41] Hughes, *Pentecostal Preaching*, p. 73.
[42] Hughes, *Pentecostal Preaching*, pp. 73-74.
[43] Hughes, *Pentecostal Preaching*, pp. 73-74.
[44] Hughes, *Pentecostal Preaching*, p. 75.

general.[45] When preachers fail to show respect for others, people eventually lose respect for the preacher.[46] Fifth, preachers must be committed to a denomination. Loyalty to a fellowship of other believers beyond one's local church is important because Christ's church is more than about one individual.[47] People are more willing to invest in the broad goals of an organisation rather than one person's goals.[48] Finally, preachers must be careful in their relationships with the opposite gender. Though Hughes is open to both male and female preachers, his comments on how to treat those of the opposite gender are addressed primarily to male preachers (though his comments could likely be applied to female preachers also). Male preachers must be careful with females in the church by: giving credit to women for their contributions; not being 'over-solicitous' with ministry requests so that the focus is not on serving the preacher rather than God; giving attention to their own marriage; ensuring that any contact with women are conducted 'in an open, professional, and upright manner'; taking time for prayer and reading Scripture; and while being careful to avoid being the subject of gossip, not allowing others' views to keep them from ministering to the needs of people.[49] Thus, Hughes commends an experience of the immediacy of God for preaching by highlighting the importance of a call of God; the experience of Spirit baptism; maintaining a fresh anointing of the Spirit; and maintaining a proper self-concept, which displays both an emphasis on the need for an immediacy of God and other concerns for the preacher. Hughes' six recommendations for preachers reveal the importance of character, which show concern for the issues facing preachers that go beyond an explicit reference to an experience of the Spirit's immediacy (though show evidence of God's call on the preacher).

Charles T. Crabtree

Crabtree provides an extensive discussion on the importance of the preacher's lifestyle throughout his book on preaching, which includes an experience of the immediacy of God through the call of God, Spirit baptism, and being continually filled with the Spirit. First, the

[45] Hughes, *Pentecostal Preaching*, p. 75.
[46] Hughes, *Pentecostal Preaching*, p. 75.
[47] Hughes, *Pentecostal Preaching*, p. 76.
[48] Hughes, *Pentecostal Preaching*, p. 76.
[49] Hughes, *Pentecostal Preaching*, pp. 78-79.

call of God is important because it gives preachers authority. Preachers receive authority from God when they respond to the 'internal' work of God through the Spirit, rather than any other 'external stimuli' – whether people, society, and tradition.[50] 'Ultimate loyalty must be to the living God, not to a tradition kept alive through an external program or process. "The letter kills [even the most beautifully structured and appealing], but the Spirit gives life".'[51] Just as Jesus received his divine mission and authority from the Father, preachers must also derive their commission and authority to preach from God.[52] Maintaining this authority from God requires regular fresh encounters with God.[53] Preachers must seek to please God rather than people, since pleasing people leads to losing authority from God and respect from people.[54]

Second, Crabtree argues that Spirit baptism is crucial for preachers because it leads to supernatural results in preaching. Spirit baptism is a gift that any Christian can receive by faith within the context of praise and prayer, whereby the initial evidence of this gift is speaking in tongues.[55] A preacher who has received Spirit baptism is different from those who have not experienced Spirit baptism.[56] Those who have not experienced Spirit baptism include the disciples whom Christ 'breathed' on and said, 'Receive the Spirit', prior to the Day of Pentecost.[57] Jesus gave his disciples an 'enduement of the Spirit' so that they were 'ordained and empowered to preach' the gospel.[58] Billy Graham's ministry is an example of this level of the Spirit's reception in a preacher, because 'the Spirit of God has attended his preaching, drawing thousands into the Kingdom by convicting, saving, and baptizing into the body of Christ'.[59] Thus, every Christian preacher has an 'enduement of the Spirit', so that the Spirit draws people to God through preaching.

---

[50] Crabtree, *Pentecostal Preaching*, pp. 14-19.
[51] Crabtree, *Pentecostal Preaching*, p. 15. Commentary is Crabtree's.
[52] Crabtree, *Pentecostal Preaching*, pp. 16-18.
[53] Crabtree, *Pentecostal Preaching*, pp. 14-19.
[54] Crabtree, *Pentecostal Preaching*, pp. 6, 14-19, 21, 98, 130.
[55] Crabtree, *Pentecostal Preaching*, pp. 164-66.
[56] Crabtree, *Pentecostal Preaching*, p. 27.
[57] Crabtree, *Pentecostal Preaching*, p. 30; Jn 20.21-23; Acts 2.4.
[58] Crabtree, *Pentecostal Preaching*, pp. 30-31.
[59] Crabtree, *Pentecostal Preaching*, p. 31.

Crabtree explains that Spirit baptism enables preachers to experience the goals of revealing Jesus and supernatural results, which Jesus promised. For Jesus expected the disciples to wait and receive 'a special enduement of power from on high' – Spirit baptism. When Jesus told his disciples to wait for Spirit baptism, the disciples could have resisted since they already experienced an 'enduement' of the Spirit. But they did not resist since they had not received this 'special enduement' of the Spirit.[60] Two linked implications of Spirit baptism for Pentecostal preaching include a revelation of Jesus and supernatural results. First, '[w]ith divine authority, the Pentecostal pulpit will reveal Jesus Christ as He is, through the power of the Spirit resulting in living revelation and truth'.[61] Second, this revelation of Jesus Christ 'will also be accompanied by the living works of Christ in supernatural demonstration' – miracles.[62]

The reason supernatural results follow preachers who have experienced Spirit baptism depends on linking two of Christ's teachings. The first is Christ's promise to his disciples that they would experience 'greater works' when he went to the Father.[63] The second is Christ's admonition that they would be better off when he left since the Spirit would come and they could experience Spirit baptism.[64] Thus, through Spirit baptism the preacher can experience 'greater works'. 'Greater works' includes a greater revelation of Christ and supernatural results for preachers who are baptised in the Spirit.[65]

Finally, Crabtree stresses that preachers must be 'continually filled with the Spirit'.[66] Since Spirit baptism is an 'initial' one-time experience, preachers must also strive to be 'continually filled with the Spirit'.[67] The goal of being continually filled with the Spirit 'can be met only by first dying daily to oneself and then being renewed inwardly through the work of the Spirit'.[68] Five dimensions are neces-

---

[60] Crabtree, *Pentecostal Preaching*, p. 31.
[61] Crabtree, *Pentecostal Preaching*, p. 33.
[62] Crabtree, *Pentecostal Preaching*, p. 35.
[63] Crabtree, *Pentecostal Preaching*, p. 36; Jn 14.12.
[64] Crabtree, *Pentecostal Preaching*, p. 36; Jn 16.7.
[65] Crabtree, *Pentecostal Preaching*, pp. 36-37.
[66] Crabtree, *Pentecostal Preaching*, p. 110.
[67] Crabtree, *Pentecostal Preaching*, p. 110.
[68] Crabtree, *Pentecostal Preaching*, p. 111.

sary to be a 'Spirit-filled' preacher: 1) a Spirit-filled character, display-
ing the fruit of the Spirit; 2) a Spirit-filled mind, since 'the truth of
God' 'can be understood only through the lens of the Spirit'; 3) being
in continual communication with God – speaking in tongues and
hearing from God 'through the instrumentality of the Spirit'; 4)
Spirit-filled direction, whereby the Spirit guides the preacher before
and during the sermon; and 5) expecting signs and wonders.[69] Thus,
an experience of the immediacy of God is crucial for a preacher's
identity and preparation, notably in their need for a call of God to
preach, an experience of Spirit baptism, and being continually filled
with the Spirit.

Haddon W. Robinson

The role of the immediacy of God for the preparation of preachers
in Robinson's thought finds it place in two ways: some are gifted by
God to be preachers and the Spirit shapes preachers through the
study of Scripture for character growth. He also delves into issues
not explicitly related to the immediacy of God, such as the idea that
preachers are heralds and that they must have a desire to connect
Scripture to contemporary life. First, the idea that some receive the
gift to preach from God is a minor point in Robinson's work, since it
can only be found in the two prefaces of his updated book on preaching.[70] Nevertheless, he acknowledges that God may gift both men and
women to preach.[71]

Second, Robinson acknowledges character growth as important
for the preacher, which is chiefly experienced through the Spirit's immediacy available through the study of Scripture.[72] Character transformation occurs primarily through the study of Scripture because
the Spirit confronts people 'primarily through the Bible'.[73] When a
preacher studies Scripture, the 'Spirit studies' the preacher.[74] The
Spirit primarily develops preachers through the study of Scripture in
Robinson's discussion on the preparation of preachers.

While not explicitly tied to the immediacy of God, Robinson
makes one brief reference about the identity of a preacher, stating

---

[69] Crabtree, *Pentecostal Preaching*, pp. 112,114-15, 116-18, 118-20, 120-22.
[70] Robinson, *Biblical Preaching*, pp. 10, 14.
[71] Robinson, *Biblical Preaching*, p. 10.
[72] Robinson, *Biblical Preaching*, pp. 26-27.
[73] Robinson, *Biblical Preaching*, p. 27.
[74] Robinson, *Biblical Preaching*, p. 26.

that they are heralds.[75] Preachers can be viewed as heralds since '[p]reach means to cry out, herald, or exhort'.[76] Preachers, thus, must 'speak as heralds', whereby 'they must cry out "the Word"'.[77] Since Robinson focuses primarily on what it takes to preach the Word (Scripture), it is understandable that the only reference he makes to the identity of a Christian preacher is that they are a 'herald' of the Word.

Finally, Robinson argues that preachers must have a strong desire to connect Scripture to life. While this point is not explicitly linked to the immediacy of God, it ultimately leads to an experience of the immediacy of God whereby people can hear the Word of God from Scripture through preaching.[78] A desire to connect Scripture to life is even more crucial than the 'gift' to preach.[79]

Thus, the only discussion on the preparation of preachers in Robinson's thought that includes the immediacy of God, is a brief reference to being gifted by God to preach and that the Spirit promotes character growth in preachers when they study Scripture. Other brief references to the identity and character of a preacher relate to preachers being heralds and that preachers must have a desire to connect Scripture to contemporary life.

Preparing a Sermon/Message

Hughes, Crabtree, and Robinson provide a number of recommendations for how a preacher may prepare and construct their message to preach. The types of recommendations they share for the preparation of sermons include the need to receive a direct message from God, understanding hearers, studying Scripture, discerning the type of preaching to use, preparing a manuscript of the sermon, and making Christ central to the message. The views of the three leaders follow.

---

[75] Robinson, *Biblical Preaching*, p. 20.
[76] Robinson, *Biblical Preaching*, p. 20.
[77] Robinson, *Biblical Preaching*, p. 20.
[78] Robinson, *Biblical Preaching*, p. 14.
[79] Robinson, *Biblical Preaching*, p. 14.

Ray H. Hughes

Hughes' views on preparing to preach a message are founded upon preachers first experiencing the immediacy of God, whereby they receive a 'message' from God for his people, and that preachers understand their audience so that the congregation experiences the Spirit's work in their lives through the preaching.[80] He also includes elements for preparation not explicitly linked to the immediacy of God, including three recommendations for studying Scripture and discerning which of four types of preaching to use. First, the most thorough study of Scripture and other resources 'will come to naught if the minister has not seen the face of God'.[81] A preacher must call upon, depend upon, and seek the aid of the Spirit for studying Scripture for the development of a message.[82] God must be sought to receive a message from him to share.

Second, Hughes also argues that preachers 'must first know and understand' their audience as they prepare, which enables them to invite the Spirit's comfort for the audience's unique needs.[83] Ministers 'must be a student of human nature', taking the time required to get to know the various issues their audiences face. Knowing the type of issues the audience is facing will provide the 'inspiration to pray and to search the Word' for what to preach.[84] Knowledge of the congregation enables preachers to share the 'promises of God' in Scripture adequately, which address the issues of the audience with the comfort of the Spirit in preaching.[85]

Receiving a message from God for preaching (an experience of the immediacy of God), though, does not preclude the need for studying Scripture in Hughes' thought. While seeking God is a necessary first step, and required during the study of Scripture, preachers who fail to study 'have no right to call upon God to make up the deficits of their idleness'.[86] Hughes thus provides three general recommendations for the study of Scripture. The first is the need to have a

---

[80] Hughes, *Pentecostal Preaching*, pp. 150-51.

[81] Hughes, *Pentecostal Preaching*, p. 93.

[82] Hughes, *Pentecostal Preaching*, p. 94.

[83] Hughes, *Pentecostal Preaching*, p. 103.

[84] Hughes, *Pentecostal Preaching*, p. 103.

[85] Hughes, *Pentecostal Preaching*, p. 103.

[86] Hughes, *Pentecostal Preaching*, p. 100.

'broad understanding of the Bible'.[87] The entire context of Scripture must be understood, considered, and used when preaching. Preachers must not just focus on a few isolated passages of Scripture when discerning the meaning of Scripture for preaching.

Second, preachers must invest in 'a good, basic library' that contains a variety of tools for studying Scripture. A few tools include: a study Bible, an exhaustive concordance, a Bible dictionary, a topical Bible, a Bible handbook, a commentary, a Bible encyclopedia, a set of word studies, individual commentaries, a Bible atlas, Old and New Testament surveys, and other books of the preacher's own special interest.[88]

Third, preachers should make use of the different types of Bible study methods available.[89] Hughes commends Richard Warren's twelve methods, which include the: *'Devotional Method'*, *'Chapter Summary Method'*, *'Character Quality Method'*, *'Thematic Method'*, *'Biographical Method'*, *'Topical Method'*, *'Word Study Method'*, *'Book Background Method'*, *'Book Survey Method'*, *'Chapter Analysis Method'*, *'Book Synthesis Method'*, and *'Verse-by-Verse Analysis Method'*.[90] While a discussion on what each of these methods includes is beyond the scope of this chapter, what is significant is that Hughes is open to a variety of methods for Bible study. The method of study chosen depends on the goals of the preacher.[91]

After studying Scripture, preachers must discern the type of preaching to use. Hughes acknowledges the role of at least four types of preaching, though he acknowledges that there are other types – which he does not describe.[92] The first is *'expository preaching'*, whereby a preacher comments on a 'full chapter' or 'lengthy passage of Scripture ... in a systematic way'.[93] The second is *'preaching from a text'*, whereby the preacher shares ideas based on a short passage of Scripture.[94] The third is *'theme preaching'*, whereby a number of passages of

---

[87] Hughes, *Pentecostal Preaching*, p. 94.
[88] Hughes, *Pentecostal Preaching*, p. 95.
[89] Hughes, *Pentecostal Preaching*, p. 96.
[90] Hughes, *Pentecostal Preaching*, pp. 97-98 (emphasis original). Also see Byrd, 'Formulation of a Classical Pentecostal Homiletic', p. 103.
[91] Hughes, *Pentecostal Preaching*, p. 98.
[92] Hughes, *Pentecostal Preaching*, p. 110.
[93] Hughes, *Pentecostal Preaching*, p. 110 (emphasis original).
[94] Hughes, *Pentecostal Preaching*, p. 110 (emphasis original).

Scripture are chosen that follow a 'logical sequence'.[95] The fourth is *'subject preaching'*, whereby the subject is chosen based on 'current events, history, or from any other point of interest upon which the minister develops his own thoughts'.[96] Ministers must choose what type of preaching should be used, even if it combines some of the types available, which can best help them reach their goals for the message.[97]

An experience of the immediacy of God for preparing a message/sermon is important in Hughes' thought, for preachers must first seek the Spirit's aid for the study of Scripture for preaching. Preachers must also know the audience well enough in order to address the needs of the audience, so that the audience can receive the Spirit's comfort through preaching. But Hughes addresses other important facets of preparing sermons – not explicitly tied to the Spirit's immediacy, though still dependent on the Spirit's aid – such as his three recommendations for the study of Scripture and the need to use the right type of preaching that is consistent with the goals of the sermon.

Charles T. Crabtree

Crabtree's approach to preparing a sermon underscores the Spirit's immediacy in four ways. And while not explicitly linked to an experience of the Spirit, he suggests three types of sermons one can use. The first way he highlights the Spirit's immediacy for sermon preparation is through an emphasis on a 'revelational hermeneutic'.[98] A 'revelational hermeneutic' comes by the Spirit who gives understanding of theological truth.[99] A revelation from the Spirit enables preachers to know 'many things' that 'the highly educated theologian cannot learn apart from the Spirit'.[100] The Apostle Peter is an example of someone who was uneducated, but gained understanding of Christ's identity and more through the Spirit's revelation.[101] Preachers gain

---

[95] Hughes, *Pentecostal Preaching*, p. 110 (emphasis original).
[96] Hughes, *Pentecostal Preaching*, p. 110 (emphasis original).
[97] Hughes, *Pentecostal Preaching*, p. 110.
[98] Crabtree, *Pentecostal Preaching*, pp. 142-44; Holm, 'Cadences of the Heart', p. 20.
[99] Crabtree, *Pentecostal Preaching*, pp. 142-44.
[100] Crabtree, *Pentecostal Preaching*, p. 143.
[101] Crabtree, *Pentecostal Preaching*, pp. 143-44.

their 'highest education' through 'an intimacy with Christ by an intimacy in the Spirit'.[102] The first place to start the preparation for a sermon is through intimacy with the Spirit.

Second, preachers must also ensure that Christ is central to the message, since the Spirit leads to witnessing to Christ.[103] For Christ stated, 'When the Comforter is come … he shall testify of me'.[104] The various aspects of Christ, such as his humanity, lordship, divinity, and redemptive work, are important to present in the sermon.[105] The Spirit will make Christ relevant for the needs of humanity, so the preacher does not need to try to make Christ relevant.[106]

Third, Crabtree shares how preachers must experience the Spirit's immediacy when studying Scripture and other resources to appropriate their learning for preaching. Preachers must study Scripture first within the context of the text with the Holy Spirit as guide, and then confer with other resources.[107] Preachers have a responsibility to study and clarify what Scripture conveys.[108] Consulting other resources only comes later in the process of study, in order to ensure that one's 'mind has been "programmed" by the Spirit' first.[109] Others' views must 'not drive the message', but 'only enhance and enrich the truth' when beginning with Scripture and the Spirit for guidance.[110] Crabtree acknowledges that Pentecostal preachers must not be lazy, presuming to rely on the anointing – an experience of the Spirit – but must be disciplined to study and prepare for preaching.[111] Even while preachers read 'books and commentaries' by others, Crabtree states, '[l]et the Spirit impress your thinking as you read others'.[112] For even as preachers consult other resources, preachers must be yielded to what the Spirit impresses while reading.[113] Preachers

---

[102] Crabtree, *Pentecostal Preaching*, p. 144; Holm, 'Cadences of the Heart', p. 20.

[103] Crabtree, *Pentecostal Preaching*, p. 145.

[104] Crabtree, *Pentecostal Preaching*, p. 145; Jn 15.26, KJV.

[105] Crabtree, *Pentecostal Preaching*, pp. 145-47.

[106] Crabtree, *Pentecostal Preaching*, pp. 147-48; Holm, 'Cadences of the Heart', p. 20.

[107] Crabtree, *Pentecostal Preaching*, pp. 194-96.

[108] Crabtree, *Pentecostal Preaching*, p. 47.

[109] Crabtree, *Pentecostal Preaching*, p. 195.

[110] Crabtree, *Pentecostal Preaching*, p. 195.

[111] Crabtree, *Pentecostal Preaching*, p. 7.

[112] Crabtree, *Pentecostal Preaching*, p. 195.

[113] Crabtree, *Pentecostal Preaching*, p. 195.

must only use ideas that 'excite' the preacher, since ideas that do not influence the preacher will not benefit the congregation either.[114] Crabtree's discussion on how to study Scripture and other resources for the preparation of sermons is brief, relative to the other subjects he addresses in his book.[115]

Fourth, preachers prepare for a sermon by creating an outline and manuscript, though the outline and manuscript must be subservient to the Spirit's direction while preaching.[116] Writing out all the details of what may be shared in the sermon helps ensure that the preacher takes the time to 'articulate difficult concepts'.[117] A manuscript, however, is not to be memorized, for preachers must be open to spontaneous leadings of the Spirit, which may not be articulated in the manuscript.[118] Thus, preparing an outline and manuscript are helpful tools to prepare for preaching, but must be subservient to the leading of the Spirit during the event of preaching.

Finally, Crabtree acknowledges at least three types of communication styles, found in Jesus' approach, which can be used for one's preparation to prepare a sermon. Though these three types of preaching are not linked to an experience of the Spirit, they can help facilitate the immediacy of God for preaching. The three types include personal conversations; 'teaching truth', which he describes as 'Bible teaching and exposition preaching;' and 'proclaiming truth'.[119] Personal conversations are about sharing the gospel with an individual – preaching to an individual.[120] Rather than trying to think about preaching to a crowd, viewing one's ministry as preaching to individuals helps keep the ministry personal.[121] Teaching truth is an approach that is more expositional, so that one may be referred to as a 'teacher-preacher'.[122] He refers to 'proclaiming truth' as 'preaching' the gospel, but does not adequately distinguish this type of preaching

---

[114] Crabtree, *Pentecostal Preaching*, p. 195.

[115] Crabtree, *Pentecostal Preaching*, pp. 193-203.

[116] Crabtree, *Pentecostal Preaching*, pp. 196-203.

[117] Crabtree, *Pentecostal Preaching*, p. 200.

[118] Crabtree, *Pentecostal Preaching*, pp. 39-40, 200.

[119] Crabtree, *Pentecostal Preaching*, pp. 67-69.

[120] Crabtree, *Pentecostal Preaching*, p. 68.

[121] Crabtree, *Pentecostal Preaching*, p. 68.

[122] Crabtree, *Pentecostal Preaching*, p. 69.

from other types of preaching he describes.[123] Nevertheless, Crabtree's approach acknowledges a variety of styles that affect one's approach in preaching. Thus, Crabtree underscores the role of the Spirit's immediacy for the preparation for preaching, highlighting the Spirit's role for a revelational hermeneutic, witnessing to Christ, studying Scripture and other resources, and how the preparation of outlines and/or manuscripts are subservient to spontaneous leadings of the Spirit while preaching. The three styles of communication used by Jesus also reveals three styles for preaching that can be used by preachers.

Haddon W. Robinson

The immediacy of God affects Robinson's approach to preparing the sermon because he believes that God reveals himself in the Scriptures, which is the primary way God communicates today. Thus, extensive study of Scripture is necessary to prepare a sermon. Robinson's understanding of the Spirit's work for the preparation of the sermon is limited to the Spirit applying the biblical concept to the preacher, as the preacher studies Scripture. Robinson includes extensive discussion on the study of Scripture and preparation of the sermon. Relating Scripture to the audience is another crucial component for preparing sermons, though is a practice not explicitly linked to the immediacy of God in Robinson's view.

First, an extensive study of Scripture for the preparation of sermons is important because the biblical concept must shape the preacher, sermon, and congregation.[124] The biblical concept shapes sermon preparation because the authority for expository preaching is derived from Scripture, not the preacher. Sermon preparation, then, is primarily concerned with studying and seeking to discern how to explain a biblical concept. Throughout Robinson's discussion on ten stages of sermon development, he does not delve into the role of the Spirit's work. But prior to the discussion on the ten stages, he explains that Spirit applies the biblical concept to the preacher during the study of Scripture. The Spirit's application of the biblical concept to the preacher 'places God's dealing with the preacher at the center

---

[123] Crabtree, *Pentecostal Preaching*, p. 69.
[124] Robinson, *Biblical Preaching*, p. 21.

of the process'.[125] When preachers study Scripture, the Spirit prepares preachers. For '[a]s we study our Bible, the Holy Spirit studies us'.[126] Though not explicit throughout the ten stages, Robinson expects the Spirit to apply the biblical concept to the preacher throughout the study of Scripture he suggests throughout his book on preaching.

Robinson outlines ten stages that the preacher should follow to study Scripture and prepare expository sermons. Because his discussion on constructing an expository sermon takes up much of his work – approximately 168 out of 245 pages – a summary of these stages follows. The first three stages deal primarily with the biblical world.[127] First, preachers must select a biblical passage to be preached, determined either by a lectionary or a preaching calendar, while also sensitive to the needs of the congregation.[128] Second, preachers must study the biblical passage within its context, followed by the use of six different tools – lexicons, concordances, grammars, word-study books, Bible dictionaries and encyclopedias, and commentaries.[129] Third, one must 'determine the exegetical idea and its development', which indicates the subject of the biblical passage and assertions made about the subject – the complement(s).[130]

The following six stages relate the biblical world, 'the modern world, and our particular world as we develop the sermon'.[131] Stage four involves asking three developmental questions of the exegetical idea. They are: 1) what does it mean?, 2) is it true?, and 3) what difference does it make?[132] Stage five is about constructing the homiletical idea, which is a memorable sentence that encapsulates the exegetical idea.[133] The homiletical idea also connects with the audience's knowledge and experience, and focuses on the response of hearers to the sermon.[134] In stage six, preachers determine the purpose of

[125] Robinson, *Biblical Preaching*, p. 25.
[126] Robinson, *Biblical Preaching*, p. 26.
[127] Robinson, *Biblical Preaching*, p. 73.
[128] Robinson, *Biblical Preaching*, pp. 53-58.
[129] Robinson, *Biblical Preaching*, pp. 58-66.
[130] Robinson, *Biblical Preaching*, pp. 66-70.
[131] Robinson, *Biblical Preaching*, p. 75.
[132] Robinson, *Biblical Preaching*, pp. 77-96.
[133] Robinson, *Biblical Preaching*, pp. 103-12.
[134] Robinson, *Biblical Preaching*, pp. 103-12.

the sermon, which must be 'in line with the biblical purpose'.[135] The seventh stage delves into how the homiletical idea 'should be handled to accomplish your purpose'.[136] The three ways the purpose can be accomplished are through sermons developed deductively, semi-inductively, or inductively.[137] Stage eight deals with outlining the sermon, which brings 'unity, order, and progress'.[138] The ninth stage includes filling in 'the outline with supporting materials that explain, prove, apply, or amplify the points'.[139] Supporting materials includes elements such as: restatement, definition, explanation, factual information, quotations, narration, and illustrations.[140] The last stage in developing a sermon is articulating the introduction and conclusion of a sermon.[141] An introduction not only introduces the preacher, subject, or first point of the sermon, but should also 'command attention', 'uncover needs' among hearers, and introduce 'the body of the sermon and its development'.[142] Conclusions 'should produce a feeling of finality'.[143] A few ways of concluding may include summarizing, an illustration, a quotation, a question, a prayer, specific directions, or helping hearers visualize how they would apply the message in their lives.[144]

Robinson also commends writing out a full manuscript of the sermon, because it helps bring order to the sermon and highlights key ideas.[145] Factors that contribute to effective manuscript-writing include: strong transitions, a clear outline, short sentences, simple sentence structure, simple words, a direct and personal style, and vividness.[146] The manuscript must not be memorized, just rehearsed.[147] The manuscript only 'contributes to the thought and wording of your

---

[135] Robinson, *Biblical Preaching*, p. 108.
[136] Robinson, *Biblical Preaching*, p. 116.
[137] Robinson, *Biblical Preaching*, p. 116.
[138] Robinson, *Biblical Preaching*, p. 132.
[139] Robinson, *Biblical Preaching*, p. 140.
[140] Robinson, *Biblical Preaching*, pp. 140-62.
[141] Robinson, *Biblical Preaching*, p. 166.
[142] Robinson, *Biblical Preaching*, pp. 166-72.
[143] Robinson, *Biblical Preaching*, pp. 175-81.
[144] Robinson, *Biblical Preaching*, pp. 175-81.
[145] Robinson, *Biblical Preaching*, p. 183.
[146] Robinson, *Biblical Preaching*, pp. 186-98.
[147] Robinson, *Biblical Preaching*, p. 186.

sermon, but it does not determine it'.[148] The manuscript does not 'determine' every thought and word, since new sentence structures and phrases will develop during the preaching event spontaneously.[149] He does not, however, indicate whether the Spirit leads to these new sentence structures and phrases. Thus, Robinson views the study of Scripture to articulate its relevance for the contemporary audience as reliant on an experience of the Spirit's immediacy in the life of the preacher. For God primarily reveals himself and addresses people today through Scripture. The Spirit applies the biblical concept to the preacher who studies Scripture for sermon preparation. Robinson's ten stages and suggestions for manuscript preparation also contribute to helping preachers bring Scripture to bear upon the lives of a congregation in an effective way.

The Preaching Event

The preaching event includes all that is involved in the sermon being delivered. Some elements that arise among the leaders include an emphasis on prophetic preaching, being yielded to the Spirit, spontaneity, and the means by which the Spirit applies the message to hearers. What Hughes, Crabtree, and Robinson highlight for the preaching event follows.

Ray H. Hughes

Hughes believes that preachers must be sensitive to the Spirit's immediacy while preaching, notable in his view of the need for prophetic preaching. Prophetic preaching represents the 'best' of Pentecostal preaching.[150] A prophetic approach to preaching is understandable – especially for Pentecostals – since prophecy is 'a distinctive gift of Pentecost'.[151] Peter acknowledged that 'sons and daughters' would now prophesy, fulfilling Joel's earlier prophecy.[152] Peter's use of Joel's prophecy indicates that this period of the church is an age when 'the presence of the Holy Spirit was to be marked by an extraordinary

---

[148] Robinson, *Biblical Preaching*, p. 186.

[149] Robinson, *Biblical Preaching*, p. 186.

[150] Hughes, *Pentecostal Preaching*, p. 138. Daniel E. Albrecht also notes that within the Pentecostal-Charismatic tradition, 'the pastor often carries the burden of the prophet during the preaching rite'. Albrecht, *Rites in the Spirit*, p. 221.

[151] Hughes, *Pentecostal Preaching*, p. 137.

[152] Hughes, *Pentecostal Preaching*, p. 137; Acts 2.17-18; Joel 2.28-32.

manifestation of prophetic power'.[153] Preaching, then, should be prophetic, as one is 'empowered by authority of the Holy Ghost to declare the mind of God'.[154] Prophetic preaching is not only marked by openness to spontaneous leadings of the Spirit, but also provides four benefits.

First, prophetic preaching requires openness to the spontaneous leadings of the Spirit.[155] A preacher must always remain sensitive to the Spirit's direction 'at the moment', which may lead in a different direction than one's earlier plan.[156] During such moments, God illuminates the preacher's mind, and 'thoughts rush on him: he can hardly speak before other thoughts present themselves for consideration'.[157] A preacher may receive messages through revelation, and 'Scriptures previously read and studied are brought to memory and unfold in beautiful splendor and symmetry'.[158] Fully explaining a preacher's experience of the Spirit during such a moment is difficult because 'words' are 'poor and inadequate vehicles for capturing the high emotional impact of such a moment in the pulpit'.[159]

Of the four benefits of prophetic preaching, the first involves relevant Scripture being brought to remembrance for the moment. Relying on the spontaneous leading of the Spirit, however, does not abdicate the preacher's need to study Scripture. Studying in preparation for preaching is important because '[t]he Spirit, except through revelation, cannot bring to one's mind that which the mind has not learned'.[160] Christ's promise of the Spirit, to teach and bring to remembrance all Christ stated undergirds this idea.[161] While preaching, the Spirit may spontaneously lead the preacher in a different direction – but the Spirit gives direction and brings to mind details of Scripture already studied by the preacher.[162] For this reason, studying Scripture in advance can strengthen prophetic preaching, even during moments of spontaneity.

---

[153] Hughes, *Pentecostal Preaching*, p. 136.
[154] Hughes, *Pentecostal Preaching*, p. 137.
[155] Hughes, *Pentecostal Preaching*, p. 139.
[156] Hughes, *Pentecostal Preaching*, p. 139.
[157] Hughes, *Pentecostal Preaching*, p. 139.
[158] Hughes, *Pentecostal Preaching*, pp. 138-39.
[159] Hughes, *Pentecostal Preaching*, p. 148.
[160] Hughes, *Pentecostal Preaching*, p. 138.
[161] Hughes, *Pentecostal Preaching*, p. 138; Jn 14.26.
[162] Also see Byrd, 'Formulation of a Classical Pentecostal Homiletic', p. 69.

Second, courage is a benefit of prophetic preaching. 'Courage is a special gift of the anointing', which prepares ministers for difficult tasks.[163] After the apostles prayed for boldness to speak God's Word, the place where they were shook, they were filled with the Spirit, and they preached boldly.[164] Peter is an example of someone who lacked courage prior to his experience of the Spirit on the Day of Pentecost. But Peter gained boldness after an experience of the Spirit on the Day of Pentecost.[165]

Third, prophetic preachers can receive a message through revelation, whereby the Spirit 'reveals the needs of a congregation to the preacher'.[166] Having knowledge of the congregation's needs – previously unknown to preachers – may be disconcerting to some. Receiving such a message may cause others to think that friends have told the preacher their needs.[167] Prophetic preaching enables preachers to preach in a way that speaks directly to the needs of congregations, which includes the conviction of sins.[168]

Fourth, prophetic preaching will produce miraculous results. At least four elements are required for miraculous results – also found in Peter's prophetic sermon on the Day of Pentecost. The four include: an experience of the gift of the Spirit, boldness, a message based on the Word, and a message centered on Jesus Christ.[169] Since miraculous results are an expectation for the altar, they are discussed in the following section.[170] Thus, Hughes highlights the Spirit's immediacy during the preaching event, presenting prophetic preaching as the best form of preaching. Prophetic preaching requires being open to spontaneous leadings of the Spirit, who helps remind preachers of relevant Scripture, gives courage, gives a message of revelation, and helps produce miraculous results.

---

163 Hughes, *Pentecostal Preaching*, p. 140.

164 Hughes, *Pentecostal Preaching*, p. 140; Acts 4.29-33.

165 Hughes, *Pentecostal Preaching*, pp. 140, 142.

166 Hughes, *Pentecostal Preaching*, p. 141.

167 Hughes, *Pentecostal Preaching*, p. 141.

168 Hughes, *Pentecostal Preaching*, p. 141.

169 Hughes, *Pentecostal Preaching*, p. 143.

170 Hughes considers Peter's message on the Day of Pentecost a prophetic sermon, and also considers the response to Peter's message as the altar call and altar. Hughes, *Pentecostal Preaching*, pp. 127, 142.

Charles T. Crabtree

Crabtree believes the preaching event must be characterised by a preacher who is yielded to the Spirit's work, which ultimately leads to the Spirit's manifestation among the congregation. First, preachers must be yielded and sensitive to the Spirit while preaching, which often requires openness to spontaneously addressing needs as the Spirit directs. This approach led Crabtree to stop a sermon to pray for healing, so that a woman was healed of Parkinson's disease and her husband was healed of a heart condition.[171] While orders of service and manuscripts are helpful, they should only be 'guides, not rules' in light of 'spiritual need and warfare'.[172]

Second, when ministers preach while yielded to the Spirit's work – ministering in the power of the Spirit – hearers will also experience the Spirit's immediacy. For when preachers preach while yielded to the Spirit, hearers will 'be convicted of sin and convinced of truth by the work of the Holy Spirit'.[173] For Christ stated that the Spirit would 'convict the world of guilt in regard to sin and righteousness and judgment'.[174] Preachers only report the good news, and must allow 'the Spirit to flow in power and conviction'.[175] When preaching truth in the Spirit, hearers can receive the truth through the 'Spirit's revelation'.[176] For while a sermon may convince someone to convert to a religion, only the Spirit transforming work can enable someone to become a 'child of God', whereby they are 'born again by the work of the Spirit'.[177] A preacher cannot witness genuine Christian transformation apart from the Spirit's present work in the hearer's reception of biblical truth.[178] Thus, the Spirit's immediacy during the preaching event is crucial in Crabtree's thought, for the preacher must be yielded to the Spirit so that hearers may respond to the Spirit's power and conviction.

---

[171] Crabtree, *Pentecostal Preaching*, p. 39.

[172] Crabtree, *Pentecostal Preaching*, pp. 39-40.

[173] Crabtree, *Pentecostal Preaching*, p. 148.

[174] Crabtree, *Pentecostal Preaching*, p. 148; Jn 16.8.

[175] Crabtree, *Pentecostal Preaching*, p. 202.

[176] Crabtree, *Pentecostal Preaching*, p. 149.

[177] Crabtree, *Pentecostal Preaching*, p. 149.

[178] Crabtree, *Pentecostal Preaching*, p. 149.

Haddon W. Robinson

The Spirit's immediacy for the preaching event in Robinson's thought is required so that the preacher depends on the Spirit, and the Spirit applies the biblical concept through the preacher to the hearers in preaching. But he also delves into several other important aspects for the preaching event that rely on communication studies and one's personality, which are explained here. First, while depending upon the Spirit, a preacher 'aims to confront, convict, convert, and comfort men and women through the proclamation of biblical concepts'.[179] Robinson does not, however, expand on how one might depend on the Spirit while preaching. Since Robinson gives no indication that the subject of the sermon can or should change during the act of preaching – other than new sentence structures and phrases that may spontaneously arise – preparing the sermon is critical.[180]

Second, the Spirit applies the biblical concept to hearers during the preaching. For the Spirit to apply the biblical concept, preachers are required to provide effective application of the biblical concept in the sermon.[181] Robinson's approach, then, necessitates effective preparation of the sermon, providing applications that deal with both theology and ethics.[182] Applications prepared beforehand must probe relationships between the biblical world and the contemporary world.[183]

Robinson also explains the relevance of communication studies for the preaching event, which is not linked to the immediacy of God. Robinson takes an entire chapter to help the preacher with their delivery style. He explains that '[t]he effectiveness of our sermons depends on two factors: what we say and how we say it. Both are important. Apart from life-related, biblical content, we have nothing worth communicating; but without skillful delivery, we will not get that content across to a congregation.'[184] Furthermore,

[i]n order of significance, the ingredients making up the sermon are thought, arrangement, language, voice, and gesture. In priority of impressions, however, the order is reversed. Gestures and voice

---

[179] Robinson, *Biblical Preaching*, p. 39.
[180] Robinson, *Biblical Preaching*, p. 186.
[181] Robinson, *Biblical Preaching*, pp. 27-30.
[182] Robinson, *Biblical Preaching*, pp. 29, 140-62.
[183] Robinson, *Biblical Preaching*, pp. 29, 140-62.
[184] Robinson, *Biblical Preaching*, p. 201.

emerge as the most obvious and determinative part of preaching.[185]

In Robinson's discussion on delivery, he frequently relies on communication studies. This should not be surprising since his PhD is in speech communication.[186] Ironically, though, in a later section of his book on preaching, he explains that only Christ through His Spirit can meet the 'hungers of an entire congregation', because '[p]reaching is ultimately His work'.[187]

Finally, while not linked to the immediacy of God, the personality of the preacher is important in Robinson's estimation because hearers reject you based on who you are during the introduction of a sermon. Introductions familiarise a congregation to the preacher. Since a congregation does 'not hear a sermon' – '[t]hey hear you' – establishing who the preacher is crucial in the introduction.[188] Preachers must ensure they do not 'appear nervous, hostile, or unprepared', otherwise listeners 'are inclined to reject you'.[189] But when preachers appear 'alert and friendly, they decide you are an able person with a positive attitude toward yourself and your listeners'.[190] Thus, Robinson includes the need for the Spirit's immediacy for the preaching event, so that preachers depend on the Spirit, and the Spirit applies the biblical concept through the preacher to the hearers. Furthermore, Robinson also gives credence to the importance of communication studies and the role of one's personality for the preaching event, which he does not directly link to the immediacy of God.

The Response to the Sermon – the Altar

The altar represents the response to the sermon, primarily where preachers within a Pentecostal context expect hearers to come forward physically to a context whereby they appropriate the message heard. Various topics arise when examining the theme of the altar in the leaders' views discussed here, such as the need for preachers to

---

[185] Robinson, *Biblical Preaching*, pp. 201-202.

[186] Haddon Robinson, *Biblical Preaching: The Development and Delivery of Expository Messages* (Grand Rapids: Baker, 1st edn, 1980).

[187] Robinson, *Biblical Preaching*, p. 223.

[188] Robinson, *Biblical Preaching*, p. 165.

[189] Robinson, *Biblical Preaching*, p. 165.

[190] Robinson, *Biblical Preaching*, p. 166.

be led by the Spirit and the altar being central for hearers to experience the immediacy of God through miracles. The views on the altar highlighted by Hughes, Crabtree, and Robinson follow.

Ray H. Hughes

Hughes highlights the immediacy of God for a response to the sermon and the altar, for hearers may experience miracles at an altar, preachers must be led by the Spirit, hearers may even respond during the preaching, and discernment is required. The importance of the altar is an important component in Hughes' thought since the altar is a key context whereby the congregation can respond to the message and experience the immediacy of God – the supernatural.[191] The supernatural – miracles, healings, signs, and wonders – '*should* and *will* follow*' the preaching of believers today.[192] An emphasis on a response to the sermon is why 'many Pentecostal sermons conclude with the congregation around the altar seeking God'.[193]

Hughes theologically grounds the need for an 'invitation, or the altar call', on a few key verses in Scripture. Peter not only preached a sermon on the Day of Pentecost, which brought conviction in his hearers, but he also included a means by which people could respond.[194] Even Jesus frequently gave opportunity to his hearers to respond to His message, such as his injunctions to 'Follow me', 'Come after me', 'Believe in me', and 'Come unto me'.[195] Hughes does not define 'the altar' for preaching, but generally views the altar as the context for responding to the sermon, whereby people can seek God and experience the supernatural.

Hughes provides six recommendations for good altar calls, which are dependent on the Spirit's immediacy because the preacher must follow the Spirit's direction. Though these recommendations are specific for evangelistic preaching, they can be adapted for altar calls with different goals. First, the altar call must be 'properly timed'.[196] The timing of the altar call must be coordinated with the Spirit's overall

---

[191] Hughes, *Pentecostal Preaching*, p. 155.

[192] Hughes, *Pentecostal Preaching*, pp. 155-56.

[193] Hughes, *Pentecostal Preaching* p. 29.

[194] Hughes, *Pentecostal Preaching*, p. 127; Acts 2.37-38.

[195] Hughes, *Pentecostal Preaching*, p. 127.

[196] Hughes, *Pentecostal Preaching*, p. 129.

direction and the 'climactic moment' of the sermon – when 'all arguments and all words peak'.[197] A call to the altar comes out of the preacher's attitude, one of love and concern for hearers, and whose yearning for response is 'heightened by the power of the Spirit'.[198] Second, the altar call must be 'definite' and 'specific', so that hearers have 'no doubt' about what the invitation is for.[199] Third, the transition between the sermon and altar invitation must be 'smooth', so that musicians are ready, songs are chosen, and distractions are minimized.[200] Fourth, a preacher must carefully consider when the invitation should conclude. Some invitations may be extended, while others should be prompt to emphasize the urgency of the message.[201] Fifth, either the preacher or altar workers must instruct those who have responded to the altar call.[202] Finally, after the altar experience there must be 'follow-up'.[203] New converts must receive instruction, prayer, and contact with a pastor and other church members.[204]

Hughes also admits that people may respond to a sermon because of the Spirit's work while the message is being preached – not waiting for the formal altar call following the sermon. Peter's sermon at the home of Cornelius exemplifies how hearers may respond to a sermon before it concludes. While Peter was preaching, 'the Holy Ghost fell on all them which heard the word'.[205] Hughes has also witnessed people respond while preaching, so that 'men or women have been known to cry out, to stand, and to run forward to an altar of prayer, conviction too heavy for them to wait'.[206] Understanding all the dynamics involved when people respond during the preaching is not possible, since the experience can only be described as the 'miracle element in Pentecostal preaching'.[207]

Finally, while Hughes expects the supernatural to follow good preaching, he acknowledges that this emphasis on the supernatural

---

[197] Hughes, *Pentecostal Preaching*, p. 129.
[198] Hughes, *Pentecostal Preaching*, p. 128.
[199] Hughes, *Pentecostal Preaching*, p. 129.
[200] Hughes, *Pentecostal Preaching*, p. 129.
[201] Hughes, *Pentecostal Preaching*, pp. 129-30.
[202] Hughes, *Pentecostal Preaching*, p. 130.
[203] Hughes, *Pentecostal Preaching*, p. 130.
[204] Hughes, *Pentecostal Preaching*, p. 130.
[205] Hughes, *Pentecostal Preaching*, p. 158; Acts 10.44.
[206] Hughes, *Pentecostal Preaching*, p. 157.
[207] Hughes, *Pentecostal Preaching*, p. 157.

can lead to excesses, which demand a means of discernment. Three guidelines assure that an emphasis on the supernatural does not lead to fanaticism, heresy, and preachers who are merely seeking 'personal and earthly ambitions'.[208] The three guidelines are: 1) preaching that 'centers in the Word', 2) preaching that 'always exalts Jesus Christ', and 3) preaching that 'is always directed and empowered by the Holy Spirit'.[209] These guidelines ensure that preachers are 'sensitive to God's will' and 'promoting the church and the Kingdom'.[210] These three guidelines give discernment for leaders when expecting the supernatural for altars. Thus, Hughes highlights the importance of the immediacy of God for the altar, for it must be led by the Spirit, so that hearers may respond to the Spirit's convicting work, whereby they experience miraculous results at an altar. Hearers, however, may respond to the Spirit's convicting work during the preaching. Furthermore, Hughes' acknowledges the potential for excess with the goal of the altar, and gives three guidelines for discerning the appropriateness of preaching with an altar as the goal.

Charles T. Crabtree

Crabtree views the altar as the crowning achievement of preaching, because the immediacy of God is notably evident at the altar where the Spirit initiates transformation and supernatural results manifest. Furthermore, altars are best led by those who have already experienced the Spirit's work in their lives.[211] Crabtree provides five recommendations for leading an altar service. First, in response to the Spirit's work of convicting people of sin and convincing people of truth through a sermon, preachers must call people to the altar where they can experience supernatural results – salvation, Spirit baptism, the gifts of the Spirit, healing, and miracles.[212] The altar is a crucial component of Pentecostalism, because supernatural results are 'the defining element that sets it apart from any other evangelical entity'.[213] Since a primary context for experiencing the supernatural is the altar, the altar becomes crucial for preachers.

---

[208] Hughes, *Pentecostal Preaching*, p. 156.

[209] Hughes, *Pentecostal Preaching*, p. 156; Holm, 'Cadences of the Heart', p. 19.

[210] Hughes, *Pentecostal Preaching*, p. 156.

[211] Crabtree, *Pentecostal Preaching*, pp. 122, 202-203.

[212] Crabtree, *Pentecostal Preaching*, pp. 148-49.

[213] Crabtree, *Pentecostal Preaching*, p. 135.

Second, an experience of the supernatural is predicated on preachers and altar workers who have already experienced the Spirit's work in their lives. For the altar is 'the capstone, the supreme reward of the many hours of prayer and study' for 'Spirit-filled preachers'.[214] 'A well-prepared, Spirit-filled pulpit will beget a well-filled, Spirit-convicting altar, an altar of repentant sinners and hungry believers.'[215] Preachers who go to an 'altar' before they preach – that place of experiencing the Spirit's work for transformation – will ensure the altar that follows their sermon is full of people experiencing transformation and the supernatural.[216] Furthermore, the best altar workers – those who pray for people coming forward to pray at the altar – are also those who have also already experienced the Spirit's work prior to praying for others.[217]

Crabtree gives five recommendations for conducting an altar call for Spirit baptism, which also reveals important considerations for conducting altar calls in general to experience the supernatural. First, '[t]he call to come forward to receive the baptism should be done in a very encouraging and non-threatening manner'.[218] A few ways to ensure the call is 'encouraging and non-threatening', include letting people know God wants to give them the Spirit baptism.[219] Preachers should also have those who will pray for others come forward in advance to help people 'feel less conspicuous'.[220]

Second, those praying at the altar with people desiring Spirit baptism should themselves be baptised with the Spirit with the evidence of tongues.[221] Those praying for people at the altar should also follow a few instructions, such as: not manipulating others to experience Spirit baptism, taking time to praise God together at the altars since that is when 'God comes in special habitation', and only praying with those of the same gender 'to avoid any kind of embarrassment or

---

[214] Crabtree, *Pentecostal Preaching*, p. 203.
[215] Crabtree, *Pentecostal Preaching*, p. 203.
[216] Crabtree, *Pentecostal Preaching*, p. 203.
[217] Crabtree, *Pentecostal Preaching*, p. 164.
[218] Crabtree, *Pentecostal Preaching*, p. 163.
[219] Crabtree, *Pentecostal Preaching*, pp. 163-64.
[220] Crabtree, *Pentecostal Preaching*, pp. 163-64.
[221] Crabtree, *Pentecostal Preaching*, p. 164.

distraction'.[222] Those leading the altar should have already experienced the response expected for hearers.

Third, preachers must ask those who have come forward to the altar for Spirit baptism whether 'they are certain they are saved and in a right relationship with God'.[223] Certainty of salvation and relationship with God engenders thankfulness to God for public prayer.[224] Following the public prayer, preachers should have seekers raise their hand if they are a 'child of God' and subsequently 'qualified' to receive Spirit baptism.[225] The act of raising their hand gives them an opportunity to give 'testimony and clarifying for themselves the reality and joy in being a member of the same family'.[226] Establishing certainty also ensures that doubts and fears are removed in place of faith.

Fourth, preachers must explain that Spirit baptism is a gift of God the Father, which believers receive by faith.[227] Part of receiving Spirit baptism also includes 'taking the gift by an act of the will and choosing to step out in faith, not knowing what to say but believing God will give the utterance'.[228] Seekers of Spirit baptism must 'launch out … in a new tongue' at some point, trusting God to give the utterance.[229] Responding to an altar call requires faith and a willingness to act on that faith.

Finally, preachers must encourage both those who have received and not received Spirit baptism. For those who have received Spirit baptism, they must be encouraged to continue to pray in tongues over time. If they fail to continue to pray in tongues, they may not experience the practical benefits of a 'Spirit-filled life', being 'content' with a one-time experience.[230] For those who have not received Spirit baptism, preachers must remind them that they must continue to seek God's promise of Spirit baptism. Those not receiving Spirit baptism should also be introduced to and hear the testimonies of those who

[222] Crabtree, *Pentecostal Preaching*, p. 164.
[223] Crabtree, *Pentecostal Preaching*, p. 164.
[224] Crabtree, *Pentecostal Preaching*, pp. 164-65.
[225] Crabtree, *Pentecostal Preaching*, pp. 164-65.
[226] Crabtree, *Pentecostal Preaching*, pp. 164-65.
[227] Crabtree, *Pentecostal Preaching*, p. 165.
[228] Crabtree, *Pentecostal Preaching*, p. 165.
[229] Crabtree, *Pentecostal Preaching*, p. 166.
[230] Crabtree, *Pentecostal Preaching*, p. 166.

have received Spirit baptism, particularly those who initially did not receive Spirit baptism at the altar.[231] Preachers must be sensitive to the various experiences at the altar that may be both joyful and disappointing.

Thus, Crabtree highlights the crucial role of the altar, because it is a key context to experience the immediacy of God – supernatural results. Altars are best led by preachers and altar workers who have experienced the Spirit's work themselves, and require sensitivity to the various needs of the congregation while leading.

Haddon W. Robinson

Robinson does not commend an altar experience in response to the sermon, for the Spirit's work is primarily experienced during the sermon whereby the Spirit applies the message to their lives in practical ways. A response to the sermon is primarily related to an application of Scripture to the various contexts of the hearers' lives. People in the congregation, however, may respond to sermons by giving feedback to the preacher to help them improve. Sermons may conclude in a variety of ways: a summary, an illustration, a quotation, a question, a prayer, specific directions, or a visualization whereby preachers help congregations imagine their application of the sermon in the future.[232] The closest Robinson gets to something of an altar experience, is his view that sometimes an appropriate response to a sermon may be falling down and worshipping God. He does not expand on this response of falling down and worshipping, acknowledging that congregations are better served by sermons that 'offer practical suggestions on how to translate scriptural truth into life experience'.[233] When the Spirit applies the biblical concept to the hearers during the preaching of the sermon, hearers can consider how they may apply the biblical concept to their lives.[234] Thus, the hearers' response to the sermon during the time of corporate worship is primarily relegated to their thought on the subject as the Spirit applies the biblical concept while the sermon is preached. For after sharing a conclusion, the preacher is expected just to stop.[235] It may be implicitly deduced, then,

---

[231] Crabtree, *Pentecostal Preaching*, pp. 166-67.
[232] Robinson, *Biblical Preaching*, pp. 175-81.
[233] Robinson, *Biblical Preaching*, p. 179.
[234] Robinson, *Biblical Preaching*, pp. 27-30, 178-81.
[235] Robinson, *Biblical Preaching*, p. 181.

that Robinson deems hearers' daily lives as the place for 'their altar' experience and response to the sermon.

The immediacy of God is experienced during the preaching – when the Spirit applies the biblical concept – so Robinson acknowledges the need for feedback on sermons for the benefit of future sermons. Preachers should give some people in their congregation an opportunity to respond to a sermon following the preaching, primarily to offer feedback for the preacher to improve sermons. Getting them to provide feedback on a sermon's effectiveness will delve into various facets, including: the aim of the sermon, the biblical text, illustrations, application, delivery, and other suggestions for improvement. Thus, Robinson gives little room for an altar experience, for he relegates most of what God does through preaching during the sermon – when the Spirit applies the biblical concept. He is also open for feedback to improve the effectiveness of future sermons. He views the response to sermons primarily for hearers' 'day–to–day' lives in the various contexts they live in.

Conclusion

After a discussion on the approach to preaching and the altar call among Hughes, Crabtree, and Robinson, all assume the immediacy of God for preaching in different ways. All three leaders discuss important facets of Scripture, the Spirit, the character of the preacher, and the congregation for preaching, but give different opinions and varying degrees of emphasis on each subject for preaching. Only Hughes and Crabtree, though, emphasise the importance of the altar for an experience of supernatural results. Robinson's response to preaching is primarily relegated to how the biblical concept applies for daily living. All three leaders' approach to preaching and the altar can be found among Pentecostal contexts, and the implications of their approaches are important to understand in order to provide an analysis of preaching and the altar found in Pentecostal churches. The next chapter builds upon the discussion of both this chapter and the previous chapter by providing an analysis of preaching and the altar for Pentecostal churches today.

7

ANALYSIS OF CONTEMPORARY PENTECOSTAL PREACHING AND THE ALTAR

Chapters five and six discussed important theological issues related to the three key leaders examined: Ray H. Hughes, Charles T. Crabtree, and Haddon W. Robinson. An emphasis on the immediacy of God found its way into all three leaders' approach to preaching and the altar in different ways, and an analysis of their views is necessary here. One of the initial thoughts one may have when comparing Hughes's, Crabtree's, and Robinson's works, is the difference in their book titles: *Pentecostal Preaching* and *Biblical Preaching*. In Hughes' and Crabtree's work, all facets of preaching and the altar must be characteristically Pentecostal. Thus, the Spirit's present work is crucial in various ways for the definition/nature of preaching, the preparation of the preacher, the preparation of the sermon, the preaching event, and the altar. In Robinson's work, the Spirit's present work is primarily related to an understanding of Scripture for the preparation of the preacher, the preparation of the sermon, and the preaching event. Though all three leaders include elements of the others' emphases, they nevertheless underscore different themes in preaching that brings authority and effectiveness to the act of preaching. This analysis begins with a discussion on the understanding and role of preaching and the altar at the Azusa Street Revival. An analysis of Hughes's, Crabtree's, and Robinson's works follows, which is discussed in light of 1) the Azusa Street Revival and 2) other pertinent resources. Throughout the analysis, the theological concerns in all three leaders are addressed, whereby in some instances the focus may be on one, two, or all three leaders. The subjects are addressed as they arise in each leader's views somewhat chronologically, examining Hughes, then Crabtree, followed by Robinson. The purpose of this analysis is to contribute toward a more robust Pentecostal theology of preaching and the altar.

A Constructive Appraisal of Pentecostal Preaching and the Altar

Sermons vs. Messages

Hughes distinguishes sermons from messages, because of his view on the need for the immediacy of God in preparation, but his approach is problematic. Hughes explains that people may develop a 'sermon' through the techniques developed from a course on homiletics. But a 'message' is received through an experience of God – when the preacher sees 'the face of God'.[1] In Hughes' work, however, he uses the language of 'sermon' to describe Peter's sermon on the Day of Pentecost. But Hughes considers Peter's sermon a model for Pentecostal preachers – something he would consider a 'message' from God. Hughes is inconsistent on what may be called a sermon or a message.

Those at Azusa Street would have affirmed Hughes' position that preachers must receive their message from God because of an experience of Spirit baptism and a fresh anointing of the Spirit, rather than rely on the techniques learned in a course on preaching. For instance, they explain that 'God does not need a great theological preacher that can give nothing but theological chips and shavings to people', because an experience of Spirit baptism is the credential needed for preaching.[2] Ministry that relies primarily on education and techniques fails to be Pentecostal preaching – the Spirit's immediacy is crucial for preaching. Those at Azusa, however, did not seek to distinguish a sermon from a message, like Hughes.

Another problem with Hughes' view is the idea that sermons developed from a thorough study are useless unless the preacher experiences the immediacy of God. Hughes' views on sermons and messages may be tempered by his admission that preaching must exalt

---

[1] Hughes, *Pentecostal Preaching*, p. 93.
[2] *AF* 1.2 (October 1906), p. 3.

Jesus Christ and be based in the written Word.[3] If preachers develop their sermon from Scripture and exalt Jesus in the sermon, the sermon is a message from God since Scripture is the Word of God, which points to Jesus Christ. The Apostle Paul even acknowledged that the proclamation of Christ is something to rejoice in, regardless of people's good or bad motives (Phil. 1.17). Christ even explained that some people may have experienced supernatural results arising out of ministry in the name of Christ, even though the minister failed to be Christian (Mt. 7.21-23). The Spirit magnifies Christ when the sermon is based on Scripture and exalts Christ – regardless of a preacher's own experience. Though the preacher may not have a sense of the Spirit's direction and empowerment, the Spirit can work in hearers, even when the preacher fails to experience a sense of the Spirit's immediacy. This discussion merely relays the fact that the Spirit can use sermons preached by someone who has not experienced the immediacy of God. When a sermon is based on Scripture and exalts Christ, the Spirit can use such a sermon to bring conviction despite a preacher's shortcomings.

Acknowledging that the Spirit can use a sermon despite a preacher's shortcomings is not an endorsement to exclude a preacher's experience of the immediacy of God for preaching. Preachers who fail to experience an encounter with God limits their effectiveness. Preachers will fail to give evidence of the Spirit's transformative work for character and power for ministry.[4]

Supernatural Results Accompanying the Preached Word

Both Hughes and Crabtree argue for the necessary role of supernatural results accompanying the preached Word among Pentecostals, which is an important issue requiring a thorough analysis here. Hughes insists on supernatural results accompanying preaching primarily based on his view of Mark 16, while Crabtree focuses on the role of Spirit baptism for supernatural results. Beginning with Hughes' approach, he insists that supernatural signs – miracles, healings, signs, and wonders – *'should* and *will* follow' the preaching of

---

[3] Hughes, *Pentecostal Preaching*, p. 156.
[4] Galatians 5.22-25; 1 Tim. 3.1-13; Jn 20.21-23; Acts 1.8.

Pentecostals today, which creates problematic tensions for preaching.[5] He argues that Pentecostal preaching is unique, primarily because of the role of the supernatural in Pentecostal preaching.[6] Further, he states that 'Pentecostal preaching has always produced miraculous results'.[7]

Hughes gives rationale for his view that supernatural results accompany Pentecostal preaching from words attributed to Christ in Mark 16. In Mk 16.16-18, 20, Christ tells His disciples to preach the gospel throughout the world, and that 'signs' – such as casting out devils, speaking in tongues, experiencing safety in the face of danger, and healing – follow those who preach the Word.[8] Pentecostal preaching will 'always produce' miraculous results 'in keeping with the Spirit and the tone of the New Testament'.[9] But there is some ambiguity in Hughes' thought, for he admits in another place that the results of preaching 'are not always immediately visible'.[10] And in a section title that addresses the idea that signs accompany the preaching of the Word, referencing Mark 16, the title reveals that signs *often*

---

[5] Hughes, *Pentecostal Preaching*, pp. 155-56. This idea is confirmed by another classical Pentecostal leader, Assemblies of God leader James K. Bridges. See James K. Bridges, 'Introduction', in James K. Bridges (ed.), *Foundations for Pentecostal Preaching* (Springfield: Gospel Publishing House, 2005), p. 13. Also see Byrd, 'Formulation of a Classical Pentecostal Homiletic', p. 80.

[6] Hughes, *Pentecostal Preaching*, p. 155.

[7] Hughes, *Pentecostal Preaching*, p. 160. William C. Turner confirms this expectation among Pentecostals, stating that 'Pentecostal worship is charged with the expectation that conversion, Spirit baptism, healing, and other works of the Spirit will be ingredients in the preaching event. Such signs and wonders are regarded as demonstrations . . . of the gospel's truth'. William C. Turner, 'Pentecostal Preaching', in William H. Willimon and Richard Lischer (eds.), *Concise Encyclopedia of Preaching* (Louisville: Westminster John Knox, 1995), p. 371.

[8] Hughes, *Pentecostal Preaching*, pp. 156-57, 162. Steven M. Kane shows that some independent Holiness Pentecostals have even included snake handling during their corporate worship services, in light of the promise of Mk 16.18. These Pentecostals would argue that getting bitten by the snake gives evidence of a lack of faith and failing to follow the Spirit. See Steven M. Kane, 'Serpent Handlers', in Samuel S. Hill (ed.), *The New Encyclopedia of Southern Culture; Volume 1: Religion* (Chapel Hill: University of North Carolina, 2011), pp. 211-12.

[9] Hughes, *Pentecostal Preaching*, pp. 155-56.

[10] Hughes, *Pentecostal Preaching*, p. 117.

accompany preaching.[11] The title does not state that signs *always* accompany preaching.[12] But within that section on preaching often accompanied by miracles, he states that 'miracles must accompany' the ministry of preaching, and 'should be expected rather than thought of as out of the ordinary'.[13] On the one hand, he states that supernatural results will always – and even must – accompany preaching. On the other hand, he indicates that signs will only *often* accompany preaching.

In order to delve into Hughes' view of signs accompanying the preached Word, it is crucial to consider the key biblical text he bases his view on: Mk 16.16-18, 20. Though Crabtree also briefly refers to this passage in Mark 16 to give rationale for supernatural results accompanying the preached Word, Hughes underscores the relevance of this passage.[14] Thus, the focus here is primarily on Mark 16 in order to treat Hughes' views.

When considering Azusa, Azusa leaders make reference to the Mark 16 reference that 'signs' will follow and accompany those who believe and preach in almost every edition of *AF*.[15] Seymour uses the language of Mark 16, stating of Azusa: 'God is now confirming His Word by granting signs and wonders to follow the preaching of the Full Gospel in Los Angeles'.[16] Seymour viewed Azusa's miracles as confirmation of Mark 16.

Hughes and leaders at Azusa expected supernatural results to accompany preaching because Jesus apparently promised this in Mark 16. The problem regarding the use of this passage in Mark 16 is that early manuscripts of the book of Mark do not include these words of Jesus. Neither Hughes nor Crabtree acknowledge the issue of authenticity, but surprisingly, one of the Azusa Street leaders did.[17] An

---

[11] Hughes, *Pentecostal Preaching*, p. 124.

[12] Hughes, *Pentecostal Preaching*, p. 124.

[13] Hughes, *Pentecostal Preaching*, p. 124.

[14] Crabtree, *Pentecostal Preaching*, pp. 181-82.

[15] *AF* 1.1 (September 1906), p. 2; (October 1906), p. 3; (November 1906), p. 4; (December 1906), p. 2; (January 1907), p. 1; (February–March 1907), p. 7; (April 1907), p. 4; (June–September 1907), p. 3; (October–January 1908), p. 4; (January 1908), p. 4; (May 1908), p. 1.

[16] *AF* 1.1 (September 1906), p. 2.

[17] Byrd also acknowledges that most Pentecostals, including Hughes, 'do not address the question of the authenticity of the longer ending of Mark'. 'Formulation of a Classical Pentecostal Homiletic', p. 80, n. 57.

unnamed female leader at Azusa responded to Holiness believers who did not believe that the Mk 16.15-20 passage was authentic.[18] The Azusa leader acknowledges that because one scholar, 'Dr. Godbey', left the passage out of his commentary and translation of Mark because 'they were not in the Sinaitic manuscript from which he translates'.[19] She explains that the passage was in 'a manuscript found in later years in a mission on Mount Sinai'.[20] The Azusa leader explains that 'we feel sure that these are the words of Jesus'.[21] She gives three reasons for her insistence on the authenticity of the Mark 16 passage: 1) Christ's words were likely removed from the 'Sinaitic manuscript … for kindling wood;' 2) the same words of Mark 16 are regularly given through tongues and interpretation at Azusa; and 3) the experience of supernatural results at Azusa confirms that signs accompany those who believe God and preach the Word.[22] Conjecture and her personal experiences at Azusa confirmed to her that Mk 16.15-20 was authentic.

The question remains, then, should contemporary Pentecostals follow suit with Hughes and those at Azusa in expecting signs to accompany the preached Word, based on the Mark 16 passage? The majority of Markan scholars conclude that Mk 16.9-20 was not originally part of Mark's gospel.[23] Some contemporary Pentecostal scholars, however, have taken time to reckon with this issue of the canonical authority of this passage, particularly because of the extensive use of the longer ending of Mark among Pentecostals. For instance, John Christopher Thomas, Kimberly Ervin Alexander, and Robert P. Menzies acknowledge that that while the longer ending may not have been written by Mark, it does not necessarily mean that it is not part of the canon.[24] Thomas and Alexander suggest that the church can

---

[18] *AF* 1.2 (October 1906), p. 3.

[19] *AF* 1.2 (October 1906), p. 3.

[20] *AF* 1.2 (October 1906), p. 3.

[21] *AF* 1.2 (October 1906), p. 3.

[22] *AF* 1.2 (October 1906), p. 3.

[23] Robert H. Stein, 'The Ending of Mark', *Bulletin for Biblical Research* 18.1 (2008), p. 83.

[24] John Christopher Thomas and Kimberly Ervin Alexander, '"And the Signs are Following": Mark 16.9-20 – A Journey into Pentecostal Hermeneutics', *Journal of Pentecostal Theology* 11.2 (Fall 2003), pp. 163, 165; Robert P. Menzies, *Speaking in Tongues: Jesus and the Apostolic Church as Models for the Church Today* (Cleveland: CPT Press, 2016), pp. 68, 72.

affirm the canonical authority of the longer ending of Mark in light of 'its antiquity, its integration of a variety of Gospel traditions, and its near universal acceptance as part of the church's canon of Scripture'.[25] There are significant reasons why one may or may not consider the longer ending of Mark authoritative Scripture. Thus, while it is beyond the scope of this chapter to address this debated issue within biblical studies, it is sufficient enough to discuss whether Hughes' views, based on Mk 16.9-20, are substantiated by 1) Mk 16.9-20 itself, and 2) whether other passages in Scripture can substantiate Hughes's claims.[26]

First, in Mk 16.16-18, 20, Christ is portrayed as promising that signs – casting out demons, speaking in tongues, and healing – 'will accompany those who believe'. Further, the writer explains that 'the Lord worked with them [the disciples] and confirmed the message by the signs that accompanied it'. This passage in Mark explains that supernatural results 'will accompany' those who believe and preach. Supernatural results are expected, but the passage fails to promise supernatural results for *every* occasion of preaching. Supernatural results appeared to accompany those who believed and preached, but not necessarily for every act of preaching.

Second, if Mk 16.15-20 is not authoritative and inspired, can Pentecostal preachers expect supernatural results accompanying the preached Word – based on other passages of Scripture? Throughout the New Testament, there are numerous indications that supernatural results can be expected to accompany the ministry of preaching. In Acts 14.3, for instance, Paul and Barnabas preach, and God grants 'signs and wonders to be done through them' in order to testify to 'the word' of God's 'grace'. Paul also explains that there are various gifts of the Spirit that enable some to minister in a way that leads to supernatural results like healing and miracles (1 Cor. 12.1-11). But Paul does not state that everyone is gifted by the Spirit to experience the same type of results through their ministry. For this reason, Hughes – as well as Crabtree and Robinson – must be open to a greater variety of the gifts of the Spirit to manifest among both the

---

[25] Thomas and Alexander, '"And the Signs are Following"', 167.

[26] For a more thorough treatment of the issues related to the ending of Mark, see Stein, 'The Ending of Mark'; Thomas and Alexander, '"And the Signs are Following"'; and Menzies, *Speaking in Tongues*, pp. 67-84.

preacher and congregation – a subject addressed in an upcoming section.[27] Finally, the variety of gifts does not mean that preachers can ignore certain activities if they are not gifted to perform them. For instance, while some may have the gift of evangelism, all believers are still called to evangelise (Eph. 4.11-13; Mt. 28.16-20). Thus, preachers should be open to supernatural results accompanying their own preaching, but not feel like it should *always* manifest as sensational healings and miracles. The Spirit may manifest in different ways.

The key issue requiring analysis of Crabtree's view relates to his view on Spirit baptism for supernatural results. He also highlights the role of supernatural results accompanying and confirming the preached Word. Crabtree argues that without the supernatural in preaching, Pentecostals would not be different from 'any other evangelical entity'.[28] The supernatural accompanies Pentecostal preaching, for the preaching of Jesus Christ 'will also be accompanied by the living works of Christ in supernatural demonstration' – miracles.[29] Through Spirit baptism the preacher can experience 'greater works' – a greater revelation of Christ and supernatural results – through the work of the Spirit in his or her ministry.[30] While Crabtree includes salvation as one of the greatest miracles – which Hughes and Robinson would likely agree with – Crabtree includes other potential miracles, healings, and the expression of the gifts of the Spirit as important for preaching, and necessary if it is to be described as 'Pentecostal preaching'. A few comments on Crabtree's proposal related to the supernatural helps provide insight into this issue.

Crabtree emphasises the experience of Spirit baptism in a preacher, which contributes to supernatural results for preaching. Delving into the validity of the doctrine of Spirit baptism and initial evidence – which classical Pentecostal Crabtree argues is tongues – is beyond the purview of this study.[31] Nevertheless, the issue of Spirit baptism is significant because he argues that those who have experienced Spirit baptism will experience supernatural results in preaching. However, even Crabtree acknowledges that the disciples exorcised

---

[27] See upcoming section on the Spirit's Work among the Congregation.
[28] Crabtree, *Pentecostal Preaching*, p. 135.
[29] Crabtree, *Pentecostal Preaching*, p. 35.
[30] Crabtree, *Pentecostal Preaching*, pp. 36-37.
[31] E.g., see Chad Owen Brand (ed.), *Perspectives on Spirit Baptism* (Nashville: Broadman and Holman, 2004).

demons and witnessed healing through their ministry prior to the Day of Pentecost – when he believes the disciples experienced Spirit baptism. Nevertheless, Crabtree does not expound on the implications of disciples experiencing miracles through their ministry prior to experiencing Spirit baptism.[32]

When considering Azusa, like Crabtree, Azusa participants argued that Spirit baptism provides power and equips preachers for ministry. But in an article in the *AF*, they acknowledge that the disciples had eight gifts of the Spirit, such as healing, discernment, wisdom, and prophecy, prior to the Day of Pentecost.[33] They exercised these gifts of the Spirit because Jesus had already given the power from the Spirit when 'He breathed on them and said, "Receive ye the Holy Ghost"', all prior to the Day of Pentecost.[34] The disciples were thus 'filled with the unction of the Holy Spirit, the anointing, before the day of Pentecost when Jesus breathed on them'.[35] The gift they did not have was tongues, which 'was reserved for the day of Pentecost to be a sign and evidence of the baptism with the Holy Ghost'.[36] Like Crabtree, however, they do not tease out the implications of supernatural signs being manifest among Christ's disciples prior to the Day of Pentecost. Rather, they give the impression that as people are being baptised in the Spirit at Azusa, supernatural signs accompany this experience of the Spirit. Whether those who are not baptised in the Spirit can experience supernatural results is ignored. The implicit implication of the Azusa leaders' teachings is that only those who are baptised in the Spirit with the evidence of tongues will witness supernatural signs accompanying ministry.

Though Crabtree tempers his argument, noting that all Christians have an 'enduement' of the Spirit, while those who are baptised in the Spirit with the evidence of tongues have a 'special enduement' of the Spirit, this is insufficient. Crabtree can argue for another dimension of power for ministry as a result of Spirit baptism – tying his view to the Acts 1.8 passage. Those who have not experienced Spirit baptism should not be understood as lacking the potential for super-

---

[32] Crabtree, *Pentecostal Preaching*, p. 73; Mk 6.7-13.
[33] *AF* 1.4 (December 1906), p. 2.
[34] *AF* 1.4 (December 1906), p. 2; Jn 20.21-23.
[35] *AF* 1.4 (December 1906), p. 2.
[36] *AF* 1.4 (December 1906), p. 2.

natural results in their preaching. Crabtree, and those at Azusa, over-promise the benefits of Spirit baptism, and subsequently under-promise the benefits available to all Christians. Pentecostals are served well by acknowledging the benefits of Spirit baptism, most notably another dimension of power for ministry.[37] But Pentecostals must not overpromise supernatural results that will lead to false expectations and disappointment.

Supernatural occurrences should be expected through faithful Christian preaching, as Hughes and Crabtree argue, for the supernatural cannot be discounted for preaching that is based on Scripture. But both Hughes and Crabtree communicate that if one does not experience supernatural results from preaching – whether salvation, miracles, healing, or an expression of the gifts of the Spirit – the preaching fails to be 'Pentecostal'. Hughes states that 'Pentecostal preaching has always produced miraculous results'.[38] Crabtree argues that 'true Pentecostalism is marked by the unexplainable, the unique, and the unexpected'.[39] Crabtree follows up the previous statement, asserting that an experience of supernatural results is the only thing that sets Pentecostalism apart from other evangelical groups.[40] The importance of supernatural results for Pentecostal preaching – particularly during the altar – has been substantiated by another Pentecostal homiletician, Aldwin Ragoonath.[41]

But there are limits to the supernatural, for Jesus stated that signs may appear among 'false Christs' and 'false prophets', and the rising of the dead may not convince people if the Word does not convince them (Mt. 24.24; Lk. 16.19-31). However, though the signs are not the message – the incarnate Word, Jesus is – signs often accompany

---

[37] The language of 'dimensions' of the work of the Spirit for preaching finds precedent in James A. Forbes Jr's work, *The Holy Spirit and Preaching* (Nashville: Abingdon, 1989). Forbes rightly explains,

It is important that we … rise above the tendency to arrange stages of spiritual growth in rigid patterns of ascending and descending values. How wisely Tillich warned us against the use of 'steps' with regard to spiritual growth. His word 'dimensions' is preferable because it avoids the temptation to play the game of 'I am more anointed than thou' (p. 31).

[38] Hughes, *Pentecostal Preaching*, pp. 155, 160.
[39] Crabtree, *Pentecostal Preaching*, p. 135.
[40] Crabtree, *Pentecostal Preaching*, p. 135.
[41] Ragoonath, *Preach the Word*, pp. 37, 75.

and confirm the preached Word as found in Scripture. While the supernatural is an important part of preaching, it is not a guaranteed response to the sermons of all faithful Pentecostal preachers.

Looking back at Azusa, as stated earlier, they expected supernatural results by their focus on signs accompanying and confirming the preaching, and Spirit baptised preachers being particularly equipped to experience supernatural results. In one entry in the *AF*, one writer emphasises that 'signs SHALL follow them that believe'.[42] Azusa participants likely chose to highlight this passage because of its inclusion of tongues as a sign. This focus on Mark 16 regrettably, though, may have led to the sometimes overemphasis on sensational works of God among Pentecostals. For the Mark 16 passage is solely focused on the more sensational miracles, rather than elements that may be deemed as less sensational, like pastoring and teaching. And as stated earlier, there are other references in Scripture that indicate experiences like miracles and healings can be expected among Christian ministers. If Azusa participants, as well as other Pentecostals like Hughes, did not primarily rely on the Mark 16 passage, they may have had a more balanced approach to the expectation for sensational miracles. They may have expected sensational miracles, but may have also been willing to acknowledge other manifestations of the Spirit that are equally necessary.

Cheryl Bridges Johns provides an insightful perspective on the role of the supernatural in her description of good Pentecostal preaching. She states, 'Pentecostal congregations expect that the preaching of the Word will bring about the reality described in the text. If the sermon is about the miracles of Jesus, they expect to see Jesus present to heal.'[43] So yes, God should be sought for supernatural results through preaching, particularly when the sermon is based on a passage in Scripture that includes such expectations. This has significant implications for preaching within Pentecostal and charismatic contexts – so much so, that it may be one key reason some have dismissed Pentecostal and Charismatic preaching practices. The implications of this subject must be further explained.

---

[42] *AF* 1.1 (September 1906), p. 2 (emphasis original).
[43] Cheryl Bridges Johns, 'What Makes a Good Sermon: A Pentecostal Perspective', *Journal for Preachers* 26.4 (2003), p. 50.

If Pentecostal preachers feel that their preaching is only 'Pentecostal' when they experience supernatural results from their preaching, they may be tempted to manipulate the context of preaching in order to gain some sort of response to the preached Word. Pentecostals and non-Pentecostals have been turned off by Pentecostal preaching due to some preachers' need to manipulate meetings in order to bring out some response, whether through 'hype', emotionalism, pushing people at altar calls so they are 'slain in the Spirit', and over-promising the results of an altar call. Expecting and hoping for a healing, though, is reasonable when preaching a message based on a story of Christ's healing in Scripture. And while healing can take place even during messages not directly about healing, some messages may need to focus on other challenges – based in Scripture – requiring transformation that some may not be considered a sensational supernatural work of God. One may need to focus on issues like feeding the poor, forgiveness, and serving, which require the Spirit's supernatural work for transformation.

Discerning the Spirit's Immediacy

Discerning the Spirit's immediacy is a common issue among both Hughes and Crabtree that requires analysis. First, Hughes is to be commended for providing a filter for discerning the Spirit's immediacy in preaching. His three guidelines to ensure that an emphasis on supernatural results does not lead to fanaticism, heresy, and selfish ambition are helpful to discern a genuine work of God in preaching and the altar. The three guidelines are: 1) preaching that 'centers in the Word', 2) preaching that 'always exalts Jesus Christ', and 3) preaching that 'is always directed and empowered by the Holy Spirit'.[44] Crabtree acknowledges the importance of the three themes in Hughes' guidelines throughout his work. But Crabtree focuses on the centrality of Christ in preaching over the Spirit's manifestation.[45] Pentecostal preaching has often been criticized for promoting unbiblical, sensational gimmicks through the ministry of preaching. Hughes' approach, however, is especially beneficial for Pentecostal preachers because his three guidelines are important elements of preaching, yet broad enough to apply for different contexts for preaching.

---

[44] Hughes, *Pentecostal Preaching*, p. 156.
[45] Crabtree, *Pentecostal Preaching*, pp. 34-35.

Reflecting back on Azusa, leaders considered it important to distinguish marks of fanaticism from marks of the Spirit's work within their community, which benefits the preacher's focus. First, being 'harsh' with others who you do not agree with is a mark of fanaticism.[46] 'A very little harshness or a critical suspicious statement about a brother will grieve the tender, sensitive Spirit'.[47] Second, another mark of fanaticism occurs when 'Jesus is not held up'.[48] The exaltation of Jesus Christ is central for the church and preaching. Azusa participants believed that there was no time to preach anything else but Christ, since the Spirit does not have 'time to magnify anything else but the Blood of our Lord Jesus Christ'.[49] Third, love was a very crucial mark of the Spirit in one's life.[50] Seymour even explains that Spirit baptism includes the experience of being 'flooded with the love of God'.[51] Fourth, humility was another important mark of the Spirit in the church community. Azusa participants acknowledged their ministry was humble, within a humble context, and that they humbled themselves before God to search His will in Scripture.[52] Fifth, holiness was crucial, as participants lived 'separate' lives from the world, the flesh, and the devil, and called others to do the same.[53] Sixth, a mark of the Spirit included the ability to recognise a genuine work of the Spirit. For if someone professes to know the Spirit, it only follows that such a person must be able to acknowledge when the Spirit is working within a community.[54]

Elements for discernment that the Azusa participants highlighted, like the centrality of Christ, love, humility, holiness, and a confirmation in one's spirit that the Spirit is indeed present, are helpful. Their description of being 'harsh', however, requires more elaboration. The Azusa participants received much criticism during the early period of the revival, and were understandably sensitive to criticism. For even Parham, who they initially confirmed as leader (and later revoked),

---

46 *AF* 1.2 (October 1906), p. 2.
47 *AF* 1.4 (December 1906), p. 45.
48 *AF* 1.2 (October 1906), p. 2.
49 *AF* 1.5 (January 1907), p. 2.
50 *AF* 1.2 (October 1906), p. 2.
51 Seymour, *The Doctrines and Discipline*, p. 42.
52 *AF* 1.2 (October 1906), p. 2.
53 *AF* 1.2 (October 1906), p. 2.
54 *AF* 1.2 (October 1906), p. 2.

opposed their ministry after visiting with them.[55] His criticism may have even been the reason they were more adamant that love, and not tongues was the more crucial evidence of Spirit baptism in a believer.[56] Scripture, however, provides several indications that criticism is not necessarily a lack of the Spirit's work – though it can be. Even Jesus and Paul critiqued the religious establishment of their day when necessary.[57] Paul's injunction in Eph. 4.15, that believers are to 'speak the truth in love', best tempers the Azusa participants' views on criticism. Preachers, and believers in general, may need to critique in love.

Hughes and the Azusa Street Revival's participants' views on discerning the Spirit's immediacy in preaching are helpful. Preachers can use the recommendations made to ensure that they are not following a path of manipulation for preaching. Many of the virtues proposed by Hughes and those at Azusa are important filters to discern authentic preaching led by the Spirit. Preachers must ensure that their preaching is established in Scripture, Christ is central, the Spirit is leading, love is exhibited, humility is sought, holiness is maintained, and a discerning of the Spirit in general is manifest in their ministry.

The Spirit's Work in the Preacher

While Hughes and Crabtree emphasise the Spirit's immediacy in the life of the preacher, Robinson's inclusion of the Spirit's work for the preacher is regrettably deficient. The two ways Robinson's work fails to offer a robust understanding of the Spirit's work in preaching is in his limited role for the preacher's spirituality upon preaching, and by overstating the importance of communication theory (discussed in the following section). Robinson emphasises the discipline of studying of Scripture, but he does not include other spiritual disciplines for the growth of preachers, such as praying. He does not discuss the need for prayer, whether it relates to prayers for the subject and content of sermons, for better understanding Scripture, or how a preacher should pray for their congregation. He does not delve into the need to experience a fresh experience of the Spirit through prayer – apart from just studying Scripture. This may be surprising, but Robinson never explicitly commends the preacher to 'pray' about the sermon.

---

[55] *AF* 1.4 (December 1906), p. 3.
[56] *AF* 1.11 (October-January 1908), p. 2.
[57] E.g., Mk 11.15-18; Mt. 23.1-36; Gal. 2.11-14.

Robinson may assume that preachers who read his book already have a vital spirituality, and will pray in coordination with his emphasis on studying the Bible – when he explains 'the Holy Spirit studies us'.[58] Studying the Bible is undoubtedly critical for one's spiritual growth, but if limited to this one practice, it is insufficient. Scripture, for instance, shows that even the twelve apostles considered the coordination of preaching with prayer was of utmost importance for them.[59] Since Robinson is coming from an evangelical context, it may seem unnecessary to him to delve into spiritual disciplines – beyond the study of Scripture – that may be assumed within his context. One's theology, however, is expressed not just by what is included, but also by what is excluded. For this reason, Robinson's work suffers from a lack of emphasis on the spirituality that is vital for a preacher – apart from the study of Scripture. This approach seems to derive from his views on the issue of authority for preaching.[60] Authority derives primarily from Scripture, which was inspired by the Holy Spirit – so that the preacher must be a dedicated student of Scripture.

Through the written Word people encounter the revelation of Jesus Christ and His redemptive work. But without an emphasis on the present work of the Spirit in preaching, 'biblical' preaching can become sterile. The religious leaders of Jesus' day knew the written Word, but they were wrong in their understanding of the Word. People need to be illuminated by the Spirit in order to comprehend the Word (1 Cor. 2.9-11). An emphasis on being yielded to the Spirit's present work for preaching is thus critical (1 Cor. 2.9-11).

---

[58] Robinson, *Biblical Preaching*, p. 26.

[59] Acts 6.1-4; Bridges, 'Introduction', pp. 13-14.

[60] William Turner's ideas on Protestantism and preaching may apply to Robinson's approach, for he argues that Protestants are not open to 'mystery' and preaching that is both theologically sound and in the Spirit. He explains in 'Preaching the Spirit: The Liberation of Preaching', *Journal of Pentecostal Theology* 14.1 (2005), p. 14, that

> Protestantism, which is centered in right preaching of the Word and right celebration of the sacraments, tends to put emphasis on correctness of confession and verifiable knowledge. The epistemology is spurred by distrust of mystery, especially when entrusted into the hands of priests to whom the people are subservient. It was enhanced by the rise of historical consciousness and modern theories of knowledge that put the human knower at the center. A consequence was decreasing capacity to speak faithfully of mystery.

Greg Heisler acknowledges that Evangelicals have typically neglected the work of the Spirit in preaching to avoid being labelled a
Charismatic or Pentecostal.[61] Charismatics also caricature Evangelicals as group that is focused on an intellectual faith merely based
upon propositions.[62] He explains that '[a] correct biblical theology of
pneumatology and bibliology must drive and under-gird any methodology of homiletics'.[63] Furthermore, '[t]he Spirit-driven methodology of expository preaching posits that the Spirit, the Word, and
the preacher must all testify to Jesus Christ in unison during the actual
preparation and proclamation of the sermon if the preacher is ever
going to preach with power'.[64] Heisler rightly includes the Spirit's
work in all aspects of preaching. And like Hughes, Crabtree, and Robinson argue, the focus of the message must be Jesus Christ.[65] Recognising the ongoing, dual role of Scripture and the Spirit for preaching
is critical, as Jesus himself stated that Scripture and the Spirit bears
witness to himself (Jn 5.39-40; 15.26).

But even Heisler's understanding of the relationship between the
Spirit, Word, and preacher is limited. Heisler refuses to dialogue with
'popular charismatic' approaches to the Spirit's work because of excesses within this movement. Some of the excesses he mentions includes those who breath on people to be 'slain in the Spirit' and for-
mulaic approaches to God, that all end up making more of individuals than God.[66] This, however, leads to his unwillingness to deal with
a Pentecostal approach to preaching that includes the place of the
gifts of the Spirit like prophecy, words of knowledge and wisdom,
and miracles.[67]

---

[61] See Greg Heisler, 'Clark Kent or Superman? A Case for a Spirit-Driven Methodology of Expository Preaching'. Paper presented at the annual meeting of the
Evangelical Academy of Homiletics, 2004. Online: http://www.ehomiletics.com/
papers/04/heisler04.php and Greg Heisler, *Spirit-Led Preaching: The Holy Spirit's Role
in Sermon Preparation and Delivery* (Nashville: Broadman and Holman, 2007).

[62] See Heisler's works, *Spirit-Led Preaching* and 'Clark Kent or Superman?'

[63] Heisler, 'Clark Kent or Superman?'

[64] Heisler, 'Clark Kent or Superman?'

[65] Heisler, *Spirit-Led Preaching*, p. 21.

[66] Heisler, *Spirit-Led Preaching*, p. 127.

[67] Cheryl Bridges Johns alludes to this idea when she states that 'Perceived excesses in revivalism and Pentecostalism have fostered an image of Spirit-centered
religion as fanatical. As a result, "Holy Spirit shyness" is often preferred over Holy
Spirit fanaticism.' Cheryl Bridges Johns, 'Holy Spirit and Preaching', in Paul Scott

Robinson, however, supervised a thesis on preaching by a Canadian classical Pentecostal, Fred Penney. Like Heisler, Penney posits the failure of texts on homiletics to include substantial thought on the role of the Spirit, favouring a more intellectual approach in order to understand the text of Scripture and a way to incorporate good communication theory.[68] Penney argues for the need to include a 'spiritual warfare cosmology', noting that the context for preaching is charged with invisible realities, such as the kingdom of darkness, which requires the need for the power of the Spirit in preaching.[69] That Robinson would supervise such a thesis at least reveals a sympathetic view towards a Pentecostal impulse that emphasises the present work of the Spirit in preaching.

Communication Theory

Robinson also overstates the importance of communication theory for preaching, and is subsequently ambiguous about the role of the Spirit for preaching. For instance, Robinson overstates the importance of non-verbal communication. When he argues that '[g]estures and voice emerge as the most obvious and determinative part of preaching', he appears to betray his own words. In a later addition in his second edition, he states that preaching is God's work and only Christ through His Spirit can effectively feed the congregation.[70] His view contrasts significantly with Hughes' and Crabtree's approach that emphasises the Spirit's present work in preaching. By overstating the role of communication theory, one may neglect the Apostle Paul's thought that preaching must be done 'with a demonstration of the Spirit and of power', so that one's 'faith might not rest on human

---

Wilson (ed.), *The New Interpreters Handbook of Preaching* (Nashville: Abingdon 2008), p. 461.

[68] James T. Flynn, *Words that Transform: Preaching as a Catalyst for Renewal* (Lanham: University Press of America, 2010), p. 20, who also writes from a charismatic background, concurs with this analysis, stating,

> many sermons lack transformational power because we preachers neglect the internal preparation necessary to give substance to our sermon's words. Our inclination to emphasize the external part of sermon preparation is evident in preaching literature. Books advocate different kinds of rhetorical method, different rules for textual treatment and exegesis, various ways to contextualize the sermon for specific cultures, and a plethora of other approaches to honing the sermon's external attributes.

[69] Penney, 'Applying a Spiritual Warfare Cosmology to Preaching'.

[70] Robinson, *Biblical Preaching*, pp. 202, 223.

wisdom but on the power of God' (1 Cor. 2.1-5).[71] To be fair to Robinson, though, he spends much time on the role of Scripture, so that his comments on communication theory may also betray his emphasis on Scripture, which is inspired by the Spirit. While incorporating good communication theory can be helpful for one's preaching, the Spirit can convict hearers through a sermon uttered through a preacher with less than admirable non-verbal skills in the pulpit.

Spontaneity and the Leading of the Spirit

In all three leaders, openness to spontaneity is encouraged, but only Hughes and Crabtree associate the importance of spontaneity with the leading of the Spirit. Hughes argues that prophetic preaching is the best form of Pentecostal preaching, which involves being open to spontaneous leadings of the Spirit while preaching. Crabtree regularly emphasises the need to be open to spontaneous leadings of the Spirit while preaching. While Crabtree acknowledges the role of preparation, he rightly reminds preachers that even Christ responded spontaneously while ministering when the need arose.[72] Robinson does not associate spontaneity in the pulpit with the Spirit, but just with the 'heat' of delivery.[73] He does not elaborate on what this 'heat' may be, but it appears to be about a preacher's excited emotions while preaching. Further, Robinson only indicates that new sentence structures and phrases may spontaneously arise while preaching. For Robinson, then, a different subject does not emerge, but paraphrases of the content prepared for the sermon.[74] Since Hughes and Crabtree consider an openness to spontaneity as crucial to being open to the leading of the Spirit, spontaneity and the leading of the Spirit must be addressed.

Looking back at Azusa, spontaneously following the Spirit's leadership for the ministry of preaching was not only crucial, but normative. Azusa leaders did not announce the subjects of sermons in advance and did not advertise any special preachers – they claimed that

---

[71] Flynn rightly notes that 'The sermon must begin as a work in the heart rather than with external work on words, rhetoric, diction, style, or form. As important as external considerations are, if they dominate the message preparation process, they can strip the message of its power'. *Words that Transform*, p. 31.

[72] Crabtree, *Pentecostal Preaching*, p. 39; e.g., Mk 1.31-37.

[73] Robinson, *Biblical Preaching*, p. 186.

[74] Robinson, *Biblical Preaching*, p. 186.

the Spirit led who should preach and what to preach during the service.[75] The Azusa approach to preaching, then, is even more dependent on spontaneity than Hughes and Crabtree. For both Hughes and Crabtree acknowledge the role of studying and preparing for a sermon in advance. It would appear, then, that what would arise among Azusa participants who are preaching, is the result of their own testimony – their experience of the Spirit's work – and regular, personal study of Scripture. Preparing a sermon, then, would be less about preparing a sermon manuscript, but preparing the person so that they are immersed both in Scripture and an experience of the Spirit. Thus, when ministers preach, what emerges in their words is a sermon that is dependent on their personal experience of the Spirit and Word.

The types of spontaneity that Hughes, Crabtree, and Robinson are open to reflect the type of preparation they all emphasise for the preacher. Both Hughes and Crabtree emphasise the need for preachers to prepare themselves through the Spirit's work, so that they are open to the spontaneous leading of the Spirit. Though both Hughes and Crabtree acknowledge the role of study and preparing a sermon manuscript, they both do not emphasise this type of preparation relative to an experience of Spirit baptism. Hughes devotes 8 out of 168 pages to an explanation of how to study Scripture for preaching, while Crabtree writes 9 pages out of 203 on studying Scripture for preaching.[76] Robinson emphasises the need for preachers to study and prepare a sermon manuscript, so that he only indicates that the language used may change when preaching. Robinson gives very little emphasis to the preparation of the preacher's character, other than how the study of Scripture for sermon preparation initiates the Spirit's work of transformation in a preacher.

The emphasis on spontaneous leadings of the Spirit, highlighted by Hughes, Crabtree, and especially those at Azusa, can lead to negative implications. Those who primarily rely on spontaneous leadings of the Spirit while preaching, rather than a thorough study and preparation for a sermon, can be led to careless treatment of the Word of God, and even error. Explaining a difficult concept in Scripture often requires time, prayer, meditation, and careful formulation of

---

[75] Bartleman, *Azusa Street*, pp. 62-63.
[76] Hughes, *Pentecostal Preaching*, pp. 93-100; Crabtree, *Pentecostal Preaching*, pp. 193-202.

one's thoughts. When people seek to be spontaneous, they may neglect carefully explaining particular nuances of Scripture and theology that is necessary for understanding the Word of God.

Pentecostal preachers, however, would be well advised to take seriously the emphases of all three leaders – as well as those at Azusa – so that they are immersed in an experience of the Spirit and the Word. What emerges when people preach spontaneously is what has been percolating in that person's heart. As Christ stated, 'it is out of the abundance of the heart that the mouth speaks' (Lk. 6.45b). And the Spirit brings studied Scripture to mind, so that one's previous engagement with Scripture will affect the effectiveness of preaching spontaneously (Jn 14.26). Thus, if preachers are not immersed in both Scripture and an experience of the Spirit, what arises out of their spontaneous preaching will be lacking. If they only emphasise the Spirit's work in their preparation, they will lack a ministry that is rooted firmly in Scripture. For even the Spirit's work contributes to bringing to mind Scripture previously encountered and studied. But more than just studying Scripture and preparing a sermon, taking the Azusa Street leaders' emphasis on regular, daily study of Scripture is important. Regular, daily study of Scripture, which is not necessarily for the study of a sermon, ensures that one's life is immersed in the Word of God. Scripture, then, is not reduced to just a tool for ministry activity. Following Hughes' and Crabtree's emphasis, though, also ensures that preaching is not relegated to the intellectual dimension of ministry. Preaching is not merely about preparing and delivering a carefully constructed speech that is based on Scripture – preaching is a 'demonstration of the Spirit and power' (1 Cor. 2.1-5). Thus, preachers should be open and yielded to the Spirit's leading while preaching – remaining rooted in Scripture – so that they truly engage in robust prophetic preaching.[77] Ensuring this type of prophetic preaching continues, can help ensure the church continues to experience renewal.[78]

---

[77] Also see Lee Roy Martin, 'Fire in the Bones: Pentecostal Prophetic Preaching', in Lee Roy Martin (ed.), *Toward a Pentecostal Theology of Preaching* (Cleveland: CPT Press, 2015), p. 51.

[78] Martin, 'Fire in the Bones: Pentecostal Prophetic Preaching', p. 63.

The Role of Scripture for Preaching

Hughes, Crabtree, and Robinson all argue that Scripture is a critical authority for preaching, but Pentecostals Hughes and Crabtree ironically spend little time delving into how one may faithfully appropriate Scripture for preaching in each of their books on preaching. Hughes dedicates 8 pages out of 168 pages for the proper approach for studying Scripture for preaching.[79] Crabtree limits his discussion on appropriating Scripture for preaching to approximately 9 pages out of 203 pages in his book.[80] Robinson, however, spends approximately 113 out of 245 pages for the means of appropriating Scripture for the sermon.[81] This illustrates why Pentecostals may use books like Robinson's in order to counter-balance the sometimes excessive emphasis Pentecostals place on the present work of the Spirit and the supernatural – to the exclusion of Scripture for preaching. But while Robinson's work offers helpful insights into studying Scripture for preachers, Hughes' and Crabtree's emphasis on preachers being continually yielded to the Spirit cannot be neglected. A more balanced Pentecostal approach to preaching is needed today – incorporating the Spirit's past (Scripture) and present work for preaching.

Reflecting back on Azusa, they did not address the need to spend time on studying Scripture so that it can be appropriated for a particular sermon. Azusa participants, as stated earlier, prized the role of spontaneity for preaching over prepared sermon manuscripts. Nevertheless, they did acknowledge the importance of the regular study of Scripture. Though Seymour highlights the important role of Scripture in a preacher's life, he does not give guidance on how to study it systematically for a particular sermon. Seymour only delves into the need for prayer and daily time in Scripture through reading, meditating, hearing, and obeying what is learned in Scripture.[82] Azusa leaders understood that a thorough knowledge of Scripture helps

---

[79] Hughes, *Pentecostal Preaching*, pp. 93-100.

[80] Crabtree, *Pentecostal Preaching*, pp. 193-202.

[81] Robinson, *Biblical Preaching*, pp. 51-164.

[82] Seymour, *The Doctrines and Discipline*, p. 107. Seymour is noted as someone known for regularly praying at the Azusa Street Mission. Rufus G.W. Sanders, *William Joseph Seymour: Black Father of the 20th Century Pentecostal/Charismatic Movement* (Sandusky: Xulon, 2003), p. 97.

202 The Holy Spirit in Worship Music, Preaching, and the Altar

provide discernment for preachers, ensuring that their preaching is not led by false experiences of the immediacy of God.[83]

Contemporary preachers can benefit from Azusa leaders' emphasis on the role of Scripture in a minister's life. Insisting that preachers follow a rigorous, daily pattern of studying Scripture can ensure that preachers are faithful to the whole counsel Scripture in their preaching. But even the most dedicated student of Scripture can be benefited by systematic preparation for preaching, which Robinson values and teaches. Robinson's approach to appropriating Scripture for preaching is systematic and rigorous – and can benefit the Pentecostal preacher. Of course, other resources for studying Scripture for sermons should also be consulted.

The Spirit's Work and Opposition

In all three leaders' works on preaching, none tackle the issue of preaching that engenders opposition and suffering. If preachers work hard at applying the principles they share, the assumption is that positive results will follow. For Hughes and Crabtree, positive results most often mean sensational, supernatural results. For Robinson, positive results most often mean that hearers are able to apply the Scripture to their day-to-day lives. The Azusa participants, however, acknowledged that while the immediacy of God could be expected through faithful preaching, opposition was another unavoidable result of faithful preaching.

Through Azusa, the early Pentecostal movement gained both followers and detractors. While they regularly cited their impressive growth and supernatural results following the preaching, they admitted that opposition was unavoidable with faithful preaching.[84] Azusa's teaching and experience can benefit contemporary Pentecostal preachers today. Success among Pentecostal preachers is often determined by numerical growth within a congregation and supernatural results. Health, wealth, and even popularity, are often deemed as the natural consequence of faithful Christian preaching among Pentecostals. But a failure to acknowledge the role of opposition fails to take seriously Christ's example and call to ministry that revealed the reality of opposition and suffering.

---

[83] *AF* 1.11 (October-January 1908), p. 2.
[84] *AF* 1.5 (January 1907), p. 3.

While Hughes and Crabtree acknowledge the importance of proclaiming the message of 'Christ and Him crucified', they fail to take
into account how Christ's example and message affects the ministry
of preaching itself. Even the Apostle Paul gave emphasis to the role
of opposition and suffering in his life. While many view Paul's conversion on the road to Damascus as the most defining aspect of his
life for ministry, he describes his experience of suffering more so
than his dramatic conversion. In Paul's writings, he only mentions his
conversion once, but explains his experience of suffering numerous
times for his readers to understand his life and ministry.[85] Paul viewed
his ministry of preaching as 'a direct expression of his continuous
participation in and imitation of the life of Jesus of Nazareth'.[86] Rather than viewing opposition to preaching a failure on the part of the
preacher, it may be best deemed as a natural result of faithful Christian preaching. Preachers, then, may understand that while supernatural results may accompany preaching, so will opposition.

The Spirit's Work among the Congregation
Hughes', Crabtree's, and Robinson's works could also be improved
by a more robust understanding of the work of the Spirit in the congregation. In Robinson's approach, the Spirit applies the message of
the preached Word to the congregation. Robinson also encourages
feedback on the sermon preached, which he does not associate with
the Spirit's work. Hughes and Crabtree focus on the Spirit's work
upon the congregation so that supernatural results occur among
them through preaching. Hughes also recognises the importance of
preachers knowing and understanding their audience so that they can
preach 'with precision' for the needs of the congregation.[87] In the
case of Hughes and Crabtree, the congregation's role in the development of the sermon is primarily passive, apart from their response to
the sermon. It may be the case that since all three leaders are writing
for preachers, they focus on the preacher's responsibility. But while
pastors of congregations should not abrogate their responsibility to
'shepherd the sheep', it is important to acknowledge the gifts of the

---

[85] Michael P. Knowles, *We Preach Not Ourselves: Paul on Proclamation* (Grand Rapids: Eerdmans, 2007), pp. 41-43; Gal. 1.15-17; 1 Cor. 4.11-13; 2 Cor. 4.8-10; 6.4-10;
11.23-28; 12.7-10.
[86] Knowles, *We Preach Not Ourselves*, p. 43.
[87] Hughes, *Pentecostal Preaching*, pp. 103-104.

Spirit among the congregation and their capability to be led by the Spirit for preaching (1 Cor. 12.7). The involvement of the congregation can lead to their active contribution to the sermon.

The Spirit's gifts for the ministry of preaching and the altar can lead to a variety of supernatural results, which include: wisdom, knowledge, faith, healing, miracles, prophecy, pastoring, teaching, evangelism, exhortation, and leadership.[88] Of course, other gifts and manifestations of the Spirit may affect the ministry of preaching, but the ones mentioned above are more explicit in their influence on preaching and the altar. Though Hughes and Crabtree acknowledge the role of various gifts of the Spirit for preaching, the discussion on the expression of the gifts of the Spirit are limited for the preacher, not the congregation.[89]

Taking Paul's teaching on the gifts of the Spirit into consideration broadens one's understanding of 'supernatural results' for preaching. Supernatural results for preaching may include healing and miracles – like Hughes and Crabtree emphasise – but it may include other results. Both Hughes and Crabtree acknowledge the role of various gifts of the Spirit for preaching, but the more sensational gifts like healing and miracles overshadow the other gifts.[90] Other supernatural results because of the Spirit's manifestation through preaching may include, for instance: words of wisdom received through preaching, a greater understanding of Scripture because of the gift of teaching, or a pastoral approach that affects one's preaching. But this does not alleviate a preacher from praying and expecting supernatural results that they may not associate with their gift from the Spirit. For instance, while some preachers may be gifted by the Spirit for evangelism, every Christian is expected to evangelise.[91] What this means, then, is that while preachers may experience greater supernatural results that are associated with their gift, they are not alleviated from praying and expecting results in other areas. Further, this shows why one preacher cannot accomplish everything needed for the church's mission. Those who are called to vocational ministry must ensure that they do not restrict the ministry of preaching to their own

---

[88] See 1 Cor. 12.1-11; Eph. 4.7-16; Rom. 12.3-8.
[89] Hughes, *Pentecostal Preaching*, p. 165; Crabtree, *Pentecostal Preaching*, pp. 169-87.
[90] Hughes, *Pentecostal Preaching*, p. 165; Crabtree, *Pentecostal Preaching*, pp. 169-87.
[91] Matthew 28.18-20.

preaching and gifts. Preachers must be willing to allow others to minister and preach with their other complementary gifts for a fuller expression of the Spirit's mission in the church.

Remembering Azusa, though they too emphasised the experience of the more sensational gifts of the Spirit, like tongues and miracles, they were open to the Spirit's work among various people as long as they experienced Spirit baptism. The Azusa participants' experience and emphasis on Spirit baptism led them to believe that anyone who was baptised in the Spirit could preach, regardless of gender, age, social status, educational background, or formal ministerial credentials.[92] Their approach to preaching led to an inclusive approach that cultivated the gifts of people of various backgrounds from within the congregation. Though Seymour was the primary preacher at Azusa, he shared the ministry of preaching with others on a regular basis.[93] Azusa's inclusive approach that encouraged a diversity of believers to contribute to the act of preaching is a good model for Pentecostals.

Furthermore, the congregation can be led by the Spirit to contribute to the sermon from its preparation to an experience at the altar. Preachers can form a team – consisting of a cross-section of the congregation – to help preachers develop sermons. A team for preaching adds creativity to the message and provides insights into blind spots that the preacher may have from their limited perspective.[94] The various gifts of the Spirit found within such a team – and the congregation in general – can contribute to the sermon in ways that one preacher's gifts cannot do. The congregation can also reflect back on the sermon through discussion and constructive feedback.

The congregation can be involved in the actual delivery of the sermon, which also finds precedent at Azusa. The African American preaching tradition is noted for this approach through the use of the 'call and response', which 'refers to a pattern of verbal interplay between preacher and congregation that occurs during the sermon and

---

[92] *AF* 1.2 (October 1906), p. 3; (September 1907), p. 3; (June–September 1907), p. 3.

[93] Robeck, *The Azusa Street Mission and Revival*, p. 115.

[94] Ed Young, Jr, 'Preaching Creatively', in Michael Duduit (ed.), *Preaching with Power: Dynamic Insights from Twenty Top Pastors* (Grand Rapids: Baker, 2006), pp. 246-48.

shapes its delivery'.[95] The use of 'progressional dialogue' – which expands on the African American approach – 'involves the intentional interplay of multiple viewpoints that leads to unexpected and unforeseen ideas'.[96] Progressional dialogue expands the congregation's involvement beyond a brief response, such as an 'amen', potentially to adding further discourse and points for the sermon. Pentecostals have precedent for this in Seymour's ministry at Azusa, whereby he provided opportunity for others to respond to sermons or even preach – following in line with the African-American approach to preaching.[97] Crabtree's regular admonition that preaching be done to please God, not people, can also ensure that this practice of including the congregation does not lead to preaching that panders to every opinion in the congregation. Including others in the sermon must be done with discernment and the intention of glorifying God.

The Spirit's Future Work for Preaching

In light of this discussion on the Spirit's immediacy for preaching, it is fitting also to delve into the Spirit's future work for preaching in all three leaders' approach. Understanding how the Spirit may appropriate sermons in people's lives in the future, which they have heard in the past, can help Pentecostals gain perspective beyond the emphasis on the Spirit's present work. Hughes and Crabtree do not delve into the Spirit's future work for preaching. The closest Robinson gets to acknowledging the role of preaching in one's life beyond the hearing of the sermon, is his discussion on finding ways that the sermon applies to the hearer's life during the week. Azusa participants also do not delve much into the Spirit's future work for preaching, for Spirit baptism was viewed as a quick route for an experience of power and language for preaching immediately. Furthermore, though Azusa participants spoke much of the end times, they focused primarily on teaching that Jesus was returning back soon.[98]

It is crucial for Pentecostal preachers to consider how the Spirit's work for preaching relates to the future. First, Jesus explained that one work of the Spirit is to bring his Word back to memory (Jn

---

[95] Robert Smith, Jr, 'Call and Response', in Paul Scott Wilson (ed.), *The New Interpreter's Handbook of Preaching* (Nashville: Abingdon, 2008), p. 297.

[96] Doug Pagitt, *Preaching Re-Imagined: The Role of the Sermon in Communities of Faith* (Grand Rapids: Zondervan, 2005), p. 52.

[97] Robeck, *The Azusa Street Mission and Revival*, pp. 115-19.

[98] *AF* 1.2 (October 1906), p. 3.

14.26). Christ's teaching on the Spirit shows that while it is tempting to desire immediate gratification from preaching, preachers must be willing to bear with delayed gratification in the response to the Word. What preachers say in the moment may not be received immediately, but may only bear fruit in the future. This acknowledgment can benefit preachers who are too enamored with instant responses to preaching that they fall into the temptation of manipulation.

Second, the Spirit's ongoing work will culminate in believers' glorification. The immediate results of preaching will not produce perfection, but has as its aim the perfection that the Spirit will bring. In Rom. 8.23, Paul explains that believers have 'the first fruits of the Spirit', and 'wait for adoption, the redemption of our bodies'. Thus, '[t]he church's very existence could be described as the Spirit's constantly pushing the body of Christ forward toward the parousia, the final fulfillment'.[99] The continuing role of the Spirit in the church reveals that the church has not reached perfection, but is on a journey towards this goal of perfection through the Spirit's enablement. For preaching, this reminds the church that the Spirit is not only critical because of his past and present work, but is also important for the church's continual journey towards perfection.[100] Pentecostal preachers who acknowledge the Spirit's mission in the church as ongoing and only finding fulfillment in the parousia, will be mindful of not placing inordinate pressure on immediate results from sermons. Preachers may then acknowledge their ministry as part of the church's journey in the Spirit's ongoing and future work in the church.

Finally, the Spirit's ongoing and future work includes the renewal of all creation. The Psalmist proclaims, 'When you send forth your spirit, they are created; and you renew the face of the ground' (Ps 104.30). The Apostle Paul, in Rom. 8.22-23, reveals that '[t]he Spirit who cries out from the breast of every forlorn human also groans within creation and yearns for the same eschatological redemption'.[101] Thus, 'creation care, no less than the traditional disciplines of Christian formation, is a way the Christian can "keep in step with the

---

[99] Chan, *Liturgical Theology*, p. 39.
[100] Chan, *Liturgical Theology*, p. 40.
[101] Steven Studebaker, 'The Spirit in Creation: A Unified Theology of Grace and Creation Care', *Zygon* 43.4 (December 2008), p. 952.

Spirit'".[102] This understanding of the Spirit ensures that one's vision for preaching is not relegated to traditional notions of transformation – things like personal salvation, physical healing, and forgiveness – but to all of creation. A fitting response to a sermon may include the ethical treatment of animals or the environment.

The Spirit's Role within the Triune God for Preaching
The Spirit's role within the Triune God for preaching must also be addressed among all three leaders. Hughes, Crabtree, and Robinson effectively focus on encountering Jesus Christ through preaching, and affirm the role of the Spirit in preaching (though in different ways as described above). But an explicit explanation of the Father's role in preaching among the three leaders is limited, which underlies an underdeveloped explanation of what the Triune God means for preaching. Hughes fails to give any indication of how preaching is affected by God who is Triune. Further, his only mention of the Father's role in his work on preaching, consists of Scriptural references that include mention of the Father. And his Scriptural references that mention the Father, however, are referenced in his work in order to make other points about preaching that do not explicitly highlight the Father's role in preaching.[103]

Crabtree is more explicit on what the Triune God means for the church, stating that the church is 'built upon the unity of God the Father and God the Son and God the Holy Spirit' – this view is significant for Crabtree because it ensures preachers are faithful to the gospel and Christian theology.[104] He also explains that Pentecostal preachers as leaders in the New Testament are 'distinguished by total dependence upon God the Father, the preeminence of Christ, and the person and work of the Holy Spirit'.[105] Crabtree describes this dependence as one that follows Christ's example who depended on the Father through prayer.[106] Dependence on the Father through prayer is found throughout Crabtree's work in his emphasis on Spirit baptism. Crabtree's inclusion of the Father is understandable,

[102] Studebaker, 'The Spirit in Creation', p. 954.
[103] Hughes, *Pentecostal Preaching*, pp. 68, 69, 127, 146.
[104] Crabtree, *Pentecostal Preaching*, p. 70.
[105] Crabtree, *Pentecostal Preaching*, p. 124.
[106] Crabtree, *Pentecostal Preaching*, p. 124.

though, since Jesus explicitly stated that the promised gift of the Father is Spirit baptism, which is a primary theme in Crabtree's work.[107] The Father's role is implicitly found throughout his work, since his work is saturated with quotations from Scripture where the Father is mentioned, such as: the Spirit who proceeds from the Father and testifies to Jesus; Jesus' explanation that those who believe in him will do greater works than him through the Spirit since he goes to the Father; and Peter's knowledge of who Jesus is as a revelation from the Father.[108] What is interesting to note in all these instances, is that he focuses primarily on explaining the relationship between the Son and the Spirit in each context, and ignores the Father's role. Crabtree's analysis of what the Triune God means for preaching is more thorough than Hughes' and Robinson's (as explained below), but requires further development.

Robinson identifies the Trinity as an important topic for preaching, and explains that the Father is one of the many visions of God – among others like him as Creator, Redeemer, rejected Lover, Husband, and King – that preachers may encounter when discerning the vision of God in a passage.[109] Overall, Robinson shares how one might include thoughts on the Triune God for the sermon content. He does not, however, show the implications that the Triune God – notably the Father – may have for the act of preaching itself.

Leaders at the Azusa Street Revival reflect Hughes and Crabtree, acknowledging the work of the Spirit and centrality of Christ for ministry. But those at Azusa fail to consider how the Trinity affects ministry, most notably the Father's role. Azusa's official publication, *AF*, for instance, only mentions the word 'Trinity' when making clear that the Spirit is 'the third Person of the Trinity'.[110] The Father's role in ministry is often only mentioned incidentally; particularly when they quote Scripture that includes the role of the Father. Like Crabtree, Azusa participants primarily reference the Father in relation to the promise of the Father – Spirit Baptism – which Christ explains in Lk. 24.49. The only reference to the Father that is repeated in every

---

[107] Crabtree, *Pentecostal Preaching*, pp. 109, 121, 154, 157, 159, 161-62.

[108] Crabtree, *Pentecostal Preaching*, pp. 34; Jn 14.12; 15.26, 36; Mt. 16.16-17.

[109] Robinson, *Biblical Preaching*, pp. 56, 94.

[110] E.g., *AF* 1.9 (June–September 1907), p. 4; (September 1907), p. 3; (May 1908), pp. 2, 3.

edition of *AF* is the association of receiving Spirit baptism as the promise of the Father.

Maintaining a Trinitarian approach to preaching ensures that preaching is not merely about what a preacher does, but a gift the Triune God gives. The Word begins with the Father, but the human response also ends with the Father, which James B. Torrance explains. Torrance frames the practice of preaching in light of worshipping a Triune God. Worship is 'a double movement of grace', which begins with: '(a) a God-humanward movement, from (*ek*) the Father, through (*dia*) the Son, in (*en*) the Spirit, and (b) a human-Godward movement to the Father, through the Son in the Spirit'.[111] This movement shows how worship is a gift that begins with the Father and finds its culmination in the Father. When viewing preaching and other forms of worship as primarily about what preachers do, ministers can become weary. Torrance explains how one Pentecostal appropriated this Trinitarian approach to worship and realised that he did not have to keep '"whipping up" himself and his congregation to live out their experience', which led to being weary and tired.[112] Torrance's Trinitarian approach to worship is a welcome view for Pentecostal preachers who are often so caught up in working up the emotions of the church to generate a response.[113] Understanding that worship is first and foremost a gift of the Triune God, ensures that preachers recognise that authentic worship cannot be manufactured. The origins of authentic worship are found in the Triune God.

In conclusion, Hughes, Crabtree, and Robinson have an underdeveloped view of the Trinity for preaching. Torrance's views help Pentecostal preaching become more robust in its inclusion of the Triune God for preaching. Torrance's views help Pentecostal preachers un-

---

[111] James B. Torrance, *Worship, Community, and the Triune God of Grace* (Downers Grove: InterVarsity, 1996), p. 21.

[112] Torrance, *Worship, Community, and the Triune God of Grace*, pp. 22-23.

[113] Michael J. Quicke also makes use of Torrance's views for preaching, and explains that without this type of 'trinitarian framework, weekly sermon work degenerates into practical Unitarianism in which they assume full responsibility. Rather, they should be practical Trinitarians, approaching the text open to the Spirit and the gift of participation in God's Trinitarian life.' Michael J. Quicke, 'Trinity', in Paul Scott Wilson (ed.), *The New Interpreter's Handbook of Preaching* (Nashville: Abingdon Press, 2008), pp. 500-501.

derstand that worship finds its origins in God alone, and not by man-ufacturing and manipulating the context of preaching in the guise of Spirit-led preaching.

Conclusion

Hughes, Crabtree, and Robinson approach the act of preaching from two different emphases: the Spirit's immediacy (Hughes and Crab-tree) and the written Word, inspired by the Spirit (Robinson). Both elements, however, are necessary for effective preaching. Pentecostals cannot dismiss their own theology for preaching, which includes the various gifts of the Spirit and supernatural. In the analysis of Hughes, it is clear that a preacher's shortcomings regarding their own experi-ence of God does not discount the supernatural results that may fol-low their preaching. Nevertheless, a failure on the part of preachers to grow in their experience of God limits their effectiveness. The analysis of Crabtree reveals that an experience of supernatural results is not restricted to those who have been baptised in the Spirit. Spirit baptism provides another dimension of power for ministry, but does not subsequently limit others' experience of supernatural results for preaching.

Since both Hughes and Crabtree are classical Pentecostals, it is understandable that they have two common issues arising out of their views on preaching. They both offer helpful insights into discerning the work of the Spirit in preaching, while Azusa gives further sub-stance for this issue. Preachers must ensure their preaching is estab-lished in Scripture, Christ is central, the Spirit is leading, love is ex-hibited, humility is sought, holiness is maintained, and a discerning of the Spirit in general is manifest in their ministry. Hughes, Crabtree, and those at Azusa, however, give the impression that sensational su-pernatural results can always be expected through ministry. The problem with a focus on sensational supernatural results fails to ac-count for three things. First, they fail to address the issue that preach-ers have various gifts. And though all preachers should pray for heal-ing and miracles, it is inappropriate for preachers to neglect the gifts they offer for preaching in order just to emphasise healing and mira-cles. Second, focusing primarily on sensational supernatural results fails to address the needs among the congregation that are not related to a sensational result, though still requiring the Spirit's transforming work. Third, a focus on sensational supernatural results fails to give account for the various issues addressed in Scripture – beyond just healing and miracles – that require a congregation's attention.

Robinson's view on preaching fails in offering a substantial discussion on the Spirit's work in the preacher and by overstating the role of communication theory. His focus on Scripture is an important reminder of the Spirit's role in inspiring Scripture, which plays a crucial role in preaching. Nevertheless, Robinson's approach focuses primarily on the role of Scripture for character transformation, which fails to give attention to the Spirit's work in various ways for preachers and preaching that Hughes and Crabtree rightly point out. This neglect is evidenced by the fact that he never once commends preachers to pray about the sermon. Furthermore, the benefit of communication theory for preaching is overstated in Robinson's views, in that it betrays his acknowledgement that the Spirit is crucial for convicting hearers.

In all three leaders' works, at least six themes arose that reveal areas of neglect and the subsequent need for development. First, the discussion on the role of spontaneity and being led by the Spirit showed why preachers must be immersed in an experience of the Spirit and the Word on a daily basis. Second, the analysis on the role of Scripture for preaching revealed that Pentecostals need to be careful not to neglect rigorous preparation and study of Scripture, which was inspired by the Spirit. Third, the examination of the Spirit's work and the experience of opposition showed that leaders must acknowledge the reality of opposition when faithfully preaching. Fourth, the discussion on the Spirit's work among the congregation explained why preachers must be willing to allow the congregation to be led by the Spirit to contribute actively to the sermon. Fifth, the analysis on the Spirit's future work for preaching showed how the Spirit's future work ensures preachers do not fall into the temptation of manipulation for the moment. Sixth, the examination of the Spirit's role within the Triune God for preaching revealed that preaching must be rooted in the acknowledgement of worship as a gift from the Triune God, so that the Spirit's role is neither diminished nor exalted to the exclusion of the Son and Father. The next section provides an overall conclusion to this study, providing key findings of the study, some limitations, suggestions for future research, and the value of this study.

CONCLUSION

Pentecostals have often been stereotyped as more interested in working up the emotions of adherents during corporate worship than espousing any defining theology. This work, however, points out that theology plays a very large role in how Pentecostals conduct themselves during corporate worship. The emphasis on the Spirit's immediacy during corporate worship is a defining feature of Pentecostalism. Probing their emphasis on the Spirit's direct and present work in Pentecostal corporate worship deepens our understanding of Pentecostalism. Furthermore, acknowledging the emphasis on the Spirit's immediacy in Pentecostal corporate worship also offers an important means of helping this movement gain a more robust theology of the Spirit and beyond for corporate worship. What follows are key findings of this study, limitations, suggestions for future research, and the value of this study.

Findings of the Study

This work probed the role of the Spirit's immediacy in North American Pentecostal corporate worship in order both to understand and to provide a constructive analysis of Pentecostalism today. In the discussion and analysis of contemporary Pentecostal corporate worship, three key elements of Pentecostal corporate worship were examined: worship music, preaching, and the altar. The views of some of the most influential and representative leaders that has shaped Pentecostal corporate worship music were probed. The views of Brian Doerksen, Darlene Zschech, and Matt Redman were examined in part two of this book. The three leaders' views were discussed and analysed because they are three Contemporary Worship Music (CWM) leaders who have shaped the type of worship music being used in Pentecostal churches today.

Ray H. Hughes and Charles T. Crabtree are representative classical Pentecostal leaders today, who have served as pastors, preachers, and presidents within two prominent classical Pentecostal denominations in the United States. Haddon W. Robinson is not Pentecostal, but his views have significantly shaped Evangelicals and Pentecostals through his influential book, *Biblical Preaching*. For the reasons mentioned above, the views of Hughes, Crabtree, and Robinson were examined and analysed in part three of this book because their views either represent Pentecostals well (Hughes and Crabtree) or have influenced Pentecostal preaching today (Robinson).

The approach of both Azusa Street and other pertinent theological resources were consulted in order to provide an analysis of the Pentecostal focus on the Spirit's immediacy in corporate worship. Including Azusa in this discussion of contemporary Pentecostalism is helpful in two ways. First, including Azusa helps contemporary Pentecostals understand how their theology compares to the theology of their predecessors. This comparison helps Pentecostals learn from the theology of their predecessors at Azusa, discerning both positive and negative elements. Second, in line with other scholars, Azusa was shown to be a source of renewal for contemporary Pentecostalism. But Azusa could not always offer the way forward because of the revival's own limitations. Thus, other pertinent theological resources were brought to bear upon this subject.

The analysis of CWM compared and contrasted the three leaders, and further brought the views and practices at Azusa and other theological resources to bear upon the subject. Doerksen helps Pentecostals focus on the role of the Father, for the Spirit's immediacy leads to intimacy with the Father. His inclusion of songs of lament helps contribute to a more balanced and genuine worship, for Pentecostals have neglected this type of worship music in favour of upbeat, joyful songs. Zschech points the way forward to discern the Spirit's immediacy in worship music. The fruit of worship music is not merely good feelings, but Christ-likeness, love, and social justice. She also shows the importance of singing in tongues, which finds precedent in both Scripture and at Azusa. Redman's focus on the Spirit as the worship leader is an important corrective to CWM today that puts undue pressure on humans to do something only the Spirit can do.

The three CWM leaders have two issues in common for analysis: the elevation of worship music and the role of prophetic songs. First, the elevation of worship music has led some to define worship solely as worship music. But worship music is only one facet of worship, for worship is a lifestyle. Second, on the one hand, the inclusion of prophetic songs of praise can be an important component to the sometimes overly-professional approach to worship music. On the other hand, while prophetic songs can be beneficial, the CWM leaders offer little discernment for these songs that are spontaneous. This work sought to help correct the two issues described above.

The analysis of preaching and the altar with Pentecostalism compared and contrasted three leaders, and also brought the views and practices at Azusa and other theological resources to bear upon the subject. The discussion on Hughes showed that he failed to account for preachers who may experience supernatural results through their preaching, despite failing to experience the immediacy of God. Crabtree's views were shown to be limited, in that he restricts supernatural results to preachers who have been baptised in the Spirit. Hughes and Crabtree also have two common issues in their views on preaching. First, Hughes and Crabtree – as well as those at Azusa – offer helpful insights into discerning the Spirit's work in preaching. Ensuring that the preaching is based in Scripture, Christ is central, the Spirit is leading, love is exhibited, humility is sought, holiness is maintained, and a general discerning of the Spirit is manifest are important features of those discerning the Spirit's work for preaching. Second, however, Hughes and Crabtree give the impression that Pentecostal preachers can always expect sensational supernatural results. Their assumption fails to address the variety of gifts among preachers and congregations that can contribute to preaching in a variety of ways – not just limited to healing and miracles. Further, the emphasis on results like healing and miracles fails to account for various other needs among the congregation.

Robinson's views fail to give account for the Spirit's work in the preacher and overstate the role of communication theory. While Robinson's focus on the relationship of the Spirit and Scripture for preaching is important, he fails to give attention to the Spirit's work for preaching that Hughes and Crabtree rightly point out. Finally, his

overreliance on the role of communication theory ends up being ambiguous with his statements on the Spirit's role of convincing hearers.

All three leaders' works revealed the need to address six themes.
First, their view on spontaneity and being led by the Spirit showed
why an immersion in Scripture and the Spirit on a daily basis is critical. Second, Pentecostals must be more careful to prepare and study
Scripture for preaching. Third, opposition to faithful preaching must
be acknowledged as one of Christ's promises – alongside the role of
supernatural results. Fourth, the congregation may actively contribute to the sermon as they are led by the Spirit. Fifth, acknowledging
the Spirit's future work can ensure that preachers do not fall into the
temptation of manipulation for the moment. Finally, recognising the
Triune God's role for preaching ensures that preachers understand
that worship is a gift from God.

Implications and Suggestions for Further Study

While this work provided several important remarks on the Spirit's
immediacy in corporate worship, it was limited in that it focused
solely on the primary components of Pentecostal corporate worship
today: worship music, preaching, and the altar. Of course, there are
other features of corporate worship that Pentecostals would include,
such as communion, financial giving, dancing, the reading of Scripture, announcements, footwashing, anointing with oil, and a benedic-
tion. While all these other components can contribute positively to
the overall expression of corporate worship, this one book could not
address all these components adequately. Thus, a focus on how the
Spirit's immediacy addresses other components of Pentecostal corporate worship today will be a beneficial future study. Research on
why other elements of corporate worship have become less dominant may prove fruitful, which may also shed light on the role of the
Spirit's immediacy in shaping Pentecostal corporate worship today.
For instance, the Lord's Supper is one activity Paul specifically states
believers should partake of regularly, but is often only practiced
monthly among Pentecostals. Corporate confession is another activ-

ity that is not regularly practiced among Pentecostals, but is quite appropriate since the acknowledgment of sin and the need for forgiveness makes sense when people truly encounter God.[1]

This book also focused primarily on the Spirit's present work in corporate worship within Pentecostalism. Pentecostal corporate worship has become an influential approach to corporate worship globally, so a study that delves into Pentecostal corporate worship from another theological lens may shed further light on how Pentecostal worship together – and what must be done for improvement. A few theological emphases that deserve further attention in connection with Pentecostal corporate worship may include the Trinity, the transcendence of God, and Christology.[2]

This work was also limited in that it focused on North American classical Pentecostals, and primarily engaged with white contemporary leaders for two reasons. First, there are varieties of Pentecostals in North America, due to the variety of cultural groups in both the United States and Canada. Pentecostals from around the world have come to North America and worship God in unique ways. More work needs to be done related to other cultural groups, being sensitive to unique cultural norms. Second, Pentecostalism is a global movement, and there is a need for greater discussion on how corporate worship is being conducted around the world. This book could not delve into the various approaches to corporate worship around the world. Extending this research to include global Pentecostal approaches to worship is beyond the scope of this work. The theology and practice of Pentecostal corporate worship around the world, however, should be examined as a potential source of renewal for Pentecostals in North America today. For example, Pentecostals may benefit from examining why non-Western Pentecostal churches are often reported to experience greater experiences of the Spirit's immediacy and numerical growth than that of Western Pentecostals.

---

[1] See James K.A. Smith, *You Are What You Love: The Spiritual Power of Habit* (Grand Rapids: Brazos, 2016), p. 97.

[2] For discussion on the role of the Trinity and Pentecostal worship, see Michael A. Tapper, *Canadian Pentecostals, the Trinity, and Contemporary Worship Music* (Leiden: Brill, 2017); and Chris E.W. Green, '"In Your Presence there is Fullness of Joy": Experiencing God as Trinity', in Lee Roy Martin (ed.), *Toward a Pentecostal Theology of Worship* (Cleveland: CPT Press, 2016), pp. 187-99.

Finally, this work was limited because the methodology for studying contemporary Pentecostal corporate worship was primarily restricted to six leaders. The methodology for studying contemporary corporate worship may be changed for further insights. Studies that examine other contemporary leaders or influential Pentecostal churches may prove fruitful for further research. A comparison and contrast of how corporate worship is conducted between Pentecostals and other Christian traditions may also provide insights that Pentecostals can learn from others.

Value of this Study for Scholarship and the Church

Examining the Pentecostal movement from a defining theological assumption within Pentecostalism – the Spirit's immediacy – is a crucial study. Scholars have acknowledged the important role of the Spirit's immediacy for Pentecostals, but have not provided a sustained treatment of this subject through a key context – corporate worship – where Pentecostals expect the Spirit's present work. This work offers an analysis of a defining theological assumption of Pentecostals through the important expressions for Pentecostals of worship music, preaching, and the altar. Scholars, ministers, and laity will benefit from both understanding and appraising the Spirit's immediacy in Pentecostal corporate worship.

An extended discussion on the Spirit's present work in Pentecostal corporate worship also helps Pentecostals gain a more substantive view of the Spirit's work. Pentecostals can often relegate the Spirit's work to experiences like Spirit baptism, signs, and wonders. Pentecostals may falsely assume that they are experts on the person and work of the Spirit, which can often lead to failing to think critically about the subject of pneumatology. This work provides theological analyses of the various roles of the Spirit in corporate worship that are often ignored by Pentecostals today.

A scholarly discussion of key Pentecostal corporate worship expressions – worship music, preaching, and the altar – is necessary. Modest scholarly work has been done so far on Pentecostal corporate worship. This book helps fill the gap on the discussion of Pentecostal corporate worship in Pentecostal scholarship, particularly related to North American Pentecostalism.

Since Pentecostal corporate worship has become one of the most influential approaches to the corporate worship of various Christian traditions globally, this study is an important contribution for understanding and appraising the Pentecostal approach to corporate worship. Those within the church will be benefited by this study, for it offers both a historical and contemporary analysis of Pentecostal corporate worship. Exploring Pentecostalism from one of its defining features – corporate worship – through one of its defining theological impulses – the Spirit's immediacy – is an important study that is fruitful for scholars, pastors, and local churches.

APPENDIX

WILLIAM J. SEYMOUR (1870-1922) AND HISTORICAL ANTECEDENTS TO THE CORPORATE WORSHIP AT THE AZUSA STREET MISSION[1]

Seymour is credited as one of the pioneers of the Pentecostal movement, one of the largest Christian movements in the world today. But an examination of Seymour's life, theology, and ministry within academia is only just beginning to appear. The development of research on Seymour is due to the attention and prominence given to Seymour by Robeck, Hollenweger, and Nelson.[2] This discussion is not limited to Seymour's life alone. Five historical antecedents to Seymour's experience and understanding of corporate worship are showcased – which also represents the backgrounds of participants at the Azusa Street Revival. The five antecedents are shown to be influential to varying degrees upon Azusa's corporate worship.

A few preliminary explanations are necessary for this discussion on historical antecedents to Pentecostal corporate worship. The approach taken here is one that takes the historical influences upon the Azusa Street Revival and Pentecostal corporate worship into account, rather than a providential approach. Some Pentecostals claim that the movement arose providentially – a supernatural approach that minimizes human agents. The providential approach arose for at least two reasons. The first is racism, as some would want to devalue the role of a black leader, Seymour. The second is triumphalism, whereby

---

[1] Cecil M. Robeck, Jr, 'Seymour, William Joseph', in Stanley M. Burgess (ed.), *The New International Dictionary of Pentecostal and Charismatic Movements* (Grand Rapids: Zondervan, 2003), p. 1053.

[2] Douglas J. Nelson, 'For Such a Time as This: The Story of Bishop William J. Seymour and the Azusa Street Revival' (PhD Thesis, University of Birmingham, 1981).

people want to exalt the role of the movement within church history.[3] But it is difficult to argue that merely one decision or event caused another – a variety of potential factors contribute to why something happens. Many factors contributed to the development of events in church history, and the Azusa Street Revival is no exception. Limitations for research on this subject include some factors that are unknown (e.g., books or dreams that may have been influential in Seymour's decisions that are not documented).[4] Nevertheless, a number of factors are briefly described that contributed to the rise of the Azusa Street Revival and its corporate worship, which better situate this discussion on Pentecostal corporate worship. This discussion on historical antecedents is brief, and can only provide glimpses of the corporate worship among various groups since the main focus of this work is on Pentecostal corporate worship.

What follows is a brief sketch of five corporate worship contexts that Seymour was likely influenced by due to his direct participation in them and by others through indirect means. The discussion delves into African American spirituality, Revivalism, Methodism, the Holiness movement, and Proto-Pentecostal groups, which all coincide somewhat chronologically with important moments in Seymour's life. The five contexts highlight significant corporate worship contexts for Seymour and are most pronounced in an understanding, though limited, of Seymour's life and ministry.[5] Furthermore, since the various contexts Seymour was exposed to did not arise out of a vacuum, how these local contexts derived their worship practices within its broader movement are also explained. So in the discussion of Seymour's African American church background, some important influences are described, such as the role of corporate worship among slaves, Hoodoo spirituality, and manifestations of the Spirit in corporate worship. To explore Revivalism, the discussion includes the role of George Whitefield, the Cane Ridge Camp Meetings, and Charles Finney's ministry. To understand the Methodist Church, John

---

[3] See Nelson, 'For Such a Time as This', pp. 93, 110, 111, 112.

[4] For further discussion on the subject of studying history as a Christian, see David Bebbington, *Patterns in History: A Christian Perspective on Historical Thought* (Vancouver: Regent, 2000).

[5] For a greater exploration into Seymour's life, few sources provide extensive details. See Nelson, 'For Such a Time as This'; Craig Borlase, *William Seymour: A Biography* (Lake Mary: Charisma, 2006); and Robeck, 'Seymour, William Joseph'.

Wesley's role is described. To delve further into the Holiness Movement, the launch of the National Camp Meeting Association for the Promotion of Christian Holiness, the Keswick Movement, the Evening Light Saints, and Martin Wells Knapp's ministry are put forward. Finally, an exploration of Proto-Pentecostal groups delves into Parham's ministry, the Welsh Revival, and the Mukti Mission Revival in India.

African American Spirituality

One of the most prominent elements of Seymour's spirituality that has been highlighted is his African American spirituality.[6] The following is a brief description of his life, and notable elements related to his experience of worship within the context of his early development within the African American church tradition. Three elements discussed here relate to his experience as an African American and its relevance for corporate worship, which include slavery and corporate worship (one that demands extra attention in light of its great influence), Hoodoo spirituality, and manifestations of the Spirit in corporate worship.

Slavery and Corporate Worship

Seymour was born on May 2, 1870 in Centerville, Louisiana.[7] He was the son of Simon and Phillis Seymour – both former slaves, who were born into slavery.[8] During the time that his family was in Louisiana, the Roman Catholic Church was the most prominent religious force in that region. Thus, Seymour's family became Roman Catholics, because slave owners were required to instruct and baptize their slaves in the Roman Catholic faith.[9] Blacks, however, were not originally Roman Catholics, and belonged to religious traditions from Africa. Understanding the religion of blacks from this period of slavery is important because it was an important link between blacks' religious experience in Africa and America. Religion was '[o]ne of the

---

[6] Hollenweger, *Pentecostalism*, 19; Vondey, *Beyond Pentecostalism*, pp. 119-22.

[7] Robeck, *The Azusa Street Mission and Revival*, p. 17.

[8] Robeck, *The Azusa Street Mission and Revival*, 19; Nelson, 'For Such a Time as This', p. 31.

[9] Robeck, *The Azusa Street Mission and Revival*, p. 21.

most durable and adaptable constituents of the slave's culture'.[10]
Though Seymour's parents were freed slaves just over four years before Seymour was born, it is important to understand religion and
worship in the context of African American slavery to appreciate
Seymour's background of African American spirituality.[11]

The Spirit's immediacy in the corporate worship of blacks during
the time of slavery in the United States must be understood by examining at least three elements: the role of the Exodus imagery, Hoodoo spirituality, and manifestations of the Spirit in corporate worship.[12] First, the most consistent biblical imagery African Americans
used to make sense of their oppressive situation was the Exodus
story, so that the Spirit's immediacy related to their empowerment.
When the Jews were enslaved in Egypt, God powerfully acted on behalf of these slaves to release them from bondage.[13] African Americans were powerless in America, in that they too were in bondage to
their captors and oppressors. But their experience of the Spirit made
a difference in their lives, viewing the Spirit as 'a sustaining source in
the midst of suffering'.[14] The Spirit's empowerment created 'avenues
of freedom and hope'.[15] The manifestation of the Spirit 'through the
body' was a practical way that the Spirit affirmed the dignity of African Americans, particularly during times of intense rejection and op-
pression by society. Azusa participants likewise highlighted the empowerment of the disenfranchised (e.g. women and blacks).[16] One of

---

[10] Albert J. Raboteau, *Slave Religion* (New York: Oxford University Press, 1978), p. 4.

[11] Nelson, 'For Such a Time as This', p. 151.

[12] This discussion primarily makes use of descriptions of worship provided by: Melva Wilson Costen, *African American Christian Worship* (Nashville: Abingdon, 2007); Luke A. Powery, 'The Holy Spirit and African-American Preaching' (ThD dissertation, Emmanuel College, University of Toronto, 2006); and Hollenweger, *Pentecostalism: Origins and Developments Worldwide.*

[13] E.K. Bailey and Warren W. Wiersbe, *Preaching in Black and White* (Grand Rapids: Zondervan, 2003), p. 10.

[14] Powery, 'The Holy Spirit and African-American Preaching', p. 29.

[15] Powery, 'The Holy Spirit and African-American Preaching', p. 29.

[16] Powery, 'The Holy Spirit and African-American Preaching', p. 35. For in-stance, Craig Scandrett-Leatherman, 'Rites of Lynching and Rites of Dance: His-torical, Anthropological, and Afro-Pentecostal Perspectives on Black Manhood af-ter 1865', in Amos Yong and Estrelda Y. Alexander (eds.), *Afro-Pentecostalism: Black Pentecostal and Charismatic Christianity in History and Culture* (New York: New York University Press, 2011), pp. 107, 109, argues that while 'African rites of passage

the primary contexts to experience the Spirit was in the gathering of slaves for corporate worship.

Hoodoo Spirituality

Second, Seymour's early years in Louisiana are also significant for the potential influence of Hoodoo spirituality. The dominant religion where Seymour lived in Louisiana at that time was Roman Catholicism, and its link with Hoodoo spirituality also underscored an emphasis on the immediacy of God. Seymour was christened on September 4, 1870 at the Church of the Assumption, a Roman Catholic Church in Franklin, Louisiana.[17] But blacks during Seymour's time often integrated the Roman Catholic belief imposed on them with a variation of Voodoo, called Hoodoo – religious beliefs inherited from Africa.[18] Whether Seymour himself practiced Hoodoo is uncertain. But it is important to understand Hoodoo spirituality, which was expressed among others in his community.[19]

The Hoodoo spirituality that Seymour would have been aware of in his early years in Louisiana would include 'symbols, spells, incantations, sympathetic magic, and root work'.[20] And though this preceding description of their spirituality is different from Christianity, they held some common beliefs and practices with the early Pentecostals. A few common beliefs include belief in a 'Divine spirit', and

---

were meant to elevate black males into manhood', slavery and the resulting lynchings sought to 'emasculate black men and keep the community of men as boys' (p. 109). One important means of resisting the violence done against black in the United States was through 'alternative rituals' (p. 109). He reflects on Charles H. Mason's reception of Spirit baptism at Azusa, stating that his experience of 'dying, of knowing someone's suffering for him, and being raised straight on his feet is characteristic of both slave conversion narratives, and rites of passage into manhood' (p. 107). Mason's experience of being

> brought up and back to life was bodily expressed not only in the tongue now loosed to speak freely, but also by the man standing to his feet and his whole body being freed to dance. In Afro-Pentecostal ritual Jesus' baptism of the Holy Spirit and the rite into manhood (the right of men) often involves dance. This can be understood as a celebration of the freedom to be a black man in the multicultural body of Jesus' (p. 107).

[17] Larry Martin, *The Life and Ministry of William J. Seymour and a History of the Azusa Street Revival* (The Complete Azusa Street Library, 1; Pensacola: Christian Life, 2006), p. 53.

[18] Robeck, *The Azusa Street Mission and Revival*, pp. 22-23.

[19] Robeck, *The Azusa Street Mission and Revival*, pp. 22-23.

[20] Robeck, *The Azusa Street Mission and Revival*, p. 23.

the role of the supernatural, which includes individual 'empowerment', 'signs and wonders, miracles and healings, invisible spirits, trances and spirit possession, [and] vision and dreams as a means of Divine communication'.[21] A few common corporate worship practices include singing, clapping, trembling, shouting, dancing, playing drums, and the use of a '"call and response" preaching style'.[22] Seymour's ministry at the Azusa Street Revival displayed some of these beliefs and corporate worship practices. Whether or not Seymour picked up his ministry practices from Hoodoo spirituality is uncertain, but he would have undoubtedly been familiar and sympathetic with them.

Manifestations of the Spirit in Corporate Worship

The last key issue to discuss is the manifestations of the Spirit in corporate worship. Manifestations of the Spirit in general could be expressed in a variety of ways: celebration, lament, unity, fellowship, singing, shouting, and of course, preaching.[23] Corporate worship was characterised by freedom for all to participate, in light of an experience of the Spirit, which is a common theme for participants' expression in corporate worship among both black slaves and participants at Azusa.[24] Descriptions of the ring shout, singing, and preaching within African American Christian corporate worship follow, and reveal the importance of a manifestation of the Spirit for corporate worship. The ring shout, for instance, is a spontaneous encounter with the Spirit whereby 'the Holy Spirit fills and empowers … worshipers'.[25] Those involved in the ring shout may stand or dance or jump 'involuntarily', or remain seated while swinging their arms and legs 'convulsively'.[26] People may describe this 'physical involvement' as 'religious ecstasy' or 'uncontrollable movements involving one's

---

[21] Robeck, *The Azusa Street Mission and Revival*, p. 23.

[22] Robeck, *The Azusa Street Mission and Revival*, pp. 23, 117-18.

[23] Powery, 'The Holy Spirit and African-American Preaching', p. 230; and William C. Turner, 'The Musicality of Black Preaching: Performing the Word', in Jana Childers and Clayton J. Schmit (eds.), *Performance in Preaching: Bringing the Sermon to Life* (Grand Rapids: Baker, 2008), p. 204.

[24] Costen, *African American Christian Worship*, p. 26.

[25] Costen, *African American Christian Worship*, p. 36.

[26] Costen, *African American Christian Worship*, p. 36.

whole person'.[27] The shout would be viewed as a 'special divine moment of happiness and joy' through the encounter and enablement
of the Spirit.[28]

Second, singing also evidenced an emphasis on an experience of
the Spirit. Singing in the African American slave context provided an
opportunity for the Spirit to move, and 'helped create a mood of
freedom, an openness to quicken an awareness of God's presence,
and for the hearing and receiving of God's grace'.[29] Robeck suggests
that the 'Negro chant', developed in African American 'praise houses'
during and after slavery, are similar to singing in the Spirit, so that
singing in the Spirit at Azusa finds roots in African American spirituality.[30]

Finally, the event of preaching also showcased the importance of
a direct and present experience of the Spirit in corporate worship.
Preachers may have had little education, but they were considered
'divinely inspired' and 'biblically articulate'.[31] Since preachers were
'called' from among the slaves, they could empathize with their oppressive situation.[32] When they preached, a 'freedom of the Spirit'
not only enabled preachers, but also a 'responsive listening of the
Spirit-filled congregations'.[33] The experience of the Spirit encouraged the full participation of slaves during corporate worship, much
like those who participated at Azusa. Overall then, the experiences
of the Spirit in corporate worship described above can be seen as
parallel with Pentecostal corporate worship. Seymour's background
of African American spirituality undoubtedly affected the approach
of corporate worship at the Azusa Street Revival.

Revivalism

The Revivalist impulse was also featured at the Azusa Street Revival,
and contributed to the emphasis on God's present work experienced

---

[27] Costen, *African American Christian Worship*, p. 36.

[28] Costen, *African American Christian Worship*, p. 36.

[29] Costen, *African American Christian Worship*, p. 33.

[30] Robeck, *The Azusa Street Mission and Revival*, p. 150; Daniels, 'Gotta Moan
Sometime', pp. 14-15.

[31] Costen, *African American Christian Worship*, p. 26.

[32] Costen, *African American Christian Worship*, p. 26.

[33] Costen, *African American Christian Worship*, p. 26.

in corporate worship. Seymour would have likely experienced this revivalist impulse in various corporate worship contexts. In Louisiana,
Seymour and his family had been loosely associated with a nearby
Baptist church, New Providence Baptist Church.[34] His family lived
close to the Baptist church, and his father was buried in the cemetery
belonging to New Providence Baptist Church.[35] And since Baptist
churches have a revivalist impulse in their history, Seymour may have
encountered this approach in corporate worship among the Baptists
in his community.[36] Seymour undoubtedly encountered the revivalist
impulse among the Methodist, Holiness, and Proto-Pentecostal
groups he associated with. To understand Revivalism and the inclusion of the immediacy of God in corporate worship, a discussion
follows describing the corporate worship at George Whitefield's ministry, the Cane Ridge camp meetings, and Charles Finney's ministry.
Though there were other contexts where Revivalism occurred – particularly camp meetings and revivals – examining these three helps to
understand this tradition of corporate worship broadly, which has
implications for Seymour's ministry at Azusa.

The Ministry of George Whitefield

Whitefield's ministry of preaching exhibited the immediacy of God
both in his preaching and the hearers' response to his sermons.
Whitefield's ministry is important for understanding a corporate worship context that became a place where both whites and blacks converted to Christianity during the First Great Awakening.[37] His ministry even had a direct impact on the worship of both the Methodist-
Holiness tradition and African American spirituality, two acknowledged antecedents to Pentecostalism. Whitefield, however, has often
been ignored in discussions on Pentecostalism. Whitefield did not

---

[34] Synan, *The Holiness-Pentecostal Tradition*, p. 93; Martin, *The Life and Ministry of William J. Seymour*, pp. 58-59.

[35] Synan, *The Holiness-Pentecostal Tradition*, p. 93; Martin, *The Life and Ministry of William J. Seymour*, pp. 58-59.

[36] Thomas R. McKibbens, Jr, 'Our Baptist Heritage in Worship', *Review and Expositor* 80.1 (Winter 1983), p. 63. For a brief introduction to Baptist history in general as it relates to corporate worship, see McKibbens, 'Our Baptist Heritage in Worship'.

[37] See Josh P.S. Samuel, 'Pentecostal Worship Roots: George Whitefield's Influence upon the African American and Methodist Traditions', Annual meeting of the Society of Pentecostal Studies, Memphis, TN, March 12, 2011.

found an institution that could carry on his name and efforts – like John Wesley and the Methodist Church – which likely contributed to the lack of recognition given to Whitefield for his accomplishments.[38] Whitefield's ministry of preaching is first described, followed by the response to his sermons.

First, Whitefield's approach to preaching was fervent and emotional, which showcased the immediacy of God to hearers. His following became so large, that he was forced to preach outdoors.[39] One of his contemporaries believed that he 'spoke with a "mighty sense of God" and a "sense of eternity"'.[40] While the preaching of his day and church – the Church of England – within the context of corporate worship was 'formal', Whitefield and other ministers of the Great Awakening demonstrated '*fervent, powerful, evangelistic preaching*'.[41]

Whitefield not only directly influenced John Wesley and the Methodists by incorporating fervent, outdoor preaching, but his ministry also resonated with African American spirituality.[42] African Americans did not initially respond in great measure to the ministry of

---

[38] Samuel, 'Pentecostal Worship Roots', p. 28.

[39] This is Wesley's explanation for this in Wesley's sermon at Whitefield's funeral. See John Wesley, 'On the Death of the Rev. Mr. George Whitefield', in John Wesley, *Sermons on Several Occasions*. No pages. Online: http://www.ccel.org/ccel/wesley/sermons.txt.

[40] Marion D. Aldridge, 'George Whitefield: The Necessary Interdependence of Preaching Style and Sermon Content to Effect Revival', *JETS* 23.1 (March 1980), p. 61.

[41] William H. Pipes, *Say Amen, Brother! Old-Time Negro Preaching: A Study in American Frustration* (repr., Detroit: Wayne State, 1992), p. 60 (emphasis original).

[42] John Wesley, *The Journal of John Wesley*. No pages. Accessed January 26, 2010. Online: http://www.ccel.org/ccel/wesley/sermons.txt (Reprint from Chicago: Moody Press, 1951); James F. White, 'Traditions of Protestant Worship', *Worship* 49.5 (May 1975), p. 280. Other preachers had used field preaching in the past, but it was Whitefield who popularized it and directly influenced scores of other preachers. Roy Hattersley, *The Life of John Wesley: A Brand from the Burning* (New York: Doubleday, 2003), explains,

> The idea was not entirely novel. George Fox, the Quaker leader, had preached 'out of doors' during the seventeenth century. Morgan, a Welsh dissenter, had revived the practice a dozen years before Whitefield spoke in Bristol. So Whitefield neither chose nor invited 'field preaching' but was forced to follow the practice out of necessity. Because of his oratorical powers, he made Bristol, at least for the moment, the center of the Great Revival (p. 147).

Christians because '[w]hite religion had been formal, cold, and unattractive'.[43] Even though Quakers, Baptists, and Presbyterians later affirmed the humanness of blacks and the subsequent need to grant them the privileges necessary for all people, these groups were not able to incorporate blacks fully into the church.[44] African Americans accepted Christianity through a connection to their own religious experiences though the fervent preaching of people, most notably Whitefield.

Whitefield preached in Philadelphia in 1766, and Gustavus Vassa, an African American slave who was in attendance, testified about his experience. Vassa explained that as he entered the church, he witnessed a 'pious man' who exhorted the congregation with great 'fervor and earnestness', sweating like Vassa had done while in slavery.[45] Vassa wondered why other preachers did not 'exert' themselves like Whitefield, and realised that congregations were small because of preachers' unwillingness to follow Whitefield's fervent approach to preaching.[46] Whitefield's worship expressed through his preaching was emotional. Whitefield's preaching brought a religion to African Americans that, as Vassa explains, 'they could understand' and 'stir them to self expression', 'enthusiasm', 'imagination', and 'passion'. Further it provided them with a 'mental escape' from their deplorable social position, and inspired them 'to assert' themselves as human beings.[47] While Puritans of that age 'invested the sermon with a monolithic voice that spoke authoritatively', Whitefield broke tradition with his style of preaching.[48] Passion and fervour became important

---

Two thousand people came to hear Whitefield preach the first time he attempted to do so, according to Wesley. Wesley, 'On the Death of the Rev. Mr. George Whitefield'.

[43] Henry H. Mitchell, *Black Preaching: The Recovery of a Powerful Art* (Nashville: Abingdon, 1990), p. 32.

[44] Pipes, *Say Amen, Brother!*, p. 62.

[45] See Vernon Loggins, *The Negro Author: His Development in America to 1900* (Port Washington: Kennikat, 1959), p. 3.

[46] See Loggins, *The Negro Author*, p. 3.

[47] Loggins, *The Negro Author*, pp. 3-4.

[48] Harry Stout, 'Puritan Preaching', in William H. Willimon and Richard Lischer (eds.), *Concise Encyclopedia of Preaching* (Louisville: Westminster John Knox, 1995), p. 397.

features of Whitefield's ministry of preaching – and the general expression of worship at his meetings.[49]

Whitefield 'built the bridge' whereby Protestantism 'could travel to a spiritually hungry and brutally oppressed people from Africa'.[50] Whitefield affirmed African Americans by connecting with them through an emotional worship pattern with which they were already familiar. African Americans did not learn something new about being emotionally expressive in their spirituality – they had already expressed their religious sentiments in such a way in Africa.[51] Through George Whitefield's ministry, though, many African Americans received the message of the gospel of Jesus Christ through a common worship pattern they were used to, and became a pattern they continued to follow as Christians.[52]

---

[49] Stout argues that Whitefield's early learning and involvement in theatre affected his preaching, whereby emotions were primary, which directed all the faculties of a human such as intellect and will. See Harry S. Stout, *The Divine Dramatist: George Whitefield and the Rise of Modern Evangelicalism* (Grand Rapids: Eerdmans, 1991), p. xix.

[50] Mitchell, *Black Preaching*, p. 34.

[51] Mitchell, *Black Preaching*, p. 32.

[52] Wesley acknowledged the many whites and blacks who came to Christian faith through Whitefield's ministry. See Wesley, 'On the Death of the Rev. Mr. George Whitefield'. Whitefield focused on the conversion of blacks souls and sought to ensure they were generally treated well as slaves – though he disappointingly never spoke out against slavery. In the conclusion of one of his sermons, Whitefield directly addressed African Americans and their need for conversion, for they may be 'children of God'. See George Whitefield, 'The Lord our Righteousness'. In *Selected Sermons of George Whitefield*. No pages. Accessed March 5, 2010. Online: http://www.ccel.org/ccel/whitefield/sermons.txt. For more information regarding Whitefield's approach among slaves, see Stephen Stein, 'George Whitefield on Slavery: Some New Evidence', *Church History* 42.2 (June 1973), pp. 243-56.

Mitchell, *Black Preaching*, gives one instance of how Whitefield's ministry influence extended within the African American Christian community:

One direct channel of transmission of this 'emotional' preaching can be traced from Whitefield's ministry in Massachusetts all the way to Andrew C. Marshall at the First African Baptist Church at Savannah. It started with Shubal Stearns (1706–1771, converted under Whitefield on his second visit to Boston in 1745) and Daniel Marshall, Stearns' brother-in-law from Connecticut (1706–1784; also converted in 1745). Both withdrew from the Congregational Church (1851 and 1852 respectively) under conviction as Baptists. Ordained as missionaries, they worked their way from New England to Winchester, Virginia, to Sandy Creek, North Carolina, to Kiokee, Georgia, where Daniel Marshall settled in 1771. There he was responsible for strengthening a small congregation and leading in the development of many other churches. One of these churches

Secondly, the response to Whitefield's ministry is also characterised as incredibly emotional, which appeared to exhibit the immediacy of God. Wesley explains: 'In some places, thousands cried out
aloud; many as in the agonies of death; most were drowned in tears;
some turned pale as death; others were wringing their hands; others
lying on the ground; others sinking into the arms of their friends;
almost all lifting up their eyes, and calling for mercy'.[53] Whitefield's
preaching provided opportunity for hearers to encounter God. Hearers' emotional response gave evidence that they were experiencing a
visitation from God through the message they heard. While many
may attribute features of Whitefield's preaching to his acting prowess,
it nonetheless communicated his own unique worship pattern
through the ministry of preaching.[54]

Both African Americans and Methodist-Holiness believers find a
common corporate worship root in Whitefield through his fervent,
emotional preaching, and emotionally responsive hearers. When
these two traditions coalesced at the Azusa Street revival, they already
had a common corporate worship root in Whitefield.[55]

The Cane Ridge Camp Meetings

The Cane Ridge Camp Meetings, considered one of the most influential camp meetings within Evangelicalism, exhibited an emphasis
on the immediacy of God through the manifestations expressed by
participants in corporate worship.[56] These camp meetings occurred
in Cane Ridge, KY in August 1801, which popularised camp meetings.[57] These meetings are credited with igniting the Second Great
Awakening.[58]

---

was the Black congregation at Silver Bluff, Aiken, South Carolina, which was
started by George Leile (p. 33).

[53] Wesley, 'On the Death of the Rev. Mr. George Whitefield'.

[54] See Stout, *The Divine Dramatist*, p. xix.

[55] Robeck, *The Azusa Street Mission and Revival*, p. 145.

[56] Douglas A. Sweeney, *The American Evangelical Story: A History of the Movement*
(Grand Rapids: Baker, 2005), p. 70.

[57] Kenneth O. Brown, *Holy Ground: A Study of the American Camp Meeting* (New
York: Garland, 1992), pp. 4-22. Brown argues that John McGee was the first to
propose the use of a camp meeting in the United States to facilitate a revival that
began in the summer of 1800. See Kenneth O. Brown, *Holy Ground, Too: The Camp
Meeting Family Tree* (Hazelton: Holiness Archives, 1997), pp. 38-43.

[58] Brown, *Holy Ground*, pp. 4-22; Sweeney, *The American Evangelical Story*, p. 70.

Barton Stone led the Cane Ridge meetings, and was inspired by revivals he had witnessed among one of his friends, James McGready, who ministered in Logan County in May of 1801.[59] Stone witnessed 'hundreds gathered' at this revival, and 'dozens of people struck down in a swoon-like state'.[60] He shared what he witnessed at this revival among those at Cane Ridge and Concord, which led to a revival where people experienced deep conviction and some who fell down or 'swooned'.[61] This revival spread, which climaxed at Cane Ridge in August of 1801.

One minister's description of the Cane Ridge Revival included 'sinners' falling, 'shrieking, groaning, crying for mercy, convoluted', and believers 'praying, agonizing, fainting, falling down in distress, for sinners, or in raptures of joy!'[62] Further, various expressions occurred in worship, such as singing, shouting, clapping hands, hugging, kissing, laughing, and counseling both the distressed and those opposed to the ministry.[63] Physical manifestations in corporate worship were rampant, and appeared to exhibit the immediacy of God.

The central themes found within this movement arising from the camp meetings include some striking parallels with the early Pentecostals: 'freedom from all creeds and coercive human traditions, restoration of simple primitive Christianity, the transforming power of the Holy Spirit, separation from the fashions of the world, and the millennial unity of believers'.[64] And like Seymour years later who focused on the work of the Spirit for unity, they too believed that unity, described as 'fire union', was 'forged only in the fire of God's Spirit'.[65] During a time of racial inequality, traditional racial lines – including gender and age distinctions – were blurred, much like what occurred at the Azusa Street Revival. The Cane Ridge revival appealed to both blacks and whites, and at least one black man seems to have preached

---

[59] C. Leonard Allen, 'Cane Ridge and the Spirit's Fire', *Lexington Theological Quarterly* 34.3 (Fall 1999), p. 131.

[60] Allen, 'Cane Ridge and the Spirit's Fire', p. 131.

[61] Allen, 'Cane Ridge and the Spirit's Fire', p. 131.

[62] Allen, 'Cane Ridge and the Spirit's Fire', pp. 131-34. Allen explains that what brought people outside for these camp meetings at Cane Ridge was a communion festival – originating among Scottish-Irish Presbyterians in the 1600s – whereby people came to celebrate communion with the context of a meal (131-34).

[63] Allen, 'Cane Ridge and the Spirit's Fire', p. 134.

[64] Allen, 'Cane Ridge and the Spirit's Fire', p. 135.

[65] Allen, 'Cane Ridge and the Spirit's Fire', p. 135.

at Cane Ridge.[66] Blacks were also influential, since 'it is probable that black people, especially women, drawing on memories of traditional African religious dance, music and spirituality, often took the lead in expressing strongly emotional and physical responses to revival preaching, which then spread to whites'.[67] Various influences were involved in the development of corporate worship patterns in these camp meetings, where both blacks and whites, men and women, brought their various approaches to what transpired.

When Stone reflected on the revivals in his later years, he described them as 'a good work – the work of God' because the fruit of these revivals included 'genuine religion'.[68] Stone affirmed that what happened was genuine not because of the dramatic experiences in corporate worship, but because of the good fruit that resulted from the revivals. Stone highlighted the transforming power of the Spirit as operative in the corporate worship practices, which affected believers so that expressive worship also became a response to the work of God at the revivals.[69] Azusa leaders appreciated the corporate worship patterns of camp meetings like those at Cane Ridge, since they contended that the ministry of Azusa included the restoration of camp meetings.[70]

The Ministry of Charles G. Finney

Charles G. Finney's ministry of preaching also emphasised the immediacy of God by popularising the 'new measures' in corporate worship.[71] First, Finney is one of the famed ministers who provided leadership during the Second Great Awakening during the 1790s. Second, the 'new measures' used by Finney require explanation.

---

[66] John Wolffe, *The Expansion of Evangelicalism: The Age of Wilberforce, More, Chalmers and Finney* (A History of Evangelicalism, vol. 2; Downers Grove: Inter-Varsity, 2007), pp. 58, 59, 60-61.

[67] Wolffe, *The Expansion of Evangelicalism*, pp. 58, 59, 60-61.

[68] Allen, 'Cane Ridge and the Spirit's Fire', p. 135.

[69] Allen, 'Cane Ridge and the Spirit's Fire', p. 135. Allen refers to: 'Barton W. Stone, The Autobiography of Elder Barton Warren Stone, ed. John Rogers (Cincinnati, 1847)' (p. 135 n. 4).

[70] *AF* 1.1 (September 1906), p. 2. Also see Brown, *Holy Ground, Too*, pp. 62-63.

[71] Richard Carwardine, *Transatlantic Revivalism: Popular Evangelicalism in Britain and America 1790–1865* (Westport: Greenwood, 1978), p. 8. See Wolffe, *The Expansion of Evangelicalism*, p. 73.

The 'new measures' popularised by Finney, and used by others during the Second Great Awakening, appeared to showcase the immediacy of God through heightened emotions throughout the services.[72] The general atmosphere was one of 'high pressure conditions', so that emotions could be roused and revival 'could explode uncontrollably'.[73] Prayers could be led by either men or women, and could last for long periods. '[P]reaching was often direct, specific, and theatrical and was often conducted by preachers who itinerated with the avowed intention of stirring churches and winning converts'.[74] Finally, ministers used the 'anxious seat' – a precursor to the modern-day altar call.[75] Ministers used the 'anxious seat' so that those who were concerned about their spiritual state could move to a front pew where they could receive exhortation and prayer from ministers and make a public commitment.[76] Though participants could use various methods, the constant among all included spontaneity, 'boldness, frenetic activity, emphasis on public pressures, and general readiness to experiment that marked the exponents of the new-measure revivalism'.[77]

Finney's ministry and 'new measures' are significant for Pentecostals. Finney valued the role of spontaneous, heightened emotions in corporate worship, which underscored the immediacy of God as he aimed at evangelism and a general response among hearers to preaching. Heightened emotions, spontaneity, and expressiveness in corporate worship became 'more institutionalized and socially respectable' through Finney's ministry, which also paved the way for other revivals

---

[72] Finney did not 'invent' these new measures, as they have been found in varying degrees among other contexts – like George Whitefield's ministry, Methodist revivals, and camp meetings – prior to him. Douglas A. Sweeney, review of *Pedlar in Divinity: George Whitefield and the Transatlantic Revivals, 1737–1770* (Princeton: Princeton University, 1994), by Frank Lambert, in *International Bulletin of Missionary Research* 20.3 (July 1996), p. 138; Wolffe, *The Expansion of Evangelicalism*, p. 73.

[73] Carwardine, *Transatlantic Revivalism*, p. 8. See Wolffe, *The Expansion of Evangelicalism*, p. 73.

[74] Carwardine, *Transatlantic Revivalism*, p. 8. See Wolffe, *The Expansion of Evangelicalism*, p. 73.

[75] Carwardine, *Transatlantic Revivalism*, p. 8. See Wolffe, *The Expansion of Evangelicalism*, p. 73.

[76] Carwardine, *Transatlantic Revivalism*, p. 8. See Wolffe, *The Expansion of Evangelicalism*, p. 73.

[77] Carwardine, *Transatlantic Revivalism*, p. 8. See Wolffe, *The Expansion of Evangelicalism*, pp. 71, 73.

like Azusa.[78] For even Azusa viewed their revival as part of a restoration of revivals of the past.[79]

The Methodist Tradition

Seymour eventually left Louisiana, moving to Memphis, Tennessee, serving as a porter for a businessman and later as a driver for the Tennessee Paper Company.[80] By 1893, he had gone 'through Indiana, Ohio, Illinois, and possibly Missouri and Tennessee working as a hotel waiter'.[81] Seymour moved to Indiana by 1895, and eventually 'converted in a colored Methodist Episcopal Church' (MEC) in Indiana.[82] Not much is known about the circumstances of his conversion. Nevertheless, the immediacy of God in corporate worship within the Methodist context revealed the importance of affective spirituality through the need for an assurance of salvation.

Seymour experienced conversion in a Methodist church, showing that infant baptism (which Seymour experienced with the Roman Catholic Church) did not determine salvation in Seymour's thought. Rather, Seymour's conversion in the Methodist church community reveals the value of the Methodist tradition's emphasis on a decision to follow Christ for salvation, and the resulting assurance of salvation received. This conversion emphasis that began in Seymour also became an emphasis at the Azusa Street Revival. Thus, one must explore the approach to Christianity and salvation found in John Wesley, the founder of Methodism.

John Wesley influenced Methodism through his own dramatic conversion, which included an affective dimension. Wesley was attending a Moravian meeting where he heard a reading of Luther's

---

[78] Wolffe, *The Expansion of Evangelicalism*, p. 71; Robert Mapes Anderson, *Vision of the Disinherited: The Making of American Pentecostalism* (New York: Oxford University Press, 1979), p. 41.

[79] *AF* 1.1 (September 1906), pp. 2, 9.

[80] Estrelda Alexander, *Black Fire: One Hundred Years of African American Pentecostalism* (Downers Grove: InterVarsity Press, 2011), p. 112.

[81] Alexander, *Black Fire*, p. 112.

[82] Charles W. Shumway, 'A Study of "the Gift of Tongues"' (AB Degree, University of Southern California, 1914), p. 173, n. a. References to the Methodist Episcopal Church are referred to by the abbreviation, MEC.

preface to Romans.[83] Wesley describes this event, explaining that 'while he [Luther] was describing the change which God works in the heart through faith in Christ, I felt my heart strangely warmed. I felt I did trust in Christ, Christ alone, for salvation; and an assurance was given me that He had taken away my sins.'[84] Wesley moved away from a mere intellectual assent to Christianity to a more intimate, affective dimension to his spirituality. In Wesley's brief description of his conversion, he reveals two dimensions of conversion that found its way into Pentecostal spirituality in Seymour: the importance of faith for justification and an 'assurance' of conversion. His conversion did not come through a baptismal rite, family heritage, or a minister's pronouncement – it came through an internal sense of conversion made possible by an experience of the Spirit. Wesley explains, '[t]he testimony of the Spirit is an inward impression on the soul, whereby the Spirit of God directly witnesses to my spirit, that I am a child of God; that Jesus Christ hath loved me, and given himself for me; and that all my sins are blotted out, and I, even I, am reconciled to God'.[85] This affective approach to salvation exhibited the Spirit's immediacy and was evident among the Azusa Street Revival participants, and has become an influential approach among all Pentecostals.

The theology and affective spirituality promoted by Wesley found its way into worship music of the Methodist tradition. Worship music was also an important part of the Methodist tradition, as John Wesley and his brother Charles Wesley were heavily involved in the production of hymns for Methodists. The Wesleys used 'hymns to teach

---

[83] The Moravians were Germans who belonged to a Christian tradition associated with German Pietism, spearheaded by Philip Jakob Spener. German Pietists stressed the importance of a distinct experience of change, becoming a new person through conversion, which went beyond outward adherence to inner change of the heart. See Steffen Arndal, 'Spiritual Revival and Hymnody: The Hymnbooks of German Pietism and Moravianism', in Hedwig T. Durnbaugh (ed. and trans.), *Brethren Life and Thought* XL (Spring 1995), p. 71; Stanley J. Grenz, 'Concerns of a Pietist with a Ph.D'., *Wesleyan Theological Journal* 37.2 (Fall 2002), p. 61; Mark A. Noll, *The Rise of Evangelicalism: The Age of Edwards, Whitefield and the Wesleys* (Downers Grove: InterVarsity Press, 2003), p. 62; Mark Boda, 'A Severe Mercy', McMaster Divinity College, Class Notes, Hamilton, Ontario, Fall 2009.

[84] Wesley, *The Journal of John Wesley*; also see William C. Placher, *A History of Christian Theology: An Introduction* (Philadelphia: Westminster, 1983), p. 246.

[85] John Wesley, 'The Witness of the Spirit', in John Wesley, *Sermon on Several Occasions*. No pages. Online: http://www.ccel.org/ccel/wesley/sermons.txt.

their theology and beliefs to the people', which often focused on salvation available to all (as opposed to the Calvinist teaching on limited
atonement), 'Christian perfection, and the witness of the Spirit'.[86]
John and Charles Wesley not only helped write hymns, but John even
translated German hymns of the Moravians and Lutheran Pietists.[87]
Charles Wesley also wrote over 5,000 hymns.[88] John R. Tyson explains
that Charles Wesley was 'the "poet laureate" of Methodism, whose
hymns gave the movement both a sound track and a public and congregational voice'.[89] Both brothers worked together to incorporate
hymns in their meetings, so that they eventually came out with popular collections of hymns.

Though Azusa participants claimed to have no need of song-
books, they used many hymns from the Wesleyan Holiness tradition.[90] There was even musical commonality among those both from
an African American and Wesleyan Holiness background, as they
both used the 'same basic style of singing' and 'sang many of the
same songs'.[91] While those of Wesleyan Holiness background at the
Azusa Street Revival would be influenced by the Methodist tradition,
it must also be stated that 'the first published liturgical document by
and for African American worshipers was a hymnal' developed by
Richard Allen, 'founder of the African Methodist Episcopal Church'

---

[86] Guthrie, 'Pentecostal Hymnody', pp. 59-60.

[87] Frank Whaling, *John and Charles Wesley: Selected Prayers, Hymns, Journal Notes,
Sermons, Letters and Treatises* (Mahwah: Paulist, 1981), p. 66. To understand the hym-
nody of German Pietism and Moravianism, see Arndal, 'Spiritual Revival and
Hymnody'.

[88] Mark A. Noll, *The Rise of Evangelicalism*, p. 18, also includes Charles Wesley as
influential for Pentecostals, stating that

> modern-day Pentecostals must be considered parts of the broader evangelical
> family since they are descended from nineteenth-century leaders who empha-
> sized holiness and the work of the Holy Spirit, and who were themselves deci-
> sively shaped by the teaching of several important leaders of the eighteenth-
> century revivals, especially John and Charles Wesley'.

Cf. 'Wesley, Charles', in F.L. Cross and E.A. Livingstone (ed.), *The Oxford Dictionary of the Christian Church* (Oxford: Oxford University, 3rd edn, 2005), p. 1739.
In order to distinguish Charles Wesley from John Wesley, full names are regularly
used throughout this work.

[89] John R. Tyson, 'The Theology of Charles Wesley's Hymns', *Wesleyan Theological Journal* 44.2 (Fall 2009), p. 58.

[90] Dove, 'Hymnody and Liturgy in the Azusa Street Revival', p. 259.

[91] Robeck, *The Azusa Street Mission and Revival*, p. 145.

in 1801.[92] And while the songs of various songwriters were found in that hymnal, he included Charles Wesley's hymns.[93] Since many participants at the revival came from a Methodist-Holiness background, it is understandable that the Methodist tradition played an important role in the type of music that they incorporated at the Azusa revival.

Seymour eventually left the MEC for two reasons: they did not 'endorse either premillennialism or special "revelations"'.[94] His views on special 'revelations' are important because it has implications for his view on corporate worship. Seymour's insistence on special revelations indicates a link with his approach to corporate worship being influenced by the Spirit's leading. His views were likely influenced by his African American church background, where divine communication through various means, such as dreams and visions, was valued. Seymour eventually found more common affinity with the Holiness Movement – related to the reasons he left the Methodist tradition – which leads to the next major section here.

The Holiness Movement

Seymour eventually transitioned from Methodism to the Holiness Movement, a movement many participants at the Azusa Street Revival belonged to, which reveals the importance of this context for understanding Pentecostal corporate worship. Two significant Holiness contexts of corporate worship Seymour has been associated with during his life are discussed here: the Evening Light Saints and Martin Wells Knapp's ministry. Seymour claims to have experienced 'the grace of instantaneous sanctification in Cincinnati', and Robeck suggests that this occurred within the Holiness ministry of the Evening Light Saints.[95] Before expanding further on the two ministries Seymour was apparently associated with, a brief description of the Holiness Movement follows.

Holiness believers showcased the immediacy of God in corporate worship by their emphasis on an experience of entire sanctification in camp meetings. The Holiness tradition arose among those who

---

[92] Costen, *African American Christian Worship*, p. 81.
[93] Costen, *African American Christian Worship*, p. 81.
[94] Shumway, 'A Study of "the Gift of Tongues"', p. 173.
[95] Shumway, 'A Study of "the Gift of Tongues"', p. 173; Robeck, *The Azusa Street Mission and Revival*, p. 29.

belonged to the Methodist tradition. They sought to reinvigorate the practice of entire sanctification, which the early Methodists highlighted. Methodists of their generation neglected entire sanctification.

> Protestant Christianity suffered a gradual decline in both membership and interest … [w]ithin the Methodist ranks, both north and south, there arose a conviction that a holiness revival of the kind that had swept much of the country in 1858 would once again set things right.[96]

Methodists who sought to re-establish the practice of entire sanctification formed the 'National Camp Meeting Association for the Promotion of Christian Holiness', which held its first and very successful camp meeting in Vineland, New Jersey on July 17, 1867.[97] A call to holiness, revival, and unity was the general appeal that led to the first camp meeting and association. One specific call appealed to people of all denominations to a 'forest-meeting', for the 'promotion of holiness', unity, and prayer 'for the descent of the Spirit upon ourselves, the church, the nation, and the world'.[98]

The Methodist view on entire sanctification originated with John Wesley. Wesley viewed entire sanctification as a second potential crisis experience, distinguished from salvation, and available for believers.[99] He succinctly described entire sanctification in one of his sermons as 'perfect love'.[100] He admitted that though this experience may not occur at conversion, a believer could experience this transformation here on earth.[101]

The Holiness movement focused on the experience of entire sanctification, which by the 1890s, they described as a second work

[96] Synan, *The Holiness-Pentecostal Tradition*, pp. 23-24.
[97] Synan, *The Holiness-Pentecostal Tradition*, pp. 24, 26.
[98] See Synan, *The Holiness-Pentecostal Tradition*, p. 25.
[99] See Placher, *A History of Christian Theology*, p. 246.
[100] He writes what this entails: 'It is love excluding sin; love filling the heart, taking up the whole capacity of the soul. It is love "rejoicing evermore, praying without ceasing, in everything giving thanks."' John Wesley, 'The Scripture Way of Salvation', in John Wesley, *Sermon on Several Occasions*. No pages. Online: http://www.ccel.org/ccel/wesley/sermons.txt.
[101] Wesley, *The Journal of John Wesley*; Wesley, 'The Scripture Way of Salvation'.

of grace associated with Spirit baptism found in Acts 2.[102] The Holiness context of corporate worship – camp meetings – to seek this experience of Spirit baptism also became an important contribution to the development of Pentecostal corporate worship.[103]

The Keswick movement arose out of the Holiness movement, which also influenced the early Pentecostals by its emphasis on the Spirit's empowerment for ministry. The Keswick movement began in 1875, and was primarily composed of non-Wesleyans.[104] They refused to link Spirit baptism with entire sanctification, as '"orthodox" Holiness' believers contended.[105] And they also rejected entire sanctification, seeing sanctification as a lifelong process that is never completed.[106] They equated Spirit baptism with a separate 'enduement of power'.[107] The Azusa Street leaders, like those in the Keswick movement, linked Spirit baptism with empowerment for ministry.[108] The Keswick approach to corporate worship included a focus on revivals, as some of the most prominent leaders included revivalists like Moody.[109] The reception of the Spirit's power for ministry during corporate worship finds correspondence with Azusa's emphasis, without the inclusion of tongues. A significant revival that came out of the Keswick movement was the Welsh Revival, which is discussed

---

[102] Synan, *The Holiness-Pentecostal Tradition*, p. 26; C.E. Jones, 'Holiness Movement', in Stanley Burgess (ed.), *The New International Dictionary of Pentecostal and Charismatic Movements* (Grand Rapids: Zondervan, 2003), p. 728.

[103] Also see Vondey, *Beyond Pentecostalism*, pp. 122-25.

[104] Anderson, *Vision of the Disinherited*, p. 40; Charles R. Fox, 'William J. Seymour: Pioneer of the Azusa Street Revival', in Vinson Synan and Charles R. Fox, *William J. Seymour: Pioneer of the Azusa Street Revival* (Alachua: Bridge-Logos, 2012), pp. 52-53.

[105] Anderson, *Vision of the Disinherited*, p. 41; Jones, 'Holiness Movement', p. 727.

[106] Anderson, *Vision of the Disinherited*, p. 41; Jones, 'Holiness Movement', p. 727.

[107] Anderson, *Vision of the Disinherited*, p. 41.

[108] *AF* 1.1 (September 1906), p. 2. In one article, the writer explains that a fourteen year old girl who was 'saved, sanctified, and baptized with the Holy Ghost' had tremendous results in ministry, and much more impressive than what a salaried minister who merely had theological training could accomplish. See *AF* 1.2 (October 1906), p. 3.

[109] C.E. Jones explains that during the early 1900s in America, 'the center most sympathetic to the Keswick teaching was Moody Bible Institute in Chicago'. 'Holiness Movement', p. 727.

later in this appendix.[110] Attention must now be given to Seymour's direct involvement in a group associated with the Holiness Movement, the Evening Light Saints.

The Evening Light Saints – Church of God (Anderson)

Seymour was involved with the Evening Light Saints – currently known as the Church of God (Anderson) – in Indianapolis and/or Cincinnati.[111] Robeck explains that Mother Emma L. Cotton, an African American preacher and pastor in Los Angeles, who was also a friend of Seymour's and early participant in the Azusa Street Mission, claimed that Seymour was 'saved and sanctified' among the Evening Light Saints.[112] But Shumway states that Seymour was converted in a Methodist Episcopal Church. Seymour may have worshipped with the Evening Light Saints while in Indianapolis, and also 'came to faith in a Methodist Episcopal Church of some sort', but 'went on to be further converted and/or "sanctified" while attending services offered by the Evening Light Saints'.[113] A few comments on who these Evening Light Saints were, and what their corporate worship was like during Seymour's time is important for this discussion – especially because Seymour possibly experienced salvation and sanctification in this context.

The Evening Light Saints, known as the Church of God Reformation Movement and more recently as Church of God (Anderson,

---

[110] Fox, 'William J. Seymour', pp. 54-57.

[111] B. Scott Lewis, 'William J. Seymour: Follower of the 'Evening Light' (Zech. 14.7)', *Wesleyan Theological Journal* 39.2 (Fall 2004), pp. 169-76. Where and when Seymour got involved with the Evening Light Saints has been up for debate. Nelson claims that Seymour was introduced to this group while in Cincinnati, while Robeck suggests that he became involved with them in Indiana – prior to arriving in Cincinnati. See Douglas J. Nelson, 'For Such a Time as This: The Story of Bishop William J. Seymour and the Azusa Street Revival' (PhD Thesis, University of Birmingham, 1981), p. 33; Robeck, 'Seymour, William Joseph'; Robeck, *The Azusa Street Mission and Revival*, pp. 29; Lewis, 'William J. Seymour', p. 169; Sanders, *William Joseph Seymour*, p. 50; and Fox, 'William J. Seymour', pp. 32, 40-46. Nevertheless, regardless of where or when he began to associate with the group is less important for this study than who these 'Saints' were and the worship practices of this group that Seymour was exposed to and possibly influenced by.

[112] Robeck, 'Seymour, William Joseph', p. 1054; Robeck refers to 'Mother' Emma Cotton, 'Inside Story of the Outpouring of the Holy Spirit (Azusa Street, April 1906)', *Message of the Apostolic Faith* 1 (1 Apr. 1939)', p. 1057. Also see Robeck, *The Azusa Street Mission and Revival*, p. 29.

[113] Robeck, *The Azusa Street Mission and Revival*, p. 29.

IN), was a '[m]idwestern movement started by Rev. Daniel S. Warner in 1880 in Ohio, Indiana, and Michigan'.[114] They were a predominantly white holiness group, that reached out to blacks.[115] They based their initial name, and vision for their Christian ministry, from Zech. 14.7b 'at evening time it shall be light'.[116] They believed that a final spiritual outpouring was being given to believers – saints – just before the close of history – evening time.[117]

The Evening Light Saints would appear to emphasise the immediacy of God in corporate worship by their stress on experiential conversion, entire sanctification, and interracial corporate worship.[118] Interracial fellowship was an especially attractive position to blacks during a time of racism in nineteenth century America. For the Evening Light Saints, interracial fellowship was an indicator of true holiness and unity among believers.[119] Seymour apparently experienced entire sanctification in their meetings after hearing these saints' testimonies, which was typical of people's participation in Evening Light Saints meetings.[120] *The Gospel Trumpet*, one of the newsletters that propagated the ministry of the Evening Light Saints, commonly claimed that 'souls were saved, sanctified, and prejudice removed'.[121] Sanctification was central to their ministry, 'for it was the cleansing of God's sanctuary that unified the Church, which set the stage for Christ's soon return'.[122] This approach to sanctification, whereby believers experienced 'prejudice removed', would attract blacks during that era of explicit racism.

Seymour would appreciate the interracial fellowship of these Saints, and may have been one of the more crucial influences upon Seymour, who likewise valued interracial fellowship for the Azusa Street believers. This tendency towards interracial fellowship for corporate worship did not begin here, though, for Seymour may have

[114] Nelson, 'For Such a Time as This', p. 164. Robeck, *The Azusa Street Revival and Mission*, p. 29.
[115] Nelson, 'For Such a Time as This', pp. 164, 48, n. 18.
[116] Robeck, *The Azusa Street Mission and Revival*, p. 29.
[117] Nelson, 'For Such a Time as This', p. 164.
[118] Lewis, 'William J. Seymour', p. 170.
[119] Lewis, 'William J. Seymour', p. 171.
[120] Lewis, 'William J. Seymour', p. 172.
[121] Lewis, 'William J. Seymour', p. 172.
[122] Lewis, 'William J. Seymour', p. 174.

chosen to attend an all black church belonging to the MEC.[123] One of the reasons Seymour may have left the MEC for the Evening Light Saints was because this Methodist tradition began to become more racially divided.[124] Seymour may have also left the MEC for the Evening Light Saints because of Warner's admonition to believers to leave churches where 'human structures and traditions impeded the free flow of God's Spirit' – another emphasis found at Azusa.[125]

Though Holiness believers like the Evening Light Saints equated entire sanctification with Spirit baptism, Seymour later distinguished entire sanctification from Spirit baptism.[126] Seymour argued that Spirit baptism was a 'gift of power', and an evidence of Spirit baptism was tongues.[127] By 1907 Seymour did, however, in line with the Evening Light Saints, state that the experience of 'Spirit baptism' should ultimately lead to changed behaviour in line with the fruit of the Spirit – which he referred to as 'the real evidence of the baptism' in *AF*.[128] But Seymour defended the inclusion of tongues as 'one of the signs that go with every baptized person'.[129] Seymour never explicitly stated that an evidence of Spirit baptism is interracial fellowship. But in his delight that people are being baptised in the Spirit at the Azusa Street Mission, he exclaimed, 'praise our God, He is now given and being poured out upon all flesh. All races, nations, and tongues are receiving the baptism with the Holy Ghost and fire, according to the prophecy of Joel.'[130] The promise of God's Spirit includes interracial fellowship for corporate worship, of which Seymour saw himself as part of at the Azusa Street Revival. Groups like the Evening Light Saints were likely a factor in Seymour's emphasis – based on the prophecy in Joel 2.28-32, where God promises the pouring out of the Spirit on all regardless of race. A few significant parallels between the Evening Light Saints and those at Azusa include: 'a policy of non-sectarianism, the equality of the races', 'the

[123] Nelson, 'For Such a Time as This', pp. 160-62.

[124] Nelson, 'For Such a Time as This', p. 162; Lewis, 'William J. Seymour', p. 169.

[125] Lewis, 'William J. Seymour', p. 173; Barry L. Callen, *It's God's Church: The Life and Legacy of Daniel Sidney Warner* (Anderson: Warner, 1995), p. 76.

[126] Nelson, 'For Such a Time as This', p. 165.

[127] *AF* 1.1 (September 1906), p. 2; *AF* 1.9 (June–September 1907), p. 2.

[128] *AF* 1.9 (June–September 1907), p. 2; Fox, 'William J. Seymour', p. 150.

[129] *AF* 1.9 (June–September 1907), p. 2.

[130] Seymour, William, 'Receive ye the Holy Ghost', *AF* 1.5 (January 1907), p. 2.

equality of women and men', and the same three ordinances of baptism, the Lord's Supper, and foot-washing.[131]

Another important issue relates to Seymour's call to ministry, which impacts who gives pastoral leadership for corporate worship. Though Nelson argues that Seymour was ordained among the Evening Light Saints, and Robeck associates Seymour's call to ministry with Knapp's ministry, what is most critical here is that his call occurred within the context of the Wesleyan Holiness movement. For this reason, Seymour's call is described here.

Seymour felt a call to preach while in Cincinnati – based on Shumway's research – which means he was either involved with the Evening Light Saints, as Nelson suggests, or with Knapp's ministry, which Robeck suggests.[132] This means that understanding the process of Seymour being called within the Wesleyan Holiness movement is important. Seymour felt called '[a]fter claiming the grace of instantaneous sanctification', which undoubtedly affected his approach to the ministry.[133] His call preceded an experience of God. Holiness believers equated entire sanctification with Spirit baptism. Thus, for Seymour at this time, he linked the importance of Spirit baptism and the evidence of holiness – entire sanctification – for those called to preach since both the Evening Light Saints and Knapp's ministry equated Spirit baptism with entire sanctification.[134] He initially did not respond to this call. Shumway writes, 'He refused to obey the call and says that God sent him the small-pox which robbed him of one of his eyes. He then consented to preach.'[135] His apparent punishment for disobeying the call may have contributed to Seymour and the participants of the Azusa Street Revival to emphasize the spirituality of ministers – such as entire sanctification and Spirit baptism

---

[131] Robeck, *The Azusa Street Mission and Revival*, p. 31. John W.V. Smith, *The Quest for Holiness and Unity: A Comprehensive History of the Church of God Reformation Movement* (Merle D. Strege (rev./exp.); Anderson: Warner, 2nd ed., 2009), p. 30.

[132] Shumway, 'A Study of "the Gift of Tongues"', p. 173; Nelson, 'For Such a Time as This', pp. 35, 165; Robeck, *The Azusa Street Mission and Revival*, pp. 31-35.

[133] Shumway, 'A Study of "the Gift of Tongues"', p. 173.

[134] Nelson, 'For Such a Time as This', p. 165; Martin Wells Knapp, *Revival Kindlings* (Cincinnati: The Revivalist, 3rd edn, 1890), pp. 309-10, 312.

[135] Shumway, 'A Study of "the Gift of Tongues"', p. 173.

– as more important than other traditional qualifications among other Christian traditions, such as education and ordination.[136]

The Ministry of Martin Wells Knapp

The ministry of Martin Wells Knapp is another potential influence upon Seymour's beliefs and practices related to corporate worship. Knapp was initially a Methodist evangelist who led a ministry in Cincinnati while Seymour lived in Cincinnati.[137] Whether or not Knapp influenced Seymour is debated, since there is no written documentation of Seymour's involvement in Knapp's ministry.[138] Claims from oral tradition, however, show that Seymour participated in Knapp's ministry.[139]

The strong parallels between Knapp's ministry and Seymour's ministry at the Azusa Street Revival also give indication of Knapp's influence upon Seymour.[140] The Methodism of that era became less concerned for racial equality and the holiness emphasis of early Methodism.[141] But Knapp's ministry would attract Seymour since he included blacks in his ministry and offered ministerial training.[142] Though Knapp belonged to the Holiness Association, he eventually left because they spoke 'against preaching the apocalyptic return of the Lord Jesus Christ, and divine (or faith) healing' – two important features of Seymour's ministry.[143] Knapp later also left the Methodist Episcopal Church in 1901 because they 'tried to prevent him from undertaking evangelistic travels unless he first gained administrative

---

[136] Scholars have debated whether or not Seymour was ordained with the Evening Light Saints due to a lack of documentation. Seymour may have been ordained with the Evening Lights – with no documentation available – or he may have at least been an itinerant gospel worker. See Nelson, 'For Such a Time as This', p. 180, n. 99; Robeck, *The Azusa Street Mission and Revival*, p. 30; Smith, *The Quest for Holiness and Unity*, p. 65.

[137] Nelson, 'For Such a Time as This', p. 163.

[138] Nelson, 'For Such a Time as This', p. 177, n. 81.

[139] Nelson explains that an oral tradition originating in the African American 'Apostolic' tradition in Indianapolis substantiates this claim. Nelson, 'For Such a Time as This', p. 163. Also see Robeck, *The Azusa Street Mission and Revival*, p. 31; Sanders, *William Joseph* Seymour, pp. 52-54; and Fox, 'William J. Seymour', pp. 32, 37-40.

[140] Nelson, 'For Such a Time as This', p. 163; Robeck, *The Azusa Street Mission and Revival*, p. 31; and Sanders, *William Joseph Seymour*, p. 53.

[141] Nelson, 'For Such a Time as This', p. 163.

[142] Nelson, 'For Such a Time as This', p. 163.

[143] Nelson, 'For Such a Time as This', p. 163.

approval'.[144] Knapp's willingness to minister despite what hierar-
chical, denominational structures have in place has some correspondence with Seymour, who sought to lead a ministry that transcended
denominational barriers and hierarchy. Oral tradition and the parallels
between Seymour's and Knapp's ministry give reason to consider
Knapp's likely influence upon Seymour regarding corporate worship
practices.

The immediacy of God in corporate worship was emphasised in
various ways in Knapp's ministry, related to his views on entire sanctification, preaching, healing, and miracles. First, Knapp distinguished conversion from Spirit baptism, equating Spirit baptism with
entire sanctification. He believed Spirit baptism included 'receiving
the Holy Ghost' and 'the obtaining of heart purity' – two things that
are 'identical'.[145] Spirit baptism not only sanctified the believer, but it
also empowered the believer for ministry.[146]

How believers experienced entire sanctification stressed the immediacy of God in corporate worship in several ways. First, he expected those who preach to have experienced salvation and entire
sanctification so they can be 'led of the Spirit'.[147] Preachers required
an experience of salvation and entire sanctification prior to their own
preaching, since they 'cannot lead others where they have not been
themselves'.[148] Second, he encouraged the use of altar calls as a response to preaching, in order for hearers to experience entire sanctification (as well as salvation).[149] Further, people must be willing to
fast, pray, and 'tarry' – wait – for the reception of entire sanctification.[150] Those seeking entire sanctification may display 'intense anticipation', and may shout, cry, and jump.[151] Knapp considered the phys-

---

[144] Nelson, 'For Such a Time as This', p. 164.

[145] Knapp, *Revival Kindlings*, p. 312. See Acts 15.8,9.

[146] Knapp, *Revival Kindlings*, pp. 309, 310, 321.

[147] Knapp, *Revival Kindlings*, p. 113.

[148] Knapp, *Revival Kindlings*, p. 113.

[149] Knapp, *Revival Kindlings*, p. 309.

[150] Martin Wells Knapp (ed.), *Bible Songs of Salvation and Victory, For God's People of Every Land: Suitable for Revivals, the Church, Sunday-Schools and the Home* (ed. Robert E. McNeill; Cincinnati: M.W. Knapp, n.d.), p. 82.

[151] William Kostlevy, *Holy Jumpers: Evangelicals and Radicals in Progressive Era America* (Oxford: Oxford University Press, 2010), pp. 32-33.

ical manifestations as 'normative for those seeking entire sanctifica-tion'.[152] Viewing physical manifestations as normative for entire sanc-tification has close affinity with the classical Pentecostal insistence on tongues as normative for Spirit baptism. Though Knapp did not refer to tongues – *xenolalia* or *glossolalia* – as the verification for Spirit bap-tism, he explained that one's speech will be affected by an experience of Spirit baptism. He suggested that Spirit baptism leads to a free-dom to 'speak and sing and pray', which may include emotional man-ifestations like shouting and crying in corporate worship.[153] Third, Knapp's reflection on how to know when one is baptised in the Spirit reveals the importance of God's present work in corporate worship. He explained that when Spirit baptism occurs, there will be 'no doubt', for 'God's presence is felt; and when one feels it, he knows it, whether a philosopher or a little child'.[154]

Second, the preacher's ministry is also affected by the importance of a direct experience of God. As stated earlier, preachers must have previously experienced salvation and entire sanctification.[155] Preach-ers should also prophesy. He described prophesying as 'inspired preaching', which is '[n]ot simply foretelling future events, but heaven-born God-sent messages from Spirit-filled hearts'.[156] In gen-eral, his views on preaching were affected by his value of the imme-diacy of God, for he believed in the importance of freedom (cf. with 'too much form' and 'ceremony') in corporate worship for empow-ered preaching, the benefit of hearing from God through visions, preaching 'in demonstration of the Spirit and power', and preaching that is based on Scripture in coordination with the Spirit.[157]

Third, Knapp highlighted the role of healing and miracles. The gift of healing 'embraces the power to claim physical healing for self or others when God reveals such to be His will'.[158] Further, the gift of miracles is 'the possession of miraculous power to do any God-

---

[152] Kostlevy, *Holy Jumpers*, p. 33.
[153] Knapp, *Bible Songs of Salvation and Victory*, p. 82; Kostlevy, *Holy Jumpers*, p. 33.
[154] Knapp, *Revival Kindlings*, p. 321.
[155] Knapp, *Revival Kindlings*, p. 113.
[156] Martin Wells Knapp, *Lightning Bolts from Pentecostal Skies; or Devices of the Devil Unmasked* (Cincinnati: The Revivalist, 1898), p. 84.
[157] Knapp, *Revival Kindlings*, pp. 112-13, 116-17, 119-20, 125-26, 129; Martin Wells Knapp, *Pentecostal Preachers* (Salem: Convention, n.d.), pp. 11, 38, 49.
[158] Knapp, *Lightning Bolts from Pentecostal Skies*, p. 84.

given work when such power is needed, whether it be to heal the sick or do the still greater work of resurrecting the spiritually dead and healing the spiritual leper'.[159] Though he was open to healing and miracles, he did not include an approach to other gifts of the Spirit that are more ecstatic in nature, particularly tongues.[160]

Finally, Knapp stated that one can have the 'best influence over others in revival meetings' by 'living right with God and man between such meetings as well as in them'.[161] Knapp ensures here, that Christian living is not merely about 'revival meetings', but encompasses all aspects of life. Seymour came to a similar approach to the Christian life, focusing less on tongues and more on love in the later stages of the Azusa Street Revival. Knapp's views on the present work of God in corporate worship finds a number of parallels with Seymour's views in the various ways described above, which shows how Seymour may have been influenced by Knapp.

Proto-Pentecostal Groups

Three groups have significant commonalities with the Azusa Street Revival, most notably the expression of tongues in the context of corporate worship, which is why they are described as Proto-Pentecostal. The three Proto-Pentecostal groups examined here is the Topeka, Kansas revival led by Parham; the Revival in Wales led by Evan Roberts; and the Mukti Mission Revival led by Pandita Ramabai. All three groups contributed to the birth of Pentecostalism. But as explained more thoroughly earlier, Azusa was the most influential upon

---

[159] Knapp, *Lightning Bolts from Pentecostal Skies*, p. 84.

[160] Knapp, *Lightning Bolts from Pentecostal Skies*, p. 84. Knapp admits he is influenced by W.B. Godbey's *Spiritual Gifts and Graces*, even encouraging readers to seek Godbey's instruction regarding the gifts of the Spirit because it includes a 'full and masterly presentation of this subject'. See Knapp, *Lightning Bolts from Pentecostal Skies*, pp. 84-85. In Knapp's analysis, though, tongues is not an ecstatic experience of speaking in an unknown language, but the ability to quickly learn a new language for the purpose of ministry – more so than the average person without this gift. Gerald W. King, 'When the Holiness Preacher Came to Town: Re-Dating W.B. Godbey's Visit to Azusa Street', *Cyberjournal for Pentecostal-Charismatic Research* 18. No pages. Online: www.pctii.org/cyberj/cyberj18/king.html; W.B. Godbey, *Spiritual Gifts and Graces* (Cincinnati: M.W. Knapp, 1895), pp. 42-46.

[161] Knapp, *Revival Kindlings*, p. 133.

the global Pentecostal movement, and most notably for North American classical Pentecostalism. All three revivals discussed here, however, are significant because they directly influenced Seymour and the Azusa Street Revival.

The Apostolic Faith Movement: The Ministry of Charles F. Parham

Parham influenced Seymour's views on theology and ministry, as Parham formally taught Seymour for a short period of time in December 1905 prior to the start of the Azusa Street Revival. Parham's influence, however, is limited with regard to the role of the Spirit's immediacy in corporate worship at Azusa. First, Parham taught Seymour at his own Bible School in Houston, Texas, where Seymour learned about Parham's view on Spirit baptism.[162] Parham believed that the evidence of Spirit baptism is tongues – *xenolalia* – so that people can preach the gospel in another human language, previously unknown.[163] Parham also included Seymour for the ministry of preaching during his time of training, though Parham required both the audience and altar time to be racially segregated.[164]

The second way Parham influenced Seymour was by the model of corporate worship and experience of Spirit baptism showcased at the Topeka, Kansas revival. Parham led the Topeka revival in 1901, which was initially viewed as a significant milestone among the Azusa Street Revival leaders. In the first issue of *AF*, issued in September of 1906, the early Pentecostals made an important statement about the origins of the movement they belonged to: '[t]his work began about five years ago last January, when a company of people under the leadership of Chas. Parham, who were studying God's word, tarried for Pentecost, in Topeka, Kan'.[165] The Azusa leaders explain that the Topeka revival participants searched the nation for Christians who had the 'true Pentecostal power', but were unsuccessful.[166] So they put aside 'commentaries and notes', and decided to wait on God, study the Word, and 'asked God to have wrought out in their hearts by the Holy Ghost'.[167] And after regular prayer over three months, a 'sister'

---

[162] Nelson, 'For Such a Time as This', p. 35; Fox, 'William J. Seymour', p. 61.
[163] Nelson, 'For Such a Time as This', pp. 37, 168.
[164] Nelson, 'For Such a Time as This', p. 168.
[165] *AF* 1.1 (September 1906), p. 1.
[166] *AF* 1.1 (September 1906), p. 1.
[167] *AF* 1.1 (September 1906), p. 1.

– described as 'sweet', 'loving', and one who had 'all the carnality taken out of her heart' – 'felt the Lord lead her to have hands laid on her to receive the Pentecost'.[168] And after their prayer for her, 'the Holy Ghost came in great power and she commenced speaking in an unknown tongue'.[169] This created a hunger among all those in the Bible school, so that three nights later, twelve more students apparently 'received the Holy Ghost, and prophesied, and cloven tongues could be seen upon their heads'.[170] The Azusa participants equated their experience with believers in Acts 2, and subsequently typical of the expectations and experiences of the early Pentecostals' worship at Azusa.[171] Praying, physical manifestations, and tarrying for long periods of time for the experience of the Spirit baptism were common features of the revivals in Topeka and Azusa.[172]

Finally, Parham's influence on Seymour's approach to the present work of the Spirit in corporate worship was not only limited, but differences led to division. Seymour initially viewed Parham as 'God's leader in the Apostolic Faith Movement'.[173] But the Azusa Street participants – particularly those publishing *AF* – changed their position by December of 1906 regarding the origins and leadership of their movement. Different views on God's present work in corporate worship led to the division, though they do not explain the full story behind their change of position. How the division occurred follows.

Seymour invited Parham to preach for the Azusa Street Revival. Seymour believed that Parham's ministry at the Azusa Street Revival would usher in a 'great revival'.[174] When Parham finally arrived, he did not like what he saw at Azusa. Parham stated that to his 'utter surprise and astonishment', conditions at Azusa proved to be worse than he expected.[175] He argued that Seymour approached him in a

---

[168] *AF* 1.1 (September 1906), p. 1.
[169] *AF* 1.1 (September 1906), p. 1.
[170] *AF* 1.1 (September 1906), p. 1.
[171] *AF* 1.1 (September 1906), p. 1.
[172] Goff, *Fields White Unto Harvest*, p. 129.
[173] *AF* 1.1 (September 1906), p. 1.
[174] Sarah E. Parham, *The Life of Charles F. Parham: Founder of the Apostolic Faith Movement*. 1930 (repr., New York: Garland Publishing, Inc., 1985), pp. 154-55. Also see Goff, *Fields White Unto Harvest*, p. 113.
[175] Parham, *The Life of Charles F. Parham*, p. 163.

'helpless' state, and Seymour apparently told Parham that he was unable to 'stem the tide that had arisen'.[176] From the platform, Parham stated that he 'saw manifestations of the flesh, spiritualistic controls, saw people practicing hypnotism at the altar over candidates seeking the baptism; though many were receiving the real baptism of the Holy Ghost'.[177] What Parham disliked most about what was going on was not anything regarding their teachings on Spirit baptism, healing, salvation, sanctification, eschatology, missions, finances, or administration, but what was occurring within the context of the worship services.[178] Parham focused on corporate worship as one of the contributing factors for the division between Parham and Seymour's ministry at Azusa.[179] While Parham's racist views affected his view of the corporate worship at Azusa, the focus here is on his explicit views on the experience of the Spirit in corporate worship.[180]

Parham also contrasted what he saw at the Azusa Street Revival with his movement, differentiating his ministry, the 'Apostolic Faith movement', with the Azusa Street Revival, which he refers to as the 'Pentecostal Assemblies'.[181] He states that people wrongfully associate his ministry with Azusa as 'kindred missions', because they fail to see the differences over various issues he explains related to origins, worship, and the use of tongues.[182] Regarding origins, he explains that his ministry began in 'Topeka, Kansas, January, 1901', while the 'Pentecostal Assemblies' began 'in a negro mission in Los Angeles, California'.[183] Regarding corporate worship, he explains that his ministry

---

[176] Parham, *The Life of Charles F. Parham*, p. 163.
[177] Parham, *The Life of Charles F. Parham*, p. 163.
[178] Also see Liardon, *The Azusa Street Revival*, p. 188.
[179] Parham, *The Life of Charles F. Parham*, pp. 163, 165, 168-70; Roberts Liardon explains that Parham was 'offended by the interracial nature of the meetings and graphically explained to his audiences that the "sin" of intermarriage in the days of Noah had been the chief cause of the Flood' (p. 82). *The Azusa Street Revival*, pp. 82, 189-91; Sanders, *William Joseph Seymour*, pp. 108-109. Sanders also acknowledges that Parham 'observed various charisms being demonstrated too openly by the congregation to suit him' (p. 108).
[180] Sanders, *William Joseph Seymour*, p. 109.
[181] Charles F. Parham, *The Everlasting Gospel* (originally published 1911; repr.; Baxter Springs: Apostolic Faith Bible College, n.d.), p. 118.
[182] Parham, *The Everlasting Gospel*, p. 118.
[183] Parham, *The Everlasting Gospel*, p. 118.

'is a dignified work, full of power and precision', while the 'Pentecostal Assemblies ... is a cross between the old-fashioned negro worship of the South, and Holy-Rollerism'.[184] Finally, regarding tongues, he states that seventy-five percent of people who claim to speak in tongues in the 'Pentecostal Assemblies' are only expressing 'chatter and jabber', have 'no Pentecostal power at all', and is essentially a 'Corinthian muddle'.[185] Parham was so adamant that the corporate worship patterns were unacceptable, that he distinguished the Azusa Street Revival and the other ministry centers associated with it as 'foreign' and 'unknown' to the movement he associated with, the 'Apostolic Faith'.[186]

Parham's views on corporate worship changed sometime between 1901 and 1906. Goff claims that Parham's change of views regarding corporate worship relates to Parham's experience in 1903; he writes, 'The original outpouring at Topeka had been, admittedly, an uncontrolled affair. But following the 'fleshly manifestations' in Nevada, Missouri, early in 1903, Parham had guarded against excessive emotion'.[187] At this meeting they witnessed 'some fleshly manifestations, and giving out of messages' they had 'not witnessed before'.[188] His wife explains that in Nevada her husband 'carefully and prayerfully tested these things', which she believes gave him a basis for knowing how 'to rebuke fanaticism'.[189]

Sarah Parham illustrates this issue concretely, explaining how she was once in prayer, and 'a power seized' her 'lower jaw', which caused it to 'tremble' and later 'shake with increased violence'.[190] Her husband apparently witnessed this, but did not 'condemn or criticize', but just prayed silently for her, so that the 'power' left her so that she ultimately gained control of herself – this proved to her that this

---

[184] Parham, *The Everlasting Gospel*, p. 118.

[185] Parham, *The Everlasting Gospel*, p. 118. Liardon points out that Parham opposed the corporate worship at Azusa, but only points out Parham's charge of 'hyper-emotionalism' as the cause. He does not link the idea of emotionalism with Parham's views on the experience of the Spirit in corporate worship, which this study exposes. *The Azusa Street Revival*, p. 188.

[186] Parham, *The Life of Charles F. Parham*, p. 168.

[187] Goff, *Fields White Unto Harvest*, p. 129.

[188] Parham, *The Life of Charles F. Parham*, p. 87.

[189] Parham, *The Life of Charles F. Parham*, p. 87.

[190] Parham, *The Life of Charles F. Parham*, p. 87.

'power' was 'not of God'.[191] This incident gives an indication that both Charles and Sarah Parham may have begun to distinguish physical demonstrations from manifestations explicitly mentioned in Scripture – like tongues – so that anything they considered excessive or emotional in corporate worship was unwelcome. In this shaking case, it was physical – something they deemed would be more evident in black spirituality or 'holy rollerism'. Parham's early ministry at Topeka, Kansas influenced the Azusa Street Revival participants' beliefs and experience of corporate worship, but his latter ministry was not as influential. And as Parham confessed, Azusa consisted of more than one influence upon the movement – notably both black spirituality and 'holy rollerism'.

There were two other revivals that occurred at the beginning of the twentieth century that influenced the corporate worship at the Azusa Street Revival, though Seymour did not physically attend these revivals: the revival in Wales and the Mukti Mission revival.

The Welsh Revival

Though Seymour never attended the revival in Wales from 1904–1905, this revival became another model for Azusa participants for an experience of God in corporate worship in four ways. Before turning to the four ways the Wales revival became a model, a brief description of this revival follows. S.B. Shaw's book, *Great Revival in Wales*, provided the story of the revival in Wales in 1904–1905. It was a popular book among participants at the Azusa Street Revival.[192] Bartleman linked the Azusa Street Revival with the Wales revival, describing the Wales revival as the beginnings of the Azusa revival, likening it to a baby where it was 'rocked in the cradle of little Wales'.[193] The revival in Wales was primarily led by Evan Roberts.[194] Bartleman reveals a letter he received from Roberts regarding the revival in Wales. It provides some important clues regarding the approach to worship they expressed, and how it could have affected

---

[191] Parham, *The Life of Charles F. Parham*, p. 87.

[192] Fox, 'William J. Seymour', p. 55.

[193] Bartleman, *Azusa Street*, pp. 21-22. Bartleman also stated he received 5,000 tracts on the revival in Wales, and that he distributed them among churches (p. 22).

[194] Bundy, 'Welsh Revival', 1187. D.D. Bundy explains that though the 'revival owed its beginnings to three Welsh revivalists: Seth Joshua, Joseph Jenkins, and Evan Roberts', the 'most important leader of the revival was Evan Roberts' (p. 1187).

those at the Azusa Street Revival. Roberts explained to Bartleman that the Wales revival has its origins in God, not people, and that God has 'come very close' to them.[195] He also contends that there is no 'creed', 'dogma', or 'sectarian doctrine' in the movement, just 'the wonder and beauty of Christ's love'.[196] Roberts believed that the revival in Wales was just 'the beginning', and that a 'great religious revival' was coming soon whereby '[t]he world will be swept by His Spirit as by a rushing, mighty wind'.[197]

The first way the Wales revival influenced others in highlighting the immediacy of God in corporate worship, is by emphasising the need for prayer in order to experience revival.[198] The second, and related to the previous point, was the role of spontaneity. Roberts maintained that he had no 'methods', so that he never prepares what he will speak, but leaves it to God.[199] Spontaneity was preferred for both prayers and preaching.[200] Third, the gifts and manifestations of the Spirit were expressed, which included 'singing in tongues', prophecy, and tongues.[201] Finally, Roberts emphasised that the marginal would be empowered by God to lead the ministry. He states that '[m]any who are now silent Christians will lead the movement', 'thousands' will even do more than them, all due to God's empowerment.[202] Roberts recognises that the 'silent' will lead revival, when they are empowered by God.[203] All four points mentioned above have parallels with Azusa's approach to the present work of God in corporate worship, and show why Azusa participants would view the Wales revival as exemplary.[204]

---

[195] Bartleman, *Azusa Street*, p. 38.

[196] Bartleman, *Azusa Street*, p. 38.

[197] Bartleman, *Azusa Street*, p. 38.

[198] Robeck, *The Azusa Street Mission and Revival*, p. 58.

[199] Bartleman, *Azusa Street*, p. 38.

[200] D.D. Bundy, 'Welsh Revival', in Stanley M. Burgess (ed.), *The New International Dictionary of Pentecostal and Charismatic Movements* (Grand Rapids: Zondervan, 2003), pp. 1187-88; Bartleman, *Azusa Street*, p. 38.

[201] Bundy, 'Welsh Revival', pp. 1187-88.

[202] Bartleman, *Azusa Street*, p. 38.

[203] Bartleman, *Azusa Street*, p. 38.

[204] For a more in-depth treatment of the connections between the Welsh revival and the Azusa Street Revival, see Jennifer A. Miskov, 'The Welsh Revival and the Azusa Street Revival: Liturgical Connections, Similarities and Developments', in Mark J. Cartledge and A. J. Swoboda (eds.), *Scripting Pentecost: A Study of Pentecostals, Worship, and Liturgy* (London: Routledge, 2016), pp. 32-52.

The Mukti Mission Revival in India

The Mukti Mission Revival highlighted the immediacy of God in corporate worship and influenced Azusa in two ways. To begin, a brief description of the Mukti Mission and its relationship with Azusa is necessary. The Mukti Mission was founded and led by Pandita Ramabai, and she was joined by a missionary to India from the United States, Minnie F. Abrams in 1898.[205] The Mukti Mission was a community for disenfranchised women in Pune, India.[206] Though Ramabai initially joined the Church of England, she associated with the Holiness movement, for she 'experienced a deeper work of the Holy Spirit at the Holiness camp meeting at Lanauli' in 1895.[207] She even enrolled her daughter at Chesbrough Seminary, a Free Methodist school in the States.[208] From 1905–1907, a significant revival occurred among the women of the Mukti Mission, and subsequently among others, including men.[209]

Azusa participants acknowledged their link with the Mukti Mission Revival. While Bartleman stated that the revival in Wales was 'rocked in the cradle of little Wales', he further states that '[i]t was "brought up" in India following, becoming full grown in Los Angeles later'.[210] And to link the revival in Wales with the Mukti Mission revival in India is appropriate, since *The Great Revival*, a booklet on the revival in Wales, was also shared and translated into a few languages used in India.[211]

---

[205] Stanley M. Burgess, 'Ramabai, Sarasvati Mary (Pandita)', in Stanley M. Burgess (ed.), *The New International Dictionary of Pentecostal and Charismatic Movements* (Grand Rapids: Zondervan, 2003), p. 1017; G.B. McGee and D.J. Rodgers, 'Abrams, Minnie F', Stanley M. Burgess (ed.), *The New International Dictionary of Pentecostal and Charismatic Movements* (Grand Rapids: Zondervan, 2003), pp. 305-306.

[206] Helen S. Dyer, *Pandita Ramabai: The Story of Her Life* (London: Morgan and Scott, n.d.); Burgess, 'Ramabai, Sarasvati Mary (Pandita)', pp. 1016-18; Anderson, *Introduction to Pentecostalism*, p. 124.

[207] Howard A. Snyder, 'Holiness Heritage: The Case of Pandita Ramabai', *Wesleyan Theological Journal* 40.2 (Fall 2005), pp. 37-39.

[208] Snyder, 'Holiness Heritage: The Case of Pandita Ramabai', pp. 37-39.

[209] Burgess, 'Ramabai', p. 1018.

[210] Bartleman, *Azusa Street*, pp. 21-22.

[211] G.B. McGee and S.M. Burgess, 'India', in Stanley M. Burgess (ed.), *The New International Dictionary of Pentecostal and Charismatic Movements* (Grand Rapids: Zondervan, 2003), p. 120. See Dyer, *Pandita Ramabai the Story of Her Life*; Burgess, 'Ramabai, Sarasvati Mary (Pandita)', pp. 1016-18; Anderson, *Introduction to Pentecostalism*, p. 124.

The first way those at Mukti provided inspiration for Azusa regarding the present work of God in corporate worship relates to the role of Spirit baptism and tongues. Ramabai explained that she witnessed people of various backgrounds – like at Azusa – coming 'under the power of the revival', from 'the most ignorant' of her 'people', to 'the most refined' and 'highly educated English men and women' who came to India for 'God's service'.[212] She states that these people 'lose all control over their bodies, and are shaken like reeds, stammering words in various unknown tongues as the Spirit teaches them to speak, and gradually get to a place where they are in unbroken communion with God'.[213] One primary difference with the Azusa Street Revival, was Ramabai's insistence that tongues was only one of many other signs of Spirit baptism. Ramabai explained: 'The gift of tongues is certainly one of the signs of the baptism of the Holy Spirit. There is scriptural ground to hold this belief. But there is no Scripture warrant to think that the speaking in tongues is the only and necessary sign of the baptism of the Holy Spirit'.[214]

The second facet of Mukti's experience of the immediacy of God in corporate worship that influenced Azusa relates to the role of physical demonstrations. In *AF*, a report from a participant at the revival in India includes revealing insights on the role of physical demonstrations in corporate worship, which influenced the approach to corporate worship at the Azusa Street Mission. They describe both the lament and joy at Mukti, which included: 'trembling' because of conviction, 'loud crying in prayer', 'loud … confessions', 'falling', 'writhing', and people 'being twisted and violently thrown down when an unclean spirit had been cast out'.[215] But there is joy described at Mukti as well, as there is '[j]oy unspeakable filling faces with glory', 'singing', 'clapping', 'shouting praises, dancing, and losing strength as under an "exceeding weight of glory"'.[216] They also share how people become 'unconscious' of others due to 'intense' intercessory prayer,

---

[212] Burgess, 'Ramabai, Sarasvati Mary (Pandita)', p. 1018.
[213] Burgess, 'Ramabai, Sarasvati Mary (Pandita)', p. 1018.
[214] See Snyder, 'Holiness Heritage', p. 46.
[215] *AF* 1.9 (June–September 1907), p. 4. The newsletter states that this description comes from a '[p]ublished report of the Mission at Mukti, Kedgaon, India', particularly from a unnamed female participant (p. 4).
[216] *AF* 1.9 (June–September 1907), p. 4.

or even 'become unconscious and fall'. They also state two conse-
quences among those who were 'babbling brooks at the time of their
convictions and conversion': 'holy living' and 'service' for evangelistic
work.[217] The above description of the physical manifestations in worship in India is vivid – and the same description could be applied to
the Azusa Street Revival. These physical manifestations, however, are
described as 'under an "exceeding weight of glory"' – reflecting a link
between physical manifestations in worship and the Spirit's immediacy, which is critical for understanding Pentecostal corporate worship.

The report from the female participant in the Indian revival maintains that people should not suppress physical manifestations, which
grieves the Spirit, for the 'work' will stop and the 'fruit of holy lives'
will not be found.[218] They explain that though 'the devil imitates the
trembling caused by the Holy Spirit when He comes in so as to over-
power the physical', individuals should not allow that to alter or question what God may be working in people.[219] Mukti was a corporate
worship context that was explicitly influential upon the Azusa Street
Revival, as Mukti gave Azusa participants a model that included Spirit
baptism, tongues, and physical demonstrations.

Conclusion

This appendix shows that several people and movements had directly
or indirectly contributed to Azusa's approach to understanding God's
present work in corporate worship. African American spirituality, Revivalism, Methodism, the Holiness Movement, and Proto-Pentecostal groups all contributed to what developed at the Azusa Street Revival.

---

[217] *AF* 1.9 (June–September 1907), p. 4.
[218] *AF* 1.9 (June–September 1907), p. 4.
[219] *AF* 1.9 (June–September 1907), p. 4.

BIBLIOGRAPHY

Adams, Charles G., 'The Burden of the Black Church', in Michael P. Knowles (ed.), *The Folly of Preaching: Models and Methods* (Grand Rapids: Eerdmans, 2007), pp. 15-28.

Akins, Debra, 'Song Story: Matt Redman's'. *Crosswalk.com*, April 28, 2003. Online: http://www.crosswalk.com/church/worship/song-story-matt -redmans-1197457.html.

Albrecht, Daniel E., *Rites in the Spirit: A Ritual Approach to Pentecostal/Charismatic Spirituality* (JPTSup, 17; Sheffield: Sheffield Academic Press, 1999).

Aldridge, Marion D., 'George Whitefield: The Necessary Interdependence of Preaching Style and Sermon Content to Effect Revival', *JETS* 23.1 (March 1980), pp. 55-64.

Alexander, Bobby C., *Victor Turner Revisited: Ritual as Social Change* (ed. Susan Thistlethwaite; American Academy of Religion Academic Series 74; Atlanta: Scholars, 1991).

Alexander, Estrelda, *Black Fire: One Hundred Years of African American Pentecostalism* (Downers Grove: InterVarsity Press, 2011).

Alexander, Kimberly E., 'Heavenly Choirs in Earthy Spaces: The Significance of Corporate Spiritual Singing in Early Pentecostal Experience', *Journal of Pentecostal Theology* 25.2 (2016), pp. 254-68.

Alford, Delton L., *Ministering Through Music* (ed. Donald S. Aultman; Cleveland: Pathway, 2002).

—*Music in the Pentecostal Church* (Cleveland: Pathway, 1967).

—'Music in Worship', in Cecil B. Knight (ed.), *Pentecostal Worship* (Cleveland: Pathway, 1974), pp. 63-75.

Allen, C. Leonard, 'Cane Ridge and the Spirit's Fire', *Lexington Theological Quarterly* 34.3 (Fall 1999), pp. 131-49.

Althouse, Peter and Michael Wilkinson, 'Musical Bodies in the Charismatic Renewal: The Case of Catch the Fire and Soaking Prayer', in Monique M. Ingalls and Amos Yong (eds.), *The Spirit of Praise: Music and Worship in Global Pentecostal-Charismatic Christianity* (University Park: The Pennsylvania State University Press, 2015), pp. 29-44.

Anderson, Allan, 'Pentecostalism', in William A. Dyrness and Veli-Matti Kärkkäinen (eds.), *Global Dictionary of Theology* (Downers Grove: InterVarsity, 2008), pp. 641-48.

—*An Introduction to Pentecostalism* (Cambridge: Cambridge University, 2004).

—*Spreading Fires: The Missionary Nature of Early Pentecostalism* (Maryknoll: Orbis, 2007).

Anderson, Kenton C., *Choosing to Preach: A Comprehensive Introduction to Sermon Options and Structures* (Grand Rapids: Zondervan, 2006).

Anderson, Robert Mapes, *Vision of the Disinherited: The Making of American Pentecostalism* (New York: Oxford University Press, 1979).

Andrews, Edward G. (ed.), *The Doctrines and Discipline of the Methodist Episcopal Church* (New York and Cincinnati: Methodist Episcopal Church, 1900).

The Apostolic Faith. CD-ROM. Destiny Image. [Originally published from 1906–1908, Los Angeles, California].

Archer, Kenneth J., *The Gospel Revisited: Towards a Pentecostal Theology of Worship and Witness* (Eugene: Pickwick, 2011).

Archer, Melissa L., *'I Was in the Spirit on the Lord's Day': A Pentecostal Engagement with Worship in the Apocalypse* (Cleveland, TN: CPT Press, 2014).

Archives of the PAOC [Pentecostal Assemblies of Canada]. Online: http://www.paoc.org/about/archives.

Arndal, Steffen, 'Spiritual Revival and Hymnody: The Hymnbooks of German Pietism and Moravianism', in Hedwig T. Durnbaugh (ed. and trans.), *Brethren Life and Thought* XL (Spring 1995), pp. 71-93.

Australian Christian Churches. 'About ACC'. Online: http://www.acc.org.au/AboutUs.aspx.

—'Our History'. Online: http://www.acc.org.au/AboutUs/OurHistory.A s px.

Australian Pentecostal Studies. Online: http://webjournals.ac.edu.au/journal s/aps.

Bailey, E.K., and Warren W. Wiersbe, *Preaching in Black and White* (Grand Rapids: Zondervan, 2003).

Baker, J.P., 'Prophecy, Prophets', in I. Howard Marshall, A.R. Millard, J.I. Packer, and D.J. Wiseman (eds.), *New Bible Dictionary* (Leicester: Inter–Varsity, 3rd edn, 1996), pp. 964-75.

Baker-Wright, Michelle K., 'Intimacy and Orthodoxy: Evaluating Existing Paradigms of Contemporary Worship Music', *Missiology: An International Review* 35.2 (April 2007), pp. 169-78.

Bartleman, Frank, *Azusa Street* (Vinson Synan (intro.); Alachua: Bridge-Logos, 2nd edn, 1980). [Originally published as *Another Wave Rolls In* (Northridge: Voice Christian Publications, 1962)].

Bebbington, David, *Patterns in History: A Christian Perspective on Historical Thought* (Vancouver: Regent, 2000).

Begbie, Jeremie S., *Resounding Truth: Christian Wisdom in the World of Music* (Grand Rapids: Baker Academic, 2007).

Bennet, Joy T., 'Voices of Praise: Israel Houghton and New Breed', *Ebony* (November 2007), pp. 191-94.

Berger, Teresa, and Bryan D. Spinks (eds.), *The Spirit in Worship – Worship in the Spirit* (Collegeville: Liturgical Press, 2009).

Bergunder, Michael, *The South Indian Pentecostal Movement in the Twentieth Century* (Grand Rapids: Eerdmans, 2008).

Best, Harold M., *Unceasing Worship: Biblical Perspectives on Worship and the Arts* (Downers Grove: InterVarsity, 2003).

Blomberg, Craig, *1 Corinthians* (The NIV Application Commentary, Grand Rapids: Zondervan, 1994).

Blumhofer, Edith L., *Restoring the Faith: The Assemblies of God, Pentecostalism, and American Culture* (Urbana: University of Illinois Press, 1993).

Boda, Mark, 'A Severe Mercy', McMaster Divinity College, Class Notes, Hamilton, Ontario, Fall 2009.

Bogart, Julie (ed.), *All About Worship* (Anaheim: Vineyard Music Group, 1998).

Borlase, Craig, *William Seymour: A Biography* (Lake Mary: Charisma, 2006).

Bowman, Robert M., Jr, *The Word-Faith Controversy: Understanding the Health and Wealth Gospel* (Grand Rapids: Baker, 2001).

Brand, Chad Owen (ed.), *Perspectives on Spirit Baptism* (Nashville: Broadman and Holman, 2004).

Bridges, James K., 'Introduction', in James K. Bridges (ed.), *Foundations for Pentecostal Preaching* (Springfield: Gospel Publishing House, 2005), pp. 11-25.

Brown, Kenneth O., *Holy Ground: A Study of the American Camp Meeting* (New York: Garland, 1992).

—*Holy Ground, Too: The Camp Meeting Family Tree* (Hazelton: Holiness Archives, 1997).

Brueggemann, Walter, *The Psalms and the Life of Faith* (ed. Patrick D. Miller; Minneapolis: Fortress, 1995).

Bundy, D.D., 'Irving, Edward', in Stanley M. Burgess (ed.), *The New International Dictionary of Pentecostal and Charismatic Movements* (Grand Rapids: Zondervan, 2003), pp. 803-804.

—'Welsh Revival', in Stanley M. Burgess (ed.), *The New International Dictionary of Pentecostal and Charismatic Movements* (Grand Rapids: Zondervan, 2003), pp. 1187-88.

Burgess, Stanley M. (ed.), *The New International Dictionary of Pentecostal and Charismatic Movements* (Grand Rapids: Zondervan, 2003).

—'Ramabai, Sarasvati Mary (Pandita)', in Stanley M. Burgess (ed.), *The New International Dictionary of Pentecostal and Charismatic Movements* (Grand Rapids: Zondervan, 2003), pp. 1016-18.

Butler, Melvin Lloyd, 'Songs of Pentecost: Experiencing Music, Transcendence, and Identity in Jamaica and Haiti' (PhD dissertation, New York University, 2005).

Byrd, Joseph Kendall, 'Formulation of a Classical Pentecostal Homiletic in Dialogue with Contemporary Protestant Homiletics' (PhD dissertation, The Southern Baptist Theological Seminary, 1990).

Callen, Barry L., *It's God's Church: The Life and Legacy of Daniel Sidney Warner* (Anderson: Warner, 1995).

Canadian Pentecostal Seminary. 'Canadian Pentecostal Seminary'. Online: http://canadianpentecostalseminary.ca/home.

Cartledge, Mark J. and A.J. Swoboda (eds.), *Scripting Pentecost: A Study of Pentecostals, Worship and Liturgy* (London: Routledge, 2016).

Carwardine, Richard, *Transatlantic Revivalism: Popular Evangelicalism in Britain and America 1790–1865* (Westport: Greenwood, 1978).

Chan, Simon, *Liturgical Theology: The Church as Worshiping Community* (Downers Grove: InterVarsity, 2006).

—*Pentecostal Theology and the Christian Spiritual Tradition* (JPTSup, 21; Sheffield: Sheffield Academic Press, 2000).

Chant, Barry, *The Spirit of Pentecost: The Origins and Development of the Pentecostal Movement in Australia, 1870–1939* (Lexington: Emeth, 2011).

Chapell, Bryan, *Christ-Centered Preaching: Redeeming the Expository Sermon* (Grand Rapids: Baker, 2nd edn, 2005).

Clemmons, I.C., 'Mason, Charles Harrison', in Stanley M. Burgess (ed.), *The New International Dictionary of Pentecostal and Charismatic Movements* (Grand Rapids: Zondervan, 2003), pp. 865-67.

Clifton, Shane, *Pentecostal Churches in Transition: Analysing the Developing Ecclesiology of the Assemblies of God in Australia* (Leiden: Brill, 2009).

Cone, James, 'Sanctification, Liberation, and Black Worship', *Theology Today* 35.2 (1978), pp. 139-52.

Consortium of Pentecostal Archives. Online: http://www.pentecostalarchives.org. Cook, Jeremy, 'Vineyard Worship Values'. Inside Worship: A Vineyard Resource for Worship. Online: http://www.insideworship.com/2011/about/vineyard-worship-values.

Cooke, Victoria, *Understanding Songs in Renewal* (Grove Renewal Series 4; Cambridge: Grove Books, 2001).

Costen, Melva Wilson, *African American Christian Worship* (Nashville: Abingdon, 2007).

Courey, David, 'What Has Wittenberg to Do with Azusa?: Luther's Theology of the Cross and Pentecostal Triumphalism' (PhD dissertation, McMaster Divinity College, 2011).

Cox, Harvey, *Fire from Heaven: The Rise of Pentecostal Spirituality and the Reshaping of Religion in the Twenty-First Century* (Cambridge: Da Capo, 1995).

Crabtree, Charles T., 'Dr. Charles T. Crabtree Biography'. No pages. Online: http://crabtreeandramona.com/charlesBio.htm.

—*Decisive Leader* (Springfield: U.S. Decade of Harvest, 1991).

—*The Pentecostal Priority* (Springfield: U.S. Decade of Harvest, 1993).

—*Pentecostal Preaching: Empowering Your Pulpit with the Holy Spirit* (Springfield: Gospel, 2003).

—*This I Believe* (Springfield: Gospel Publishing, 1982).

Crawford, Evans E., *The Hum: Call and Response in African American Preaching* (Nashville: Abingdon, 1995).

Crosby, Robert, 'The Pentecostal Paradox: As the Global Chorus Grows, American Tongues Fall Silent'. No pages. Online: http://www.patheos.com/Resources/Additional-Resources/Pentecostal-Paradox-Robert-Crosby-01-27-2012.

Dallimore, Arnold A., *George Whitefield: God's Anointed Servant in the Great Revival of the Eighteenth Century* (Westchester: Crossway, 1990).

Daneel, M.L., *All Things Hold Together: Holistic Theologies at the African Grassroots* (Pretoria: Unisa, 2007).

Daniels, David Douglas, III, '"Gotta Moan Sometime": A Sonic Exploration of Earwitnesses to Early Pentecostal Sound in North America', *Pneuma* 30.1 (2008), pp. 5-32.

Dawn, Marva J., *Reaching Out Without Dumbing Down: A Theology of Worship for the Turn-of-the-Century Culture* (Grand Rapids: Eerdmans, 1995).

David C. Cook, 'David C. Cook Acquires Integrity Music from Integrity Media Inc'. Online: http://davidccook.ca/news.php?area=&aid=928.

Davis, Gerald L., *I Got the Word in Me and I Can Sing It, You Know: A Study of the Performed African-American Sermon* (Philadelphia: University of Pennsylvania, 1985).

—'Trusting the Spirit to Lead Us', *The African American Pulpit* 12.1 (2008–2009), pp. 50-53.

Dayton, Donald, *Theological Roots of Pentecostalism* (Grand Rapids: Francis Asbury, 1987).

Doerksen, Brian, 'BrianDoerksen.com'. Online: http://briandoerksen.com.

—'The Call to Worship the Father', in Julie Bogart (ed.), *All About Worship* (Anaheim: Vineyard Music Group, 1998), pp. 53-58.

—'Faithful Father'. Mercy/Vineyard Publishing, 1996.

—'Faithful One'. *Equip: Vineyard Worship Resources*, 2004.

—'Father, I Want You to Hold Me'. Mercy/Vineyard Publishing, 1989.

—'Focusing Your Worship Ministry on God'. *Christian Musician Summit: CMS Overlake 2007 Mini-Sessions*. November 9–10, 2007. Online: http://www.youtube.com/watch?v=PtDhS4X816c.

—*Make Love, Make War: Now is the Time to Worship* (Colorado Springs: David C. Cook, 2009).

—'Song Writing', in John Wimber (ed.), *Thoughts on Worship* (Anaheim: Vineyard Music Group, 1996), pp. 87-103.

—'Songs of Lament: An Interview with Brian Doerksen (Part 2)'. Interview by Jim Coggins. May 15, 2008. Online: http://canadianchristianity.com/songs-lament-interview-brian-doerksen-part-2-3424/.

Doerksen, Brian, Daphne Rademaker, Karen Mitchinson, and Steve Mitchinson, 'How Long O Lord?' Integrity's Hosanna! Music, 2002.

Dove, Stephen, 'Hymnody and Liturgy in the Azusa Street Revival, 1906–1908', *Pneuma* 31 (2009), pp. 242-63.

Dunn, James D.G., *Jesus and the Spirit: A Study of the Religious and Charismatic Experience of Jesus and the First Christians as Reflected in the New Testament* (London: SCM, 1975).

—*1 Corinthians* (New Testament Guides; Sheffield: Sheffield Academic Press, 1995).

Dyer, Helen S., *Pandita Ramabai: The Story of Her Life* (London: Morgan and Scott, n.d.).

Dyrness, William A., *A Primer on Christian Worship: Where We've Been, Where We Are, Where We Can Go* (Grand Rapids: Eerdmans, 2009).

Eastern Ontario District – PAOC. Online: http://www.eod.paoc.org/ca mps.html.

Erickson, Gary D., *Pentecostal Worship: A Biblical and Practical Approach* (Hazelwood: Word Aflame, 1989).

Erickson, Millard J., 'Charismatic Gifts', *The Concise Dictionary of Christian Theology* (Wheaton: Crossway, rev. edn, 2001), p. 31.

—'Charismatics', *The Concise Dictionary of Christian Theology* (Wheaton: Crossway, rev. edn, 2001), p. 31.

Escobar, Samuel, review of *Pentecostalism: Origins and Developments Worldwide* (Peabody: Hendrickson, 1997), by Walter J. Hollenweger, in *Missiology* 28.1 (January 2000), pp. 115-16.

Eskridge, Larry, 'God's Forever Family: The Jesus People Movement in America, 1966-1977' (PhD diss.; Stirling University, Scotland, 2005).

—'Slain by the Music', *Christian Century* (March 7, 2006), pp. 18-20.

Evans, Mark, *Open Up the Doors: Music in the Modern Church* (London: Equinox, 2006).

Farias, Andree, 'Think About God: Pioneer Doerksen on What's Wrong with Worship Music', *Christianity Today* 51.7 (July 2007), p. 59.

'The Fatherless Child: It is a Unique Cultural Moment for the Church to Act like a Family', *Christianity Today* 51.10 (October 1, 2007), p. 25.

Faupel, D. William, *The Everlasting Gospel: The Significance of Eschatology in The Development of Pentecostal Thought* (Blandford Forum: Deo, 2009).

Fee, Gordon D., *God's Empowering Presence: The Holy Spirit in the Letters of Paul* (Peabody: Hendrickson, 1994).

Finney, Charles G., *The Memoirs of Charles G. Finney* (ed. Garth M. Rosell and Richard A.G. Dupuis; Grand Rapids: Zondervan, 1989).

Fitzmyer, Joseph A., *First Corinthians* (The Anchor Yale Bible 32; New Haven: Yale University Press, 2008).

Flower Pentecostal Heritage Center. Online: http://ifphc.org.

Flynn, James T., *Words that Transform: Preaching as a Catalyst for Renewal* (Lanham: University Press of America, 2010).

Forbes, James A., Jr, *The Holy Spirit and Preaching* (Nashville: Abingdon, 1989).

Fox, Charles R., 'William J. Seymour: Pioneer of the Azusa Street Revival', in Vinson Synan and Charles R. Fox, *William J. Seymour: Pioneer of the Azusa Street Revival* (Alachua: Bridge-Logos, 2012), pp. 17-167.

Fragar, Russell, 'About Russell'. Online: http://www.russellfragar.com.

—'Holy Spirit Rain Down'. Hillsong Music Publishing, 1997.

George, A.C., *Trailblazers for God: A History of the Assemblies of God of India* (Kothanur: SABC, 2004).

Godbey, W.B., *Spiritual Gifts and Graces* (Cincinnati: M. W. Knapp, 1895).

Goff, Jr., James R., *Fields White Unto Harvest: Charles F. Parham and the Missionary Origins of Pentecostalism* (Fayetteville: University of Arkansas, 1988).

—'Parham, Charles Fox', in Stanley Burgess (ed.), *The New International Dictionary of Pentecostal and Charismatic Movements* (Grand Rapids: Zondervan, 2003), pp. 955-57.

Green, Chris E.W., '"In Your Presence there is Fullness of Joy": Experiencing God as Trinity', in Lee Roy Martin (ed.), *Toward a Pentecostal Theology of Worship* (Cleveland: CPT Press, 2016), pp. 187-99.

—*Toward a Pentecostal Theology of the Lord's Supper: Foretasting the Kingdom* (Cleveland: CPT, 2012).

Grenz, Stanley J., 'Concerns of a Pietist with a Ph.D.', *Wesleyan Theological Journal* 37.2 (Fall 2002), pp. 58-76.

Griffith, R.M., and D. Roebuck, 'Women, Role of', in Stanley Burgess (ed.), *The New International Dictionary of Pentecostal and Charismatic Movements* (Grand Rapids: Zondervan, 2003), pp. 1203-209.

Grogan, Geoffrey W., *Psalms* (The Two Horizons Old Testament Commentary; Grand Rapids: Eerdmans, 2008).

Gros, Jeffrey, review of *Pentecostal Churches in Transition: Analysing the Developing Ecclesiology of the Assemblies of God in Australia* (Leiden: Brill, 2009), by Shane Clifton, in *Pneuma* 32.2 (2010), pp. 303-304.

Guthrie, Joseph R., 'Pentecostal Hymnody: Historical, Theological, and Musical Influences' (DMA dissertation, Southwestern Baptist Theological Seminary, 1992).

Hattersley, Roy, *The Life of John Wesley: A Brand from the Burning* (New York: Doubleday, 2003).

Hawthorne, Gerald F. and Ralph P. Martin, *Philippians* (Word Biblical Commentary 43; Nashville: Thomas Nelson, rev. edn, 2004).

Heath, Gordon L., 'History of Evangelicalism'. McMaster Divinity College, Class notes, Winter 2010.

Heisler, Greg, 'Clark Kent or Superman? A Case for a Spirit-Driven Methodology of Expository Preaching'. Paper presented at the annual meeting of the Evangelical Academy of Homiletics, 2004. Online: http://www.ehomiletics.com/papers/04/heisler04.php.

—*Spirit-Led Preaching: The Holy Spirit's Role in Sermon Preparation and Delivery* (Nashville: Broadman and Holman, 2007).

'The Heresy of Application: An Interview with Haddon Robinson', *Leadership Journal* 28.4 (Fall 1997) 20. Online: http://www.christianitytoday.com/le/1997/fall/7l4020.html.

Higgins, Thomas W., 'Kenn Gulliksen, John Wimber, and the Founding of the Vineyard Movement', *Pneuma* 34.2 (2012), pp. 208-28.

Hillsong, *Shout to the Lord: The Platinum Collection featuring Darlene Zschech* (Hillsong Music Australia, 2000).

—*Simply Worship 3 (Live)*. Hillsong Music Australia, 2010.

—*Touching Heaven, Changing Earth (Live)*. Hillsong Music Australia, 2010.

'Hillsong Church'. Online: http://hillsong.com.

Hillsong Live. 'About Hillsong LIVE', Online: http://live.hillsong.com/about.

Hocken, P.D., 'Charismatic Movement', in Stanley Burgess (ed.), *The New International Dictionary of Pentecostal and Charismatic Movements* (Grand Rapids: Zondervan, 2003), pp. 477-519.

Hollenweger, Walter J., 'The Critical Tradition of Pentecostalism', *Journal of Pentecostal Theology* 1 (1992), pp. 7-17.

—*Pentecostalism: Origins and Developments Worldwide* (Peabody: Hendrickson, 1997).

—'Pentecostals and the Charismatic Movement', in Cheslyn Jones, Geoffrey Wainwright, and Edward Yarnold, SJ (eds.), *The Study of Spirituality* (Oxford: Oxford University Press, 1986), pp. 549-54.

Holm, Randall, 'Cadences of the Heart: A Walkabout in Search of Pentecostal Preaching', *Didaskalia*. 15.1 (Fall 2003), pp. 13-27.

Hope Unlimited Church, 'About Us'. Online: http://www.hopeuc.com/#/home/about-us.

Horn, Ken, 'Charles T. Crabtree: A Focus on Fiscipleship and Unity', *Pentecostal Evangel* (September 2007). No pages. Online: http://pentecostalevangel.ag.org/Articles2007/4873_Crabtree.cfm.

Houghton, Israel, *A Deeper Level* (New Kensington: Whitaker House, 2007).

Houghton, Israel and Aaron Lindsey, 'Deeper'. Aaron Lindsey Publishing, 2007.

Houston, Bobbie, *Heaven is in This House* (Maximised Leadership, 2001).

—*I'll Have What She's Having: The Ultimate Compliment to any Women Daring to Change Her World* (Nashville: Thomas Nelson, 2008).

Houston, Brian, *For This I Was Born: Aligning Your Vision to God's Cause* (Nashville: Thomas Nelson, 2008).

Houston, Brian and Bobbie Houston, 'Brian and Bobbie'. Online: http://brianandbobbie.com.

Howard, Felicia, 'Hillsong's Darlene Zschech Leaves After 25 Years of Service', *The Christian Post* (October 28, 2010). Online: http://www.christianpost.com/news/hillsongs-darlene-zschech-leaves-after-25-years-of-service-47404.

Hughes, Ray H., 'The Baptism with the Holy Ghost', in Ray H. Hughes (ed.), *Who is the Holy Ghost? A Study of the Person and Work of the Holy Spirit* (Cleveland: Pathway, rev. edn, 2004), pp. 143-54.

—*Classical Pentecostal Sermon Library* (vol. 1; Cleveland: Pathway, 2011).

—'The Holy Ghost and Power', in Ray H. Hughes (ed.), *Who is the Holy Ghost? A Study of the Person and Work of the Holy Spirit* (Cleveland: Pathway, rev. edn, 2004), pp. 79-88.

—'How to Receive Power', in Ray H. Hughes (ed.), *Who is the Holy Ghost? A Study of the Person and Work of the Holy Spirit* (Cleveland: Pathway, rev. edn, 2004), pp. 121-29.

—*Pentecostal Preaching* (Cleveland: Pathway, rev. edn, 2004).

—'Speaking In Tongues', in Ray H. Hughes (ed.), *Who is the Holy Ghost? A Study of the Person and Work of the Holy Spirit* (Cleveland: Pathway, rev. edn, 2004), pp. 113-19.

—'Speaking With Tongues at Will'. Online:http://rayhhughes.com/uploads/SPEAKING__WITH__TONGUES__AT__WILL.doc.

—(ed.), *Who Is the Holy Ghost? A Study of the Person and Work of the Holy Spirit* (Cleveland: Pathway, rev. edn, 2004.

Hughes, Tim, 'Heart I am to Worship'. Thankyou Music, 2000.

Hybels, Bill, 'Endorsements', in Darlene Zschech, *Extravagant Worship: Holy, Holy, Holy is the Lord God Almighty Who Was and Is, and Is to Come* (Bloomington: Bethany, 2002), p. 13.

Ingalls, Monique M., 'Introduction: Interconnection, Interface, and Identification in Pentecostal-Charismatic Music and Worship', in Monique M. Ingalls and Amos Yong (eds.), *The Spirit of Praise: Music and Worship in Global Pentecostal-Charismatic Christianity* (University Park: The Pennsylvania State University Press, 2015), pp. 1-25.

Ingalls, Monique M., and Amos Yong (eds.), *The Spirit of Praise: Music and Worship in Global Pentecostal-Charismatic Christianity* (University Park: The Pennsylvania State University Press, 2015).

Integrity Music, 'About: Our Mission'. Online: http://integritymusic.com/about/.

Irvin, Dale T, review of *Introduction to Pentecostalism* (Cambridge: Cambridge University, 2004), by Allan Anderson, in *Journal of Pentecostal Theology* 16.1 (2007), pp. 46-50.

Jacobsen, Douglas G. (ed.), *A Reader in Pentecostal Theology: Voices from the First Generation* (Bloomington: Indiana University, 2006).

—*Thinking in the Spirit: Theologies of the Early Pentecostal Movement* (Bloomington: Indiana University, 2003).

Jakes, T.D., 'Preaching to Mend Broken Lives', in Michael Duduit (ed.), *Preaching with Power: Dynamic Insights from Twenty Top Pastors* (Grand Rapids: Baker, 2006), pp. 65-73.
—T.D. Jakes Ministry, Inc. Online: http://www.tdjakes.org.
Johansson, Calvin M., 'Singing in the Spirit', *Paraclete* 24.2 (1990), pp. 20-23.
—'Music in the Pentecostal Movement', in Eric Patterson and Edmund Rybarczyk (eds.), *The Future of Pentecostalism in the United States* (Lanham: Lexington, 2007), pp. 49-69.
Johns, Cheryl Bridges, 'Holy Spirit and Preaching', in Paul Scott Wilson (ed.), *The New Interpreters Handbook of Preaching* (Nashville: Abingdon 2008), pp. 460-65.
—'What Makes a Good Sermon: A Pentecostal Perspective', *Journal for Preachers* 26.4 (2003), pp. 45-54.
Jones, C.E., 'Holiness Movement', in Stanley Burgess (ed.), *The New International Dictionary of Pentecostal and Charismatic Movements* (Grand Rapids: Zondervan, 2003), pp. 726-29.
Kalu, Ogbu, *African Pentecostalism: An Introduction* (Oxford: Oxford University Press, 2008).
Kane, Steven M., 'Serpent Handlers', in Samuel S. Hill (ed.), *The New Encyclopedia of Southern Culture; Volume 1: Religion* (Chapel Hill: University of North Carolina, 2011), pp. 211-12.
Kärkkäinen, Veli-Matti, 'Pneumatologies in Systematic Theology', in Michael Bergunder, Allan Anderson, and A.F. Droogers (eds.), *Studying Global Pentecostalism: Theories and Methods* (Berkeley: University of California Press, 2010), pp. 223-44.
Keener, Craig S., *1–2 Corinthians* (The New Cambridge Bible Commentary; Cambridge: Cambridge University Press, 2005).
King, Gerald W., 'When the Holiness Preacher Came to Town: Re-Dating W.B. Godbey's Visit to Azusa Street', *Cyberjournal for Pentecostal-Charismatic Research* 18. No pages. Online: www.pctii.org/cyberj/cyberj18/king.html.
Knapp, Martin Wells (ed), *Bible Songs of Salvation and Victory, For God's People of Every Land: Suitable for Revivals, the Church, Sunday-Schools and the Home* (ed. Robert E. McNeill; Cincinnati: M.W. Knapp, n. d.).
—*Lightning Bolts from Pentecostal Skies; or Devices of the Devil Unmasked* (Cincinnati: The Revivalist, 1898).
—*Pentecostal Preachers* (Salem: Convention, n. d.).
—*Revival Kindlings* (Cincinnati: The Revivalist, 3rd edn, 1890).
Knight, Carolyn Ann, 'Preaching as an Intimate Act', in Cleophus J. LaRue (ed.), *Power in the Pulpit: How America's Most Effective Black Preachers Prepare their Sermons* (Louisville: Westminster John Knox, 2002), pp. 89-100.

Knight, Cecil B., 'The Wonder of Worship', in Cecil B. Knight (ed.), *Pentecostal Worship* (Cleveland: Pathway, 1974), pp. 7-15.
Knight, Henry H. III (ed.), *From Aldersgate to Azusa Street: Wesleyan, Holiness, and Pentecostal Visions of the New Creation* (Eugene: Pickwick, 2010).
Knowles, Michael P., *We Preach Not Ourselves: Paul on Proclamation* (Grand Rapids: Eerdmans, 2007).
Kostlevy, William, *Holy Jumpers: Evangelicals and Radicals in Progressive Era America* (Oxford: Oxford University Press, 2010).
Kydd, Ronald A.N., *Charismatic Gifts in the Early Church: An Exploration into the Gifts of the Spirit During the First Three Centuries of the Christian Church* (Peabody: Hendrickson, 1984).
—'Pentecostal Assemblies of Canada', in Stanley M. Burgess (ed.), *The New International Dictionary of Pentecostal and Charismatic Movements* (Grand Rapids: Zondervan, 2003), pp. 961-64.
Lakeshore Pentecostal Camp. Online: http://www.lakeshorepentecostalcamp.com.
Land, Steven Jack, *Pentecostal Spirituality: A Passion for the Kingdom* (Cleveland: CPT Press, 2010).
LaRue, Cleophus J., *The Heart of Black Preaching* (Louisville: Westminster John Knox, 2000).
—(ed.), *Power in the Pulpit: How America's Most Effective Black Preachers Prepare their Sermons* (Louisville: Westminster John Knox, 2002).
Leoh, Vincent Beng, 'Ethics and Pentecostal Preaching: The Anastatic, Organic, and Communal Strands' (PhD dissertation, The Southern Baptist Theological Seminary, 1990).
Lewis, B. Scott, 'William J. Seymour: Follower of the "Evening Light" (Zech. 14:7)', *Wesleyan Theological Journal* 39.2 (Fall 2004), pp. 167-83.
Levin, Tanya, *People in Glass Houses: An Insider's Story of a Life in and out of Hillsong* (Melbourne Victoria: Black, 2007).
Liardon, Roberts, *The Azusa Street Revival: When the Fire Fell* (Shippensburg: Destiny Image, 2006).
Liesch, Barry, 'How We Arrived at Worship Choruses'. Online: http://208.86.154.138/~worship/how-we-arrived-at-worship-choruses.
—*The New Worship: Straight Talk on Music and the Church* (Grand Rapids: Baker, exp. edn, 2001).
Lindbeck, George A., *The Nature of Doctrine: Religion and Theology in a Postliberal Age* (Philadelphia: Westminster, 1984).
Lindhardt, Martin, 'Introduction', in Martin Lindhardt (ed.), *Practicing the Faith: The Ritual Life of Pentecostal-Charismatic Christians* (New York: Berghahn, 2011), pp. 1-48.
Lischer, Richard, 'Introduction: The Promise of Renewal', in Richard Lischer (ed.), *The Company of Preachers: Wisdom on Preaching, Augustine to the Present* (Grand Rapids: Eerdmans, 2002), pp. xii-xvi.

Loggins, Vernon, *The Negro Author: His Development in America to 1900* (Port Washington: Kennikat, 1959).

Long, Thomas G., *The Witness of Preaching* (Louisville: Westminster John Knox, 2nd edn, 2005).

Los Angeles Times articles:

'Claim Power to Raise Dead'. 24 September 1906. *Los Angeles Times*.

'"Holy Kickers" Baffle Police'. 12 July 1906. *Los Angeles Times*.

'"Holy Roller" has it Bad'. 14 August 1906. *Los Angeles Times*.

'Police Asked to Raid Reds'. 6 August 1906. *Los Angeles Times*.

'Rolling and Diving Fanatics "Confess"'. 23 June 1906. *Los Angeles Times*.

'Weird Babel of Tongues'. 18 April 1906. *Los Angeles Times*. In Frank Bartleman, *Azusa Street*, 198–200. Alachua: Bridge-Logos, 1980.

'Women with Men Embrace'. 3 September 1906. *Los Angeles Times*.

Lovett, Leonard, *Crock Pot Preaching: Toward a Preaching Methodology* (Cleveland: Derek, 2009).

Macchia, Frank D., *Baptized in the Spirit: A Global Pentecostal Theology* (Grand Rapids: Zondervan, 2006).

—'Signs of Grace: Towards a Charismatic Theology of Worship', in Lee Roy Martin (ed.), *Towards a Pentecostal Theology of Worship* (Cleveland: CPT Press, 2016), pp. 153-64.

Macchia, Michael D., 'Pentecostal', in Paul F. Bradshaw (ed.), *The New SCM Dictionary of Liturgy and Worship* (London: SCM Press, 2005), pp. 83-85.

Mahaffey, Jermone Dean, 'George Whitefield's Homiletic Art: Neo-Sophism in the Great Awakening', *Homiletic* 31.1 (Summer 2006), pp. 11-22.

Maranatha Music, 'About Maranatha! Music'. Online: http://maranathamusic.com/about.

Martin, Larry, *The Life and Ministry of William J. Seymour and a History of the Azusa Street Revival* (The Complete Azusa Street Library, 1; Pensacola: Christian Life, 2006).

—'Preface to this Volume', in Larry Martin (ed.), *The Doctrines and Discipline of the Azusa Street Apostolic Faith Mission of Los Angeles, California* (The Complete Azusa Street Library, 7; repr., Joplin: Christian Life, 2000).

Martin, Lee Roy, 'Fire in the Bones: Pentecostal Prophetic Preaching', in Lee Roy Martin (ed.), *Toward a Pentecostal Theology of Preaching* (Cleveland: CPT Press, 2015), pp. 34-63.

—(ed.), *Toward a Pentecostal Theology of Preaching* (Cleveland: CPT Press, 2015).

—(ed.), *Toward a Pentecostal Theology of Worship* (Cleveland: CPT Press, 2016).

McBride, Calvin S., *Frank Avant vs. C.H. Mason: Mason and the Holy Ghost on Trial* (New York: iUniverse, 2009).

McClain, William B., 'African American Preaching and the Bible: Biblical Authority or Biblical Literalism', *The Journal of Religious Thought* 49.2 (1992–1993), pp. 72-80.

McCoy, Andrew M., 'Salvation (Not Yet?) Materialized: Healing as Possibility and Possible Complication for Expressing Suffering in Pentecostal Music and Worship', in Monique M. Ingalls and Amos Yong (eds.), *The Spirit of Praise: Music and Worship in Global Pentecostal-Charismatic Christianity* (University Park: The Pennsylvania State University Press, 2015), pp. 45-59.

McGee, G.B. and S.M. Burgess, 'India', in Stanley M. Burgess (ed.), *The New International Dictionary of Pentecostal and Charismatic Movements* (Grand Rapids: Zondervan, 2003), pp. 118-26.

McGee, G.B. and D.J. Rodgers, 'Abrams, Minnie F', Stanley M. Burgess (ed.), *The New International Dictionary of Pentecostal and Charismatic Movements* (Grand Rapids: Zondervan, 2003), pp. 305-306.

McKibbens, Thomas R., Jr, 'Our Baptist Heritage in Worship', *Review and Expositor* 80.1 (Winter 1983), pp. 53-69.

McMullen, Cary, 'Holding their Tongues', *Christianity Today* (October 2009). No pages. Online: http://www.christianitytoday.com/ct/2009/october/5.15.html.

Melick, Richard R., *Philippians, Colossians, Philemon* (New American Commentary, 32; Nashville: Broadman and Holman, 1991).

Menzies, Robert P., *Speaking in Tongues: Jesus and the Apostolic Church as Models for the Church Today* (Cleveland: CPT Press, 2016).

Menzies, William W. and Robert P. Menzies, *Spirit and Power: Foundations of Pentecostal Experience* (Grand Rapids: Zondervan, 2000).

Menzies, William W., and Stanley M. Horton (eds.), *Bible Doctrines: A Pentecostal Perspective* (Springfield: Logion Press, 1993).

Miller, Thomas William, *Canadian Pentecostals: A History of the Pentecostal Assemblies of Canada* (Mississauga: Full Gospel, 1994).

Ministry Today, 'Former Church of God Leader Ray H. Hughes Sr. Dies'. Online: http://ministrytodaymag.com/index.php/ministry-news/190 99-former-church-of-god-leader-ray-h-hughes-sr-dies.

Miskov, Jennifer A., 'The Welsh Revival and the Azusa Street Revival: Liturgical Connections, Similarities and Developments', in Mark J. Cartledge and A.J. Swoboda (eds.), *Scripting Pentecost: A Study of Pentecostals, Worship, and Liturgy* (London: Routledge, 2016), pp. 32-52.

Mitchell, Henry H., *Black Preaching: The Recovery of a Powerful Art* (Nashville: Abingdon, 1990).

Moring, Mark, 'Interview: Redman's Reasons'. Online: http://www.christianitytoday.com/ct/2011/julyweb-only/redmansreasons-july12.html.

Nelson, Douglas J., 'For Such a Time as This: The Story of Bishop William J. Seymour and the Azusa Street Revival' (PhD Thesis, University of Birmingham, 1981).

Neumann, Peter D., 'Encountering the Spirit: Pentecostal Mediated Experience of God in Theological Context' (PhD Thesis, University of St. Michael's College, 2010).

—'Whither Pentecostal Experience? Mediated Experience of God in Pentecostal Theology', *Canadian Journal of Pentecostal–Charismatic Christianity* 3 (2012), pp. 1-40.

Newport, Frank, 'Black or African American?', *Gallup* (September 28, 2007). Online: http://www.gallup.com/poll/28816/black-african-amer ican.aspx.

Ngien, Dennis, *Gifted Response: The Triune God as the Causative Agency of Our Responsive Worship* (Milton Keynes: Paternoster, 2008).

Nichol, John Thomas, *Pentecostalism* (New York: Harper, 1966).

Noll, Mark A., *The Rise of Evangelicalism: The Age of Edwards, Whitefield and the Wesleys* (Downers Grove: InterVarsity Press, 2003).

—*Turning Points: Decisive Moments in the History of the Christian Church* (Grand Rapids: Baker, 2nd edn, 2000).

Northpoint Bible College. 'Accreditation'. Online: http://northpoint.edu/ about/accreditation.

—'Charles Crabtree'. Online: http://northpoint.edu/academics/faculty/charles-crabtree.

Oss, Doug, 'Communicating the Message'. Assemblies of God Theological Seminary. Fall 2005.

Pagitt, Doug, *Preaching Re-Imagined: The Role of the Sermon in Communities of Faith* (GrandRapids: Zondervan, 2005).

Parham, Sarah E., *The Life of Charles F. Parham: Founder of the Apostolic Faith Movement*. 1930 (repr., New York: Garland Publishing, Inc., 1985).

Passion, 'About'. Online: http://www.268generation.com/3.0/#!about/ story.

Pentecostal Assemblies of Newfoundland and Labrador, 'Tyndale University College and Seminary'. Online: http://www.paonl.ca/content/tyndale.

Penney, Fred, 'Applying a Spiritual Warfare Cosmology to Preaching' (DMin thesis, Gordon-Conwell Theological Seminary, 1999).

Pipes, William H., *Say Amen, Brother! Old-Time Negro Preaching: A Study in American Frustration* (repr., Detroit: Wayne State, 1992).

Pitts, William L., Jr, 'Baptist Origins and Identity in 1609: The John Smyth/Richard Clifton Debate', *Perspectives in Religious Studies* 36.4 (Winter 2009), pp. 377-90.

Placher, William C., *A History of Christian Theology: An Introduction* (Philadelphia: Westminster, 1983).

Pollock, John, *George Whitefield and the Great Awakening* (Garden City: Doubleday and Company, 1972).

Poloma, Margaret M., 'North American Pentecostalism', in Adam Stewart (ed.), *Handbook of Pentecostal Christianity* (DeKalb: North Illinois University Press, 2012), pp. 155-58.

—'The Symbolic Dilemma and the Future of Pentecostalism: Mysticism, Ritual, and Revival', in Eric Patterson and Edmund Rybarczyk (eds.), *The Future of Pentecostalism in the United States* (Lanham: Lexington, 2007), pp. 105-21.

Powery, Luke A., 'The Holy Spirit and African-American Preaching' (ThD dissertation, Emmanuel College, University of Toronto, 2006).

—'Lament: Homiletical Groans in the Spirit'. Paper presented at the annual meeting of the Academy of Homiletics, Boston, MA, November 21, 2008.

Pulikottil, Paulson, 'One God, One Spirit, Two Memories: A Postcolonial Reading of the Encounter Between Western Pentecostalism and Native Pentecostalism in Kerala', in Veli-Matti Kärkkäinen (ed.), *The Spirit in the World: Emerging Pentecostal Theologies in Global Contexts* (Grand Rapids: Eerdmans, 2009), pp. 69-88.

Quicke, Michael J., 'Trinity', in Paul Scott Wilson (ed.), *The New Interpreter's Handbook of Preaching* (Nashville: Abingdon Press, 2008), pp. 498-502.

Raboteau, Albert J., *Slave Religion* (New York: Oxford University Press, 1978).

Ragoonath, Aldwin, 'Pentecostal Preaching in North America' (DTh Thesis, University of South Africa, 2001).

—*Preach the Word: A Pentecostal Approach* (Winnipeg: Agape Teaching Ministry, 2004).

Redman, Matt, 'Bio'. Online: http://www.mattredman.com/bio.

—'Cell, Congregation, Celebration: Worship Leading in Three Contexts in Matt Redman (comp.), *The Heart of Worship Files* (Ventura: Regal, 2003), pp. 115-16.

—'Heart of Worship'. Thankyou Music, 1999.

—*Inside Out Worship* (vol. 2; Eastbourne: Kingsway, 2005).

—'Insights: Congregational Worship as Journey', in Matt Redman (comp.), *Inside Out Worship* (vol. 2; Eastbourne: Kingsway, 2005), pp. 162-63.

—'Cultivating a Quiet Heart', in Matt Redman (comp.), *The Heart of Worship Files* (Ventura: Regal, 2003), pp. 177-80.

—*Facedown* (Eastbourne: Kingsway, 2004).

—'Gifted Response'. Thankyou Music, 2004.

—'Lord Let Your Glory Fall'. Thankyou Music, 1998.

—'The Real Worship Leader', in Matt Redman (comp.), *The Heart of Worship Files* (Ventura: Regal, 2003), pp. 80-83.

—'Thoughts on Songwriting (Part 1): Making Melody', in Matt Redman (comp.), *The Heart of Worship Files* (Ventura: Regal, 2003), pp. 32-33.

—*The Unquenchable Worshipper: Coming Back to the Heart of Worship* (Ventura: Regal, 2001).
—'Worship-Leading Essentials: (Part 1) The Gentle Persuasion of Authority', in Matt Redman (comp.), *Inside Out Worship* (vol. 2; Eastbourne: Kingsway, 2005), pp. 16-20.
—'Worship-Leading Essentials: (Part 2) The Awakening Power of Truth', in Matt Redman, *Inside Out Worship* (vol. 2; Eastbourne: Kingsway, 2005), pp. 28-32.
—'Worship-Leading Essentials: (Part 3) The Shepherding Instincts of a Pastor', in Matt Redman (comp.), *Inside Out Worship* (vol. 2; Eastbourne: Kingsway, 2005), pp. 49-50.
—'Worship-Leading Essentials: (Part 5) The Powerful Insights of the Prophetic', in Matt Redman, *Inside Out Worship* (vol. 2; Eastbourne: Kingsway, 2005), pp. 96-100.
—'Worship-Leading Essentials: (Part 9) The Constant Expectation of the Heavenly', in Matt Redman (comp.), *Inside Out Worship* (vol. 2; Eastbourne: Kingsway, 2005), p. 164-68.
Redman, Robb, *The Great Worship Awakening: Singing a New Song in the Postmodern Church* (San Francisco: Jossey-Bass, 2002).
Reed, David A., *'In Jesus' Name': The History and Beliefs of Oneness Pentecostalism* (JPTSup, 31; Blandford Forum: Deo, 2008).
—'Oneness Pentecostalism', in Stanley M. Burgess (ed.), *The New International Dictionary of Pentecostal and Charismatic Movements* (Grand Rapids: Zondervan, 2003), pp. 936-44.
Revival Library, Online: http://www.revival-library.org.
Riss, R.M., 'Finished Work Controversy', in Stanley M. Burgess (ed.), *The New International Dictionary of Pentecostal and Charismatic Movements* (Grand Rapids: Zondervan, 2003), pp. 638-39.
Robeck, Cecil M., Jr, *The Azusa Street Mission and Revival: The Birth of the Global Pentecostal Movement* (Nashville: Thomas Nelson, 2006).
—'Azusa Street Revival', in Stanley M. Burgess (ed.), *The New International Dictionary of Pentecostal and Charismatic Movements* (Grand Rapids: Zondervan, 2003), pp. 344-50.
—'Bartleman, Frank', in Stanley M. Burgess (ed.), *The New International Dictionary of Pentecostal and Charismatic Movements* (Grand Rapids: Zondervan, 2003), p. 366.
—'Prophecy, Gift of', in Stanley M. Burgess (ed.), *The New International Dictionary of Pentecostal and Charismatic Movements* (Grand Rapids: Zondervan, 2003), pp. 999-1012.
—'Seymour, William Joseph', in Stanley M. Burgess (ed.), *The New International Dictionary of Pentecostal and Charismatic Movements* (Grand Rapids: Zondervan, 2003), pp. 1053-58.

Robert, Dana L. and M.L. Daneel, 'Worship among Apostles and Zionists in Southern Africa, Zimbabwe', in Charles E. Farhadian (ed.), *Christian Worship Worldwide: Expanding Horizons, Deepening Practices* (Grand Rapids: Eerdmans, 2007), pp. 43-70.

Robinson, Haddon, *Biblical Preaching: The Development and Delivery of Expository Messages* (Grand Rapids: Baker, 1st edn, 1980).

—*Biblical Preaching: The Development and Delivery of Expository Messages* (Grand Rapids: Baker, 2nd edn, 2001).

Robinson, Haddon, Bill Hybels, and Stuart Broscoe, *Mastering Contemporary Preaching* (Portland: Multnomah, 1989).

Rudd, Douglas, *When the Spirit Came Upon Them: Highlights from the Early Years of the Pentecostal Movement in Canada* (Burlington: Antioch Books, 2002).

Samuel, Josh P.S., 'African American Preaching and Preachers with Mass Appeal: An Examination of the Preaching of T.D. Jakes and Billy Graham through the Lens of African American Homiletical Theory' (MTS thesis, Wycliffe College, University of Toronto, 2003).

—'Pentecostal Worship Roots: George Whitefield's Influence upon the African American and Methodist Traditions'. Annual meeting of the Society of Pentecostal Studies, Memphis, TN, March 12, 2011.

—'The Spirit in Pentecostal Preaching: A Constructive Dialogue with Haddon Robinson's and Charles Crabtree's Theology of Preaching', *Pneuma* 35.2 (2013), pp. 199-219.

Sanders, Rufus G.W., *William Joseph Seymour: Black Father of the 20th Century Pentecostal/Charismatic Movement* (Sandusky: Xulon, 2003).

Scandrett-Leatherman, Craig, 'Rites of Lynching and Rites of Dance: Historical, Anthropological, and Afro-Pentecostal Perspectives on Black Manhood after 1865', in Amos Yong and Estrelda Y. Alexander (eds.), *Afro-Pentecostalism: Black Pentecostal and Charismatic Christianity in History and Culture* (New York: New York University Press, 2011).

Seymour, William J. *The Doctrines and Discipline of the Azusa Street Apostolic Faith Mission of Los Angeles, California* (ed. Larry Martin; The Complete Azusa Street Library, Vol. 7; repr., Joplin: Christian Life, 2000).

—'Receive ye the Holy Ghost', *AF* 1.5 (January 1907), p. 2.

Shumway, Charles W., 'A Critical History of Glossolalia' (PhD diss., Boston University, 1919).

—'A Study of 'the Gift of Tongues'' (AB Degree, University of Southern California, 1914).

Simpson, William C., Jr, 'John Wesley and Pentecostal Power', *Living Pulpit* 13.2 (Ap-Je 2004), pp. 34-35.

Smith, James K.A, *You Are What You Love: The Spiritual Power of Habit* (Grand Rapids: Brazos, 2016).

Smith, John W.V., *The Quest for Holiness and Unity: A Comprehensive History of the Church of God Reformation Movement* (Anderson: Warner, 2nd edn, 2009).

Smith, Robert, Jr, 'Call and Response', in Paul Scott Wilson (ed.), *The New Interpreter's Handbook of Preaching* (Nashville: Abingdon, 2008), p. 297.

Snyder, Howard A., 'Holiness Heritage: The Case of Pandita Ramabai', *Wesleyan Theological Journal* 40.2 (Fall 2005), pp. 30-51.

Sorge, Bob, *Exploring Worship: A Practical Guide to Praise and Worship* (Canandaigua: Oasis House, 1987).

—*Following the River: A Vision for Corporate Worship* (Greenwood: Oasis House, 2004).

Soulen, Richard N., 'Black Worship and Hermeneutic', *Christian Century* 87.6 (1970), pp. 168-71.

Spencer, Jon Michael, *Protest and Praise: Sacred Music of Black Religion* (Minneapolis: Fortress, 1990).

Stein, Robert H., 'The Ending of Mark', *Bulletin for Biblical Research* 18.1 (2008), pp. 79-98.

Stein, Stephen, 'George Whitefield on Slavery: Some New Evidence', *Church History* 42.2 (June 1973), pp. 243-56.

Stephens, Randall J., *The Fire Spreads: Holiness and Pentecostalism in the American South* (Cambridge: Harvard University, 2008).

Stewart, Jimmy, 'Darlene Zschech Leaving Hillsong to Co-Pastor Church', *Charisma Magazine* (November 3, 2010). No pages. Online: http://www.charismamag.com/site-archives/570-news/featured-news/12096-darlene-zschech-leaving-hillsong-to-co-pastor-church.

Stewart, Warren H., *Interpreting God's Word in Black Preaching* (Valley Forge: Judson, 1984).

Stocker, Abby, 'Assemblies of God Surge, But Speaking in Tongues Slumps', *Christianity Today* (August 2013). No pages. Online: http://www.christianitytoday.com/gleanings/2013/august/assemblies-of-god-speaking-in-tongues-spirit-baptisms.html.

Stout, Harry S., *The Divine Dramatist: George Whitefield and the Rise of Modern Evangelicalism* (Grand Rapids: Eerdmans, 1991).

—'Puritan Preaching', in William H. Willimon and Richard Lischer (eds.), *Concise Encyclopedia of Preaching* (Louisville: Westminster John Knox, 1995), pp. 394-97.

Studebaker, Steven, 'Charismatic Theology'. Course at McMaster Divinity College, Hamilton, ON, Fall 2008.

—(ed.), *Defining Issues in Pentecostalism: Classical and Emergent* (Eugene: Wipf and Stock, 2008).

—*From Pentecost to the Triune God: A Pentecostal Trinitarian Theology* (Grand Rapids: Eerdmans, 2012).

—'The Spirit in Creation: A Unified Theology of Grace and Creation Care', *Zygon* 43.4 (December 2008), pp. 943-60.
Sweeney, Douglas A., *The American Evangelical Story: A History of the Movement* (Grand Rapids: Baker, 2005).
—Review of Frank Lambert, *Pedlar in Divinity: George Whitefield and the Trans-atlantic Revivals, 1737–1770* (Princeton: Princeton University, 1994), *International Bulletin of Missionary Research* 20.3 (July 1996), pp. 137-38.
Synan, Vinson, 'Appendix B: Azusa Street in *Way of Faith*', in Frank Bartle-man, *Azusa Street: An Eyewitness Account* (Alachua: Bridge-Logos, 1980), pp. 203-204.
—(ed.), *The Century of the Holy Spirit: 100 Years of Pentecostal and Charismatic Renewal* (Nashville: Thomas Nelson, 2001).
—'The Charismatic Renewal after Fifty Years', in Vinson Synan (ed.), *Spirit-Empowered Christianity in the 21st Century* (Lake Mary: Charisma, 2011), pp. 7-24.
—'Classical Pentecostalism', in Stanley M. Burgess (ed.), *The New International Dictionary of Pentecostal and Charismatic Movements* (Grand Rapids: Zondervan, 2003), pp. 553-55.
—*The Holiness-Pentecostal Tradition: Charismatic Movements in the Twentieth Century* (Grand Rapids: Eerdmans, 1997).
—'Introduction', in Frank Bartleman, *Azusa Street: An Eyewitness Account* (Alachua: Bridge-Logos, 1980), pp. xi-xxxix.
Tapper, Michael A., *Canadian Pentecostals, the Trinity, and Contemporary Worship Music* (Leiden: Brill, 2017).
Tennent, Timothy C., *Theology in the Context of World Christianity: How the Global Church is Influencing the Way We Think about and Discuss Theology* (Grand Rapids: Zondervan, 2007).
Thomas, John Christopher, '1998 Presidential Address: Pentecostal Theology in the Twenty-First Century', *Pneuma* 20.1 (Spring 1998), pp. 3-19.
Thomas, John Christopher, and Kimberly Ervin Alexander, '"And the Signs are Following": Mark 16.9-20 – A Journey into Pentecostal Hermeneutics', *Journal of Pentecostal Theology* 11.2 (Fall 2003), pp. 147-70.
Tomberlin, Daniel, *Pentecostal Sacraments: Encountering God at the Altar* (Cleveland: Center for Pentecostal Leadership and Care Pentecostal Theological Seminary, 2010).
Torrance, James B., *Worship, Community, and the Triune God of Grace* (Downers Grove: InterVarsity, 1996).
Trask, Bradley T., 'Pentecostal Preaching and Persuasion', in James K. Bridges (ed.), *Foundations of Pentecostal Preaching* (Springfield: Gospel, 2005), pp. 169-90.
Tribble, Sherman R., 'Diverse Worship Styles among African-American Baptists', *Baptist History and Heritage* 1 (Summer/Fall 2002), pp. 42-47.

Turner, William C., 'The Musicality of Black Preaching: Performing the Word', in Jana Childers and Clayton J. Schmit (eds.), *Performance in Preaching: Bringing the Sermon to Life* (Grand Rapids: Baker, 2008), pp. 191-209.

—'Pentecostal Preaching', in William H. Willimon and Richard Lischer (eds.), *Concise Encyclopedia of Preaching* (Louisville: Westminster John Knox, 1995), pp. 369-72.

—'Preaching the Spirit: The Liberation of Preaching', *Journal of Pentecostal Theology* 14.1 (2005), pp. 3-16.

Tyson, John R., 'The Theology of Charles Wesley's Hymns', *Wesleyan Theological Journal* 44.2 (Fall 2009), pp. 58-75.

Underwood, A.C., *A History of the English Baptists* (London: Kingsgate Press, 1947).

Valdez, A.C., Sr with James F. Scheer. *Fire on Azusa Street* (Costa Mesa: Gift Publications, 1980).

Versteeg, Peter, 'A Prophetic Outsider: Experience and the Boundaries of Meaning in a Local Vineyard Church', *Pneuma* 28.1 (Spring 2006), pp. 72-88.

Vineyard Resource Canada, 'Our History'. Online: http://vineyard.ca/index.php.

Vineyard USA, 'Vineyard History'. Online: http://www.vineyardusa.org/site/about/vineyard-history.

Vondey, Wolfgang, *Beyond Pentecostalism: The Crisis of Global Christianity and the Renewal of the Theological Agenda* (Grand Rapids: Eerdmans, 2010).

—'Pentecostal Sacramentality and the Theology of the Altar', in Mark J. Cartledge and A.J. Swoboda (eds.), *Scripting Pentecost: A Study of Pentecostals, Worship, and Liturgy* (London: Routledge, 2016), pp. 94-107.

—*People of the Bread: Rediscovering Ecclesiology* (New York: Paulist, 2008).

Wacker, Grant, *Heaven Below: Early Pentecostals and American Culture* (Cambridge: Harvard University, 2001).

Ward, Pete, *Selling Worship: How What We Sing Has Changed the Church* (Milton Keynes: Paternoster, 2005).

Ware, S.L., 'Restorationism in Classical Pentecostalism', in Stanley M. Burgess (ed.), *The New International Dictionary of Pentecostal and Charismatic Movements* (Grand Rapids: Zondervan, 2003), pp. 1019-21.

Warrington, Keith, *Pentecostal Theology: A Theology of Encounter* (London: T & T Clark, 2008).

Way of Faith, October 11, 1906. in Frank Bartleman, *Azusa Street* (Alachua: Bridge-Logos, 1980), pp. 203-204.

Webber, Robert E., 'Blended Worship', in Paul A. Basden (ed.), *Six Views on Exploring the Worship Spectrum* (Grand Rapids: Zondervan, 2004), pp. 173-91.

Welchel, Tom, *They Told Me Their Stories: The Youth and Children of Azusa Street Tell Their Stories* (USA: Dare 2 Dream, 2010).

'Wesley, Charles', in F.L. Cross and E.A. Livingstone (ed.), *The Oxford Dictionary of the Christian Church* (Oxford: Oxford University, 3rd edn, 2005), p. 1739.

Wesley, John, *The Journal of John Wesley*. No pages. Accessed January 26, 2010. Online: http://www.ccel.org/ccel/wesley/sermons.txt (Reprint from Chicago: Moody Press, 1951).

—'On the Death of the Rev. Mr. George Whitefield', in John Wesley, *Sermons on Several Occasions*. No pages. Online: http://www.ccel.org/ccel/wesley/sermons.txt.

—'The Scripture Way of Salvation', in John Wesley, *Sermon on Several Occasions*. No pages. Online: http://www.ccel.org/ccel/wesley/sermons.txt.

—'The Witness of the Spirit', in John Wesley, *Sermon on Several Occasions*. No pages. Online: http://www.ccel.org/ccel/wesley/sermons.txt.

Whaling, Frank, *John and Charles Wesley: Selected Prayers, Hymns, Journal Notes, Sermons, Letters and Treatises* (Mahwah: Paulist, 1981).

White, James F., 'Traditions of Protestant Worship', *Worship* 49.5 (May 1975), pp. 272-82.

Whitefield, George, *George Whitefield's Journals* (repr., London: Banner of Truth Trust, 1960).

—'The Indwelling of the Spirit, the Common Privilege of All Believers', in *Selected Sermons of George Whitefield*. No pages. Accessed March 5, 2010. Online: http://www.ccel.org/ccel/whitefield/sermons.txt

—'A Letter to John Wesley', in *George Whitefield's Journals* (repr., London: Banner of Truth Trust, 1960).

—'The Lord our Righteousness', in *Selected Sermons of George Whitefield*. No pages. Accessed March 5, 2010. Online: http://www.ccel.org/ccel/whitefield/sermons.txt

—*Selected Sermons of George Whitefield*. No pages. Accessed March 5, 2010. Online: http://www.ccel.org/ccel/whitefield/sermons.txt

Wilson, Paul Scott, *A Concise History of Preaching* (Nashville: Abingdon, 1992).

Wimber, Carol, 'The Flame of God's Presence', in Christy Wimber (ed.), *The Way In is the Way On: John Wimber's Teachings and Writings on Life in Christ* (Boise: Ampelon, 2006), pp. 106-108.

Wimber, Christy (ed.), *The Way In is the Way On: John Wimber's Teachings and Writings on Life in Christ* (Boise: Ampelon, 2006).

Wimber, John, 'Christ-Centered Worship', in John Wimber (ed.), *Thoughts on Worship* (Anaheim: Vineyard Music Group, 1996), pp. 9-14.

—'Worship: Intimacy with God', in John Wimber (ed.), *Thoughts on Worship* (Anaheim: Vineyard Music Group, 1996), pp. 1-7.

—*Thoughts on Worship* (Anaheim: Vineyard Music Group, 1996).

Wimberly, Edward P., 'The Dynamics of Black Worship: A Psychosocial Exploration of the Impulses that Lie at the Roots of Black Worship',

Journal of the Interdenominational Theological Center 14.1-2 (Fall-Spr 1986–1987), pp. 195-207.

Witvliet, John D., 'Beyond Style: Rethinking the Role of Music in Worship', in Tim A. Dearborn and Scott Coil (eds.), *Worship at the Next Level: Insight from Contemporary Voices* (Grand Rapids: Baker, 2004), pp. 163-79.

Wolffe, John, *The Expansion of Evangelicalism: The Age of Wilberforce, More, Chalmers and Finney* (A History of Evangelicalism, vol. 2; Downers Grove: InterVarsity, 2007).

Wong, Daniel L., 'Preaching'. Tyndale University College and Seminary. Fall 2008.

Wright, Bonnie, 'Experiencing God: An Ethnography of Pentecostal Worship, Race, and Place' (PhD dissertation, Wayne State University, 2003).

Yong, Amos, *Beyond the Impasse: Toward a Pneumatological Theology of Religions* (Grand Rapids: Baker, 2003).

—'Conclusion: Improvisation, Indigenization, and Inspiration: Theological Reflections on the Sound and Spirit of Global Renewal', in Monique M. Ingalls, and Amos Yong (eds.), *The Spirit of Praise: Music and Worship in Global Pentecostal-Charismatic Christianity* (University Park: The Pennsylvania State University Press, 2015), pp. 279-88.

—*Discerning the Spirit(s): A Pentecostal–Charismatic Contribution to Christian Theology of Religions* (JPTSup, 20; Sheffield: Sheffield Academic Press, 2000).

—*The Spirit Poured Out on All Flesh: Pentecostalism and the Possibility of Global Theology* (Grand Rapids: Baker, 2005).

—*Spirit–Word–Community: Theological Hermeneutics in Trinitarian Perspective* (Eugene: Wipf and Stock, 2002).

York, Terry W., *America's Worship Wars* (Peabody: Hendrickson, 2003).

Young, Ed, Jr, 'Preaching Creatively', in Michael Duduit (ed.), *Preaching with Power: Dynamic Insights from Twenty Top Pastors* (Grand Rapids: Baker, 2006), pp. 241-54.

Yun, Koo Dong, 'Pentecostalism from Below: *Minjung* Liberation and Asian Pentecostal Theology', in Veli-Matti Kärkkäinen (ed.), *The Spirit in the World: Emerging Pentecostal Theologies in Global Contexts* (Grand Rapids: Eerdmans, 2009), pp. 89-114.

Zeigler, J.R., 'Valdez, A.C., Sr', in Stanley M. Burgess (ed.), *The New International Dictionary of Pentecostal and Charismatic Movements* (Grand Rapids: Zondervan, 2003), p. 1169.

Zimmerman, J.A. and T.E. Johnson, 'Sacraments, Sacramentality', in William A. Dyrness and Veli-Matti Kärkkäinen (eds), *Global Dictionary of Theology* (Downers Grove: InterVarsity, 2008).

Zinchini, Cassandra, 'Taking Revival to the World: Australia's Largest and Most Influential Church Extends Its Reach to London, Paris and Kiev', *Christianity Today* 51.10 (October 2007), pp. 34-40.

Zschech, Darlene, *The Art of Mentoring: Embracing the Great Generational Transition* (Bloomington: Bethany, 2011).
—'Biography'. Online: http://www.darlenezschech.com/biography.
—*Extravagant Worship: Holy, Holy, Holy is the Lord God Almighty Who was and Is, and Is to Come* (Bloomington: Bethany, 2001).
—*The Kiss of Heaven: God's Favor to Empower Your Life Dream* (Bloomington: Bethany, 2003).
—'100 Huntley Interview with Darlene Zschech Part 1'. Online: http://www.youtube.com/watch?v=yXHHE4Qvwoo&feature=related.
—'The Role of the Holy Spirit in Worship: An Introduction to the Hillsong Church, Sydney, Australia', in Teresa Berger and Bryan D. Spinks (eds.), *Spirit in Worship – Worship in the Spirit* (Collegeville: Liturgical, 2009), pp. 285-92.
—'Darlene Zschech'. Online: http://www.darlenezschech.com.
—*Worship: Hillsongs Australia Leadership Series* (Castle Hill: Hillsongs Australia, 1996).

Index of Biblical References

Index of Authors

www.ingramcontent.com/pod-product-compliance
Lightning Source LLC
Chambersburg PA
CBHW060042100426
42742CB00014B/2668